a special gift

presented to:

_____

from:

_____

date:

_____

My voice shalt thou hear in the morning, O Lord;
in the morning will I direct my prayer unto thee, and will look up.
—Psalm 5:3

morning *praise*

The Women's Devotional Series

To order, call **1-800-765-6955.**
Visit us at **www.reviewandherald.com**
for more information on other Review and Herald® products.

morning
praise

EDITED BY *Ardis Dick Stenbakken*

REVIEW AND HERALD® PUBLISHING ASSOCIATION
HAGERSTOWN, MD 21740

The authors assume full responsibility for the accuracy of all facts and quotations as cited in this book.

Texts on the back cover copy are from the *Holy Bible, New International Version.* Copyright © 1973, 1978, 1984, International Bible Society. Used by permission of Zondervan Bible Publishers.

This book was
Edited by Jeannette R. Johnson
Copyedited by James Cavil
Cover design by Patricia S. Wegh
Cover photo by Jupiter Images
Electronic makeup by Shirley M. Bolivar
Typeset: Minion 11/13

PRINTED IN U.S.A.

10 09 08 07 06   5 4 3 2 1

R&H Cataloging Service
Stenbakken, Ardis Dick, 1939-   ed.
      Morning praise, edited by Ardis Dick Stenbakken.

      1. Devotional calendars—SDA.   2. Devotional calendars—women.
3. Women—religious life.   4. Devotional literature—SDA.   I. Title.

242.643

ISBN 10: 0-8280-1981-9
ISBN 13: 978-0-8280-1981-1

The Truly Extreme Makeover

Who shall change our vile body, that it may be fashioned like unto his glorious body, according to the working whereby he is able even to subdue all things unto himself. Phil. 3:21.

TECHNOLOGY HAS MADE remarkable advances through the years. I am particularly amazed at how the body can be surgically altered to meet the physical/emotional expectations of the person receiving the surgery. But even with the best physical alterations, the heart of a person cannot be changed by earthly hands.

Although my body may have a few quirks, I am grateful that I have one, and that it is intact. I look forward to being in heaven, where everything, including our bodies, will be made new. In the meantime I look forward to God working in my life in this world to prepare me for the next by working on my stony heart. The preparation will require a truly extreme makeover of my natural ways. I hold on to the promise in 2 Corinthians 5:17: "Therefore if any man be in Christ, he is a new creature: old things are passed away; behold, all things are become new." I can look over the past few years and see how God has made many changes in me and in my life. Seeing those changes gives me hope that He will continue His work in me. Knowing this helps me to be patient with others around me who are sometimes difficult to deal with.

Even though I have seen change, I know I'm not changed as completely as God would have me. The challenge that I constantly face—and I face in this new year—is to allow God to make the changes in me that I need. It seems more comfortable to stick with my familiar character defects than to get out of my comfort zone and become the new creature God wants me to be. Surrendering is faith in action—and I need both.

I could really use a faith lift today! God, thank You for not giving up on me, even when I have given up on myself. Please help me to surrender daily and to stay focused on the true purpose of my existence. Help me to do those things that will bring me closer to You, and to avoid the things that keep us apart. Thank You for the hope I have in Jesus and for giving me the ability to have the truly extreme and essential makeover that the world cannot give.

MARY J. WAGONER ANGELIN

?Thought: What would you need to do at the start of a new year to have the promised heart makeover?

Power in the New Year

Forgetting the things which are behind, and stretching forward to the things which are before, I press on toward the goal. Phil. 3:13, 14, ASV.

WHEN A YOUNG PERSON was asked recently "What does the new year mean to you?" she replied that it was just 365 more days.

I thought a lot about her response and wondered if things in her life had become so hopeless that each day rolled mindlessly into the next. Was she feeling powerless because she had no control over her circumstances? What about New Year's resolutions? Surely resolutions would help her feel as though it was not just another day. Were there things in her life that so weighed her down that her thoughts were only of making it through this day? An earthly goal—and certainly a heavenly goal—was too much for her to even glimpse, let alone think that the great God would have time for her.

If she only knew. Would anyone tell her that the God that she did not feel she had the strength to know was really the God of down-and-outers? If she knew this, the new year would not be just another 365 days; it would be the beginning of something good.

Are we like the young woman with little hope of ever succeeding? Will this year become just another 365 days? What keeps us tied to the past, robbing us of a present or the possibility of a future? Have we been so traumatized that we are more comfortable thinking on past trauma than focusing on the present? Have we allowed our past to keep us in the past? Somehow we have to do as Paul says in Philippians 3:13: Forget the things that are behind, and stretch forward to the things that are before. Press on toward the goal.

Only with God's power can we move forward and not be weighed down by our past. We need God's power every day, and we certainly do as we begin another year. With His power this coming year will not become just another 365 days. It can be the year in which we are delivered from ourselves so that God can use us. JANET MCKINON SIGH

(?) Thought: Read Philippians 3:13 and 14 in several different versions. Which version best describes your goals for this year? Should this become one of your New Year's resolutions?

Hold the Line, Please

Be still before the Lord and wait patiently for him. Ps. 37:7, NIV.

INTERNAL PEACE, EXTERNAL COMPOSURE, beautiful surroundings, a comfortable easy chair, and a well-written book. What a wonderful life! Until the shrill sound of the telephone disrupts the peaceful atmosphere. I jump up as if I had been pricked. I've waited for an important phone call for days. I stumble over my own feet. At the fourth ring I reach the telephone and pick it up.

The voice at the other end sounds soft and completely strange, unfamiliar to my ears. And as I try to concentrate on the voice, the burning words tumble into my innermost being: "This is your daughter!" My daughter? The daughter who pursues her own path, unrelentingly and resolutely; from whom I have not heard a word for almost 15 years? I knew only that she was alive.

The beautiful, clear voice tugs at my heart, overwhelms me completely. Yes, it is my daughter. Jubilation, joy takes hold of me, floods my soul. Somebody I had considered lost forever called me, wanted me, needed me.

The call I had been expecting faded in importance. It was nothing compared to this bubbling joy that hit my heart so unexpectedly.

An old hymn by Paul Gerhardt came to my mind: "Joyfully my heart will beat at this time when all angels sing for joy." Yes, there must be joy in heaven now. My Father, who loves me so much, is leading my daughter back to me.

The joy ignited, our voices tumbled topsy-turvy over each other, and the phone call became extremely long. We will see each other and dare to start over again.

I had carried this heartbreaking situation in my mind for many years. I had prayed and pleaded, but nobody answered my call. Passing time had not yet been ripe for this new encounter. But the Lord knows when the time is ripe. This is my experience.

And so I am overjoyed to have trusted in the word of the Lord and to have waited on Him. I am happy that I did not try to solve the situation by myself.

CHRISTEL MEY

? Thought: Are you willing to wait for something you desperately want? Have you asked God for it?

Living Water

But whoever drinks the water I give him will never thirst. Indeed, the water I give him will become in him a spring of water welling up to eternal life. John 4:14, NIV.

CAREFULLY I MEASURED the bread flour, ground the various grains, and deposited them into the special pan to make multigrain bread in my lovely breadmaking machine. I added the salt, milk powder, margarine, honey—checking the recipe list. It was my favorite recipe that I had used numerous times, and it always came out perfectly. I even remembered to add the dry yeast that goes into the little top pocket after I had placed the pan into its frame and closed the lid. I plugged in the cord and pushed the start button. I saw the timer on top light up and also checked my clock to determine when four hours would end and my bread would be baked.

When the four hours was almost up I stood nearby to listen for the familiar beep. Although there was a faint aroma in the kitchen, it was not like baking bread usually smells. Happily, I heard the beeping and anticipated a lovely loaf of fresh bread as I pulled the plug and lifted the lid. But what was *that* stuff? Dry, browned powder sunk low in the pan! Immediately I knew the problem. I had forgotten the water, the last item on the recipe list except for the yeast. In my haste to make sure I had the yeast, I had skipped the water. I scolded myself, shed some tears, and walked back and forth, confessing my dismay as the pan cooled on the rack.

Later, as I cleaned up the mess, I realized that the machine had faithfully gone through its routine as always. I was glad that it would work again. I vowed to remember all the ingredients next time, to the last item on the list.

Water. How important it is! Like the living water that Jesus can give to my spiritual life. Water about which He told the woman at the well. Jesus told her, "If you knew the gift of God and who it is that asks you for a drink, you would have asked him and he would have given you living water" (John 4:10, NIV). As in our text, He promised that with that water I'll never thirst again. How I need it!

Come, Living Water, I pray. Flow through me like a river. I've been thirsty so long! I don't want to be dry like those poor bread ingredients, waiting for the water that never came. BESSIE SIEMENS LOBSIEN

Open Your Mail

Thy words were found, and I did eat them; and thy word was unto me the joy and rejoicing of mine heart. Jer. 15:16.

IT PROMISED TO BE the event of the decade. There was going to be a grand inauguration ceremony. The country rustled with plans, projections, and programming. It would be an occasion of pomp and pageantry. Invitations were sent to heads of government, civic organizations, and church leaders. Everything had to be just perfect.

It seemed natural to me that my husband and I would be invited. Some of our friends gleefully informed us that they had received invitations. I mentally compared our status with theirs, dismayed that our family had not qualified for a similar honor.

After a few weeks of diminishing expectancy, I summarily dismissed hope of attending the inauguration. I secretly admitted that I must have begun to think of myself more highly than I ought to think. I resigned myself to watching the auspicious event on television.

A week after the occasion I noticed a stack of unopened mail lying almost abandoned on a little table in our study. *Where had this mail been hiding all these weeks?* Panic seized me. *What if there are some critical unpaid bills?* As I quickly sorted the mail, I noticed a large brown government envelope. I gasped as I ripped it open. There it was—the elusive invitation to the inauguration! That was not all. Enclosed were tickets for seats in the reserved section.

I had lost a golden opportunity because I had carelessly neglected to open my mail. What a lesson that was for me! Sometimes in our busy rush we Christians neglect to open our mail, the Bible. We fail to notice God's essential Word. Just think of the love notes, the precious promises, cheery tidbits, historical data, crucial forecasts, and successful formulas for happy families that go unnoticed because we neglect Bible study. The plans for the mansions our Father has gone to prepare escape us. We do not see the itinerary for our flight through eternity, and we forget about the celestial weekly reunion when "from one sabbath to another shall all flesh come to worship before me" (Isa. 66:23). Worst of all, by not opening our mail, God's Word, we miss the invitation "And the Spirit and the bride say, Come" (Rev. 22:17).

Lord, please help me meditate daily on Your Word.

GLORIA LINDSEY TROTMAN

When the Streetlights Come On

Blessed is the man whom thou chastenest, O Lord, and teachest him out of thy law; that thou mayest give him rest from the days of adversity, until the pit be digged for the wicked. Ps. 94:12, 13.

AS A CHILD I LOVED playing with my friend Patricia. There was nothing too adventurous or challenging for either of us. Her grandmother lived alone, and Patricia would spend the nights with her during the week. One evening I asked Mom if I could go with her and play until it was time to come home. Mom agreed but quickly said, "Make sure you're home before dark and before the streetlights come on." So off we went.

We were having so much fun that we didn't realize the streetlights had come on. Suddenly Patricia turned toward the window and yelled, "Selita, it's dark!" We knew what that meant. I rushed out the door, jumped off the porch."

There was Mom coming toward me. I began to explain how we were having so much fun that we had lost track of time, and I was getting ready to run home as fast as I could. Mom calmly said, "Come on; let's go home." As we started walking, I noticed something in Mom's hand behind her back. Words began to shoot out of my mouth like water in a dishwasher on the pots-and-pans cycle as I pleaded my case. However, all Mother would say was "I told you to come home before dark," and she began to spank me as I walked toward home. I didn't want to get a spanking, and especially didn't want to give my friends the pleasure of witnessing the event. So I started running fast, thinking that Mother would just walk home. But she started running right behind me.

I didn't think anyone could ever come close as Mom to meaning what they said, but God is the same way. He admonishes us to start the day with Him in prayer, reading His Word, and meditating on His goodness. Life's distractions will keep us sidetracked if we permit them to. Before we realize it, it is dark, and the streetlights are on. The Holy Spirit warns us that we have been away too long, that it's time to commune with God. God doesn't run down the street of life, spanking us all the way home, but there are times that He chastens and simply loves us back into union with Him. I suppose that's what Mom was doing too. SELITA FAY ATCHLEY HARPE

God's Embrace

Thou hast beset me behind and before, and laid thine hand upon me. Ps. 139:5.

TIMES WERE DIFFICULT IN 1975 when we arrived in Nova Lisboa (currently Huambo), Angola, and people throughout the entire country were seeking refuge there. Everywhere, we found "controls" from different factions that were quartered there and who fought among themselves. My two children, who were 3 and 6 years of age, went with me by car to congratulate my sister-in-law, who was celebrating her birthday. As night approached I decided to return home by a route that was not so busy.

In the distance I saw seven men, armed with machine guns, in the middle of the road. Their guns were poised as though they were ready to shoot. I asked the Lord to protect us and told the children not to cry or to be afraid, because Jesus would take care of them while Mommy talked to the guards.

I was aware of some situations our friends had faced. Some had been killed, and others had spent many days in isolated locations and were beaten and mistreated.

When I stopped, a soldier approached. "Good afternoon," he said. "Could you take us to the next neighborhood?" I returned his greeting and stated that I wasn't familiar with the neighborhood.

"We will show you where it is," he said.

Looking him straight in the eye, I said, "There are seven of you and three of us; the car can take only five. I do not know what to do. The children have to go home, and I have to go to the school."

"Forget it; don't worry about it. Do you have 20 escudos for us to catch the bus?"

I took out my wallet and gave the money to him. Then he said, "You can go on without any worry; no one is going to harm you."

Shaking from fright, I drove on, the children still quiet. In the rearview mirror I could see the seven soldiers in the middle of the road, guns pointed at the ground.

I thanked God for the marvelous manner in which He took care of us. Truly the Lord was there, surrounding us and giving us His special embrace in this complicated situation. He will do the same for you; He loves all of us and takes special care of His children.   MARIA COSTA SALES CARDOSA

(?) Thought: Memorize today's text. Someday you may need God's embrace in a crisis.

Peace and Safety

I go to prepare a place for you. John 14:2.

I REMEMBER WATCHING THE 1984 Winter Olympics on television; it was the year Jayne Torvill and Christopher Dean became international stars with their stunning ice skating. What a beautiful city Sarajevo, Bosnia, seemed to be! Between events the television cameras showed us magnificent old buildings by the river Miljacka that winds through the city. Eight years later Sarajevo was back on television, this time not because of a happy world event. The city was under siege.

I first met Suzanna from Sarajevo a few years ago, and we became good friends. Born and raised in Sarajevo, she is the eldest of two daughters. Before the war they were just an ordinary family, getting on with their lives. Suzanna studied at the University of Sarajevo, obtained her economics degree, and taught in a city high school. She married her sweetheart not long after she began teaching. By then her younger sister was studying English and Italian at the university. Suzanna told me how clever her sister was, how languages came naturally to her.

Overnight her life changed forever as hundreds of tanks, mortar, and other weapons surrounded the city. Electricity was cut immediately, followed soon after by telephones, gas, and water. Their neighbors became their enemies; and a few weeks later their house was fired on by a tank. Tragically, Suzanna's sister was killed by shrapnel. And so day after day, month after month, Suzanna and her family lived under siege. They blocked the windows with sandbags and somehow survived by living in the solid back of the house. They were always hungry; daytimes were spent in long lines, waiting for bread and water. They ate things they would normally never eat. Suzanna knew that God was looking after them, because the little family never got sick. The siege lasted just under four years, and Suzanna and her husband, after spending a very long two years in a refugee camp, were eventually able to immigrate to Australia.

Many people such as Suzanna are displaced from their homes and countries; but Jesus promises us that in heaven everyone will have a special place. "I go to prepare a place for you." Isn't that the very best thing we can look forward to? Safely at home with Jesus forever more.   LEONIE DONALD

(?) Thought: If you lost your home, what, and who, would you depend on?

The Answer Is on the Way

And it shall come to pass, that before they call, I will answer; and while they are yet speaking, I will hear. Isa. 65:24.

THE BIOLOGY TEACHING WORK contract was soon to end. Kemar had finished his degree in religion and was scheduled to leave for service in the ministry. He had served my department very well as a part-time student teacher.

I was faithless enough to think that there could be no other like him—he had all anyone needed in a teacher. I was scared and worried. *Where on earth am I going to find a replacement?* I worried and worried until I remembered to pray about the matter. Sound familiar?

As I was at my office desk one morning, still worrying, I turned to God in prayer. My eyes were wide open, just like the office door. "Jesus, You know that Kemar is leaving. I can't be selfish, Lord; You need him to minister Your words to Your people. But I need a replacement, and I need someone like Kemar—or better than he, if there is such a one."

I was still praying when a lively, noisy, pleasant but assertive man walked into my office. All smiles, he said, "Hi, Mrs. Clarke; my name is Patterson, and I believe you have a job for me!" I stopped praying and laughed like biblical Sarah did because I could not believe God was coming through so quickly.

After the usual formalities and investigations associated with employment, he was hired. He is now the best I know in teaching not only biology but chemistry as well!

"What a friend we have in Jesus, all our sins and griefs to bear; what a privilege to carry everything to God in prayer! O what peace we often forfeit, O what needless pain we bear, all because we do not carry everything to God in prayer."

If only I had prayed earlier I would have been spared all the anxiety, pain, and worry.

"'Tis so sweet to trust in Jesus, just to take Him at His word; just to rest upon His promise, just to know, 'Thus saith the Lord.'"

I am still learning to trust Jesus, still learning to lean on my Lord. How is it with you?   JACQUELINE HOPE HOSHING-CLARKE

(?) Thought: Are you having challenges, or is there something for which you have been praying, perhaps a long time now? Be patient and trusting. Jesus is never late; the answer will come.

Vessels of Love, Compassion, and Mercy

Yet, O Lord, you are our Father. We are the clay, you are the potter; we are all the work of your hand. Isa. 64:8, NIV.

A DAILY CALENDAR featuring my favorite artist sits on the kitchen table. It is full of color, charm, and wit. I save the daily thought sheets throughout the year to make decoupage plates as gifts for friends, for special occasions, and just for fun.

I fashioned a plate for my guest bathroom. The first choice of decor was a bouquet of lavender hydrangeas for the center to match my bathroom colors and theme. Then I chose to complete the art with "pondering thoughts" for thinkers visiting the facilities.

One Sunday morning I was blow-drying my hair and aimlessly staring at the plate in its wrought-iron holder on the wall. Bordering the plate is a picture of a clay pot, its edges trimmed in red and green. A pale-blue morning glory, climbing from its emptiness, encircles the plate. The inscription etched along the vine caught my eye: "We shape emptiness into a pot, but it is the emptiness inside that holds whatever we want."

The Bible refers to us as clay, our Father as the potter. We are the work of His hands. Too often our emphasis is on our bodily containers and their beauty and perfection, forgetting that the emptiness inside is what holds the heart of love we want. We can label and manipulate Christians into various molds that we need—Sabbath school teachers, elders, pianists—but it is the heart that holds the spirit, the attitude, and the loveliness that we want. We can teach them all the right moves and tricks—just the right words to say, the proper things to do—with teaching guides, seminars, and programs. We can make them appear flawless, but only God's Spirit of love, grace, gentleness, and forgiveness filling the emptiness inside can make us truly Christlike.

My husband once sang in a men's quartet called Vessels of Mercy. Together they sang a beautiful song titled "Make Me a Vessel of Mercy." The words of the song go something like this: "Fill me with love and compassion, and fashion my heart to be a vessel worthy of You." The Potter, the clay, love, compassion, and some mercy.

Lord, fashion us into the work of Your hands, vessels of mercy and worthy of You.   JUDY GOOD SILVER

Sort Through the Clutter

Let us throw off everything that hinders and the sin that so easily entangles, and let us run with perseverance the race marked out for us. Heb. 12:1, NIV.

WHEN WE MOVED INTO our new home, I vowed that nothing would come in that didn't belong there. And I stuck to it—well, for a while at least. But that vow wore down over the months, and it was time to de-clutter once again. As I gave my office "the test," I was amazed at all the stuff I had accumulated. It took a couple days to go through old files, reorganize my desk and drawers, and sort through the stacks of paper growing here and there.

As I dug into the task at hand, I realized that a lot of the stuff was not all that important; much was unnecessary; and, it made my office look messy. Because each day I focused on getting the urgent accomplished, other things got pushed aside and left undone. Piles of nonessentials grew, and after a few months the room that I had so carefully planned and decorated to welcome me had become an unpleasant place.

I sorted, tossed, reorganized, filed, thoroughly cleaned, and tossed some more. Unlike most other people, I actually enjoy de-cluttering. When I completed my office, it was neat, attractive, and organized. Once again it welcomed me!

The next morning I was chatting with the Lord about a few things when the Holy Spirit vividly showed me how similar our lives are to a messy office. We get so focused on daily living, so into a routine that appears to work, that we fail to see the chaos around us. To us it appears normal. Over time we end up barely functioning in a rut; just getting through the day becomes our biggest challenge. Eventually we get so weighed down by all the stuff that clutters our lives that we border on being out of control. Can this be pleasing to God?

Just as I had to take time to clean out my office, we must also take time to clean all the nonessential stuff out of our daily lives. On a regular basis we need to sit down with the Lord and go through all the things that clutter our lives and sap our energy, weeding out what keeps us from operating at peak efficiency.   NANCY VAN PELT

(?) Thought: Do you need to clean house, getting rid of stuff that might be holding you back and keeping you from being all you could be? God wants and needs the very best we can give Him.

The Lost Pin

Or suppose a woman has ten silver coins and loses one. . . . And when she finds it, she calls her friends and neighbors together and says, "Rejoice with me; I have found my lost coin." Luke 15:8, 9, NIV.

MY MOTHER HAD GIVEN my husband and me a pair of solid gold pins. They were shaped like half hearts and bore the inscriptions "MIZ" and "PAH." On the back was the text from Genesis 31:49. We wore them all the time for sentimental reasons.

One day the inevitable happened—I lost mine and was very distraught. My husband comforted me by saying he would not wear his own until I found mine. I knew I could have lost it in any number of places. I was learning to drive at the time, so I had taken it off because it was continually being knocked off by the seat belt. It had fallen out of the vehicle more than once, so I had decided to take it off and place it in my handbag before my driving sessions. I searched those places I thought it could be, but to no avail. Then it hit me—*I* would not be able to find it no matter how hard I looked, so I might as well let God do His "needle in the haystack" job for me. I prayed in faith and left it completely up to God.

One afternoon not long after, I had to complete some business in the city at a government office. I had made a short visit there some days before. As I approached the receptionist, I felt impressed to inquire about my lost pin, which I described. She immediately informed me that she had found it. I expressed my joy as I said aloud, "Thank you—and thank You, Jesus." I told her it was God who had directed her to hold it because I had placed it in His hands when I had discovered it was lost. She rejoiced with me. I later returned and gave her a religious book, for which she was grateful. When I told my husband that I had found my precious pin, he calmly said he knew I would, so there was no need to worry. I have lost and found other items since, but this experience was poignant.

It reminds me that God cares about even the smallest details of our lives, and we should never fail to involve Him in everything. He is always willing and able to answer the prayer of faith. Today we need to develop a personal relationship with Him and rejoice in this knowledge.

BRENDA D. OTTLEY

? Thought: Do you have something to rejoice about today? Tell the Lord!

Things of the Past

And their sins and iniquities will I remember no more. Heb. 10:17.

AS I ENTERED THE SMALL pathway I had a strange feeling that I was not approaching a normal place of business. I wasn't certain why this particular location seemed different. Perhaps its location in a rural area outside of the city made it appear more attractive. Maybe it was the interior of the shedlike building and the sunlight as it struggled through the dirty fiberglass roofing. Or maybe it was the makeshift wooden ground covering that attracted me. As I wandered farther among the vintage doors and windows, I caught a glimpse of a huge stained glass door and finally realized what caused my special attraction to this place.

Somehow the items here seemed to have more personality, and I wanted to know about the past of each item that caught my eye. Where had that magnificent mahogany door with hand-painted stained glass once hung? Had it marked the entrance to the home of a government official, a rich plantation owner, or a wealthy widow of the influential São Paulo high society? Who had cleaned it with care throughout the years? Had it been removed because it was no longer useful, or had it been replaced with something more modern?

What about the large window that was still covered with the dirty gray remnants of what was once an expensive white curtain? Why would someone leave a curtain at the window, knowing that a house was to be demolished?

Suddenly it occurred to me that their past does not make a difference to me in their current state. I needed to accept these beautiful furnishings exactly for what they were and not be concerned about where they had been. "Perhaps it's better to leave the past in the past," I rationalized.

I remembered our wonderful, loving Savior, and how He accepts us for what we are. He puts our past in the past. Once we ask for forgiveness He doesn't keep remembering the things we've done in the past. Micah 7:19 tells us that our sins are buried in the depths of the sea.

We were all magnificently created; however, we have become stained, tarnished, and rusted through. If we have asked for forgiveness these mistakes have been forgotten by our Savior. He wants to take us away from this demolition-yard earth and give us a beautiful heavenly home that He is preparing. There we will be completely restored. BETH VOLLMER CHAGAS

Life's Jigsaw Puzzle

All things work together for good to them that love God. Rom. 8:28.

I PUT PIECE NUMBER 1,000 into the remaining hole in the jigsaw puzzle and sat back to admire my accomplishment. It was a lovely picture of an early-American farm scene, complete with a horse-drawn cart and a watermelon patch with several pickers bending over the vines.

It brought back memories of my childhood days. I thought of the large watermelon patch my father always put in and remembered those hot summer days when he would bring out a big green just-picked watermelon and cut it open. My mouth watered as I remembered how we sat together as a family on the back steps of our house enjoying the juicy red fruit.

The picture also brought to my mind memories of our family sitting around the table on cold winter days putting together a jigsaw puzzle of some faraway place such as Venice, Italy, or Paris, France. It made me long to visit those places. When I actually got to visit Venice and stood on the plaza and fed the pigeons, I suddenly found myself in the jigsaw puzzle picture of my childhood memories. I was overcome with the emotions it recalled of family togetherness and loved ones long gone.

Life is like a jigsaw puzzle, I thought. Some parts of it are easy to fit together, like small motifs of flags, a boat, a bright flower, or a person. But other parts, like dark patches of forest, the gray mass of mountains, or large expanses of water, are much harder. Some pieces seem to fit nowhere until the very end. It seems sometimes that the number of pieces of life's puzzle expands. What we thought was the picture of our lives we were putting together turns out to be so different from what we imagined.

What we so easily put together now shows up to be only a small segment, but brilliant against the darker portions around it. Sometimes we can't really appreciate the brilliant blessings of life until we see them against our times of sorrow and difficulty.

Lord, I'm finding some strange pieces right now in the jigsaw puzzle of my life. They just don't seem to fit into my life's plan. I can't see the whole picture as You do. I know when all is over, and I see the completed picture of my life, I will treasure every piece and see how You used even the difficulties and dark times to make of my life a picture of true beauty. DOROTHY EATON WATTS

Songs in the Night

Thou art my hiding place; thou shalt preserve me from trouble; thou shall compass me about with songs of deliverance. Ps. 32:7.

DOES GOD REALLY SPEAK to us? Yes, I know He does; lately He has been speaking to me through songs. Furthermore, the experience has shown me that we are affected by the music we listen to.

I am originally from a family of Haitian descent, and the first few years of my life we attended a French-speaking church. Later we started going to English-speaking churches. Then a few years ago, in an attempt to recapture some of my Haitian culture, I joined the Peace Corps. Although I didn't get the assignment to the French-speaking country I requested, I carried with me a French hymnal instead of an English one. I used it for my devotions and marveled that I remembered many of the songs we sang long ago. Many times I recognized tunes, although I didn't always know the meaning of the words.

One morning I found myself awake about 3:00, unable to go back to sleep. As I was lying there, many thoughts came to my mind. I had been feeling a bit down and unsure about what I was doing with my life. A tune came to my mind before I was finally able to fall asleep again. Waking up to do my devotions, I was determined to find that song in the hymnal. I didn't know the words to the tune, but I knew it came from the Lord because after only two turns of the pages (and by looking at the words of the chorus and using my slight ability to read music) I found it! *"Poursuivon notre course avec perseverance."* Then the chorus: *"Regardons, a Jesus . . . couronnant de vainqueur"* ("pursuing our race, with perseverance" and "look to Jesus, winner of the crown"). Just what I needed to hear! That song carried me all day.

Again I woke up in the middle of the night, feeling lonely. Another tune came to me: *"Mon Sauveur m'aime, Quel ferme appui pour ma foi!"* ("My Savior loves me, what firm support for my faith!")

If I had still been listening to the music of the world I would likely have awakened with the tunes of songs that spoke of violence, strife, or things that I could do with a man who was not my own. These thoughts could only drag me further down as I faced the day. I praise God for giving me the wisdom to feed my mind with His words, and not the words of the world.

MIRLÈNE ANDRÉ

Frustrations

Ask, and it shall be given you; seek, and ye shall find; knock, and it shall be opened unto you. Matt. 7:7.

SEVERAL YEARS AGO I purchased a kit to create a diamond-lace afghan. The kit included yarn and instructions. After I crocheted the first five rows, daily demands forced me to put it aside until later. The kit joined the other to-do projects in the bottom of a closet. There it stayed until I had completed and published two books. Determined to take a well-deserved break from writing, I dug into the closet to discover the unfinished afghan.

An excellent winter project! I thought. I removed the yarn and hook from the storage bag. To my horror, the instructions were missing. *Where did I put them? Surely I kept the yarn and instructions together!* I searched other boxes and bags in the closet and sorted through patterns and more patterns. I rummaged through the closet and drawers but found nothing.

Frustrated yet determined to find the missing instructions, I claimed the promise in today's text. I prayed, "Lord, You know I've looked everywhere for those instructions. Please show me where I put them. Thank You!"

After another search in the closet and in all the likely drawers, I sat down and asked myself, *Where was I seated when I crocheted the first few rows of that afghan?* I remembered sitting on the living room couch, next to our cozy woodstove.

Suddenly a quiet voice whispered, "Look in the couch stand next to where you began work on the afghan." I opened the door to the stand, lifted a few books, and there, between the books, I discovered the instructions! "Thank You, Lord, for guiding my thoughts." With directions in hand I recently completed the soft all-maroon afghan.

Matthew 10:30 says, "The very hairs of your head are all numbered." Awesome Father in heaven! He's so compassionate and caring. He who deems it important to number the hairs of our head is aware of the self-inflicted frustrations in our lives. He is ever ready to help us resolve annoying problems. All we have to do is claim His promises and ask in faith.

NATHALIE LADNER-BISCHOFF

(?) Thought: How has God shown an interest in your small frustrations and daily endeavors?

Does Jesus Care?

Then they cried out to the Lord in their trouble, and He saved them out of their distresses. Ps. 107:19, NKJV.

ONE OF MY FAVORITE AUTHORS once wrote, "Nothing that in any way concerns our peace is too small for Him to notice." Many times I have learned how true that is, and I am so happy that I can go to God with all my cares and that He listens to me. This was brought to my attention once again just recently.

A woman in our weekly Bible study class sold her condo and was moving from a city about 15 miles from us. It was going to cost her $1,000 for a moving company to move her, so my husband called together a group of men from our church, and they moved her at no charge. She was so excited! No one had ever done anything like that for her before, she said. However, she still had to unpack every box that was sitting in her new garage.

A short time later a well-known Christian singing group was in a nearby city, and we invited our friend to go with us to hear them. She wasn't sure she could, because she needed to drive to another state to be with her father during his heart surgery, but then she decided she would go anyway and leave on her trip early the next morning. She thoroughly enjoyed the concert.

On the way home, around 11:00, she told us she still had to do laundry before she could leave and, worst of all, she was out of checks in her checkbook and absolutely had to find more before she could leave. They were in a box somewhere in the garage, but she had no idea where.

As she got out of the car, my husband prayed that she would have a safe trip and that her father's surgery would go well. Then I added, "And dear Father, please show her which box her checks are in so that she can get to bed soon and have a good rest before she leaves."

When we arrived home a few minutes later there was a message on our answering machine: "You are not going to believe this, but after you left I walked out to the garage, and the very first box I was impressed to look in had my checks in it." ANNA MAY RADKE WATERS

?Thought: Make a list of what God has done for you lately.

A Sewing Machine and Needle

I will greatly rejoice in the Lord, my soul shall be joyful in my God; for he hath clothed me with the garments of salvation, he hath covered me with the robe of righteousness. Isa. 61:10.

EVERY SO OFTEN ONE of my girls reminds me of a special dress she had while growing up. Ardie remembers the dark-plaid dress with the row of buttons across the front. She called it her piano dress. And I remember the pink dress with the dark-brown pinafore. Gail inherited some of Ardie's outgrown dresses, but she had special ones as well. How I loved to sew for my children, sometimes stitching late at night. They were always well dressed because their mother had a knack with a sewing machine and needle. In fact, their brother Bill was the only boy in school who had marble bags to match his shirts.

It was no secret that I browsed the better children's and department stores to observe the dresses with their costly price tags. Then I'd find similar material in fabric stores and copy the originals, making whatever changes I thought necessary. Oh, yes, I designed some of the dresses too, but always it was fun to dress my girls up in copies of originals. My sewing skills accompanied the girls right through their high school days. I well remember the dark-green velveteen dress that followed one daughter into college. What a joy it was to make banquet formals that would pass the severest critic—and without a costly price tag.

The old sewing machine still works, even though it dates back to the nineteenth century. It has been modernized with electricity that replaced the treadle. It accomplished its purpose when sewing little dresses back then, and it accomplished its purpose for Mother, too. We have both grown older, the machine and I. One of us doesn't work as well anymore, but well enough to turn out beautiful quilts and whatever else needs to be sewn or mended.

God isn't concerned with our outward appearance or how we are dressed. He looks on the conditions of the heart. That is what counts most with Him. Christ's robe of righteousness will cover our nakedness if we are in tune with Him. All will be originals woven on a heavenly loom without a seam.

LAURIE DIXON-MCCLANAHAN

(?) **Thought:** Study Isaiah 61:10 and 11 and think about how God is preparing you for your robe of righteousness.

Physiotherapy for the Soul

Therefore we do not lose heart. Though outwardly we are wasting away, yet inwardly we are being renewed day by day. 2 Cor. 4:16, NIV.

IT HAD BEEN ONE of those days. The pool had been troubled—the angel had been there and gone, and he was still there.

Everything always passed him by, and the people who were supposed to help him pushed him out of the way. Another 38 years of waiting loomed. Then the Stranger came. He asked, "Do you want to get well?" (John 5:6, NIV).

"Sir," the invalid replied, "I have no one to help me into the pool when the water is stirred. While I am trying to get in, someone else goes down ahead of me" (verse 7, NIV).

Haven't you had one of those days, weeks, or even years? You've been injured by life, you've heard of a way out, and then other people who need the help less than you do push you out of the way.

Then the Stranger comes. "Get up! Pick up your mat and walk!" (verse 8, NIV). What a breath of fresh air. Not knowing where you got the strength, you get up and start all over again.

Today Jesus is saying to you, "Get up. Take whatever may have been your physical or emotional pain, and walk." There will be joy as you discover the strength you did not realize you had. It will also be difficult; there will always be the Pharisees telling you that you are breaking their rules, asking you what right you have to be well.

Listen to what God says: "[Those] who bind themselves to the Lord to serve him, to love the name of the Lord, and to worship him, . . . these I will bring to my holy mountain and give them joy in my house of prayer" (Isa. 56:6, 7, NIV).

There will be days when you feel broken and hurt, but God has promised physiotherapy for your soul. He is the one who can really bring you deep joy. As Paul has assured us: "All this is for your benefit, so that the grace that is reaching more and more people may cause thanksgiving to overflow to the glory of God. Therefore we do not lose heart. Though outwardly we are wasting away, yet inwardly we are being renewed day by day" (2 Cor. 4:15, 16, NIV).

JUDITH PURKISS

(?) **Thought:** If Jesus were to ask you "Do you want to get well?" how would you respond?

Looking Young, Yet Blind

For now we see through a glass, darkly; but then face to face: now I know in part; but then shall I know even as also I am known. 1 Cor. 13:12.

I HAD BECOME MORE conscious of cleaning my glasses while reading, or even pushing my hair aside to be able to see clearly. Only when I went to the doctor did I find out the sad truth.

We had just returned from a visit to Thailand, where our son was working. He had taken care of a number of things concerning our health and even our appearance, including new glasses that were a little more up-to-date. With all the rest and the good food we enjoyed, we even looked younger. This was confirmed by the welcome we received at the church once we returned home. The first elder announced from the pulpit, "Welcome to the Poddars! They went from here as old people and came back as young people." We had a good laugh, of course.

Despite "becoming young" again, I soon learned that I had developed cataracts. This was certainly a blow, but I had to accept it, whether I liked it or not. After the surgery I had to wear dark glasses, as the other eye was not ready for the surgery yet. Never having worn dark glasses in my entire life, I was a bit shy to wear them. One doctor commented that I looked stylish, which made me laugh; but I received more and more comments when I reached home. Yet when I put away the dark glasses, my eyes hurt. I did not ask to be looking young and stylish but to be healed.

When I reached home, the first thing I noticed was that my house looked as if it were newly painted. My clothes looked new and extra colorful. The curry I made looked as if I had put in too much curry powder, and even my toothbrush handle was unusually yellow in color.

I recognize I still have another serious cataract sin problem that the Lord will completely remove at His coming. Right now I see through a dark glass at the imperfect world and the pollution that increases day by day. I look forward to when I will be transformed to a new body and yet preserve my identity. I will be known as I am known now—but younger, of course, and with perfect eyesight to see near and beyond to the limitless space. Above all, I will behold my great and wonderful Savior, who made it possible to be there. Praise the Lord!

BIRDIE PODDAR

Redeemer of Dreams

The Lord will command His lovingkindness in the daytime, and in the night His song shall be with me—A prayer to the God of my life. Ps. 42:8, NKJV.

I JERKED AWAKE, my heart racing. Drenched in sweat, yet cold, I sat up and reached a shaky hand to turn the clock: 3:30 a.m. By now I knew the pattern. Even if I could manage to calm down and fall asleep, the nightmare would return. I sighed, got up, and picked up my Bible, but couldn't concentrate. For a week I'd had my sleep interrupted by nightmares.

Later that day I told a friend about it. "Have you considered that this might be a spiritual attack?" he asked. Surprised, I admitted I hadn't. He suggested I pray about it, so that night as I prepared for bed I did. "Lord, this seems kind of silly to me, but I just can't handle this anymore. Please, guard my dreams tonight." With that I fell asleep.

That night the nightmare started again. I was on the top floor of a huge mansion with many other people. Filled with fear, I knew somehow I needed to get out, but stairways that should have led down twisted around so I always ended up where I started. I asked the people to help, but they ignored me. The terror had built up to an almost unbearable level when I felt a tap on my shoulder. Turning around, I saw a man who looked like Jesus, dressed in jeans and a T-shirt. He pointed toward the flight of stairs I'd tried before, and said, "Follow Me." Instantly calm, I followed Him down many levels until we came to a large door. He opened it, and we stepped out into the yard. I turned around, but He had disappeared. I looked at the mansion and saw it slowly sink into the ground. Feeling incredible peace, I sat down and looked up into a brilliantly blue sky and sang.

When I woke, I was filled with joyful praise for my God and hummed a tune that seemed familiar. When I found the song in my hymnal, I was astounded by the first verse: "Be Thou my vision, O Lord of my heart; naught be all else to me save that Thou art, Thou my best thought, by day or by night, waking or sleeping, Thy presence my light."

The nightmares continued for three days after that, but in every one the ending was changed by a miracle, turning my fear into praise. I woke each morning amazed by the love of my God who cares so much about me that He keeps me safe even in my dreams.   EVE PARKER

Parties, Donkeys, and God's Love

King Belshazzer gave a great banquet for a thousand of his nobles and drank wine with them. . . . Suddenly the fingers of a human hand appeared and wrote on the plaster of the wall. Dan. 5:1-5, NIV.

THIS WAS NOT A SMALL dinner party! It was a huge banquet held at the royal citadel in Babylon. One thousand of the king's nobles and the king's wives and concubines were in attendance. Because the king's women attended, it is likely that the wives of the nobles were there also. So the guests may have numbered more than 2,000.

Imagine the party: the guests all reclined on cushions beside the tables. The king ate alone (or perhaps with his favorite woman) on a dais. The meal consisted of many courses and a great deal of wine. I'm sure that the guests had become "mellow," and that this wasn't a quiet affair. Undoubtedly there was entertainment, because Middle Eastern kings had trained musicians and dancing girls in their harems.

In the middle of all this, Belshazzar decided to make a mockery of the Jewish people, their religion, and their God by commanding that the golden cups and vessels taken from the Temple in Jerusalem be brought in to be used for the party.

The Bible doesn't tell us of God's efforts to influence Belshazzar prior to this time. He must have known about Nebuchadnezzar's experiences and his eventual love for God. Perhaps Belshazzar simply ignored that part of his family history. So God chose to warn him by sending an angel to visit the party and write a warning on the wall in the presence of Babylon's most influential citizens. Belshazzar couldn't ignore this message.

There are other stories in the Bible about God having to resort to creative measures to catch His people's attention: wrestling with Jacob, speaking through a donkey, blinding Saul/Paul with a bright light.

I wonder how often God has felt that I needed a donkey to confront me because I've forgotten about the role that He has played in my life.

CLARICE BRENNEISE TURNER MURPHY

Thought: Think about what God has done to get your attention. Could there be an easier way?

The Salt

You are the salt of the earth. But if the salt loses its saltiness, how can it be made salty again? It is no longer good for anything, except to be thrown out and trampled by men. Matt. 5:13, NIV.

ANOTHER WINTER, I SIGHED. Don't get me wrong; even though I come from a tropical place, I love winter. Really. I love to feel cozy in my pajamas, or just snuggle on the couch with a good book, or take time to play Scrabble. However, what I don't like is shoveling snow. And it's just my luck that most of the time when we get a snowstorm, my husband is traveling somewhere.

Today was one of those times I needed some help shoveling. I woke up to find about six inches of snow on the ground. My husband was in Zimbabwe, and we have a 10-car driveway. With help from a friend, we did finish shoveling—but with a backache. Off to work I went. At the office, however, they announced that they recommended all employees go home early because the roads were icy. I dreaded going home; I wished I could just stay in the office, but it was not possible. First, my dog, Rafiki, was waiting for me; and second, I needed to take care of the ice in the driveway before someone slipped and got hurt.

On my way home I stopped by the store to get a new shovel. I noticed people buying salt and heard people saying they needed it to melt the ice. But because I was raised in the tropics, I didn't really understand. However, I bought a 25-pound bag anyway, just to try it.

I was amazed, really amazed. As I sprinkled salt on the crystal ice I could literally hear the cracking sound as the ice melted. *Thank You, dear Father,* I whispered. *This salt is a great help. Now I don't have to suffer another back-ache. All I need to do is to sprinkle some salt and the problem is gone.*

Matthew 5:13 reads "You are the salt of the earth" (NIV). If we are the salt of the earth, we bring joy to those who are around us. We melt cold hearts and warm them with the love of Christ. People will love to have us around because they can hold on to us; they don't have to slip in this icy world. We are their friends, their encouragers, their supporters.

JEMIMA D. ORILLOSA

?Thought: How might you be the "salt of the earth" today? Do you ever feel you have lost your saltiness? If so, what can be done about that?

Sit

They went to a place called Gethsemane, and Jesus said to his disciples, "Sit here while I pray." Mark 14:32, NIV.

EARLY ON WEDNESDAY mornings I meet with my "support group." We six women laugh and weep and often pray for each other. Jesus had a small support group, too, and in Mark 14 we see His group in action.

He brought His closest friends as far as they could go without intruding on an experience that needed to be very private. As intense as His encounter with His Father was, He tore Himself away three times to seek the strength that comes from simply having friends near.

I find it curious that Jesus did not ask them to pray for Him as He approached His trial. He simply said, "Sit here while I pray. . . . Stay here and keep watch" (verses 32-34, NIV).

Did He assume they would be praying for Him, and thus didn't mention it? Or was it because His impending struggle was between Him and His Father?

When He returned the first time and found them asleep, He did tell them to pray. But not for Him. Rather, He told them to pray for themselves—that they would "not fall into temptation" (verse 38, NIV). If they had prayed as instructed, would Peter have been spared the shame of denying his Friend and Lord?

Though it must have disappointed Jesus to find His friends asleep while He agonized, He didn't respond in anger. Rather, after a mild scolding ("'Simon,' he said to Peter, 'are you asleep? Could you not keep watch for one hour?'" [verse 37, NIV]) He showed He understood by His gentle comment "The spirit is willing, but the body is weak" (verse 38, NIV).

When He returned again and found them asleep, "they did not know what to say to him" (verse 40, NIV). He was right. Their bodies were weak; they had no excuse. Jesus simply turned back to His task, perhaps comforted by the knowledge that they were trying, even if it didn't seem enough.

In our present day, when we face trials and call on supportive friends (or we are the willing but weak friend?) it is worth remembering that it is not our prayers nor our encouraging or advising words but our faithful presence that conveys the needed message and supplies the needed courage. Sometimes "being there" is the most valuable gift we can give another.

DOLORES KLINSKY WALKER

She Keeps Going and Going!

The Lord is my strength and my shield; my heart trusted in him, and I am helped: therefore my heart greatly rejoiceth; and with my song will I praise him. Ps. 28:7.

WHO HASN'T SEEN THE AD on TV featuring the Energizer bunny rolling along, playing the drum, the one who "keeps going and going" because he has such good batteries powering him?

The Energizer bunny reminds me of my friend and former neighbor, Selah, who is more than 90. While recently visiting her I asked, "Selah, do you have any special secrets as to what has enabled you to live such a long, healthy life?"

She smiled and said, "Yes. I try to eat right and drink plenty of water and get enough sleep. I also believe a person needs fresh air and sunlight and plenty of exercise."

Selah lives in the country; she stays active cleaning her house, cooking, and taking care of her small vegetable garden. She still drives her car on short trips to the doctor, post office, and grocery store. Only recently has she allowed someone to come in to help her clean.

"Do you ever have trouble with achy joints?" I asked.

"My exercises take care of that," she replied. "I do about 100 arm circles a day to keep my shoulder supple, and 500 to 600 bicycle pedals each day. That keeps my legs and feet limber. So I don't have many problems with arthritic bones. I'd say keeping going is very important."

This active senior has certainly done that. A former school teacher, she married, farmed, raised children, and now enjoys 15 grandchildren and 13 great-grandchildren.

When I asked if she had any other secrets, she told me the most important one of all: "I'm a Christian, and I try to keep happy."

Selah has a good singing voice and enjoys doing special music with members of her family. Last June her church held a homecoming, and Selah was part of it, praising God in song. She has found God to be a never-failing source of power.

I think of her and realize that many seniors aren't that fortunate. We should try to help them and remember all of them in prayer.

Lord, we thank You for being the source of life and strength. May we, like Selah, use these gifts not only for ourselves but also to bless others. Amen.

BONNIE MOYERS

What if I Soil Your Dress?

Truly, I say to you, unless you turn and become like children, you will never enter the kingdom of heaven. Matt. 18:3, ESV.

SHE SECURED THE FIRST place on the board examination, and all those who knew her believed she had the brains and the efficiency to reach the zenith. She first came to me as a preschool child. Her parents, discerning her potential, wanted her to be occupied with something useful during the day. So they sent her to the school at an early age.

She cried every morning when her parents left her at the entrance of the classroom. She didn't want anything to do with the class or its occupants. I knew she was observing every activity amid tears. I knew because I got every day's report from her parents. They knew the names of all 25 children in the class and what they did during classtime or playtime. She talked about the toys, the snack, and a lot about her teacher. And she cried all the time. She would not sit on the seat assigned to her. Instead, she'd walk around with me, holding on to my sari. She found comfort in climbing onto my lap and settling there. She even wiped her face, nose, and tears with my sari.

One day I told her, "Shoba, you are soiling my sari." Quick came the response: "What if I soil your sari? You can always wash it, can't you?" It was so innocent, so commanding and full of meaning. It sounded as if she were saying, "Don't you know that soiled things should be washed and cleaned?"

Of course dirt should be removed. We feel unclean and messy as long as it is there. The only way to feel comfortable is to have things clean. Shoba soils the cloth; I clean it. I soil my spiritual garments, and who does the cleaning? I am happy I have the answer: I have a washer ready and available at my door with the great promise "I will wash them and make them as white as snow" (see Isa. 1:18; Ps. 51:7). We can claim that promise and thank the little Shobas around the world who keep reminding us of promises. Believe, like Shoba, that a washer is readily available. Go to Him and be cleansed.

MARGARET TITO

? Thought: What do you have that needs cleaning? How often do we try to clean up messes ourselves?

Thy Word Is a Lamp

Ye are the light of the world. A city that is set on an hill cannot be hid. Neither do men light a candle, and put it under a bushel; but on a candlestick; and it giveth light unto all that are in the house. Matt. 5:14, 15.

I NOTICED WHILE FEEDING the two larger feeder fish that only one light out of two was burning in the fish aquarium. The fish were placed into the aquarium on the darker side, and they quickly swam to the lighted side and stayed together. The larger fish swam over and frightened the smaller ones by having one for its meal. On occasion a smaller fish would leave the school of fish and wander out toward the darker side—and not return. Sometimes the larger fish would tease the smaller ones in order to scatter them, and one would end up becoming the meal of the larger fish.

The big divide came when the larger fish stayed on the darker side and the smaller ones stayed on the lighted side. Everything was quiet for a while. The larger fish went as far in the darkness as possible so as not to be seen, and waited so that when a small fish strayed, leaving the company of the light and school of fish, he would swim directly into the mouth of his enemy and be destroyed.

The devil, too, is shrewd. He appears not as a big fish but as a roaring lion, seeking whom he can devour. But he also blends in with the surroundings so as not to be noticed, and when the unsuspecting Christian appears, he destroys her before she has a chance to escape.

The devil loves darkness. God has given us light. In our everyday lives we meet the devil and his many imps who are trying to get us to disobey God's Word. The church is a lighthouse and storehouse where we need to go and get spiritually recharged or our batteries will lose their charge and die. And we will be left in the dark.

"Thy word is a lamp unto my feet, and a light unto my path" (Ps. 119:105). *Lord, please keep me in the light of Your will. Thank You. Amen.*

BETTY G. PERRY

Thought: Read John 1 and note all the contrasts of light and dark. How do we share our spiritual lights?

Comfort in the Dentist Chair

My God shall supply all your need. Phil. 4:19, NKJV.

GOING TO THE DENTIST is one of my least favorite things to do. As I faced an upcoming dental appointment I kept thinking, *Maybe something will come up, and I won't have to go.* But nothing interfered with my appointment. As I drove to the dentist's office I kept a prayer on my lips. On this particular day I was having a crown preparation done. This procedure involves much grinding and a smell that makes me feel sick.

As I sat in the chair, waiting, I began to feel very nervous and wished someone had come with me to hold my hand! I again found myself talking to God about my frustrations and fears. While I was praying, a thought came to me: *Ask the dental assistant for a radio!* That seemed unusual, but I decided to ask anyway. She responded, "Yes, I think we have one around here somewhere." After a short time she returned, carrying a small radio. I thanked her and put on the headset and turned to my favorite religious station. As I began listening, this song ministered to my soul: "When peace, like a river, attendeth my way, when sorrows like sea billows roll—whatever my lot, Thou hast taught me to say, It is well, it is well with my soul."

Wow! That was comforting. It was difficult to believe, but the next song was a special blessing too. "Peace! peace! wonderful peace, coming down from the Father above; sweep over my spirit forever, I pray, in fathomless billows of love."

Each song, each verse, seemed to meet my needs. I was really feeling God's comfort, and His words were just what I needed. God had arranged for this music to be played exactly when I needed His presence and reassurance.

"Praise be to . . . the God of all comfort, who comforts us in all our troubles, so that we can comfort those in any trouble with the comfort we ourselves have received from God" (2 Cor. 1:3, 4, NIV). SHARON FOLLETT

(?) Thought: Is there someone with whom you can share God's comfort? And have you told God what you feel your needs are so that He can bless you too this day?

Witnessing

Let the words of my mouth, and the meditation of my heart, be acceptable in thy sight, O Lord, my strength, and my redeemer. Ps. 19:14.

MY HEART THRILLS WHEN members at church tell of their experiences of witnessing. One told how he had witnessed to a friend with a stubborn heart, and years later this man gave his heart to God. Oh, how I wish I had experiences to tell; but you see, I live a very ordinary life and never have an opportunity to find someone to witness to.

I work part-time in an office with three young women. I've been there 10 years, and Susan and Rebecca are like family—they know me very well. Gale, the temporary, is of a religion I know very little about, so sometimes we compare our beliefs over lunch.

A friend who enjoys seafood very much couldn't understand when I said I am interested in vegetarian meals. I suggested she read Leviticus 11.

A casual friend called one day about something related to my job. She had once been married to a minister of a different church than mine, and somehow we got to talking about beliefs. She had some "why" questions: "Why do you do this?" and "Why don't you do this?"

I have two part-time jobs, one of which is interviewing elderly people in hopes of finding them a job. The other day while I was filling out paperwork for a woman, she told me how she enjoys cooking for her church suppers. I mentioned we have potluck dinners at our church each week. One topic led to another, and 30 minutes later we got back to doing paperwork.

When my daughters were small, they became good friends with the little girls who lived across the street. They went to church with us and, as they got older, attended our church's elementary school. I seldom see them now that they are grown, but a couple years ago I saw Diana at a birthday party. She hugged me and told me I had been a great influence on her life. I cried.

Yesterday my grandson was excited about a beautiful, vivid rainbow he had seen in the sky. He didn't know about God's promise that the earth would never be destroyed by flood.

I just realized—I *am* witnessing! Most of these are average, ordinary-day happenings, nothing unusual, but I just never thought of witnessing in that way before.

Lord, help me to witness in my daily life so that others will see You in me and learn to love You as I do. NELDA BIGELOW

Lost but Not Forgotten

For I know the thoughts that I think toward you, says the Lord, thoughts of peace and not of evil, to give you a future and a hope. Jer. 29:11, NKJV.

IT SEEMED TO BE a trivial thing, lost keys. It wasn't as though I couldn't live without them, but they were special to me. They were my original set of car keys, and the ornament had today's text engraved on it—my favorite. The keys represented a promise from God when I boldly went to His throne and asked for a first-ever brand-new car.

The winter was beyond normal even for Rochester, New York. We had continual snowstorms that made everyone weary. I had gone to work very early that late January morning. And as I had done frequently, I gathered my briefcase/purse, locked my car doors, put my keys inside my coat pocket, and headed toward the building.

My workday was so intense that I never emerged until late that evening, and then I discovered that several inches of snow had fallen. When I went to retrieve my car keys from my coat pocket, they were missing. I searched everywhere but found no keys. I even went back to the parking lot and kicked the snow surrounding my car. No keys. I gave up the search, vowing that I would look again in the morning light. I pulled out a spare set of keys and drove home.

The next day my hopes were dashed when I saw that the parking lot had been plowed. Nevertheless, I searched where my car had been parked, but still no keys. I pondered whether or not my keys were now lost in the 30-foot pile of snow at the end of the parking lot. For months I kept looking at that mound of melting snow, wondering if my keys were there.

April soon came. Spring was officially here, but the constant pressures of work and life emotionally drained me. My spiritual well-being was melting, and just like my keys, I felt lost. I was beginning to question my worth to God. So I whispered, *Father, I need to see a miracle. Forgive my doubting, but I just need to see something that lets me know that You still love me.*

As I entered the building, my eyes caught a glimpse of something on the receptionist's desk. Yes, you guessed it! There lay my keys—rusted, dirty, and beat-up. But my miracle!

Although my life seemed like those lost keys, once again God revealed His promise that He loves us and cares for the dirty, rusty, and beat-up moments in our life.

EVELYN GREENWADE BOLTWOOD

The Lions' Den

My God sent his angel, and he shut the mouths of the lions. They have not hurt me, because I was found innocent in his sight. Nor have I ever done any wrong before you. Dan. 6:22, NIV.

I WASN'T LOOKING FORWARD to this. The hastily called planning session was only minutes away. The palms of my hands felt damp and clammy; my heartbeat echoed in my ears. What would they ask? What would I say? The anxiety was building, and I felt as if I were suffocating. Yet no one knew the internal turmoil and pressure. As I passed a mirror I was amazed at how calm I looked outwardly. *Dear God,* I shouted in my mind, *You delivered Daniel; deliver me.* The project had to come together in three days. Pride, reputation, and money were on the line.

I had talked about some possible strategies with two colleagues. Now they retreated to a distant corner, taking on an air of neutrality. I was definitely on my own. The designated leader motioned to me as three others found places to sit, and another paced back and forth like a caged lion, obviously angry. *Deliver me, God,* I prayed. I looked up, hoping to see that chariot of fire "coming for to carry me home." It was not to be.

"I'll carry you through," a small voice whispered, almost drowned out by the leader's gruff command, "OK, Maxine, let's hear what you think our course of action should be."

I scanned the room as I opened my mouth to speak. I remember my lips moving, but my ears could not hear what they were saying. To this day I cannot tell you what I said. Yes, there were angry exchanges, but for the most part they sat and listened attentively, looking for any cause to pounce. With God's help, by the end of that meeting I had gotten what I needed.

I had prayed for a miraculous deliverance; instead, I had been carried safely through a very tense situation. His way was far better, for I had learned a lot. With just as much dread as Daniel must have felt as they lowered him down into the lions' den, I had dreaded that meeting; but my true deliverance was to be found in the den—I had to trust the Creator of the lions.

Dear God, we do not know what challenges today will bring, or what lionlike individuals we will have to face, but please help us to remember that You've tamed lions before, and You can do it again—praise be unto Your holy name.

MAXINE WILLIAMS ALLEN

Jerusalem, We Have a Problem

Call on me in the day of trouble; I will deliver you. Ps. 50:15, NRSV.

WE WERE IN CHURCH that Sabbath, February 1, 2003, when our minister entered the pulpit and announced: "At 8:59 this morning the *Columbia* broke apart somewhere above Texas. There were no survivors." Our space coast congregation inhaled in a collective gasp. The orbiter had disintegrated only 16 minutes from landing. The astronauts hadn't even had a chance to say "Houston, we have a problem."

We experienced a gamut of emotions—shock, disbelief, anger, and grief —in numbed silence. Then tears flowed down as prayers went up.

Later, as I scoured the papers for details, I found myself particularly drawn to notes on four of the downed heroes. I received a multiforwarded e-mail from a woman who had attended a Steve Green concert just 12 hours after the loss of *Columbia*. The Christian artist, a friend of Captain Rick Husband's, told the audience that the captain's wife had chosen Green's song, "God of Wonders," for one of the crew's wake-up calls. Husband had described how overwhelming it was to view God's vast creation from space.

I read that the two women, the flight surgeon and the aeronautical engineer, who were from different parts of the world (Wisconsin, United States, and Karnal, India), had bonded through their zest for detail and their love of a science that uncovers the awesome universe.

At the memorial at the Kennedy Space Center, Rabbi Zvi Konikov described his quandary at Ilan Ramon's question. The Israeli astronaut wanted to observe the Sabbath of his people. "How does one mark the Sabbath in space, with every 90 minutes another sunset; every 10 and a half hours a Sabbath? Jerusalem, we have a problem!" he quipped.

Ramon's answer to his own query was a deep one. "No matter how fast we're going, no matter how important our work, we need to pause and think about why we're here on Earth."

Yes, we must call on our Creator Redeemer, the God of sunsets, lightning and space, and He will help us to fulfill our mission.

Humanity, we have the solution!   GLENDA-MAE GREENE

Giving Voice to Praise

Shout with joy to God, all the earth! Sing the glory of his name; make his praise glorious! Ps. 66:1, 2, NIV.

EACH DAY I ALWAYS begin my personal devotions with a time of praise. The psalmist tells us to "enter his gates with thanksgiving and his courts with praise" (Ps. 100:4, NIV).

Over the years I've found that praise at the beginning of my devotional time gives me an attitude of joy and thankfulness for what God has done in my life. It is no surprise, therefore, that I love the book of Psalms. I have read and reread those psalms many times over the years and have found something to praise God for in almost every verse I read.

But I've also found that hymns and sacred songs help me experience the same joy and thankfulness. Some days during my devotional time I do nothing but sing one hymn after the other. From praise to forgiveness to supplication to thanks—it's all there.

I think my greatest joy in going through our church hymnal has been finding hymns I have never sung before, and just reading the words aloud. It never ceases to amaze me that the hymns I've passed over for years because I didn't know them have some of the sweetest and most meaningful words.

One hymn writer exhorts us to "tell out, my soul, the greatness of the Lord! Unnumbered blessings give my spirit voice" (Timothy Dudley-Smith, "Tell Out, My Soul"). Another of my favorites says, "Lord of creation, to You be all praise! Most mighty Your working, most wondrous Your ways! Your glory and might are beyond us to tell, and yet in the heart of the humble You dwell (Jack Copley Winslow, "Lord of Creation").

Again and again I find that the writers of the hymns know my feelings, express my thoughts, and give voice to my praise and thanks to God, my king. At times when my pen cannot express what lies deep within I have found a hymn that says in words so eloquently what I feel deep inside my soul.

And so I cannot help praising my God. I praise Him for inspiring the many writers and musicians who wrote these words and put them to music for me to use to "tell out, my soul."

Have you tried to sing your devotional time? If not, then a joyous experience awaits you!   HEATHER-DAWN SMALL

The Rock

The Lord is my rock, my fortress, and my savior; my God is my rock, in whom I find protection. 2 Sam. 22:2, 3, NLT.

TO THE LOCAL ABORIGINAL people it is ancient Uluru. Nineteenth-century European explorers named it Ayers Rock to honor a political leader of the day. To many modern visitors it is simply "The Rock." One of the world's largest monoliths, Uluru rears up 1,131 feet (348 meters) from a level plain in central Australia above the red desert sand. At more than 5.5 miles (9 kilometers) in circumference, its vast bulk is visible for many miles. Its looming presence has an almost personal quality—it isn't difficult to see why Uluru is of sacred significance to Aboriginal people and revered as the haunt of their ancestral beings.

For thousands of years this rock has provided shelter to plants, birds, land animals, and humans alike. Ancient paintings can still be seen in caves around its base, evidence of generations past who sought refuge from searing summer heat and the chill of desert nights. A permanent waterhole at its foot is a lifeline for native animals. Shallow niches high on its stony flanks make safe homes for birds. Greenery clings to every crack where moisture trickles, and to every indentation where a little rainwater collects.

Uluru is an enormous, solid mass, impervious to heat, cold, wind, and fire—yet it is a thing of extraordinary beauty. Part of its mystique is because of the way its color changes in response to changing light. Red-brown at noon, it becomes almost mauve, gathering purple shadows as evening approaches, then glows with orange fire at sunset, and again at sunrise.

Was it to a rock like this that the Bible writers raised their eyes as they meditated on the eternal God? "For who is God except the Lord? Who but our God is a solid rock?" (2 Sam. 22:32, NLT). "Look, a righteous king is coming! And honest princes will rule under him. He will shelter Israel from the storm and the wind. He will refresh her as a river in the desert and as the cool shadow of a large rock in a hot and weary land" (Isa. 32:1, 2, NLT).

Lord, this world still brings many troubles that are like wind and storm and scorching heat. I am so thankful that You are always there, strong and secure, a place of shelter and safety. Be my rock and refuge today, I pray.

JENNIFER M. BALDWIN

Trouble With the Neighbor

With his mouth the godless destroys his neighbor, but through knowledge the righteous escape. Prov. 11:9, NIV.

MY HUSBAND WAS ABOUT to retire, and for many months we had been looking for real estate that would be our definitive residence. Finally we found a house that met our needs, and the amount was within our budget. We closed the deal and moved. With great joy we looked at our house and said, "Finally we are living in a house that is completely ours! Here we have peace and calm—and good neighbors!"

During the first days everything went well. Then a couple who were our friends came to visit. By mistake they rang the intercom doorbell of the next-door neighbor, a woman who lived alone. (I had seen her only once.) She immediately came to our house and rang the doorbell insistently. When I opened the door, I heard a yelling, screeching voice telling me that she had been disturbed. I apologized, attempting to calm her. In vain. Our visitors felt very awkward because she had already treated them badly outside.

When our visitors left, I decided to pray about this situation. It made us come down to earth about our neighbors. It seemed that the tranquillity and the peace had left rather quickly! *We are no longer going to have peace!* I thought. And how to now reestablish the relationship with the neighbor? I confess that the idea of selling the house passed through our minds.

The next morning I got up and prayed, asking God to guide me so that I could become friends with that neighbor. I asked Him to soften her heart. I had just begun my tasks when the telephone rang. Upon hearing our neighbor's voice, I froze. I had given her our number just two days before, and it was the first time that she had called me. She apologized profusely and said that she was embarrassed for having acted in such a manner. In the end I was the one who apologized for the error of my visitors.

I thanked God for the almost immediate response to my prayer. Today I breathe with relief because peace has again returned to our home and its surroundings.

ARLETE FRANCISCO LEÃO

? Thought: When you have had difficulty with someone, have you prayed about it? Would knowledge of God (Prov. 11:9) help you do it differently the next time?

United in Christian Love

Behold, how good and how pleasant it is for brethren to dwell together in unity! It is like the precious ointment upon the head, that ran down upon the beard, even Aaron's beard: that went down to the skirts of his garments; as the dew of Hermon, and as the dew that descended upon the mountains of Zion: for there the Lord commanded the blessing, even life for evermore. Ps. 133.

CHRISTIAN WOMEN FROM 22 countries in west-central Africa gathered together in 2004 in Grand Bassam, Ivory Coast, to worship, learn, network, and pray. Many women traveled there by air, but some of us had to go by road. We couldn't afford the exorbitant airfare and had to risk taking the bus from Nigeria. Thirty women gathered to travel together.

Trouble started shortly after we left home when one of the bus tires went flat. Then, after we had traveled nonstop for about 28 hours, the bus broke down for five hours. We were tired, dusty, thirsty, hungry, and weak. And we were discouraged. Many complained. We were almost like the children of Israel who were complaining en route to Canaan.

If you've ever tasted the Lord you know that He is good. Just when our morale was completely low, He showed us that He is still in control and that we were not to worry. There were a few houses near where we sat under a big shady tree. Because the place was cool, many of us from the bus had gone there to relax. The women from the houses were friendly, and in spite of our broken English we learned that one of them was a Christian too. Praise the Lord! From that point on we were no longer tired. We were excited!

This woman (whose name I don't know) boiled water for us so we could wash. She prepared her bed and arranged chairs for some to sleep and relax, and she even went to prepare food for us. We couldn't communicate much with language, but we could smile. Other women joined in our excitement and became friendlier than before. The hours, which seemed to be dragging now flew by, and it was time to go. Our kind friend came with her friends to wave us off.

This experience reminded us that God was with us, and that there is always pleasure—even if everything seems to go wrong—when brothers and sisters live together in the unity of Christian love.   BECKY DADA

? **Thought:** If you feel the way the Israelites did when crossing the desert, how could today's text give you hope?

Wings of Protection

He will shield you with His wings. He will shelter you with His feathers. His faithful promises are your armor and protection. Ps. 91:4, NLT.

ONE WINTER DAY my two-mile walk was filled with the screaming calls of the red-shouldered hawk. Looking up, I saw a pair dipping and soaring above me while loudly proclaiming their interest in each other. Maybe, I hoped to myself, *this loudmouthed couple will nest in our neighborhood.* To my delight, a few weeks later I saw one fly into a nearby palm tree with sticks in its beak.

A few months later I was shocked to find a beautiful young red-shouldered hawk lying with wings outstretched under the palm tree. The breast feathers were so downy they looked like fur. A few flight feathers had grown out on its wing tips but probably were not developed enough to help it fly.

Why had this happened? I will never know for sure, but I discovered some possible causes for its death. The strikingly beautiful rusty red, black, and white hawk lacks parenting skills. They build very sloppy nests that make it easy for a baby bird to fall over the edge in stormy weather or for a rambunctious chick to push a sibling out in an attempt to get more food. There is another sad fact: at times, if mother and father are too stressed in feeding three chicks (which this nest held), they have been known to dump one out.

As I thought about these handsome hawks and their poor parenting, I was struck by the stark contrast with my heavenly Father in His care and concern for His children. David describes our security in the storms of life with these words: "The Lord is my rock, my fortress, . . . in whom I find protection" (Ps. 18:2, NLT). My Father encourages us to love our brothers and sisters, not to compete for power or position: "Don't be selfish. . . . Be humble, thinking of others as better than yourself" (Phil. 2:3, NLT). My Father would never hurt one being because of His stresses. Instead, He sent His Son on a mission to rescue the whole human race. He would have allowed this most precious, only begotten Son to suffer the agonizing tortures of the cross for just one child of His.

Today I want to place my life under the shelter of my Father's wings. I want to use His faithful promises as armor against the assaults of the enemy. How about you?

DONNA LEE SHARP

Truth

And in their mouth was found no guile: for they are without fault before the throne of God. Rev. 14:5.

I REMEMBER MY CHILDHOOD experience with the cookie jar quite vividly. Having a sweet tooth led me into trouble one sunny day. The house was very quiet as I quickly climbed onto the cupboard where my mom had just put a jar of freshly baked cookies. This was my day to be caught. The jar tumbled down, and the noise alerted a neighbor to the danger. The small ooze of blood on my knee didn't hide the truth of what my intentions had been. I had to speak the truth, because I had been caught.

But it shouldn't be that way. Truthfulness is a vital virtue for Christian growth. It is evident that the Lord hates lying lips. Have you ever wondered why truth, with a little portion of a lie, automatically becomes a full package of a lie and nothing else? But plain truth will always remain truth. God requires that truthfulness shall mark His people even in the greatest peril. Zechariah 8:16 says, "Speak the truth to each other and render true and sound judgment in your courts" (NIV).

What are some of the things that may cause us to speak untruthfully? The list is endless, but to mention one: fear. It could be fear of losing a job, fear of losing a close friendship, fear of losing out on something that could be to your advantage. But remember, heaven has the power to demonstrate miraculous deliverances when faith is active. God has power to rescue you from a situation that may cause you to be untruthful.

When we steadfastly keep the will on the Lord's side, every emotion we feel will be brought into captivity to the will of our Lord Jesus Christ. We will then find our feet on solid rock. May the Lord help us to always speak the truth to one another in love, for He clearly indicates that He is a God who hates lying lips.

BERYL ASENO-NYAMWANGE

(?) Thought: If you are feeling guilty over an untruth, what might you do about it? Read 1 John 1:9 for a suggestion.

God's Leadings

Bless me and enlarge my territory! 1 Chron. 4:10, NIV.

DRIVING 120 MILES TO WORK in winter proved exhausting, yet I felt God's hand leading me. I think of the times I followed the snowplow clearing Interstate 17, but I enjoyed my work and fellow workers. I realized I had no desire to look for a job elsewhere in my field of expertise. Then an ad in the local paper for WEST (World Education Student Travel) local coordinators caught my eye. A few days after mailing my inquiry, I received a call and met with the WEST representative. "A WEST local coordinator," he said, "finds summertime host families for students ranging in age from 14 to 18 from other countries, such as France and Spain."

Because I enjoyed teaching this age group, having taught college for more than a decade, I took the challenge. Before the students arrived, I asked the Lord to make this an opportunity for the youth in my charge to know the Lord and to bless my plan to invite the students to attend church with me. I found host families easily, and shared my plan with them. They saw this as their "day off" and readily agreed. When the students arrived, the host families drove their student to meet me at my church on Saturday morning.

For reassurance of God's approval, like Gideon I asked for a specific sign from God: I asked for the preacher to talk about Daniel and his three friends in his sermon. My heart overflowed with thanksgiving as the minister opened his sermon with the story of Daniel's three friends and their steadfast faith through the ordeal of the fiery furnace. We stayed for the church fellowship lunch, which the students enjoyed. "Could we do this again?" they asked. Church members with teenagers invited their new French and Spanish friends to spend the rest of the day with their families.

The host families enjoyed their first summer students and looked forward to another summer like it. Three students returned the next summer and invited their host families to visit them in their own homes. I thanked God for leading in my life, and I ask that I may meet some of my WEST students in the earth made new. CONSUELO RODA JACKSON

?Thought: Is there some creative way you can use your job to introduce someone to Christ?

Answers to Prayer

Surely he took up our infirmities and carried our sorrows. Isa. 53:4, NIV.

IT WAS A FRIDAY AFTERNOON, and my children were already gathered in the living room while I was in my bedroom changing our youngest, little Luci, 3 months old.

Unexpectedly, one of the boys came into the room, twirling his jacket with all of his might. Children are children, and in the joy and liveliness of their childhood years, they don't see the consequences of their playing. The heavy metal zipper, as though aimed at a target, hit my left eye, which immediately began to fill with blood.

The pain was extreme; it's impossible to describe. Even now, 40 years later, I can still remember the situation clearly. Because of the excruciating pain I fell, not knowing what to do. Within a matter of seconds it seemed that my eye had exploded and that I would lose it and become blind.

My husband was now by my side, taking care of our daughter. When he saw the condition of my eye, he quickly called a taxi to take us to the ophthalmologist. The doctor didn't minimize the problem. He gave me emergency treatment, prescribed medication, and required me to remain in bed for at least 10 days, the time necessary for the injury to heal.

"But Doctor, I have six children!" I protested.

"However, you have only two eyes," the doctor responded.

So we called my mother, who never denied help during difficult times. On Sabbath she stayed with me while my husband and the children went to church and requested prayer for my recovery. I spent the entire day in the darkened room, as the doctor had prescribed. That night my husband took off the bandage to apply the medication and, praise God, there was not even a trace of blood.

The doctor was amazed. "This is a miracle! It is a miracle!" he repeated. That reached my ears like a sweet song. I was happy to know that my sight would return to normal. And it has. I use my two eyes without any problem. The Lord protects and cares for His children. He provides their necessities.

NILSE TOLEDO WOERLE

(?) Thought: Thank the Lord for a time when He has healed you or some other family member.

Angels Among Us

I am going to send an angel in front of you, to guard you on the way and to bring you to the place that I have prepared. Ex. 23:20, NRSV.

IT SEEMED AS THOUGH everything was going wrong that Sabbath morning. My husband and I were to lead the singing for the first church service, and he was to play his trumpet for special music for the second service. But now he was too ill to get out of bed.

"Lord," I prayed as I left the house, "I need Your help this morning. Only a miracle will get me to church in time to find a replacement for Shane." As I approached my car, I noticed it was leaning on one side. "Oh, no—a flat tire! This is perfect! Just what I need!" I groaned.

As I drove at five miles an hour to the gas station, I prayed, *Lord, remember the miracle I asked You for this morning? I really need Your help now.*

When I finally arrived, the line of cars waiting to have air put in their tires was longer than I could wait for. *Hello, Lord? Are You there? Can I get some help down here?* I exclaimed in desperation. I was about to cut in line when a voice inside my head said, "No, Gladys, you should ask." Without hesitation I got out of my car and walked toward the driver.

"Buenos dias!" I greeted him as I smiled and explained my predicament.

"No hay problema, señorita; adelante ["No problem, ma'am; go ahead"]," he replied agreeably.

I struggled to pull into line and jumped out of my car to grab the air hose. "No, señorita! No, miss! You would get your beautiful dress dirty, and then how are you going to sing at church?" I looked up and saw the same driver beside me. He grabbed the hose, ran to my car, and began to put air into my tire. While he pumped and checked the pressure, he asked me about our church and our beliefs. I gladly shared with him. He continued to ask questions until he finished getting my tire to the right pressure.

"Gracias, señor! Usted ha sido un angel ["Thank you, sir! You have been an angel!"]!" I told him as I got back into my car.

As I drove away I recognized that angels are surely among us. We may not know who they are or when we may find one, but the Lord knows—and He sends them just in time. Even though I ended up doing both services, I was mightily blessed by the Lord that Sabbath day.

GLADYS S. (GUERRERO) KELLEY

49

Vitiligo

And there came a leper to him, . . . saying unto him, If thou wilt, thou canst make me clean. Mark 1:40.

VITILIGO IS A SKIN DISEASE that affects skin pigmentation. It is more prominent on dark skin where the pink pigmentation is considered unsightly. Because the condition sometimes starts with a rash, I had seen a doctor, but I didn't know I was developing this disease. Then one morning when I woke up and looked into the mirror I was shocked to see that I had lost all my facial pigmentation. Other tiny spots showed on my arms and legs. I became depressed and felt like an outcast, wondering if I would ever regain my complexion; and what would be the reaction from the public? I felt I was scary and different from other people.

My cousin escorted me to a dermatologist, and while I was sitting in the waiting room it felt as if everybody were looking at me. They couldn't help having some facial reaction of fear or pity for me.

I tried different practitioners and had skin tests done. One particular practitioner referred me to a dermatologist who made an emergency booking. When I arrived at this specialist's office, I had no sooner walked into the consulting room than I was diagnosed with "postinflammatory vitiligo." I almost fell to the floor. Fortunately, a chair was nearby. I sank into the chair, having now lost all hope that I would ever be myself again.

I was so depressed that I told the Lord, "Just let me die." For days I was in despair. Finally I remembered to talk to my Savior about my condition. I asked for forgiveness for the way I had spoken to Him, and pledged to leave all in His care.

Somehow I felt a difference. I also decided that I should go to church. I thought, *What if I have lost my pigmentation permanently? Will I sit at home and never go to church again?* I hoped that my fellow worshippers would get used to me.

I almost felt as though I was living in Bible times—I felt separated from the community, as the lepers had been. I understood the feeling they had gone through. Nevertheless, one leper returned and thanked the Master for the cleansing. When I left my health in His care, it improved.

How important it is today to ask the Savior to help—regardless of the problem.

ETHEL D. MSUSENI

Dark to Light

And you, my son Solomon, acknowledge the God of your father, and serve him with wholehearted devotion and with a willing mind, for the Lord searches every heart and understands every motive behind the thoughts. 1 Chron. 28:9, NIV.

EVEN THOUGH DARK, SMELLY, and old, the barn had always been my place to hide. I loved the smell of hay, the dusty atmosphere, and the sunlight streaming through the cracks between the old wood slats. At first the dark interior looked dusty and dim. But when my eyes adjusted, the shadows between the hay bales came alive. I never knew what I would find. Sometimes I'd see bird eggs cracked and open, the refuge of the baby bird. Sometimes I'd find forts other people had made, or I would make my own. I'd lie there, curled in a ball, trying to keep from being seen, but I was never completely hidden. From the outside looking in, darkness was all I saw.

The knotted beams holding the rafters provided a shelter for many different creatures, animal and human alike. One wall was almost completely open to the pasture, allowing me to watch the horses. Openings in two of the walls were large enough to back a trailer through. The one remaining side was almost complete, but even then there were holes.

The wooden framework, the open rafters, all symbolized the way I felt. I was always open to others. I was a shelter for my family, for my sister's depression and my mother's loneliness. I was open on three sides. I felt guilty for having one side covered. It made me feel dark inside, as if I were hiding. I could be a shelter as long as no one looked too deeply. I didn't want anyone to see how dark I really was inside. I was afraid that no one would ever want to be with me if they really knew all the secrets my heart held. Yet I would look around the barn and see the sunlight streaming in through the cracks. No matter how dark it got in the barn, I knew there was hope; I knew the light would find a way in. Looking into the old barn, all I saw was darkness. But looking out, past the wooden pillars, past the bales of coarse golden hay, past the dirty rumps of my four-legged friends, I could see the sunlight streaming into the barn and into my life. — ELIZABETH DAVIS

Thought: Are there dark places in your soul? What solutions might you find today that would bring you light?

One Minute for Myself

To love him with all your heart, with all your understanding and with all your strength, and to love your neighbor as yourself is more important than all burnt offerings and sacrifices. Mark 12:33, NIV.

FOR ALL THE MULTITASKING done by mothers, grandmothers, wives, career folks, and church members who believe firmly in loving their neighbors, let's not forget the last two little words after this great commandment: "as yourself." When these two words are forgotten, we get ourselves into such a hectic lifestyle that we give and give without stopping at the filling station of grace; then we tend to run ourselves empty.

In the 1980s *The One Minute Manager* was very popular reading among management circles. Following the wake of its success a number of other "one-minute" books were published. Among them was *One Minute for Myself.* The contents of this book spoke to me as I assessed the multiple demands on my plate. Taking that one minute for myself and my needs was equally important and needed priority if I were to have the strength to minister to others and their needs.

It meant taking the time to feed myself spiritually so that I would have spiritual food to share. It meant inviting the Holy Spirit into my life so that I could recommend Him to another. It meant taking care of my own emotional needs so that I could offer a shoulder for someone to cry on. It also meant taking that minute or two to relax, taking a power nap, listening to some elevating music, or stopping and smelling the flowers before moving on to attend to the demands of others.

Yes, we are called to minister to others with needs, but how can we accomplish that when we ourselves are running dry? When we find ourselves losing our tempers, feeling physically drained or emotionally parched, it is God's way of telling us that we need to fill our spiritual tanks—and then our physical and emotional tanks. It is a priority that must be attended to.

So let's take that minute for ourselves today to recharge before we move on. That time spent will be very worthwhile as we gather more power from the Spirit that is at work within us to accomplish far more than all we can ask or imagine (Ephesians 3:20).   SALLY LAM-PHOON

(?) **Read** Ephesians 3:20 and try to imagine what the Spirit might accomplish through you.

My Orchids

The Lord did not set his affection on you and choose you because you were more [beautiful] than other peoples. . . . But it was because the Lord loved you. Deut. 7:7, 8, NIV.

IT WAS THE FOURTH time that my two orchids had bloomed, and it looked as if this were going to be the most glorious display ever. Fourteen blossoms had already opened, and there were 26 more buds. Every time I walked into the bathroom I stopped to check on their progress. And I noticed something different about the fifteenth blossom—it faced the opposite direction of all the other purple beauties. What was the matter? Why was it so odd?

As I thought about this flower head I realized the positives of the situation. I could see the back of the flower without having to bend and twist. And even the back was beautiful and helped me appreciate all the other blossoms more. I then began to think about some people, some women particularly, who seem so odd, so different; they always seem to be looking the other direction. And yet if we give them a chance, we can discover a unique point of view, a beauty that is different, and even come away from an acquaintance with them appreciating more the others in our lives. And the bottom line is that God created each blossom, each woman, exactly as He wants, because He loves each one.

Just when about half my orchid blossoms had opened, we had to move almost across the continent. We carefully packed the orchids in boxes, wrapped the boxes in blankets, and put the boxes in the car in the back of the moving van. Oh, how I wanted those orchids to survive!

Alas! The February night the van spent in Kansas City was too cold, and the orchids froze. Oh, how sad they looked! And how sad I felt!

But you know what? Orchids are replaceable. In fact, within a month I already had three more. Maybe they will be better than the original two—and maybe they won't. But the people around us are not replaceable—each is unique and special and loved by the Savior, and each deserves our special care and attention. Satan does all he can to obliterate the beauty God has planned. Some people are damaged, but we can still find beauty in their lives; sometimes we have to look a little harder, but it is worth it. God did not choose us because of our beauty or any other aspect of *us,* but because *He* loves us. A good thing to remember on Valentine's Day!

ARDIS DICK STENBAKKEN

Turned Around

I say to you that if two of you agree on earth concerning anything that they ask, it will be done for them by My Father in heaven. Matt.18:19, NKJV.

"MY LIFE HAS COMPLETELY tuned around since attending prayer meeting!" Kathleen blurted out as she gave me a sideways glance and grinned her pleasant toothless smile. I had just picked her up to take her to prayer meeting when she began a litany of her blessings.

It had not been that long ago that Kathleen had been depressed and plagued with hearing voices that she described as repeating her thoughts out loud. In telling the prayer group about her problem she lamented, "The voices are very loud, and this is very annoying." As was our custom when a special need arose, we placed Kathleen in the center of our prayer circle and prayed for deliverance from her depression and voices.

Kathleen was living in a partially finished, moldy, musty, and scantly furnished basement apartment. Here was another call for special prayer. One member of the prayer group thought Kathleen should be eligible for housing at a local complex sponsored by U.S. Department of Housing and Urban Development and had Kathleen's name placed on a list for any future vacancies. Surprisingly, in a few weeks an apartment was available. It was so much fun giving Kathleen a home-furnishing shower with the help of the prayer group and a Sabbath school class.

With her voices stilled, and her depression lifted, and living in a cozy, attractive apartment, Kathleen acknowledges she has experienced firsthand the transforming power of prayer.

Interestingly, the prayer group's main focus was to pray for our pastors, as well as the numerous prayer request cards turned in each week. Praying for any needs of the prayer group was a sideline of sorts, but has become a huge faithbuilder for the power of prayer. Even though the prayer group is small and made up of a very diverse assortment of individuals, we've had astonishing answers to prayer—healings from cancer, employment needs met, addictions recovery, and, of course, Kathleen's turned-around life.

Sadly, prayer meetings seem to be diminishing. What blessings are missed when we neglect the power of group prayer! For Jesus promises "where two or three are gathered together in my name, there am I in the midst of them" (Matt. 18:20).

BONNIE HUNT

Bearing the Fruit of Love

You did not choose me, but I chose you and appointed you to go and bear fruit—fruit that will last. Then the Father will give you whatever you ask in my name. This is my command: Love each other. John 15:16, 17, NIV.

A FEW YEARS AGO I first met an atheist. (Imagine—not to believe in God! Surely no one *really* feels this way!) George was a tall, slender man nearing 70 years of age, though he appeared much younger. Perhaps this was because he was a very active man who looked as though he enjoyed good health. George told me emphatically that he did not believe that there is a God, and he wanted to make sure that no one tried to speak to him of religion. He would mind his own business, and we were to mind ours.

He moved in on the ninth floor of our retirement center and kept quite to himself at first. One day I heard one of the women tell how George saw her trying to bring her groceries in with her walker. He took them inside for her, and even put them away.

"Really?" her friend said. "But don't you know that he doesn't believe in God?"

George's reputation for helping others spread rapidly throughout the building. Many of the women became dependent upon him to help them. But we respected George's wishes and gave him his space. He said, "I have always preferred to be alone. I don't need God or people." He always had a ready smile and a helping hand, but still he professed, "There is no God."

I was shocked to come in one morning and learn that George had been taken to the emergency room with a massive heart attack. In the cardiac-care unit he looked as white as the sheets, his body strapped to all sorts of heart monitors and machines. "Ms. Barbara, I'm glad you are here," he said, "for I have a confession I must make to you." Immediately I felt uncomfortable. What was he going to say? "I lied to you when I told you I didn't believe there is a God. But you have shown me there is, and I feel His presence here with me now."

Choking back my tears, I said, "Oh, George, there is no way you could have exhibited such love and concern for others the way you have without its being God's love beaming through you!" He was a man who protested with his mouth "There is no God," but who bore the fruit of the love of God.

BARBARA SMITH MORRIS

An Apple of His Eye

For whoever touches you touches the apple of his eye. Zech. 2:8, NIV.

IN TODAY'S GLOBAL VILLAGE, where innocence seems to evaporate a couple years after birth (thanks to the age of speed and information technology), I was amazed to find a woman of 40 who had never seen an apple in her entire life.

Contrary to the belief that missionaries are sent to "teach" and to "preach," our experience in Uganda has been that of learning new lessons every day. Because of our birth and upbringing in a country whose past has a lot in common with Uganda, my husband and I have not found it difficult to adjust to the lifestyle. One of the gifts we have received here is Nyabo.

Nyabo (literally meaning "lady," or "madam") has helped us at home—more as a companion than a maid—for more than five years. Nyabo is raising a family of six children. With her estranged husband showing up only once in a while, the entire responsibility of raising her family and sending her children to school lies on her feeble yet firm shoulders. But it is her deep faith in God that keeps Nyabo going.

While in need of every coin she can lay her hands on, Nyabo makes sure that not a single penny, carelessly thrown around, is lost from our house. Working most times on an empty stomach, Nyabo fixes the heaps of vegetables and fruits in the kitchen. She sees bananas getting rotten but does not help herself to one unless offered. Nyabo is honesty personified.

One day, when feeling a little generous, I offered Nyabo an apple. She looked at it and smiled and then asked me quietly, "Madam, what fruit is this?"

"Don't you know, Nyabo?" I raised my eyebrows. "This is an apple."

"Oh, thank you, madam. I want to take this home to my children. They have never seen an apple either." Rooted to the ground, I thought of her children going to the primary school nearby and learning a lesson of the alphabet: A for apple . . .

Apple. I'm sure this woman, who had never seen or tasted an apple before, is herself the apple of God's eye. A true Christian, an epitome of faithfulness and honesty and hard work, Nyabo is a rare apple.

VINITA GAIKWAD

? Thought: Have you seen such an apple lately? Are you the apple of His eye? How do you know?

God Cares for Us

He performs wonders that cannot be fathomed, miracles that cannot be counted. Job 5:9, NIV.

ONE DAY MY HUSBAND got a small wagon to transport mineral water from a fountain near our town. Since he was going to attach the wagon to the motorcycle, I decided to ask him to take me along. I didn't think of the danger—a small motorcycle pulling a wagon on a dirt road. I planned to take our 8-month-old baby, too, whom I had always taken with me wherever I went.

I left some chores undone, and we departed on our little pleasure trip. When we stopped by a friend's house to get empty bottles for the water, my friend insisted that we leave the baby with her, but her insistence was in vain—we took little innocent Elisa with us.

It had not been 10 minutes before we came to a section of the road that was filled with small bumps and a large amount of sand on the side. Suddenly the motorcycle hit the washboardlike bumps, and we were bounced up and down. My husband swerved to the edge of the road, and we slid in the sand. This all happened within a split second, but it was long enough for me to regret my terrible decision and to cry out for God's help. My husband raised his legs, and I lifted my daughter up high so that if we crashed the motorcycle would not land on her.

We crashed. My husband scratched his knees, I broke my shoulder blade, and a screw punctured my knee. But the impossible had also happened: Elisa was not hurt—not even a scratch. Nor was she frightened.

On the way to the hospital I had room in my heart only for thanksgiving, for praise to a God who does such wonderful things, to a God of such infinite mercy. As I heard my husband express anger over the incident, I could, with the eyes of faith, perceive the love and care of a Father who even in the face of an irresponsible act cared for His precious children. I did everything I could to protect my baby, but God did more: He protected the three of us.

Lord, help me to believe that You will care for me always, even when I do not realize the irresponsible acts that I commit. Help me to praise You for so many marvelous things that have taken place in my life.

AURÍSIA SILVA BRITO RODRIGUES

Lesson on Happiness From a Dog

Therefore we do not lose heart. Though outwardly we are wasting away, yet inwardly we are being renewed day by day. For our light and momentary troubles are achieving for us an eternal glory that far outweighs them all. So we fix our eyes not on what is seen, but on what is unseen. For what is seen is temporary, but what is unseen is eternal. 2 Cor. 4:16-18, NIV.

OVER THE PAST FEW MONTHS my life has been in transition, and I've felt as if I'm lost. Every direction I go has dead-ended in nothing. It's dispiriting, and lately I've felt discouraged. I'm a morning walker, but even my walks haven't cheered me up.

At least that's how it was before my attention was jolted by the blessings of a neighbor's straying dog. When I would start my walk, up she would bound, wanting to be petted and begging for attention. Throughout my walk she was right behind or just in front of me. I was continuously struck by her happy attitude. She always seemed so permanently happy and carefree. I was walking with the weight of the world on my shoulders, and she was simply enjoying the air and having me around. To run, to play, to smell, to be, were her goals. Mine were more like to plan, to work, to attain, to accomplish. I found myself being drawn toward her easygoing attitude.

This got me thinking. God wants me to be unencumbered by material gain and constant striving for attainment and worldly applause. My happiness is to be in Him. When I depart from Him, I cannot find peace and contentment. He wants me to go through life knowing that there's a much greater world to come, not just this one that's filled with so much pain and heartache. That is the world I am to prepare for and to seek.

With my head to the ground, feeling sorry for myself, I'd lost my sense of greater purpose. Teresa of Avila once wrote, "Be not perplexed, be not afraid, everything passes, God does not change. Patience wins all things. He who has God lacks nothing. God alone suffices."

Like my walking companion, I need to remember that I walk not alone but with an awesome God who will never leave me nor forsake me. I feel so lost when I stray from my Source of contentment and joy.

I still am in transition, but I now know I need not be discouraged and downtrodden, for I know One who will ultimately work out all things for the best.

RISA STORLIE

Deliverance Granted

And call upon me in the day of trouble: I will deliver thee, and thou shalt glorify me. Ps. 50:15.

ONE SABBATH WHILE WORKING with prison's ministries I heard one of the prisoners give a testimony in the chapel. He talked about how he used to literally stay in trouble. He claimed to have been most disobedient and spent much of his time in the bars and clubs, drinking and having a so-called good time.

One day while under the influence of alcohol he became involved in a dispute with another intoxicated individual. Soon it became physical. Unfortunately, he killed the man. As he spoke he was extremely remorseful. His words and emotions indicated that he really didn't mean to kill anyone. He immediately realized what he had done and stood over his opponent, suddenly sober and trembling. The police soon arrived on the scene and without much questioning they roughly handcuffed the young man and took him to the police station.

He confessed to us that many had prayed for him. He accepted Christ as his personal Savior and began attending services in the chapel. Baptism soon followed. He began encouraging other prisoners to give their lives to the Lord.

One day he found himself standing before a judge. The judge gave him a long stare and finally said, "I have wrestled with God all night. He told me to let you go; therefore, I am dismissing your case. If you ever come into my court again I will throw the book at you!" The prisoner went home, fell on his knees, and praised and thanked God for His love and compassion.

A few years have passed since this occurrence. My sister recently handed me a tape and said, "I'm sure that you will recognize this young man." She had mentioned him before, but I didn't have a clue whom she was referring to. Hearing his voice and listening to his preaching allowed me to identify him. I praise God for bringing him through difficult times.

I shed tears of joy as I listened to the tape. God forgave him for his sin, and brought him out of darkness into His marvelous light, and now, years later, this young man is letting his light shine so that others can see it and glorify our Father who is in heaven. What an awesome God!

DAISY SIMPSON

Thought: God grants deliverance. What do you think is the difference between the person who receives deliverance and the one who does not?

God Is in Control

We wait in hope for the Lord; he is our help and our shield. Ps. 33:20, NIV.

IT WAS A TYPICAL February morning—clear and cold, with a thin layer of snow that had fallen the night before. My husband and I were slightly nervous about letting our son drive himself and his sister to school as usual. He hadn't had much experience driving in wintry conditions, and while he was usually a careful driver, we hesitated to turn him loose on the slick streets. But the salt trucks had made their rounds and I was relatively sure that the main roads were clear, so I agreed to let him drive. I would follow him out to the main road and call for help if he slid into a ditch.

We had morning worship, and I specifically prayed for a safe trip to school and work. Then we set off, caravan-style, up the hilly country road that intersected the end of our long driveway. The gravel road winds up and over a couple of low hills before coming to a stop sign just over the top of one hill. The crossroad from the left side is a blind approach over the crest of another hill, and cars frequently fly over the hill without slowing down.

As I crested the hill behind Ron, I saw a heavy gravel truck fly by on the street ahead. To my horror, I saw my son's car coast down past the stop sign without slowing at all. It barely missed the back end of the passing salt truck. There was a slick spot in the road, and my own car fought to maintain its traction as I slowly approached the stop sign. Had we been just a few seconds earlier Ron's car would have slid out in front of—not behind—the heavy salt truck and likely been crushed beneath it. You can be sure that I spent the rest of my journey praising God for His miraculous intervention and care for my children riding in that car.

There is nothing more terrifying than realizing you are out of control, whether you are driving a car or attempting to steer your life. Things are whirling around you at lightning speed, causing you to question your ability to ever again be in control. Just when you are about to crash, something pulls you out of the spin and sets you on the path again. No matter how out of control we are, God is in control and will never let us down.

FAUNA RANKIN DEAN

? Thought: In what way is today's verse a promise of control? How can you best apply it to your life today?

Fighting

Be strong and of a good courage. Joshua 1:6.

ASSERTED IN THE UNITED STATES' Declaration of Independence are the rights to "life, liberty, and the pursuit of happiness." The inspiration for that phrase came from the writings of an English philosopher, John Locke, who clearly stated that a man's rights were to life, liberty, and property.

Courage, strength, prosperity, and good success are ours through Christ. As we meditate on God's Word day and night, observing all that is written therein, it is possible to obtain our inheritance here, as well as in the New Jerusalem. It came at a precious price, and we have only to fight the good fight of faith to receive all that God desires to bestow upon us.

On October 24, 1929, commonly known as "Black Thursday," the New York Stock Exchange suffered through the first of a series of steep declines that made the nation aware that a major economic catastrophe was in progress. There are documented stories of the choices people made when this historical event took place. When they discovered their finances had been depleted overnight, some individuals chose to take their own life, leaping to their deaths from skyscrapers. Some found their solace in alcohol and ended up as bums and beggars on the street.

I know there are times when we become overwhelmed with the challenges of life. But God knows our frame and remembers that we are dust. We will have our times of greater energy and hope, and our times of feeling depleted and lost. As we grow and mature, we learn to see many peaks and valleys across the landscape of life as we fight for our inheritance.

God is looking for warriors—men and women who cannot, and will not, be bought or sold. Individuals who are not afraid to stand up and be counted. Christians who are willing to fight for their God-given rights, who can confidently say with Holy Spirit perseverance, "Give me liberty (in Christ Jesus), or give me death."

With great anxiety and self-distrust we too, like Joshua, can look forward to the work before us. Our fears will be removed by the assurance of God: "As I was with Moses, so I will be with thee: I will not fail thee, nor forsake thee. . . . Unto this people shalt thou divide for an inheritance the land, which I sware unto their fathers to give them" (Joshua 1:5, 6). All is to be ours as we fight for our earthly and heavenly inheritance. Only "be strong and of a good courage."   CEREATHA J. VAUGHN

In Him I Will Trust

I will say of the Lord, "He is my refuge and my fortress; my God, in Him I will trust. Ps. 91:2, NKJV.

ONE MORNING MERVYN complained of a stomachache. Thinking that it may be the stomach flu, his mom suggested that he get a blood test. To her utter dismay, the doctor, after checking the results, said that Mervyn should be rushed to the hospital. There he was finally diagnosed as having renal failure—his kidneys were malfunctioning.

This was devastating news for a 21-year-old and everyone in the family. The doctors finally concluded that he needed a kidney transplant. But even this sad news didn't shake their utmost trust in God.

His mother, Vinitha, mentioned her son's condition to a woman who felt impressed to submit a short article about Mervyn to the community newspaper, hoping that someone would be willing to donate a kidney. When she approached the newspaper office, the reporter was interested in personally interviewing him. Soon the reporter interviewed both Mervyn and his parents and printed a front-page article, including photos. It was an inspiration to read the reporter's comments, especially about Mervyn and his parents' strong faith in God.

After getting his name on the national donor list, the family was informed that it could take at least five years to get a kidney. Even this news did not affect their firm faith in God.

Three months later, after a church service, a young man came up to Vinitha and said that he would be willing to donate his kidney. He said that even if he had to die from surgery complications, he was willing to donate. Vinitha was baffled by this young man's offer. She felt as if an angel was talking to her through this complete stranger. He was so eager to help that he personally visited Mervyn. Now everyone is praying that their kidneys will match perfectly, and that the surgery will be successful.

Whatever problems we may face, if we implicitly trust in God He will see us through and will strengthen our faith even more by the way He guides and helps us with our problems. Today's text is one of many beautiful verses in the Bible about trusting in God: "I will say of the Lord, 'He is my refuge and my fortress; my God; in Him I will trust.'" STELLA THOMAS

? Thought: Do I really believe this text? Do I really trust Him? In everything?

Covered

He shall cover thee with his feathers, and under his wings shalt thou trust. Ps. 91:4.

RECENTLY MY HUSBAND and I went with a group of about 100 church members on a chartered bus shopping trip to Pennsylvania. As we rode along the highway, it began to rain. No one seemed concerned, because we were on the bus and out of the rain, and we had confidence in the skill of our driver. Fortunately, by the time we arrived at the King of Prussia mall we were going to, it was dry outside, and the outing proved very fruitful and enjoyable for everyone.

As I drove to work the following day it rained again. Once again I was not bothered, since I had sufficient time to arrive without rushing. Thoughts began to fill my mind about the idea of being covered. Even though it was raining all around me I was not concerned, because I was "covered" by the protection my car provided. After I arrived at work I had to use my umbrella, which sheltered me somewhat but not completely. I've seen umbrellas destroyed by the fury of wind and rain and left, useless, by the side of the road. These remind me of the futility of our attempts to protect ourselves in a world fraught with assaults by the enemy.

I thought about the wonderful grace of God that's available to cover us all through our lives, even as we experience difficult and sad times. As we strive to be more like Him daily and abide under His shelter, we need not worry or fret about the turbulent rains of trial, temptation, turmoil, and trouble that threaten to overtake us. We are safe as long as we are covered by His grace and maintain a right relationship with Him. Though we are in the world, we have dependable coverage that protects us from being crushed by the stresses and cares of the world.

Yes, the wind and rain will come, more often than we expect, or even more than we feel is fair at times. We may even ask, "Lord, why me?" But as we remember that even our best efforts are insufficient to keep us from getting wet from the rains of strife, we can also be reminded that through the protective coverage of the marvelous grace of God we can be strengthened, protected, and unspotted by the world.

Lord, please keep us ever mindful that we cannot make it in our own strength, but that Your grace and mercy remain available to us as a buffer between us and our trials, and as a protector to cover us when we would be shattered.

GLORIA STELLA FELDER

Miracles Happen

And whosoever shall give to drink unto one of these little ones a cup of cold water only in the name of a disciple, verily I say unto you, he shall in no wise lose his reward. Matt. 10:42.

IN 2003 I HAD the privilege of working as a volunteer. The local church Community Services offers assistance to needy people in the community, so as I worked there I always attempted to do the most possible so that people were always well attended and left feeling comforted.

One Sabbath morning an individual came to me saying that a man wanted to talk with the person who worked in Community Services. I knew that the man had left his wife at home with a baby. He was a former prison inmate, and he and his family were hungry. I felt bad because I knew that the shelves in the Community Services food storage area were empty. There was nothing there, not even a pound of beans.

I explained to him that at the moment I had no way to help him, but that within the next several days there would probably be some food to give away. As I returned to what I had been doing, the face of that man came to my mind again. It was a face that reflected the presence of obvious hunger. I began to think: *If this man and his family are hungry, God knows this, and He knew that the man would come to me. So God would not allow him to go home empty-handed and hungry. The God I know would not do that.*

I headed for the Community Services food storage area, with the key in my hand. I prayed as I went: *Lord, if this man is really in need of food, You, Lord, already know this, and I am certain that You have already provided something for him.*

In the food storage area I found two bags with everything the man needed. I thanked God and went to his home and said, "God sent some food for you!"

Lord, thank You for individuals who make themselves available to relieve the hunger of others. Thank You for giving me the joy of seeing the smile of gratitude of these, Your children. TÂNIA MICOL S. BARTALINI

(?)Thought: We are an extension of the hands of God. He acts through us when we place ourselves in His service. What do you plan to do for Him today?

My Garage Floor Devotions

Cleanse me with hyssop, and I will be clean; wash me, and I will be whiter than snow. Ps. 51:7, NIV.

WE MOVED INTO OUR new house almost two years ago. Everything was as we wanted it. Everything, that is, except the garage floor. I wanted it stained. "Why bother?" my daughter, who shares the house with me, wanted to know. "Why bother?" my son, who knew he would have to move the bookcases and heavy boxes, inquired hesitantly. But I wanted it stained.

A great idea, I told myself as the floor glistened in spotless beauty sometime later. "A good idea," several visitors confirmed as they looked at the easy-to-clean surface. "An excellent idea," a girlfriend echoed as she made plans to do the same. "An amazing idea!" my daughter finally concluded as she walked over the newly smoothed surface in her bare feet.

I still feel myself smiling every time I see the floor. I even hear myself singing (something I rarely do). My daughter insists that I find more reasons than ever to go to the garage. That got me wondering: *What is it about a nicely stained floor that makes me so pleased? Is it the fact that both the inside and the outside are pleasing to my eyes?* I reflected on my questions until I found myself asking a critical question: Was my own life filled with rough-looking spots that needed to be smoothed out instead of being just painted over? In penitent prayer I searched for the rough spots that now seemed more obvious than before.

Often we find unsightly character flaws in our lives that need to be attended to. Washing the easy-to-clean floor yesterday, I took some time to commune with my Savior. *I'm so glad I bothered to stain this floor,* I told Him, *but I'm even gladder that You bothered to save me. Thank You for paying the price to remove all my blemishes, leaving me clean and spotless in Your eyes.*

Even more fervent now are the grateful thanks I send to my heavenly Father, who sees both the inside and the outside of my life. Each time I go to the garage I praise God for His marvelous idea that is our plan of salvation. I praise Him for washing me clean and covering me with the robe of His righteousness.

Thank God for garage floors!

CAROL JOY GREENE

Smell the Roses

And my people shall dwell in a peaceable habitation, . . . and in quiet resting places. Isa. 32:18.

ONE DAY I WAS REMINDED of the saying "Take time to smell the roses." I was eating lunch beside a window in an activity center where I work. What I observed made me smile, as I have eight part-time jobs, and my days are nonstop.

A boy, about 7 years old, was trudging over the frozen snow, pulling a cart with wheels. It was difficult for him, as inside were heavy newspapers that he was delivering to the homes nearby. As his slumped-over body and his cart bumped over the rough snow, he stopped and carefully laid the handle over the cart, turned around, and walked away, abandoning his possessions there on the snow.

He rounded the corner of the building, heading toward something I couldn't see. I went over to another window to watch him. He stopped beside an area that earlier in the year had been a mud puddle but now had a thick layer of ice over it. Then he proceeded to tap, tap, tap and break all the ice on the puddle, obviously having great fun.

When it was all broken and some water came sloshing up between the cracks, he played in it for a while, then looked around for another puddle. Finding another small one, he repeated his actions. Looking around once more, he could see no more ice, so with a body shrug he sauntered back to his bundle. Passing the broken puddle ice, he gave it a little smirk.

This little episode taught me that it's important to take time out of my busy schedule to smell the roses, relax with a cup of herbal tea, light a candle, and run a bubble bath—break a little ice on a puddle.

It can be rewarding to observe a squirrel as he goes about his day, or park beside a pond or a creek in between appointments, watch the birds, and let your mind unwind. Go for a walk and behold what the Lord has put there for your pleasure. I sometimes pull over by the roadside on my paper route, turn on some nice music, flip back the seat, close my eyes, and pray or just relax for a few minutes, thinking about the little boy and the puddle of ice.

VIDELLA MCCLELLAN

?Thought: Have you seen any puddles of ice lately? What did you do to them? What will you do the next time?

Dear Jesus? Amen!

And you remember that ever since you were a child, you have known the Holy Scriptures, which are able to give you the wisdom that leads to salvation through faith in Christ Jesus. 2 Tim. 3:15, TEV.

SOME TIME AFTER our daughter's first birthday, my husband and I started experiencing financial difficulties. We had made a risky investment, but because we were sure that God was leading us, we survived one day at a time through faith in His promises.

About that same time our little girl started imitating us when we prayed. She would kneel, fold her hands reverently, and say, "Dear Jesus? Amen!" It would crack us up every time. Imani even did it at church, and some members were impressed by how nicely she was learning about Jesus.

But one day when I was feeling especially discouraged, Imani taught me a lesson. She knelt down beside the bed and said "Dear Jesus? Amen!" Then she jumped up, applauded herself as she always did, and walked away. And then it struck me: We had placed our lives in God's hands and had promised to do His will, no matter the cost. And although some months were harder than others, we could still say "Amen!" We were all healthy, we always ate three meals a day, there was always enough gas in the tank, and our bills got paid—somehow. "Amen!"

Many times we promise to follow God's lead, but when difficulties arise we begin to doubt and wonder if God is really in charge. Sometimes we try to grab our lives back in the hope of improving our future, as if it were up to us. But if we'd hold on only a little longer and let God work, we'd discover all the great and mighty things He has planned for us (Jer. 33:3), and then we would realize that God doesn't really need our suggestions on how to solve our problems.

I would love to tell you how this story ended, but it's not over yet. We're still living one day at a time, our lives are still in God's hands, and we praise and worship Him for all He's done and for what He has yet to do. *Dear Jesus? Whatever You have planned, amen!*   DINORAH BLACKMAN

(?) **Thought:** A month is ending. Can you say "Amen" to what has happened this month? How about placing the new month in His charge?

Answered Prayer

Before they call, I will answer; and while they are yet speaking, I will hear.
Isa. 65:24.

FOR WEEKS I'D BEEN PRAYING for my house to be rented. Some people who had looked at it decided that the size was not right for them, or had not rented it for other reasons. One morning as I returned from my walk I decided to take a different route that would take me through a housing development. As I walked on, my mind was enveloped with the thought that another month was ending, my mortgage had to be paid, and the house was still not rented. I started talking to God aloud, reminding Him of my need.

Just as I neared the main road, I heard someone calling me. I turned around to see who had called, then waited until she caught up with me. She explained her reason for stopping me. She had some problems and was seeking answers to her prayers. I found myself encouraging her that God would answer her prayer but that He wanted her to wait. I explained to her that I too was waiting on God for an answer. I told her that I had prayed to have my house rented, but that God had not yet sent me the right tenant.

Immediately she told me that her sister urgently needed a house. She gave me her sister's telephone number, and I contacted her the moment I reached home. I arranged to show her the house that same day. We had some anxious moments as she contemplated how her furniture could fit into the small space. Her friend, who had come along, really seemed to think that the task was going to be impossible. I watched with bated breath as they deliberated. As the prospective renter inspected the house, she looked up the road, and it suddenly dawned on her that the house was close to the house of her son's grandmother, which was a plus for her. Eventually she moved in, the furniture fitted beautifully into the space, and the deal was done.

To me, this was a direct answer to my prayer. At first I felt I was talking to Someone who was not listening, but now He suddenly heard when I spoke loudly. However, I know God had heard my prayer, but my impatience had not matched His perfect timing. Surely it was He who had inspired me to take a different route that morning as part of the answer to my prayer.

Today as we face life's challenges let us be patient and wait on our on-time God, who always hears and answers the prayers of His children.

LILITH R. SCARLETT

If I Could Only . . .

A [woman] who has friends must [herself] be friendly, but there is a friend who sticks closer than a [sister]. Prov. 18:24, NKJV.

SHE WAS THE FIRST person to greet me and become my friend. She was sincere, frank, and very openhearted. We were very much alike, so we became close friends. We shared our secrets and joys, as well as sorrows. She became my prayer partner. As the days went by our families, too, became close friends. I could count on her whenever I needed her, and she came to me when she needed anything.

We were separated because of our professions, yet we kept in touch with each other. After retiring we again could visit, but neither of us was well, and the visits became less and less frequent.

One Sabbath when I planned to spend the day with her, her sister phoned and told me that Saro was very sick and had been admitted to the hospital. I went to the hospital and, after great difficulty, obtained permission to go to the special ward to see her. She had cancer and had not told me. It was pathetic to see her suffering. Tubes were inserted, and she was having a difficult time breathing. She couldn't speak; she struggled to tell me something but could not. She waved her hands and tried to express something—but it was too late.

One week earlier I had seen her at her home. She was sitting on the bed and singing. As soon as she saw me she said, "I was praying for some company, and God sent you. I am glad you came. Please pray for me." We knelt and prayed, after which she hugged and kissed me. We both were in tears. That Sabbath three persons offered prayers for her.

When I think of her I always have a guilty feeling over not being with her more often when she was suffering. If only I had visited her more. If only I had a chance to speak to her and ask what she wanted to tell me. I lost my best friend. I have no one now to call and share my worries and sorrows. I have no one here, but when I read the Bible, I find Jesus, my best friend. I can go to Him at any time and tell Him what I want and unburden myself.

WINIFRED DEVARAJ

(?) **Thought:** Do you need to spend time with a friend today? How about a special Friend?

Before You Call

Before they call I will answer, while they are yet speaking I will hear. Isa. 65:24, RSV.

IT WAS A QUIET AFTERNOON in my house in Mexico. I was caring for my toddler son when the quiet was interrupted by a loud rapping on my front door, followed by an urgent request from our neighbor for our car keys so he could drive my husband to the emergency room. There had been an accident in the woodshop, and my husband had lost most of his thumb in a wood planer.

In the hours that followed, friends pitched in to babysit while I sat in the emergency room with my husband, who drifted in and out of consciousness. When he was awake enough to speak, he asked me repeatedly not to let anyone operate. His fear was that the thumb was so badly damaged that they would amputate what was left. He is an instrumental musician and teacher, so his thumb is critical to his ability to do his job. The medical staff stopped the bleeding, then cleaned and bandaged his wound. They advised us to find a specialist to discuss treatment options. In the next several days I made many phone calls and drove my husband to a small U.S. town just across the border in Texas. There we found a surgeon who specialized in microsurgery and hand reconstruction. Three surgeries and many months later, thanks to God's grace and the surgeon's skill, my husband's thumb was once again fully functional.

After the last surgery we had a chance to chat with the surgeon about the fascinating events that had led him to a residency in surgery and microsurgery, followed by more specialized training in hand reconstruction. He mentioned that he had not really planned to live in this small border town, but that things had "just worked out" for him to begin a practice there not long before my husband's accident. Over the years since that frightening and job-threatening accident, we have talked many times about God's leading in our lives. God is good, and He is faithful! Before we even knew we would need such a specialized doctor, God was answering our prayer for healing and a skillful surgeon. How good it is to know that whatever may happen in our lives, God has already anticipated our needs! The God who hung this planet in space and who knows the beginning from the end has such an interest in us that He plans in advance to answer our cries for help. He has promised that before I call—before *you* call—He will answer. Rest today in that promise!

SANDRA SIMANTON

Small Stuff

Let the words of my mouth and the meditation of my heart be acceptable in Your sight, O Lord, my strength and my Redeemer. Ps. 19:14, NKJV.

I WAS SITTING ON a stool on the patio of the condo where I live, relieving my flowers of their dead leaves and branches. Suddenly the door just beyond my condo opened, and a man emerged. "Oh!" I said, "you startled me." He laughed a bit and re-marked how smoky the air was. "Yes," I agreed. "They just said on the news that the fires had started up again."

We began a conversation, and he commented on what he had heard about the fires. As we talked I tried to remember where I had seen him before. My curiosity grew until finally I blurted out, "I don't recognize you."

He laughed again and, with a flick of his hand toward my next-door neighbor's condo, he replied, "I'm her son."

"Ron," I said, having often heard his mother speak of him. "I've seen you come and go. How is your mother?"

He then explained that he and his mother were trading cars. Her car, a comparatively new model, had received a couple of dents in her efforts to park it in the garage below. Rather than wreck it, she decided she preferred driving her son's older car. After a bit more conversation he got into his mother's car and left.

Later, when I went back into my house for a break, I realized what had happened. In a small segment of time I had met someone new and touched others' lives for a moment, just as mine, too, had been touched by the bit of conversation we had shared. I realized this is what we are here for, and so many times we never give these momentary contacts any thought. Each word, each smile, each short bit of laughter, touches someone and triggers a response for good or ill. God is in the small stuff, too. I hope I remember.

EVA ALICE COVEY

? Thought: Is our text for today really about "small stuff"—or "big stuff"? What difference does it make in your life as to how you regard it? Think about some casual conversations you've had lately. How do we determine what is acceptable to God—what He wants us to do?

Right on Time

My God shall supply all your need according to his riches in glory. Phil. 4:19.

MY HUSBAND AND I decided to do some home renovations. We contracted out the kitchen counters, carpet, and hardwood floor. Rationalizing that it couldn't be all that hard to put down ceramic tiles, we took on that job. We measured the floor, bought the necessary supplies, and headed home to tackle the job with instructions I had printed from the Web. We were on a tight schedule to finish the bathrooms before the professionals came.

We consulted with a few friends and got varying suggestions. Then we discovered that we needed to put in a subfloor. By this time we realized that we were in way over our heads. We didn't have a clue how to lay the subfloor or the tiles. We prayed for guidance and approached people we thought could assist. No one had the time to help us out.

When we went to the hardware store one evening, my husband stopped to talk to an older gentleman. I became rather impatient, thinking of all the work we had to do at home. Why was he wasting so much time talking to this stranger? Little did I know that this stranger was the answer to our prayers. When my husband and I caught up to each other, he informed me that the man recognized him because he had sung at his church some time back. They struck up a conversation, and the man indicated that he was a carpenter, among other things. Just the person we needed! *Father, forgive me!*

My husband explained our situation to him, and the man offered to come by the house one evening. True to his word, Dennis came and put down the subfloor in both bathrooms. He came back another evening, laid out the tiles, and marked all the ones that needed to be cut. He showed us how to apply the adhesive and install the tiles. He came several times to lend a hand at no charge. The bathrooms were completed just in time, and everything was professionally done. What a mighty God we serve!

God knows what we need even before we call upon Him. We don't know when or how He will answer, but we can rest assured that *He will answer.*

SHARON LONG (BROWN)

(?) Thought: If you are praying for something, do you have faith to believe that your answer is already on the way? Sometimes God doesn't answer us in the way we expect!

Sheltered in the Arms of God

For thou hast been a shelter for me. Ps. 61:3.

DURING OUR EVENING MEAL I glanced over at our 15-year-old daughter, Judy Lynn, and noticed that she was crying softly. "What's the matter, honey?" I asked. I really didn't need to ask. She'd been having intermittent abdominal pains for several weeks, and the doctors couldn't diagnose the problem. Now the pains were back, and they were preventing her from eating. "It hurts," she said.

"Honey, I know it hurts, but can you show me exactly where it hurts?" She put her hand on the right side of her body, between the hip bone and the navel. I was at her side in a few seconds with my full attention on the implications of her disclosure. I touched softly at first, then with three fingers I pressed down very fast, a bit harder, letting up very quickly. This procedure was used to diagnose my appendicitis three and a half years before Judy Lynn was born. Her response confirmed this was the problem. I briefly comforted her, then ran for the phone and told our doctor my findings. He told me to bring her to the hospital without delay.

I quickly gathered a few things she would need, and my husband carried Judy Lynn to the station wagon, laying the seat down so that she could recline and be more comfortable.

During the 20-minute ride the tape player in the car was playing soothing religious music softly in the background, and my attention was on driving safely and keeping a careful watch on Judy Lynn. Then something about the music made me sit up straighter and listen more carefully to the words: "For I'm sheltered in the arms of God." Most of the tension that had been building slowly dropped off my back and shoulders. Why should I bear this weight alone? God was there with us in the car as we were driving to the hospital. He was at home with my husband and the two younger children, keeping them sheltered as they slept. He would be with the hospital staff, too, as they cared for Judy Lynn.

Everything went very well in the surgery. Soon we brought Judy Lynn home, and she was well enough to return to school and the other activities she enjoyed.

LILLIAN MUSGRAVE

Thought: How do we make sure we never forget that we are constantly sheltered in the arms of God?

The Seat Covers

John saw Jesus coming toward him and said, "Look, the Lamb of God, who takes away the sin of the world!" John 1:29, NIV.

THE FIRST NEW CAR I drove off the showroom floor was a little red Buick Skylark. How proud I was of that car! My husband surprised me with a gift of fluffy white lambskin seat covers soon after I got the car home, and they set off the maroon interior beautifully.

A few days after we had the seat covers installed, my 4-year-old granddaughter, Kimi, went for a ride with me. Kimi loved pretty things. She surveyed the seat covers and fingered the softness of the lambskin silently. "Grandma," she asked, "did they have to cut a sheep to make your seat covers?"

In amazement I eyed her. No way could I lie. "Well, yes, Kimi," I finally managed to answer her, "I guess someone did have to cut a lamb to make these seat covers."

Kimi sat in silence, looking straight ahead as I started the car. "Grandma," she finally said, looking at me sadly, "I don't think God likes you to cut sheep to make seat covers."

Suddenly I didn't like my new seat covers anymore. Fortunately, they didn't wear well, and I replaced them with human-made fleece covers.

Over the next few years I often thought of Kimi's response to my seat covers. Then one day I heard a man pray an unusual prayer. He thanked the Lord for dying and giving us His fleece. In my mind's eye my white fleece seat covers appeared, and I realized that they represented the fleece of the Lamb of God. Unless a knife was applied to the Lamb, I couldn't be covered by His fleece. His death made my salvation possible.

In my imagination I was back in Eden. The first sinners had just discovered that they were naked. Innocent Eden animals were brought forward and killed, and from their skin God fashioned garments for Adam and Eve. Jesus Himself is the Lamb who was slain for my sins, the Lamb without spot or blemish. His beautiful fleece, His perfect righteousness, was made into a covering for you and me.

Yes, Kimi, I silently said to the long-ago-4-year-old, *I see it now. They did have to cut a Lamb to make a covering for you and me.*

CARROL JOHNSON SHEWMAKE

A Fresh Start

I came here baptizing with water, giving you a good bath and scrubbing sins from your life so you can get a fresh start with God. John 1:31, Message.

I HAD INFORMED my supervisor that I was planning to resign my position. After nine and a half years I was seeking a job at another company. Perhaps even in a different state. New horizons and bigger challenges. A fresh start.

So began the tedious chore of throwing out files that would not be needed again and setting up the remaining files for whoever would take my position. I browsed through the folders. At times there were things I wanted to keep, but I reluctantly tossed them into the rapidly growing pile of discarded paper. Why leave outdated or unnecessary office files to take up valuable space? And why take personal files home to my already-jammed file cabinet when I would probably never need them again?

Deciding what to keep and what to toss was painstaking and time-consuming. But it had to be done! My nails chipped and split from the constant push and pull on the folders and from the paper clips and staple removal. My hands and wrists ached, my knees were stiff from staying in the same position for much too long, and my back felt like it was going to break in two.

I was consumed with the task for hours. Finally it was done! I breathed a sigh of relief. Stacks of old folders and hanging folders were strewn about the floor, and mounds of paper clips were on my desk, reminding me of how much had been accomplished. And the recycle can was overflowing. I was sure the cleaning crew would wonder why so much had been thrown out at one time. Never again would I let files accumulate without taking time to discard what was no longer needed. It was too much trouble!

As I tidied up my desk area before going on to my other tasks, my mind wandered to thoughts of baptism—to a clean slate, to a new start. Even then, I had spent time agonizing—what could I keep, what did I have to toss? And why couldn't I hold on to it and get rid of it later? Had I known that nothing really mattered except Jesus, I would have gladly tossed it all!

Lord, I long for a fresh start again. As I sift through all that life has set before me today, help me to choose wisely, toss out anything that I don't need, and rededicate myself to You.

IRIS L. STOVALL

Guinea Hens

And all things, whatsoever ye shall ask in prayer, believing, ye shall receive.
Matt. 21:22.

AFTER MY HUSBAND RETIRED, we decided to move to the country, where one of our children, a teacher at a private school, and his lovely family were living. On moving day, as we started unloading the truck that held all our worldly goods, we were greeted by a flock of guinea hens. They wanted to get in the truck and got under our feet as we went back and forth into the house with our household goods.

After being in our house for a few days we knew we were in for some "fun." Whenever those birds heard us, or whenever they heard our radio (we tried to play it so softly), or whenever they spotted us, they'd come running with such squawking that, if we were on the phone, we couldn't even hear. They'd peck on our patio door relentlessly, or try to roost on our front porch glider. I'd have to get my broom out and chase them off.

Our neighbors had some good laughs watching all of this, and even my husband thought it was funny. So I decided to take matters into my own hands, as praying them away didn't seem to be working.

I asked my grandson for the use of his BB gun. Well, the BBs only fell out at my feet. So I asked for the use of his air rifle. I guess I'm a weakling, because I couldn't pump it up. I was in a quandary as to what to do. Then I got an idea. Surely God would say yes to this.

I went to our son's house, where our two lovely granddaughters, who are 4 and 7 years old, live. "Girls," I said, "would you do something for Grandma? I want you to pray and ask Jesus to take the guinea hens away before they drive Grandma crazy! You don't want Grandma to go crazy, do you?" So they promised to pray. Lo and behold, the Lord took the guinea hens away. We haven't seen or heard them since.

I'd been asking Jesus to take the guinea hens away, but for some reason He didn't do it for me. When I enlisted help from my two granddaughters, the guinea hens left. I decided that maybe He wanted me to share prayer with the girls so they could see firsthand how God answers.

JANET THORNTON

? Thought: Have you asked anyone to join you in prayer? Do you have enough faith to do that? What if God says no?

He Hears Us!

Then you will call upon me and come and pray to me, and I will listen to you. Jer. 29:12, NIV.

WHEN WE RETURNED from a long trip to visit our daughters who lived in another state, we left the bus station and took a taxi to our home in a neighborhood outside of the downtown area.

We handed the taxi driver three suitcases and a travel bag. The trip had been long and tiring, and we couldn't wait to get home, unpack, and rest. When we got out of the taxi, the driver paused, opened the back door, and gave us just three suitcases.

"What could have happened?" we questioned. "Where is the travel bag? You placed the three suitcases and a travel bag in the car, didn't you?"

"Yes," he answered, "however, as we rounded a curve along the road, the back opened, and the bag must have fallen out."

"What will we do now?" I asked, very concerned, trying to think of some solution.

"I'm going to go back to the terminal by the same route that we took. I'll attempt to discover what happened, or see if the travel bag has been found by someone. We'll talk again soon," he promised.

I was very upset. I cried out to God, because He knows all and can do everything, and we could do nothing. In my request I told Him of the certainty that I had regarding His providence.

And what I expected happened. He heard our prayer. The bag was found and was delivered to us the same day. A man had found it along the highway and taken it to the taxi office at the bus station. Praise the Lord, there are still conscientious people today! Certainly the Lord directed that man who willingly took the bag to the lost-and-found sector of the taxi company.

I knelt and thanked the Lord for fulfilling the promise recorded in today's text: "Then you will call upon me and come and pray to me, and I will listen to you."

The promise of the Lord is certain. He blesses those who trust in Him, and He attends their prayers and supplications.   IVONETE VIANA

(?) Thought: When you have cried out to God, have you really believed that He was going to answer your prayers? What happened?

No Temptation

No temptation has seized you except what is common to man. And God is faithful; he will not let you be tempted beyond what you can bear. But when you are tempted, he will also provide a way out so that you can stand up under it. 1 Cor. 10:13, NIV.

GOD IS WONDERFUL! He not only provides us with an escape route from temptation; He provides us with one we can "stand up under." We don't have to crawl out from under it by our fingernails, getting scraped elbows. He has pulled back the oppressor's affliction from us far enough to enable us to "stand up under it." Those who are oppressed by temptation at every corner know how debilitating it is. It feels as though there is no end to it, and that even though we ask God to deliver us from it we return to it. Why? Is it that we don't know of this escape route God provides for us? Is it that we don't sense that God can deliver us?

I once believed that I was the only one going through the trials of morality and spirituality. I thought, *If God really is love, why doesn't He save me from these things?* Then He brought today's verse to my mind. I hadn't separated temptation from sin. I had lived a life in which temptation became sin. This verse cleared the way for life-changing events. Temptation that is placed before me is experienced by not only me but others also. I don't have to waste time wondering how to get away from it. God has already done that.

Friend, if you are tempted don't let it become sin. And if it is now sin, no matter what it is, know that you aren't alone. Even though we feel as though we can't stand it anymore, we need to remind ourselves constantly that God holds back the oppressor's impact on us so that he cannot tempt us beyond what we can survive. God is our source of survival, our escape, and our recovery from any temptation we experience—lust, adultery, greed, gossip, jealousy, envy—all of them.

Blessed Lord of all, thank You, thank You for this escape route from the oppressor's deceptions. Strengthen us because we believe in You; we believe in Your power and authority.   JULIE NAGLE

(?) Thought: Think of the things that are particularly tempting to you. Have you asked Jesus to deliver you from these temptations? How has He provided a way out? Now the hard question: Have you taken advantage of this escape route?

Chosen

"All things are lawful for me," but not all things are helpful. "All things are lawful for me," but I will not be enslaved by anything. 1 Cor. 6:12, ESV.

THE GREAT DAY OF our picnic arrived. I was very eager to go out with a group of friends—a very enthusiastic group. We were going to a waterfall to spend the day in nature, playing games, hiking in the woods, and bathing in the water among the rocks. I didn't know how to swim, but I hoped to have a very enjoyable Sunday.

When we arrived at the meeting place, one of the vehicles that had been rented was gone—the group had already departed, leaving seven of us behind. Since the second vehicle never came, we decided to take advantage of the day at another location. The food and everything was ready; we could still spend the day together. We went to a nearby waterfall, although some of the group didn't like the idea because it was a somewhat dangerous location.

When we arrived we went into the lake that was formed by the waterfall and began to play with an empty coconut shell, as though it were a ball. Without realizing it, I was distracted and drifted into a spot where the water was deeper. My energetic friend also became distracted. We did not realize that we were getting farther from the lakeshore. Suddenly I could no longer feel the bottom. Desperation took over, and I began to go under. I was scared! I sank to the bottom for a few seconds and couldn't get back up. I began to pray and ask for forgiveness for everything that I had done wrong because I felt that I was going to die.

It was then that a tall man approached me and pulled me out of the deep water. I believe that man was my angel, because soon after the fright had passed, we went to find him to thank him, and he was no longer to be found.

I was only 13 years old, but I knew then that God had a plan for my life, and I felt the hand of God that day. John 15:16 states, "You did not choose me, but I chose you and appointed you to go and bear fruit—fruit that will last. Then the Father will give you whatever you ask in my name" (NIV). I am chosen as well as redeemed.   LEONÍZIA GENEROSO

? **Thought:** What has God done for you that convinces you that He has chosen you and has a plan for your life?

Standing in the Gap for the Dying

Then He came to the disciples and found them sleeping, and said to Peter, "What! Could you not watch with Me one hour?" Matt. 26:40, NKJV.

MY FATHER-IN-LAW lay dying in the hospital after a long illness that had followed a severe stroke. It had been a painful year, and the doctors didn't expect him to survive. This was an especially stressful time for my husband, as his dad had become ill less than a month after his mom had passed away. His parents had been married for 50 years.

The day before my father-in-law was to be removed from the machine that was prolonging his life and his suffering, my husband of 16 years requested that I go to the hospital to pray. Our prayer had changed from a plea to heal to one for salvation. That day I struggled between the duty to pray and a great yearning to shut off the lights, cower under my covers, and hide. Hide from the hurts that Dad's certain death would bring to us and to our two children. Hide from my husband's tears and hurt for his only living parent.

Discouraged, I dropped down on the living room couch, begging sleep to help me forget. Then I thought of my husband and the promise I had made to him. Without even checking my hair or clothes, I gathered my courage and my Bible and drove to the hospital.

Once there, I sang and recited verses. I claimed promises of forgiveness, salvation, and resurrection, inserting Dad's name in the appropriate spots. The more I sang, the stronger I felt. Then I prayed and kissed Dad goodbye.

Later that afternoon my husband came home and asked (more a statement than a question), "You did OK with Dad today?"

"Fine," I answered. He then intimated that while he worked he had been praying with me. He agreed with me in prayer, pleading for Dad's salvation.

I smiled as I remembered the internal battle I'd fought before I visited Dad. Then my thoughts came to the Savior. At His worst time His closest friends, the disciples, couldn't wait and pray for Him. How He was depending on them for strength and comfort!

ROSE THOMAS

(?) **Thought:** If someone asks you to pray for them or for someone else, what is your response?

The Lord Went Before

And the Lord went before them. . . . He took not away the pillar of the cloud by day, nor the pillar of fire by night. Ex. 13:21, 22.

"LET'S TAKE OUT A Bible promise from the box and think about it all week long until sundown worship," suggested my family that Friday evening.

The text I drew was Exodus 13:21 and 22. I thought it was very strange: I didn't see how a text that referred to the Israelites in the desert could apply to my life today.

The next morning my 10-year-old daughter showed me her hands which were covered with red spots. *She must have slept on them* was my first thought. *Nothing to worry about.* As I helped her get ready for school, I noted that her feet also had red spots. *First her hands, now her feet.* At this point I became concerned.

I got out books and began to read about childhood illnesses. All the symptoms indicated rubella. As I was three months pregnant with twins, I began to despair. *Exactly now, in the third month of pregnancy. Why not before? Why not later?* I thought.

I immediately sought medical attention. "We have to wait 15 days for the results of your tests. Everything indicates that it is rubella, but don't worry about your daughter—she'll be fine. My concern is you and your condition," stated the doctor. That only increased my despair.

I remembered so many stories of mothers who had contracted rubella during pregnancy. Their children were born disabled, some hearing- or sight-impaired. In my case there would be two babies. It was then that I remembered the Bible verse that I had taken out of the little promise box at last week's sunset worship. At the time I hadn't understood the message from God to me, but things were becoming clear. I began to see the care that God had for the children of Israel in a desert so far away, and this same God continues to be as caring today. I took hold of His hand and called out to Him day and night. Praise the Lord who cares for each one of us!

I'd had contact with the rubella virus; however, the virus had been overtaken, and I didn't develop the disease.

ISABEL CRISTINA DE ALMEIDA MACHADO

Thought: Are you going through a desert experience? Where might you be able to see the pillar of cloud or fire?

In the Valley

Even though I walk through the valley of the shadow of death, I will fear no evil, for you are with me. Ps. 23:4, NIV.

"YOU HAVE A BRAIN TUMOR." The words fell out of the doctor's mouth in slow motion. Two year later the moment is still surreal. I still get chills when I recall that conversation with my neurologist.

I'd had a history of migraines after two childhood accidents that both resulted in concussions. About two and a half years ago, however, the headaches had become more intense, more frequent, and were accompanied by a variety of new symptoms. My doctor sent me to have an MRI—and the rest, as they say, is history.

When I heard those life-changing words, I became numb and felt as if I were dreaming. When I began to "wake up," I was flooded by feelings of panic, fear, confusion, and the question I dared not ask aloud: *Am I going to die?* Other thoughts played in nonstop chorus: *I'm only 34 years old! I don't want to leave my son! What about my life with my future husband? My parents can't bear this.* It was as though I'd been thrown into the middle of the ocean and I couldn't swim.

Overwhelmed, I cried out to Jesus, my Maker, my Friend, and my Savior, and He heard my cry. He lovingly wrapped His arms around me and reassured me of His love and presence. As the tears poured down my face, He reminded me of His promises. He provided me with a strong, spiritual network of family and friends who constantly prayed for me. He gave me a team of compassionate, skilled physicians. Many of my family and friends prayed for my healing, but I prayed for God's will, knowing full well what the outcome could mean. I also prayed that God would use both me and my illness for His glory.

Things have calmed down now, and I have regained a sense of normalcy. So far all the tests have shown no evidence of cancer. I still have an MRI every six months to monitor the tumor. It is still present, but it hasn't grown larger. My situation has not changed, but I am completely at peace. My faith in God was shaken, but it has grown to heights I never imagined. God loves me. He will never leave me. Even in the valley of the shadow of death, He is with me.

Lord, thank You for Your presence and the peace that comes from knowing You. ANGELA C. HARDIN JONES

A Seminar Just for Me

Even so it is not the will of your Father who is in heaven that one of these little ones should perish. Matt. 18:14, NKJV.

AT A NATIONAL TEACHER'S conference I attended a one-hour seminar on testing and statistics. I sat on the second row in front of the other conference attendees. The presenter, who had a Ph.D. behind his name, arose and began his presentation. I soon realized it was way over my head. At those infrequent times when I understood three of his sentences in a row, I'd give the presenter a smile of appreciation and slightly nod my head just to be polite.

Midway through the lecture I began noticing something so strange that at first I thought it was a figment of my imagination. The longer the presenter spoke, the more he looked at me. In fact, as he finished reading his final page of notes, he was focusing on my face.

"Are there any questions?" he finally asked, looking directly at me. Since no one behind me posed a question, I mustered a simple one about the presenter's methodology.

He kindly answered it, then thanked his audience for "staying by." Instinctively, I began to applaud his efforts, but no one joined me. Embarrassed, I stopped and looked over my shoulder. I was the only conference attendee remaining. Everyone else had left!

"As I said," emphasized the presenter, "thank you for staying by."

Before leaving, I went up and shook his hand and thanked him for what he'd done.

Once the Godhead prepared a "seminar" for the salvation of sinful humankind. The Presenter was Jesus Christ. He came to the "conference room," Planet Earth, and talked about love and relationship and sacrifice, concepts that sinners really couldn't understand. By the end of His earthly presentation most of the earlycomers had deserted. In fact, at the cross He was virtually alone. Yet if you or I had been the only ones left, He still would have gone through with the whole painful ordeal. And He did. What commitment to His purpose! What love for the wayward sinner!

No, I wasn't able to understand enough of the seminar presenter's information that day to make a difference in my teaching that year. Yet I, one of the least of these, am able to understand enough of what my Savior did, just for me, to make a difference in my life . . . eternally.

CAROLYN RATHBUN SUTTON

Chiquitín

So don't be afraid; you are worth more than many sparrows. Matt. 10:31, NIV.

MY BROTHER, ADOLFO, his wife, and children were out for a walk. It had rained, and there was a strong wind blowing, so the family had to watch for fallen tree branches. Suddenly a branch hanging from a tree caught their attention. As they got closer, they saw a nest with a little featherless bird. Adolfo lifted the branch, sure that the baby bird could die there if it didn't have more care. So his wife said to the boys, "Go ahead; I'll catch up. I'm going to see if I can put the nest and the bird in a more secure location."

She returned to the house with the bird in her hands, turned on a lightbulb, wrapped the little bird in a cloth, and placed it close enough to the lightbulb to keep it warm. Then she quickly left to catch up to her family.

When they returned to the house, everyone was very curious to see how the baby bird was. What a surprise! The little bird was alive and very hungry. The boys made "baby food" from cornmeal, and with a toothpick they put the food in its small beak.

They named the bird Chiquitín (tiny little one). To everyone's joy, Chiquitín ate very well and grew each day. Little feathers began to appear, and soon the baby bird began to fly. It flew from one place to another, landing on the heads and shoulders of the family. As they sat at the table to eat, Chiquitín flew to the table and ate the crumbs. Everyone was very fond of him, cared for him, and spoiled him with love.

One day a flock of small birds just like Chiquitín flew near the house and landed in the garden to eat some seeds. Adolfo took Chiquitín to the garden so that he could begin to learn how to relate with other birds. It didn't take long before he was happily integrated into their society. When the little birds took off to continue on their journey, Chiquitín followed them, certain that he had found his true family. As he flew to great heights, his friends who had saved him watched with smiles and tears.

Thank You, Lord, for assuring us that just as You care for the little birds, You will also take care of us. CLARA HORNUS DE FERREYRO

God Knows of Our Needs

O give thanks unto the Lord, for he is good: for his mercy endureth for ever.
Ps. 107:1.

WHEN I WAS A STUDENT, I had to work to support myself and pay for my studies. Since I came from a poor family, this was the only way for me to continue studying. I attended a boarding school and worked there several hours each day to earn the scholarship I needed.

At 5:00 on a Sabbath afternoon it was time to begin work in the cafeteria. My colleagues were already there, busily getting work done ahead of time for the supper that we would serve in a few minutes. We all rushed to be able to take care of everything before the students arrived for the evening meal.

After dinner we closed the cafeteria and began cleaning. Within a few minutes the kitchen manager asked us to serve some visitors who had arrived late and hadn't gotten dinner. I was a little aggravated, but I stopped what I was doing and waited on them. As I hurried, my sandal broke. This was a great problem because this was the only pair of sandals I had. I didn't have any funds to buy another pair, and I couldn't appeal to my parents. They had no financial resources and lived far away. I stopped for a minute and asked God to help me resolve this problem. I put on a pair of boots used for heavier duties in the cafeteria and continued my work.

The visitors had been impressed by the manner in which I had served them, and decided to help me by leaving a monetary contribution. I was completely surprised and didn't know what to do. I thanked them for their kindness and praised God for His prompt answer.

But God's answer didn't stop there. A few minutes later a coworker appeared with an almost-new pair of sandals. She said that she had three pairs and was thinking of giving a pair to someone. Through the grace of God she chose me.

It is impressive how God knows our necessities and takes care of us even in such simple situations, providing us with items we need for personal use. All we need to do is trust Him, and He will help us solve our problems.

Thank You, Lord. You care for Your children and look after their smallest necessities.
ELLEN ANDRADE VIANA

Lost

After the celebration was over they started home to Nazareth, but Jesus stayed behind in Jerusalem. . . . And when they couldn't find him, they went back to Jerusalem to search for him there. Luke 2:43-45, TLB.

HAVE YOU EVER LOST your child? If so, you'll remember the fear that gripped your heart. My first experience was at a flea market when my twins were 2. Just as the story in Luke, the children were passing between relatives when suddenly we realized that Royce was missing. Everyone went looking up and down the rows of merchants' booths. Finally I went to the front gate to make an announcement or phone the police—and there he was, sitting at the booth! A man had found him a block away, trying to cross the busy street to where our van was parked. Knowing something was wrong, the man brought him back to the gate, thinking someone would come looking for him.

Just as frightening as losing your own child is losing someone else's child! Eight years later, when my daughter was about 6, her cousin, Kelley, came to stay for a few days. There was a grand opening at a nearby store, so we went early, standing in line to be among the first to enter and receive the free gifts. We were a group of three adults and six kids in a crowd that was jostling and pushing. Suddenly we realized that Kelley was missing. My heart sank. Here my cousin had trusted me with her daughter, and I had lost her! Praise God, in minutes my name was called on the public-address system, and I was able to pick Kelley up at the cashier's desk just a few feet away.

Can you imagine Mary's terror when she realized she had lost the Son of God? God had trusted her, a human, with His precious Son, and she had lost Him! From a mother's heart, can you feel how long those days must have seemed until she finally found Him? And can you understand why she sounded upset when she asked, "Son, why have You done this to us?"

Being human, Mary and Joseph had become absorbed in their daily activities and lost sight of Jesus, both physically and spiritually. Times haven't changed. We lose sight of Jesus when our self-generated needs, ambitions, and responsibilities deprive us of prayer and devotional time. As with Mary and Joseph, it takes us much longer and more effort to find Him again than it did to lose Him in the first place.

BETH VERSTEEGH ODIYAR

My Bushtit Lesson

If we confess our sins, he is faithful and just to forgive us our sins, and to cleanse us from all unrighteousness. 1 John 1:9.

TO ME, THE VERY ESSENCE of motherhood is displayed in a bird's nest—in reality the mother bird makes a baby bed. Sometimes even a scenic one. Maybe it's the oneness I feel, that caring bond of nurture, love, and a mother's protection that warms my heart.

Housed in my half bath off the kitchen (appropriately named "The Bird Bath" because of its decor) is my varied collection of bird's nests.

One afternoon my friend Cheri and I noticed something odd in her backyard garrya bush. It looked like an dirty, gray tube sock with a tennis ball in the bottom. A closer look revealed a penny-size hole on the upper backside. We exclaimed in unison, "A bird's nest!"

Our bird book confirmed "the thing" to be a bushtit nest. Cheri asked if I wanted it, and I was thrilled. We cut the branch extra-long because I intended to anchor it in a heavy container.

Days later I took the nested branch to the shop so my husband could anchor it. I had just begun pulling weeds from the flowerbed when I heard Glen exclaim disgustedly, "You ladies!"

I dashed back to the shop, and there on the floor at his feet was a tiny egg, splattered on the cement with the yolk still intact.

"Oh, no!" I moaned. "I had no idea there were eggs in that nest!" Carefully Glen lifted the nest and out rolled eight more white, smaller-than-jelly-bean-size eggs. We looked at each other with sickened expressions.

One egg broke as I removed the insides, so I ended up with seven tiny white eggs nestled on moss at the branch base—seven little reminders that I had made some faulty assumptions. The nest was not last year's and, though I couldn't see inside the nest, eggs were present. My eager selfishness to have the nest for display resulted in canceled plans of a little bushtit baby bed full of chirping life. (Bushtits are communal nesters, so I had disappointed more than one mother!)

The unique bushtit nest and its seven little eggs will be a constant reminder that even when I make mistakes and presume incorrectly toward my friends, I have a loving God who understands and forgives the intents and motives of my often-selfish heart.   MARYBETH GESSELE

The Best Place in the World

And lo, I am with you alway, even unto the end of the world. Matt. 28:20.

CERTAINLY THE BEST PLACE in the world is at the feet of the Savior. Like every human being, we dream of many things, and my husband's dream was to study theology and become a pastor. The greatest problem with this was that my *husband* dreamed of this—but I didn't want to leave my hometown and be far from my family, whom I love very much. I'd always lived near them.

I'd been praying about this for about a year. I asked God to light our way and show us His will for our lives. I felt God opening the doors in such a manner that we at times could not understand. My husband took the college entrance examination in Brazil, but didn't qualify to enter. Within one week God changed the direction of our lives, and we went to a university in Chile. We left everything behind—house, family, relatives, friends, work—and went to another country, seeking to fulfill my husband's dream. A good friend of mine told me that if it were God's will He would open doors. However, if we saw the doors closing, this would be because it was not God's will.

The first week in Chile was difficult. Everything was different—the language and the customs—and I cried because I missed everyone I'd left behind in Brazil. I wanted to return. I prayed constantly, asking God for His comfort because my heart was in anguish and I thought only of giving up. At the same time, however, I asked God for the answer, because I knew the answer was with Him.

One morning my husband went to make a reservation for airline tickets to return to Brazil. He met a pastor's wife who asked about me. My husband told her that I was sad, crying a lot, and that I wanted to return to Brazil. She asked him not to purchase the tickets—she wanted to talk to me first. That conversation was the answer that I needed from God on that day. She encouraged me a great deal, gave me her support, and told me her life experience as a pastor's wife. When we finished our conversation, she prayed with me, and I felt relieved.

On that day I reached the conclusion that "the best place in the world is at the feet of the Lord." If we seek Him, if we serve Him, and if we have Him within our hearts, even though we are in distant locations and far from our loved ones, we can be happy. MARÍSIA OLIVEIRA H. CARVALHO

The Lost Coin

And when she has found it, she calls her friends and neighbors together, saying,
"Rejoice with me, for I have found the piece which I lost!" Luke 15:9, NKJV.

WHEN I THINK OF that lost coin celebration, I think of the dramatized parables that I always enjoyed back in my primary Sabbath school Bible class. But this time around, the parable of the lost coin had a profound meaning. This past spring I had a surprise when I was suddenly reunited with a lost friend from way back in our high school days.

You see, we were the best of friends. I had grown to like and count on her during our teenage years. We were inseparable. We shared secrets, laughed, and participated together in various church activities. Our families, too, appreciated and understood how special this friendship was (and still is today).

While in missionary work with my husband for several years, I lost contact with her. I tried for more than a few years to locate her, but to no avail. The only dear things I had were photos taken during our senior year. Yes, I had other friends, but this one friendship was out of the ordinary. I had often wondered how she was. Was she married? Did she have any children? Oh, how I missed her!

While reading unsolicited and forwarded e-mails one day I came across a familiar name. I wondered if she could be the one. The day I received that e-mail was a high day. It reminded me of the parable of the lost coin. When you are searching for something, never give up until you have found it. I was soon calling friends and family, letting them know how the lost had been found. I wanted everyone to share in this joy.

As in the lost coin story, I can't wait to see the joy in my Father's face when He scoops me up in His arms and never lets me go. And there in that great city we will be able to spend eternity with all our friends and family and never part again.

SIBUSISIWE NCUBE

(?) Thought: The coin did not know it was lost. Is it possible for us to be lost and not know it? God, however, knows and is constantly looking for us if we are. Who do you suppose will have more to celebrate—those who are saved, or God?

The Face-lift

The Lord is my shepherd; I shall not want. Ps. 23:1.

IT WAS EARLY SPRING. Oh, how I had looked forward to making extensive repairs on the house—weather permitting. The top of the foundation around the base of the house was detached from the walkway. The steps on the front stoop were broken as a result of chemicals in the snow-melting salt, and aluminum was peeping out from underneath what paint was left from my attempt to clean the siding on the front of my home. It looked awful. And I have not even mentioned the faded awning that hung over the front door. I thought about replacing it altogether and prayed about it, as I do everything. I soon found myself sharing my concerns with my neighbor. I knew that financially I was looking at astronomical figures.

Answers to my prayers were coming as quickly as I petitioned the Lord, though. I was able to get repairs on the foundation and the stoop almost immediately. The job was done well and at a reasonable fee.

To my surprise, the siding wasn't a big problem either. My neighbor encouraged me to take a small piece of the siding to the local home improvement store and have them match it with paint. I never guessed that aluminum siding could be painted. What a difference a few coats of paint made. I decided to keep the awning, which was painted as well. I couldn't imagine the beauty my eyes beheld as the sun beamed brightly against it. The face-lift on my house brightened up the whole block.

I thought about what a spiritual face-lift would do for me. Jesus will make the necessary repairs around my sinful foundation. My broken steps are under construction as I bow on my knees, confess my sins, and ask for forgiveness. My request is the same as David's: "Create in me a pure heart, . . . and renew a steadfast spirit within me" (Ps. 51:10, NIV).

My prayer today is: *As the Son shines on me, let those with whom I come in contact see the beauty of my spiritual face-lift.* You can get one too. It's only a prayer away!

CORA A. WALKER

(?) Thought: Whether a renovation or a faith lift, it is always good to think first of the foundation. Read Matthew 7:24-27 and Luke 6:46-49 and think seriously about whether your spiritual home's foundation is built on sand or rock.

Duckling for Dinner

The wolf will live with the lamb, the leopard will lie down with the goat, the calf and the lion and the yearling together; and a little child will lead them. Isa. 11:6, NIV.

LAKESIDE WALKS PROVIDE me with a sense of serenity like nothing else. My mind goes into a creative mode as I walk, and contentment is my lot. I wonder if that's how Jesus felt as He walked along the Sea of Galilee or by the Jordan River? I thank Him for these water spots that give me comfort. Then one day I saw a lakeside sight that taught me an object lesson in a dark way.

A bevy of Muscovy ducks, intent on foraging their dinner, were unaware of their adventurous duckling. Sunshine filtered through the trees circling the lake. Couples strolled along the walkway, children laughed as they played tag. The scene seemed so serene. The wee black baby duck paddled swiftly away from the communal dinner. So newly hatched, but with such an adventurous spirit! Close by, the piercing eyes of a predator bird fastened on the wee one, and he moved stealthily toward his prey. His object—duck for dinner.

A shrill call cracked the air, made by a foreigner in the crowd—a white duck. She craned her neck high as she cried and swiftly flailed her large white wings in a valiant attempt at shooing away the stalker.

Within moments the predator bird swooped low across the lake—and scooped up the baby Muscovy in its talons. I shivered as I watched, and I too cried out. In swift flight the thiefbird landed high in a live oak tree, holding a mouthful of broken-necked baby duck. Tears traced my cheeks. I felt unnerved.

We Christians know that someday there will be no such scenes. Birds will not prey on birds, animal on animal, or humans on humans. There will be no terror for man or beast. The disturbing scene brought another thought to my mind: If the adult ducks had been watching their charge the adversary probably couldn't have carried through with its intent. I liken it to the mature members and the "baby" members in the church. Sometimes a new seeker becomes discouraged and quits attending services. A few may inquire, "I wonder what happened to so-and-so?" Yet time goes by, and no contact is made. That's when Satan, the predator bird, seizes his opportunity and snatches the weak one—a broken victim.

Are we watching? Are we crying for each other?   BETTY KOSSICK

Let's Be Prepared

No one knows about that day or hour, not even the angels in heaven, nor the Son, but only the Father. Matt. 24:36, NIV.

IN THE 1980S OUR TEAM of girls chose a city in which we would sell religious books. My three sisters and I stayed in a church located in the downtown area. The church was on the upper floor, and a school operated on the lower level.

One night, after a tiring day of work, we and 20 other girls all went to sleep. During the very early hours of the morning we were awakened by the sound of footsteps, things being dragged across the floor, and male voices, though we couldn't understand what was being said.

We became frightened. The door wasn't very sturdy, and we heard someone messing with the door handle. Now we were dreadfully frightened, wondering what would happen next. What if they were thieves? Did they know there were only girls there? What did they want? It seemed that they were taking the piano and the pews. Would they do something to us? Many of the girls began to cry as we attempted to calm each other and prayed constantly for God to protect us.

Finally it was quiet. We were exhausted, but no one could sleep. Finally, when the new day broke, we reached a consensus: we should open the door. After all, nothing had happened to us, and we had to leave the room sometime. To our surprise, we learned that some church members had rearranged the furniture in the sanctuary for the funeral of an elderly woman. The noise had nothing to do with what we had imagined!

That experience was very difficult, but after everything was clarified it even seemed amusing. We learned several lessons. God in His infinite goodness protects His children in all situations. While selling books, we were all blessed and protected by our Father in heaven.

We know that Jesus has promised to return one day, and His Word tells us that many will be surprised; some will flee, and others will cry out for the rocks to fall on them so that they will not see His face. It is my prayer that we not be taken by surprise with the arrival of the One for whom we have waited so long. We need to be ready to receive Him and hear Him say, "Come, ye blessed of my Father, inherit the kingdom prepared for you from the foundation of the world" (Matt. 25:34).

AUCELY CORRÊA FERNANDES CHAGAS

Coming Soon

They shall see the Son of man coming in the clouds of heaven with power and great glory. Matt. 24:30.

I WAS ON MY FIRST tour of Europe, and I doubted if I would ever be back again. Our itinerary started in London, and we planned to be at Westminster Abbey when the royal family was to exit after the service at noon.

Everybody boarded the tour bus early, ready to hit the road. We got to the Abbey just after 9:00, two hours before the expected appearance of the royal family, so we could get the best places before the crowd really began to fill up the better viewing spots. Our group thought that the family might just be arriving, so we'd have two opportunities to get a good look at the queen, the prince, the princess, and the two young princes. Ten o'clock. Eleven o'clock. No royal family. We decided that we'd missed the grand entrance. Nevertheless, we waited another hour for their departure. When it was past noon and the royal family still was not in sight and people were leaving, our group left too, disappointed.

We went on to Italy, spending a few hours in Venice and other places, but our ultimate goal was to reach Rome to see some historical spots. We were also hoping to see the pope in Vatican City.

Our tour guide informed us that Pope John Paul II greeted visitors through a certain window in his living quarters. We asked the guide to take us to a place where we could be close enough to talk to him, or at least be able to recognize him. We were led to a spot right in front of the window with the waiting crowd.

We waited in the hot sun for more than an hour. When the time came for the pope to appear, we were told that *he was on vacation!* Once again our tour group was disappointed.

Joel 2:1 has a message for us to "sound an alarm in my holy mountain: . . . for the day of the Lord cometh, for it is nigh at hand." Jesus says in Matthew 24:42: "Watch therefore; for ye know not what hour your Lord doth come."

We are waiting for the grand appearance of our Lord Jesus Christ. He will not disappoint us if we are well prepared.   ESPERANZA AQUINO MOPERA

The Blessing of Fellowship

For this day is holy unto our Lord: neither be ye sorry; for the joy of the Lord is your strength. Neh. 8:10.

A DINNER-OUT EVENT was planned by women's ministries last week. It had been announced in the church bulletin two weeks in a row. I knew the date, but I really didn't check the calendar, thinking that the date was still far away. So I was surprised when Arlene, who arrived for the women's prayer partners meeting held on Tuesday at our house, reminded us about the up-coming event on Thursday, just a couple days away. I hadn't even thought about it! I felt as if I were being awakened from a stupor, and I needed to get my act together.

How thankful I am to God for blessing my life with women's prayer partners, which has been my chain of support in many ways. Since we started this group four years ago, we've reminded each other of our schedules. This group of women has been supporting one another as we fellowship and pray in one accord for each other and our church as a whole, including world leaders.

That particular Tuesday night we really enjoyed our study, and we worshipped in prayer, experiencing God's presence in our midst. As we concluded the meeting, again Arlene indicated her willingness to drive four prayer partners from our respective residences to the restaurant on Thursday evening.

Arlene drove out of her way so willingly, blessing all of us with God's love, producing multiple joy of the Lord in us. The conversations and laughter as we headed to the restaurant pronounced God's presence, which continued when other women's ministry members joined us at the dinner. Our Christian bond was reaffirmed as we fellowshipped, for we acknowledged that the "joy of the Lord is [our] strength" (Neh. 8:10).

We ended the dinner with more laughter as we celebrated one of our members' eighty-first birthday. We were strengthened in our relationship with one another, promoting spiritual growth. We were surely blessed with God's love, for we experienced real joy in our hearts.

Lord, thank You for showing us the importance of fellowship as we reach out to one another and experience the joy of the Lord, who strengthens us.

EUNICE URBANY

After My Own Heart

I have found David the son of Jesse a man after my own heart. Acts. 13:22.

SHE SITS ON THE FLOOR of my living room on a velvet pillow, a beautiful chestnut-red Doberman pinscher. Her eyes follow me without a flicker of warmth or recognition. She knows the dog obedience commands and does them well: come, sit, down, stay, enter kennel, give, drop it, and heel. I haven't owned her very long, and it's delightful to put her through her paces—but I haven't reached her heart.

She is not a good substitute for the black-and-tan Doberman, Sheba, who was my buddy for 10 years. I'm still trying to replace the bond that Sheba and I shared as companions and friends. She was a loving and obedient dog, after my own heart.

Outside is Mr. Blue Eyes, a cream Doberman pinscher pup with blue eyes. He is gangly, awkward, unruly, energetic, and beautiful. Although he tries (occasionally) to please me, just about everything he does is wrong. Teaching him obedience commands, I try to be patient. He catches on quickly—when he wants to. Sometimes I feel like giving up.

Muddy paws, scratched back door, chewed TV cable, chewed cell phone—this is the price I pay for eventually molding him into a truly elegant, obedient dog. He has a long way to go. An unruly rogue, he is determined to have his own way, and this gets him into much trouble. Yet he comes back to me, repentant (sometimes), to stare lovingly into my eyes, lick my hand, and lean by my side.

He got out of his yard the other day and headed down the street. I called him, and he came back. There was no leash holding him. He had his freedom to run with the traffic and run far away, but he didn't. He returned at my call.

It is as God said about David: he is "a man after my own heart," in spite of all the mistakes and sin. Mr. Blue Eyes is a dog after my own heart, in spite of the trouble he gets himself into.

And the quiet, elegant dog in my living room? I will keep talking to her, stroking her, and taking her for walks. Someday she will be my friend. God doesn't stop seeking us, who sometimes also do all the right things, but our hearts are far from Him.

EDNA MAYE GALLINGTON

? Thought: Would you rather be an obedient woman, or a woman after God's own heart? Why?

It Mattered to God!

Do not worry about anything, but pray and ask God for everything you need, always giving thanks. Phil. 4:6, NCV.

WHAT AN EXPERIENCE it was to be visiting the city of Quebec with 16 students from my French class! On Friday I purchased bus passes for going to church so that everything would go smoothly on Sabbath morning.

When it was time for all 19 of us to get off the bus, I didn't notice that my eyeglasses had slipped out of my raincoat pocket. Upon arrival in the sanctuary, I went to retrieve my glasses and, to my consternation, they were not to be found! To my horror, I realized that they must be on the city bus. I said a quick prayer as I told the pastor about my predicament of not being able to see the French stanzas I had written for the grade 9 special music I was helping with. He lent me his glasses.

Meanwhile, some of the grade 7 boys said they'd seen some glasses on the city bus floor upon exiting. Naturally they never thought the glasses belonged to their teacher! I prayed again that I might find them, unbroken, through the lost-and-found department. I must admit that my faith was only up to about 8 percent, because, after all, it was really my fault that the glasses were lost. The bad habit of taking those glasses off my nose was catching up with me.

After a delightful church service and potluck, our group went to wait for the bus. "That's our driver across the street," someone said. I jotted the bus number down. Later the same driver picked us up on the return from her loop. Imagine my surprise when I started to explain my loss and she pointed to a pair of glasses hanging by her tickets. Yes, they were mine, and they were intact. All I could say was "This answer to prayer is truly a miracle. To think that someone brought you these before they were stepped on!"

God cares about everything, even the smallest details of our lives. I believe that this answer to prayer was for the students, as well as for the mom who had said to me earlier, "Wouldn't it be a miracle if you found them on the same bus on our way back?" Most of all, I know that this miracle was to strengthen my faith in our awesome God, who cared about me and my glasses.

MURIEL HUGUENIN

Like a Tree

He shall be like a tree planted by the rivers of water, that brings forth its fruit in its season. Ps. 1:3, NKJV.

HAVE YOU EVER FELT TALENTLESS and uncreative? Have you ever listened to a gifted speaker, looked at a piece of art, read an inspiring book, or heard a moving song and wondered in amazement at the person's ability to do those things? Often the very experience of being blessed by another's gifts leaves us focusing on our own inability to do those very things. Even if we are aware of our gifts there's the matter of comparing ourselves with ourselves. Of course, in the end, we will almost certainly come up short.

It is a fact that we are not all the same. We are not all creative in the same ways. We don't all have the same gifts. But there is one thing we all are: we are all gifted. When we give our lives to Jesus we are given at least one gift. And with use and exercise that gift grows and multiplies. In Christ we are always living and growing. As a matter of fact, Scripture describes us as trees planted to thrive and grow by the rivers of waters, where we are always nourished.

Even so, we don't all bear fruit in the same way or even at the same time—especially not at the same time. How boring it would be if all the trees only bloomed, or showed their best colors, in only one month a year! God made the seasons so that each could rest and draw strength and nourishment for those times when it is their turn to shine.

God is so good! Just as the trees remind us of continuing life, we can stay fresh and strong even during the winter months of our lives. Even when it looks as though we are not contributing anything at all, in reality we really are!

Just as the florist carefully mixes in the simple green of a fern or some other leafy plant to complement the flowers in a vase, there are times we are simply to be a part of the backdrop, enabling those whose turn it is to flower and bloom even better for the cause of Christ.

Yet all the while, we can know that without the support of those "filler" plants the arrangement would not have nearly so great an impact. Each plant is important. Each of us is important too. God will always remember where He has planted us. He will never forget where He's arranged us in His glorious garden. As long as we stay rooted in the Water of Life, we can grow confident that we are giving life and strength and beauty to all who pass our way.   EMILY FELTS JONES

My Guardian

Your enemy the devil prowls around like a roaring lion looking for someone to devour. 1 Peter 5:8, NIV.

EVERYTHING WENT WELL in our travel until we reached Guwahati, Assam, around noon. When we came out of the airport, the Garo Section treasurer who met us said that we could not proceed to Tura, west Meghalaya, because of a politically motivated strike. So we checked into a hotel. The following morning the treasurer said, "There is no transportation tonight, either, and the strike is indefinite." I told the men that we must get there somehow before nightfall. I could not disappoint the women waiting for me there. God helped the treasurer get a vehicle.

The road was rugged and the ride bumpy. We hardly saw any vehicles on the road. Around 2:30 we entered Dudnoi and found the shops closed. We continued without much thought to the strike. A police officer stopped us at a crossroad and advised us to wait until 5:00 that evening, and told the driver to park the vehicle at the police station just around the corner. Instead the driver made a U-turn and drove back to look for a place to eat. Finding none, he drove toward our destination. Suddenly 15 angry young men came from different directions and blocked the road. One of them motioned for us to pull the vehicle to the side.

The driver stopped the vehicle and got out. My blood froze. *This is the end of our lives,* I thought. *What will these angry young men do to strangers? Will they burn us alive with the vehicle for violating the strike? Or will they show mercy and spare our lives and burn only the vehicle?* One of the young men asked for the car key. To our surprise, the driver handed it over without the slightest hesitation. The young man passed the key on to another, and the gang walked away without a word. Three hours later they returned the key, and we resumed our journey. *Thank You, God, for Your protection,* I prayed.

The road we journey now is rough and rugged, with trials, temptations, affliction, pain, and misery. Satan places all these before us to hinder our heavenward journey, not wanting any of us to reach our destination. But we should be neither alarmed nor discouraged. Remember, God is always in control over every situation. He protects us every step of the way.

We reached the destination in time for the scheduled meeting. My faith is strengthened. HEPZIBAH G. KORE

Bethel, God's House

My people will dwell in a peaceful habitation, in secure dwellings, and in quiet resting places. Isa. 32:18, NKJV.

MY LIFE HAD BEEN RIDDLED with problems for many years, but in March 2004 God delivered me. In gratitude I named my house Bethel, God's house. My brother and his wife came over to help me dig three large flowerbeds in front of the house. As we placed the roses, azaleas, and other flowers in the ground, I named each bed. There was Mahanaim to the south, Shalom in the center, and Peniel to the north. Now everything was beautiful and peaceful.

Two months later disaster struck again. The city decided to use one acre of their 23 acres of land directly across from Bethel to build a heavy equipment maintenance station. I had never heard of a rezoning plan—the letter must have been lost in the mail.

Apparently they came to clear the land while I was at work. Tears streamed down my cheeks as I looked at the downed trees. I had chosen this site for my house six years earlier because it was the perfect spot to enjoy nature and commune with my Father. Now ugly, heavy trucks were to keep me company. I was very distressed. Though I called real estate agents and talked about selling the house, I knew I didn't want to move. Too depressed to do anything but pray, I asked others to pray with me. Then I got to work. With God's help, I was going to fight for my house.

I began talking to city officials, and eventually was able to contact the one in charge of the project. His reply was curt: "This is our land. We will continue with the plan."

I got people in the neighborhood to sign a petition against the city maintenance unit. I wrote a letter to the city manager. Another city official came out to explain that this was their land, and they could do whatever they wished. I answered, "This is God's land." He replied, "I can't argue with that," and left. I even called the deputy mayor at his home.

At the meeting the following Tuesday, the city manager apologized. He said that he'd seen my beautiful house, and that the city would stop the plans. The project director changed his mind too. He said that they would even replace the trees they had cut down.

Yes, God is always in control.

PHOEBEE JOCELYN-MUSCADIN

April Fools'—A Day Late

A cheerful heart is good medicine. Prov. 17:22, NIV.

HAVE YOU EVER ASKED God to show you that He has a sense of humor? I did, and this is what happened.

The day after April Fools' Day, when the mail arrived, I found myself holding a Government of Canada envelope addressed to "The Estate of the Late Linda Gay Mentes." Well, it was a little thought-provoking, to say the least, to see my name written there! I opened it—and there was my income tax return.

At the end of the printout and summary it noted: "If you have any inquiries, call 1-800-XXX-XXXX." I did have a few inquiries. I called and explained things to the woman who answered. She gasped, "Oh, no!" I told her that just that very morning I had written in my prayer journal that I needed the Lord to help me have a better sense of humor. "Just hold on," the woman said. "I'll put you through to a supervisor." I explained to the supervisor that this was so funny. On the very day I prayed this prayer, I received this unique piece of mail.

She typed my information into the computer and, sure enough, when my husband did our income tax returns he put both his and my birthdays on the wrong line—he put them in the deceased line. However, his return came back fine. Even funnier, before we sent the income tax returns in, I signed on the dotted line that "all the above information" was true. I was vouching that I had died on February 26, 1955.

They told me to send the check back and they would reissue it. But first I made a photocopy of the check to tape into my prayer journal. I explained the situation to my husband and said, "Nice try, honey! Trying to knock your wife off—and then taking all of her inheritance!"

We all laughed so hard every time we told the story. April Fools'—a day late. I've said it before, and I'll say it again: the Lord has a real sense of humor. Why don't you try asking Him to show you?

"Good humor isn't a trait of character; it is an art which requires practice" (David Seabury).   GAY MENTES

(?) Thought: Do you believe God has a sense of humor? Share some examples with a friend who needs cheering up.

Asthma Attack

Be careful for nothing; but in every thing by prayer and supplication with thanksgiving let your requests be made known unto God. Phil. 4:6.

THE FIRST WEEK of April I had the privilege of going with the twelfth graders to Uttarkashi for a retreat. We drove our vehicles to Gangotri, which is about 12,000 feet (about 3700 meters) above sea level and is the place from which the main Ganges River flows. This also happens to be a Hindu pilgrimage center to which people go to worship their gods and from which they carry Ganges water to their homes for different purposes.

We were happy and excited after seeing Gangotri. We were also happy that we'd had no casualties on our way. When we were about an hour away from our destination, Priyanka Chand had an asthma attack. She used her inhaler and got some relief, but about five minutes later she suffered a second attack. The inhaler gave her less help this time. She drank water and poured some on her face. Then the attack came for the third time. This time it was very severe. The inhaler didn't work at all, and the water had no effect on her. I kept looking at her face and continued my silent prayer. Somehow we walked over to my Tempo Traveler, where the boys were seated. Sitting next to her, I asked everyone to pray and put my arm around her as I offered a prayer from a sincere heart. She felt as though she was not going to live, that she was breathing her last. After I prayed, I told her not to give up but to trust in God, that He was going to make her better. I kept encouraging her by my words.

It wasn't even two minutes later that she mustered a few words: "Madam, I am feeling better now." I do know that God answers prayer, but so soon? But then it made me think: God is really great, and of course God is love. That's why He had given her His immediate healing touch. Then I asked her to offer a prayer of thanks to the Lord.

This experience has really made my faith strong in the Lord. Priyanka had no further attacks after this incident.

Lord, Creator of this universe, help us to be firm in our faith and to rely on Your promise. This is my daily prayer.   REBECCA SINGH

April (4)

My Savior

Because we trust in the living God, who is the Savior of all men, especially of those who believe. 1 Tim. 4:10, NKJV.

"YOUR SAVIOR IS DEAD!"

I looked at my mother, puzzled. She is a good and devoted Christian woman, and I didn't know what she meant. Then she reminded me of something that had happened in my early childhood.

I was only 2 years old and was very fond of sweet fruits. In our garden there was a large mulberry tree that produced large, juicy, tasty black mulberries. All the children from our neighborhood came to pick up this tasty fruit. I couldn't climb the tree then, so the bigger children picked some fruit for me. If you've ever eaten mulberries, you know that it leaves some of the juice on your hands. And as my mother taught me, I wanted to have clean hands. So I went to wash, but not at the sink. Near our house was a water channel that was about five feet (1.5 meters) deep and 10 feet (three meters) wide. That was where I went to clean my hands.

You can imagine what happened next. I slipped on the slippery cement edge of the channel, fell into the water, and was washed downstream almost 160 feet (50 meters). No one saw what happened, but Someone from above saw me and prepared a deliverance. God sent my neighbor, a passionate fisherman, to the right place at the right time. He had come home from work on his bicycle loaded with many shopping bags. He saw something rolling in the water and thought, *That must be a great fish from the Bistrita River!* Then he saw a piece of cloth. He told himself, *That must be my daughter's doll.* Then he saw my face, and suddenly he realized what had happened. He let all his goods fly and jumped right into the water to save me.

My parents and relatives have told me this story many times. And I knew right from my childhood that I am in debt to someone for my life.

And now my mother had told me that my savior was dead. What sadness came upon my heart. The neighbor had never accepted the real Savior, in spite of our friendship and urging. And now he was dead!

But we have a greater Savior who died once for the sins of the whole world. And He is risen and is alive forever! We are in debt to Him for our lives. How shall we thank Him? By giving ourselves entirely to Him. May God bless us in doing this!

VIORICA AVRAMIEA

My Precious Tablecloth

Though your sins be as scarlet, they shall be as white as snow; though they be red like crimson, they shall be as wool. Isa. 1:18.

RECENTLY I WENT IN SEARCH of my lily-white, hand-cro-cheted tablecloth. I hadn't used it for quite a long time, and I thought it would perfectly complement the decor of the dining room that I was putting together for a special meal.

With the same pride that I felt when I completed it and showed it to my husband, I took it out of the drawer and headed to the dining room. I dusted the table and removed the chairs to give me space to lay out my prized trophy.

As I unfolded the cloth, my heart sank with disappointment. The table-cloth was spotted with all types of stains—yellow ones, yellowish-brown ones, and even gray ones. There was no pride in its display now. Ah! Now I remembered what had happened. I had realized, after discovering the stains, that trying to remove them would have damaged the delicate threads. So I had put it aside and had forgotten about it.

My spotted tablecloth caused me to reflect on myself. Although born as a spotless baby, a prize to my parents, I grew, and became tainted with sin. The stains of sin marred my character and spoiled me.

It was inevitable that my precious tablecloth would be prone to spills of gravies, juices, and different food textures that would leave stains of all colors and shapes. Likewise, it was inevitable that I would be stained with sins, being born in a sinful state. The reassuring difference between me and my tablecloth is that if I am willing, God will not push me aside and forget that I exist. He has promised to clean me up, wash me in His blood, and present me faultless. With pride He will present me to His father.

I folded my cloth and put it back in the drawer, reminiscing on its former beauty. I cannot restore my tablecloth to its original glory without destroying it. However, one day my Savior will remove every trace of sin from my life, never to be remembered, and present me spotless. A brand-new me will be created.

Dear God, today my heart is overwhelmed with gratitude; I live in anticipation of a time when You will present me spotless and sinless—as a new born baby. I live for that day. GLORIA GREGORY

Turning Enemies Into Friends

But all things are from God, who through Jesus Christ reconciled us to Himself [received us into favor, brought us into harmony with Himself] and gave to us the ministry of reconciliation [that by word and deed we might aim to bring others into harmony with Him]. 2 Cor. 5:18, Amplified.

LAST WEEK MY HUSBAND and I went to see Mel Gibson's *The Passion of the Christ.* I expected I would cry; instead, I sobbed. I figured there would be times when I would block the view from my eyes; instead, I buried my head in my husband's shoulder.

Many years ago I had read about the brutality of a Roman crucifixion. Those words imprinted pictures on my mind that have never been erased. And the barbaric way in which Jesus was treated on the way to His death as portrayed in the movie will be lodged in my mind forever. But the strongest picture in my mind is the way in which Jesus responded to all those people who were in relational conflict with Him. That is the way He responded to you and me when we were enemies of God—and to those who caused Him pain as He journeyed to Calvary.

From the Garden of Gethsemane to the cross, Jesus went from one relational conflict to another. It was like watching a catalog of difficult relationships in rapid succession. There was the betrayal by Judas, whom He loved; the desertion of those who promised to be there for Him. There was the racial hatred; the verbal and physical violence. There were the times He was lied to, made fun of, condemned for doing good and accused of doing evil. Whatever He did, He could not win. Yet He showed no undercurrents of restrained anger or desire to get revenge.

And finally, when He was on the cross, when He had been scourged, beaten, spat upon, pushed to the ground; when He had been whipped so that His skin was shredded and bleeding; when His enemies were laughing, joking, mocking, taunting Him, He looked down at them, then looked up to God in heaven and cried out, "Father, forgive them."

Never once did Jesus seek retaliation for the way in which He was treated—only reconciliation. As a result, some of those enemies became His closest friends.

At times we all have to deal with those who cause us pain. We often wonder how to deal with them. If we look at Jesus, that question will be answered.

MARY BARRETT

The Pomegranate

A golden bell and a pomegranate, a golden bell and a pomegranate, upon the hem of the robe round about. And it shall be upon Aaron to minister: and his sound shall be heard when he goeth in unto the holy place before the Lord, and when he cometh out, that he die not. Ex. 28:34, 35.

THE SCARLET FLOWERS of the pomegranate *(Punica grana-tum)* contrast with the deep-green leaves of this large shrub. It is native to Asia and widely cultivated for its edible fruit. The round pomegranate fruit is the size of an orange, with a hard reddish-yellow-brown rind. Inside, the numerous seeds are each enclosed in a juicy pulp with a mildly acid flavor. It derives its name from Middle English: *pomegranard. Pome* for apple, and *grenate* for having many seeds. It is eaten raw, and when it's squeezed to drink, the juice resembles blood. A syrup flavored with pomegranates is called grenadine syrup.

The pomegranate is referred to in 11 Old Testament books. This shows the importance of this fruit. In Exodus 28:33 we read that the hem of the high priest's robe was embroidered with pomegranates. Pomegranates were used to ornament the pillars in King Solomon's Temple (1 Kings 7:20). The spies who went to explore the land of Canaan returned with a single cluster of grapes so large that two men had to carry it on a pole. They also had some pomegranates and figs to prove that the land was fertile (Num. 13:23). Yes, the pomegranates grew in abundance in Canaan. So the pomegranate is a special fruit!

I feel so privileged to have a tall pomegranate tree growing in my backyard. I admire the pretty blossoms, then the tiny red-orange, waxlike cups (the fruit in its primary stage) until it swells out to the size of a large orange. Sometimes when the strong winds blow, the blossoms are shaken off. But once the fruit is matured, it is steadfast on the bough. When it is over-ripe it cracks open, and some of the red juice flows out. The pomegranate tree also has sharp thorns on its branches.

The pomegranate reminds me of the sacrifice Jesus made—the crown of thorns that was shoved on His head, and His precious blood spilled for me on the cruel cross of Calvary.

Thank You, Jesus for dying in my stead so that I may have eternal life. What wondrous love!   PRISCILLA E. ADONIS

Paid in Full

For God so loved the world, that he gave his only begotten Son, that whosoever believeth in him should not perish, but have everlasting life. John 3:16.

WHILE CHECKING OUT at a local store, I decided to pay with my debit card and get $20 cash back. The cashier started processing my card, then told me the card was not functioning, and declined it. So I proceeded to use a credit card for the purchase.

Later, inspired by the Holy Spirit to check my debit card account with the bank, I found that the merchant had charged for that purchase, plus the $20 I had wanted in cash. I later took both receipts and my bank statement back and talked with the merchant's manager. He, of course, tried to defend the error. He later agreed that an error had occurred and wanted to allow me merchandise instead of cash, as it would prevent showing up as a cash shortage. I refused merchandise, and he reimbursed my cash in full.

Sometimes, after paying the monthly bills, you may receive a letter from a merchant stating that you still owe. Or maybe you have remitted and your payment has crossed in the mail, but until it is received you are liable for that debt.

Before the death of Jesus Christ, the people had to bring a sacrificial lamb without blemish to be offered as atonement for sins. Without the shedding of blood there would be no forgiveness. If they were poor and couldn't afford a lamb, they could offer a dove or a pigeon. God sent His son Jesus, His only begotten Son, as the sacrificial Lamb to take away our sins. He had to shed His innocent blood and die on a cruel cross for *our* sins—not His. Because of Jesus' death on the cross, nothing will cross in the mail. All is fully paid.

We have all sinned and come short of God's glory on so many things. Sometimes we sinned unknowingly and didn't ask forgiveness. The Holy Spirit knows our intentions and intercedes for us. Jesus' death on the cross has paid our debt in full. "Jesus paid it all, all to Him I owe; sin had left a crimson stain; He washed it white as snow" (Elvina M. Hall, "Jesus Paid It All").

How much do I owe? I owe my life. Dear Lord, we all have sinned and come short. Please forgive and grant us a clean slate—paid in full. Thank You. Amen.

BETTY G. PERRY

Boats and Bridges

The Lord is my rock, and my fortress, and my deliverer; my God, my strength, in whom I will trust. Ps. 18:2.

I'VE NEVER BEEN VERY fond of boats—any size, any shape, or any style. And I especially don't care for small rowboats. But shortly after we were married, I consented to go fishing with my new husband when we visited his grandmother, who lived near one of his favorite fishing spots.

I got a bit nervous as I watched Harold push that little boat out to the rim of the water and asked me to step in. That was my introduction not only to fishing but also to a rowboat and the water beneath the boat, and I haven't cared for any of it since.

However, through the years I've found it necessary to ride ferryboats from time to time. I actually survived going from Charlevoix to Beaver Island, Michigan, not once but twice. My uneasiness was intensified on the last trip when we got lost in a dense fog and the captain missed the dock. On our many vacations in Michigan we had to go by ferry to get from the lower part of the state to the Upper Peninsula, so I was one happy camper when they built the big bridge connecting the two.

Occasionally a family member or friend will chide me for not wanting to go to Hawaii or on a cruise to some of the beautiful islands. My answer is always the same: "When they build a bridge, I will go."

I have known for some time, however, that it isn't the boat that causes the problem—it's the water beneath and around the boat that's the culprit.

You may say, "But there's water beneath and around the bridge." True, but each end of a bridge is connected to dry land, and that's where my security lies.

I heard a pastor preach a sermon on that subject one time. He referred to Jesus as our bridge. I hadn't thought about it in exactly that same way before, but it made me stop and think: Jesus is my security because He's my connection between where I once was and where He wants me to be. He's definitely my bridge.

CLAREEN COLCLESSER

Thought: What do you fear? How can Jesus help you overcome?

Tell Me the Old Story

Blessed is he that readeth, and they that hear the words of this prophecy, and keep those things which are written therein: for the time is at hand. Rev. 1:3.

READING IS ONE OF MY favorite activities. My late husband was aware of this, so at various times he would ask me to read to him. One time he jokingly told the children, "Your mother loves to read—she even reads all the advertisements."

We traveled out of state by car quite a bit. As my husband did the driving, I was busy reading signs, whether on stores, buses, billboards, or wherever there was something to read. I recall a sign on the bumper of a car in front of us that got my attention: "God is not through with me yet." I've thought about those words often and find myself thinking of how much God loves me, how patient, kind, and longsuffering He is, and I thank Him for not giving up on me.

After retirement, I babysat my three grandchildren during their preschool years. I enjoyed reading stories to them, making sure they heard at least two stories before going-home time. My granddaughter started writing short stories in elementary school, and she evidently sensed that I liked to read, because she began giving me a copy of each story as she wrote it. I began filing her stories. Now she is in college and has no time to write, so I decided one day to pull out one of her stories to reread (it had become one of my favorites). After I had read it, my thoughts focused on one of my first graders, who had her favorite story. Whether at story time or sharing time, she always mentioned her favorite story. When her time came to share, to my surprise one of her classmates blurted, "We don't want to hear your old story today!" This little first grader is grown up now and probably still has a favorite story, but I pray that like me, she has chosen the old, old story of Jesus and His love as her favorite.

Thank You, Jesus, for Your wonderful story. No matter how old, I enjoy reading it again and again, joining in with the songwriter's words, "I love to tell the story; 'Twill be my theme in glory to tell the old, old story of Jesus and His love." *

ANNIE B. BEST

---

*Katherine Hankey, "I Love to Tell the Story."

The Ugly Duckling

Beloved, now are we the sons of God, and it doth not yet appear what we shall be: but we know that, when he shall appear, we shall be like him; for we shall see him as he is. 1 John 3:2.

THERE IS A CHILDREN'S BOOK called *The Ugly Duckling*. The story tells of a plain, gray bird egg that hatched among six duckling eggs. The ducks didn't accept the new bird, and the chickens and turkeys in the barnyard picked on him too.

Finally the bird ran away and lived all alone. He didn't realize that he wasn't meant to live in a barnyard. In the winter he froze to the ice, but an old man came along and broke the ice to free him. Once an old woman invited him to stay in her yard to lay eggs, but chased him off when she saw he was a male and wasn't useful to her.

Then a father brought the big bird into his house to play with his children, but the bird became frightened and knocked over a pitcher of milk. They realized he wasn't meant to live in a house. The baby bird did lots of resting and waiting, not knowing that all along he was changing.

One day he flew to a pond where there were adult swans. He thought, *They are too beautiful to accept me, but maybe they'll let me stay on this side of the pond and admire them.* Then, when he hung his head in shame, he saw his reflection in the water and was surprised to see that he looked just like the swans! They swam over to welcome him as the most beautiful of them all.

This is our story. We were destined to be Christlike, but we were born in a sinful world. We were meant to be in fellowship with perfect beings. We don't look right or do the right things, according to the world's standards. Sometimes God allows hecklers to force us on to where we're supposed to be. Sometimes He sends helpers when we're in danger. Besides how we look, the fact that we don't do what others think is useful is another reason we're rejected.

We weren't meant to live in this sinful world, and we seem to make a mess of things. Each experience brings us closer to who we really are. As we go through our life we don't know that Someone is helping us handle what comes to us. We don't notice we're changing. But someday when Jesus and the angels come, they'll welcome us, declaring that we are the most beautiful of all because of the experience we've been through on earth.

The promise has finally come true: "When he shall appear, we shall be like him."
LANA FLETCHER

My Housecleaning

And see if there be any wicked way in me, and lead me in the way everlasting. Ps. 139:24.

WOW! SEEING THE TREES in their new mantle and smelling the air permeated with spring fragrance inspired me to get into my housecleaning.

In the course of housecleaning I found a cardboard box in the attic packed with clothes and shoes that I had planned to give away. In my busy program I'd forgotten all about it. The box had lain there for years. Inside I found mildewed clothes and shoes, plus a host of cockroaches. So I burned the box. After I had scrubbed every nook and cranny, my house was thoroughly cleaned.

Having the housecleaning done, I took a few moments to relax on the terrace and feast my eyes on the beautiful landscape, the cattle grazing in the fields, and the rolling hills against the blue horizon. The scene before me seemed uncontaminated with sin. I felt rebuked to realize that my life is in contrast to it. I therefore made an about-face to do my spiritual house-cleaning, to make amends for faults I've overlooked. And so here I go:

Dear Sir,

Enclosed, please find a check for those peaches that I enjoyed on your farm (secretly, with my roommate in high school days). I'm sorry. Thank you.

And then I moved on to type another note:

Dear Sir,

Enclosed, please find a check for the peanuts that I enjoyed (secretly, with my roommate in college). I'm sorry. Thank you.

I put the notes inside the addressed envelopes and dropped them into the mailbox.

With relief I went back to the terrace. Meditating upon my life, I asked myself, *What should I do to keep my spiritual house free from accumulating junk?* It struck me that I should see not only from my angle but through other people's eyes as well. And so I did just that.

Thus realizing my weakness, I have no one but God to turn to. I ask, "Search me, O God, and know my heart: try me, and know my thoughts: and see if there be any wicked way in me, and lead me in the way everlasting" (Ps. 139:23, 24). I must leave my "housecleaning" in His hands to make it perfect.

ANNIE M. KUJUR

Let Me Finish

Set a guard over my mouth, O Lord; keep watch over the door of my lips. Ps. 141:3, NRSV.

MY CONCLUDING STATEMENT sputtered, unspoken, to a stop. A girlfriend and I were having a heated (and I mean heated) debate about the benefits of feedback. I knew what I was talking about. So did she. As I started to offer the final statement (the clincher, I thought), she said firmly, "Let me finish."

I drew a deep breath as she completed her statement. It was then that I realized that we had been talking about the same thing during the entire interaction. We were just using different terms. Because I hadn't been listening keenly enough, I'd been hearing what she was saying, but hadn't been processing her words. I hadn't been acting out the principle that I was arguing about. I hadn't been listening to her. I hadn't been valuing her input. In my haste to share my perspective, I hadn't been deciding when to speak and when to stay silent. I'd wanted to speak.

I pondered that incident for weeks. Finally I apologized to my friend. Sweet soul that she is, she admitted that she remembered nothing of my brusqueness. Relieved, I thought of a statement made by someone in our Sabbath school class: "Consider the text in Isaiah 1:18 as the NRSV puts it: 'Come now, let us argue it out.' Look at it with your mind's ear. Listen to the call, 'Come.' I hear a gentle debate between two people who value each other."

I knew that my mind's ear wasn't working well when I argued with my friend. Nor was my value system.

All at once I remembered the request a girlfriend used to make as she recounted compliments she'd been given. "Let me have my moment," she would beg. I recall that as I would hear about her beautiful moment, I would reflect on a similar moment that I'd experienced. And I would have to share it. Right then. "Let me have my moment," she would plead. I thought I had learned that lesson, but I hadn't.

God has a way of reminding us that we are accountable for our knowledge and the way we use it. But, praise God, He also reminds us that the end is only the beginning. He still has not given up on us.

Remind me, Father, that I have two ears and one mouth for a reason. Help me to be genuine when I say, "Speak, Lord, for Your servant is listening."

GLENDA-MAE GREENE

My Cherry Tree

Trust in the Lord with all your heart, and lean not on your own understanding; in all your ways acknowledge Him, and He shall direct your paths. Prov. 3:5, 6, NKJV.

But my God shall supply all your need according to his riches in glory by Christ Jesus. Phil. 4:19.

IN THE EARLY SPRING of 1999 my husband and I decided to sell our house of 19 years. We had been on long-term disability since 1994, and our pension income was just half the salary we used to have. We were barely able to make ends meet with the existing mortgage.

After praying, we contacted a real estate agent and put up the "For Sale" sign. At the same time we started looking for a smaller house, as our children had gone to their own nests. We wanted to settle down in a three-bedroom bungalow, eliminating climbing stairs, since my husband had recently had open-heart surgery. We also wanted to relocate closer to our church.

It didn't take long to find our house of choice, a bungalow with a huge backyard. It took only five minutes to view the house. The former owner didn't care to tell us about the mature trees that were still leafless in the early spring. We were content that we would have plenty of space for gardening. I told my husband that I wanted to make sure we planted a cherry tree, just as our former neighbors had. So we went to our lawyer to sign the sale papers, then left for our yearly vacation to the Philippines.

June 30—the closing date—came, and we were ready to move into our bungalow. My sister, my niece, and my daughter-in-law went ahead of us to the house while we went to pick up the key. When we got there, we found them at a cherry tree, feasting on the ripe dark-purple cherries right in the yard of our new house!

I am humbled to know that God supplies our needs according to His riches in glory by Jesus Christ. We were able to pay off the mortgage on the former house, and our bungalow is mortgage-free. We have a few thousand dollars of pocket money and plenty of organic vegetables every summer. And the cherry tree is a monument to God's grace and everlasting love. Truly God is awesome.

EMRALINA PANGAN IMPERIO

God's Presents

Sons are a heritage from the Lord, children a reward from him. Ps. 127:3, NIV.

HERE I AM, ALONE. I just took my daughter to join a group of students who work selling books during the vacation period so they can obtain funds to pay for their studies. They are a large group of very enthusiastic youth. Now I am here alone, looking at one of my pots of African violets, walking around the kitchen, not knowing what to do. There is no one here to make a snack for, nor anyone to tell to "go take a bath" or to put to bed early because of school the next morning.

I almost allowed myself to cry and lament the fact that I am alone; however, instantly I remembered my colleagues, the angels, and a smile came to my face and I stopped to thank God. I felt extremely privileged. While many mothers at this hour of the night don't know the whereabouts of their children and are concerned and fretting, or have finally lain down on the empty bed, I know where my children are, and I'm very happy about this.

I once heard someone preach that God has a room in heaven filled with beautiful packages just waiting for us to ask for them. I think that perhaps these presents are our reward, wrapped in beautiful packages with enormous golden bows.

My son is studying in the best boarding school in the world, and my daughter is preparing to go there also. Soon the house will be empty—just me, the angels, and my violets. I wonder what it must have been like for Jochebed to leave Moses at such an early age; for Rachel to be uncertain of Joseph's destiny; or for Hannah to leave little Samuel at the tabernacle. These children were precious presents whom God had entrusted to their mothers. However, if their mothers had not let their children go, the children would not have become the great men that we remember, and we would not have these beautiful examples to strengthen us.

My daughter and the other young people have almost 30 days of school vacation. They could be doing many different things, or nothing at all, but they chose to work for God by selling religious books. Well-trained and motivated, they make a mighty army! God shall crown their efforts.

I have really enjoyed the "presents" the Lord has entrusted to me, and I'm proud and happy for the choices that they have made; however, tonight I will still fall asleep crying. REGIANE RAMOS OLIVEIRA

Rainy Reflections

And we, who with unveiled faces all reflect the Lord's glory, are being transformed into His likeness. 2 Cor. 3:18, NIV.

IT HAD RAINED on the Island. Not the usual half-hour tropical downpour. The whole day had been a tropical downpour. In the evening, after the rain ceased, I managed to circumvent major puddles to attend a class at the university.

When I reached the campus, the low-lying meadow that stretches in front of the university buildings was completely inundated. Strangely, I had never noticed how many shops there were along the street at the end of the meadow, or their extensive use of bright lights. Then I realized those lights were not all shops, nor was there an extensive use of bright lights—half of them were shop lights reflected in the flooded meadow. They gleamed and glittered and twinkled and were multiplied by reflections of street lamps and automobile lights.

And the trees! I hadn't observed before that there were so many trees. But those weren't all trees, either. Every tree was reflected in the water. Soft, fluffy cloud reflections, aided by a just-right full moon and the misty atmosphere, added enchantment to that usually colorless area.

Those reflections fascinated me. I would know something about trees if I had never seen one before. I could to some extent approximate their shape and contour, the branch formation and the leaf distribution. Reflections are always a reproduction of the original.

This watery demonstration helped me gain a better comprehension of the reflection of God's character as depicted by His Son. Jesus said, "I and my Father are one" see John 14:9). And what have I seen? Unfathomable love, benevolence, longsuffering, forgiveness, mercy, justice, and so much more.

Scripture says I am to reflect the Lord's glory (2 Cor. 3:18). With my pettiness, fears, and frustrations, I'm not even producing a faint reflection of such a character. Across the flooded meadow I witnessed only the reproduction of physical attributes. Jesus demonstrated God's spiritual characteristics. I thank Jesus that He left such a clear demonstration of God's moral qualities. And He challenges me to behold that reflection and be transformed.

A transformation with eternal dimensions! *Lord, keep me focused until I see You in reality.*   Lois E. Johannes

Forgive Whom?

For if you forgive men when they sin against you, your heavenly Father will also forgive you. But if you do not forgive men their sins, your Father will not forgive your sins. Matt. 6:14, 15, NIV.

FORGIVENESS IS A WORD that's easy to say but oh, so hard to put into practice. Sometimes hate, anger, bitterness, and resentment can well up until you feel as if it will choke you. "You don't know what they did to me," you insist. "You don't know what they said" or "How they hurt me," or, or, or— We all have a story to tell.

But is it worth telling? Jesus knows. He knows not only what "they" did or said but also what *you* did or said. And He died for both. He loves the person you're not forgiving every bit as much as He loves you. Remember the Lord's Prayer: "Forgive us our debts, as we forgive our debtors"? God will forgive us to the extent that we forgive others—even the person we like the very least. That's a hard thing to hear. But He longs to forgive us—and for us to forgive others.

Forgiving someone does *not* necessarily mean putting yourself back in a situation where the person can hurt you again (actions have consequences), but it does mean letting go of the ugliness and treating that person as the child of your God that they are.

I've heard it said that not forgiving someone out of spite is like swallowing rat poison and expecting the rat to die. It doesn't hurt the rat; it only hurts you. Let it go. Let God pry your white-knuckled fingers from around that nugget of hate, and allow Him to throw it away. It's not worth hanging on to. Let Him replace it with a peace that surpasses all understanding—with love, peace, and joy. It may not happen overnight, but it will happen. And the things He replaces it with really are worth hanging on to. Forgive yourself, let God forgive you, and let go of your unforgiving spirit toward others.

VICKI MACOMBER REDDEN

? **Thought:** Forgiving someone when they really have done you wrong is difficult—humanly impossible. Remember, you are not saying they did no wrong; you are freeing yourself from the situation. If you are struggling with forgiveness, here are some verses to study: I John 1:9, Psalm 51, Mark 11:25, Matthew 6:16, Luke 6:35-38, and Proverbs 20:22.

From Darkness to Light

And thine ears shall hear a word behind thee, saying, This is the way, walk ye in it, when ye turn to the right hand, and when ye turn to the left. Isa. 30:21.

"COME ON, SWEETHEART," I told her. "Let's go see the pretty fish. Nothing can happen to you down here; I'm holding on to your hand very tightly!"

I recently took my 4-year-old daughter to a nearby freshwater aquarium. At first Hannah was happy and excited to be there. But when we descended into the dark corridors, Hannah was ready to leave. In addition to the darkness, sounds of running water from various speakers made her nervous. She clutched my hand tightly and held back, not interested in going any farther.

Though still reluctant, Hannah eventually allowed me to lead her to see the pretty stingrays, moray eels, and more. Soon she was *oohing* and *aahing* with the rest of the children who were pressed up against the gigantic tank.

After admiring these fish for a while, we followed a path that led us to an open, brighter area. I was sure Hannah would be happy to see the brightened environment, but she hung back again. "It's noisy," she said, putting her hands over her ears for emphasis. The waterfall cascading from a nearby exhibit was indeed loud, but I encouraged her to continue on with me. My normally obedient child still refused, so I picked her up in my arms and forged ahead. As we turned a corner, Hannah's pout turned into a bright smile. Two little otters were swimming and playing and entertaining all. Hannah began laughing at their antics. "See, honey?" I told her. "Look what's in here. You would never have seen this if we had stopped when you wanted to."

I'm the same way with God sometimes. When life gets a little dark and I can't see ahead of me or my surroundings seem dim, I become frightened. Like my daughter in the aquarium, I refuse to budge, even when I know He's holding my hand. Even when He brings me into the light, I still find something to complain about: the noise, the brightness. But I must keep holding His hand.

After we turn a corner, I can finally smile again. It is then that God says, "Look what you've discovered! You would never have seen this if we had stopped when you wanted to."

TRICIA WILLIAMS

God Commanded the Bull

He shall give his angels charge over thee, to keep thee in all thy ways. Ps. 91:11.

WHEN OUR CHILDREN, David and Hannah, were 4 and 2½ years old respectively, we were living in a rented house in a big compound that didn't have a compound wall. Many times stray dogs, cows, and bulls had a free run of it. A maid took care of our children when we were away at work. We left for school at 8:00 in the morning and came back at 5:00 in the afternoon. It was not the best arrangement for our children, but the circumstances demanded it. Before I went to work, I used to tell David to take care of his little sister, Hannah. Whenever I forgot to tell him, he would come running to me and remind me to tell him. I knew he took his responsibility seriously, and usually he took his sister for long rides on his tricycle. But I often doubted the ability of a 4-year-old in a difficult situation. With a heavy heart I left for work every day, sending a silent prayer toward heaven to protect the children from any danger.

As I went outside to wash clothes one Sunday, David and Hannah were playing tag in front of the house. I saw a big brown bull with large horns enter the compound, but I didn't think much about it. The next thing I saw was the bull staring menacingly at Hannah, getting ready to charge. I was too frightened to move. Taking in the situation, David dashed toward the bull, scolding and screeching. "She's my baby! Go back! Go back!" Both children looked like grasshoppers in front of the big bull. David caught hold of Hannah's hand and pulled her backward while continuing to shout at the bull.

To this day I cannot explain in my human understanding what made the bull retreat. The only way I can explain it is that God restrained the bull from doing harm. For a moment David was an instrument in the hand of God. Like a big automobile, the bull backed up on its hind legs and took to its heels. I often wondered how busy the children's guardian angels must have been caring for them every day while we were away at work. I thank the Lord for His care for them.

SOOSANNA MATHEW

? Thought: This is an amazing story! God does care for His children not only physically but spiritually as well. Have you ever felt like a small child fighting the big bully Satan? What promises can you claim for spiritual escape?

Listening and Learning

Let the wise listen and add to their learning, and let the discerning get guidance. Prov. 1:5, NIV.

EVERY TIME PEOPLE VISIT our home they notice our parakeet, Happy, whose cage hangs from the ceiling at eye level. Invariably they are attracted to him and start the usual bird talk. "Pretty bird. What's your name? Hello." Happy looks at them intently and gets as close as possible, cocking his head and watching their every move. As they continue to talk, he continues to listen. Finally the obvious question comes: "Does your bird talk?"

I always answer, "Yes, quite a bit." That really gets them going, trying in earnest to get even an unintelligible word out of him, but he just continues to listen as they repeat the same things again and again. This is very amusing to me, because as long as they are talking, he is listening. He won't talk until they quit. If they stick around a while they'll eventually hear him happily chattering to himself. Not only is Happy courteous to others; he's also learning from them. How many of us are that wise?

I know a woman who loves to talk. So when I'm with her, I listen. After I leave, I feel sorry for her, because all she's done is repeat what she already knows. She's gotten no input from me, nothing new to think about. That's sad for her and depressing for me, because it's hard to listen to monologues. Conversations are much more stimulating.

Prayer can easily become one-way communication too. The Lord always listens to us, but do we listen to Him? Do we pause long enough to hear answers to our questions and receive direction for our lives? He longs to help us along the rough road of life, and must get frustrated when we don't stop to get His input.

When our daughter was young, there were times when she didn't want to hear what we were telling her. Then she would put her hands over her ears and loudly proclaim, "I can't hear you," in an effort to cancel us out. I think we sometimes do the same thing to God, only a little more subtly. Relationships can't grow under those circumstances, and we certainly can't get guidance, either.

"Lord, please teach us to listen to You in the same way that You listen to us, so that we can have a great conversation and know Your will for our lives."

DONNA MEYER VOTH

God Uses Spencer

It shall come to pass that before they call, I will answer; and while they are still speaking, I will hear. Isa. 65:24, NKJV.

IT WAS SUNNY AND WARM that Sabbath morning, the sky clear and beautifully blue. I could hear birds chirping among the dogwood trees, and the fragrance of blossoming flowers gave me a sense of peace. I was indeed happy for the Sabbath. As I made my way to church the feeling of Sabbath rest continued. I smiled as I listened to my favorite CD and began to sing along, praising God in song.

Upon entering the church, I was warmly and enthusiastically met with hugs, handshakes, and "Happy Sabbath" greetings. I truly felt welcomed by my church family. The Sabbath school class offered a lively and stimulating discussion, and we were all challenged never to give up! With that challenge captivating my thoughts, I entered the sanctuary and sat on one of the purple-cushioned pews. In the stillness of the moment, my emotions subtly began to transition. In spite of being seated in a filled sanctuary, I suddenly felt alone. Lonely. The feelings initially caught me off guard. *How could I feel alone and lonely in such a filled and friendly church?* I asked myself. I looked toward the back of the sanctuary and saw my brother and his family, but didn't feel compelled to move. I was struggling in silence. Within moments of my struggle there was a gentle tapping on my shoulder. It was my brother and his son, Spencer. Before I could speak, Spencer reached out to me and with those 2-year-old hands patted my loneliness away.

What I didn't realize was that at the moment of my struggle my sister-in-law was asked to sing with the choir. As she left her pew, Spencer spotted me and told his daddy, "I want Auntie!" and with those simple words he sprang from his daddy's lap and over to his auntie just when I needed him most.

God truly hears our heartfelt prayers. He will provide for us, I know, because He used Spencer to take away my loneliness one Sabbath morning.

TERRIE RUFF

? **Thought:** Worship can be very lonely for many people. Look around in your church. Whom do you see who is alone? Do all the members sit in their usual places, or do they reach out to others? What about you?

My Little Pet Dog

And all things, whatsoever ye shall ask in prayer, believing, ye shall receive. Matt. 21:22.

IT WAS ON ONE of those very rainy days that my poodle, Benji, seeing the gate opened, escaped from home. The day went by without any news, night arrived, and I lost hope of being able to find the dog. It was a very difficult time for me and my granddaughter, Beatriz. Another day and night passed without learning anything. It seemed that we would never again see Benji. How difficult it is to wait for the presence of those whom we love so much!

Beatriz, crying, said to me, "Grandma, I've asked God so much to help Benji come home, but He doesn't want to hear my prayers." I took advantage of that moment and very calmly attempted to explain to her that God many times delays in answering our requests so that He can test our faith. "And this is what God is doing with you. Don't give up on praying, because He is merciful, and certainly He is going to answer."

Another day went by. We decided to place an announcement on the local radio station, offering a reward. Our apprehension increased with each moment that passed. A few hours after we placed the announcement on the radio, some boys arrived at our home with Benji! With great joy we paid the promised reward. My granddaughter and I thanked God for bringing our dear Benji back to us. Beatriz was immensely happy. Hugging me she said, "Grandma, it's really good to know that God hears our prayers. We should always have faith in Him!"

Lord, I want to thank You for this experience that served to give me and my granddaughter the understanding that all we ask for in Your name is granted according to Your will. I ask that each day I may grow in faith, and that I may always trust in Your wonderful promises! Thank You, Lord, for being concerned with the little things that make up much of our daily life. I love You, Lord, and I will glorify You all the days of my life.

MARIA SINHARINHA DE OLIVEIRA NOGUEIRA

(?) Thought: God does care about us and the little things of our lives, and He does answer prayer—but not always as we ask. Suppose you had been this grandmother and Benji had never returned. What would you have said? What would this do to your own faith?

Keep Your Eye Single

Draw nigh to God, and he will draw nigh to you. James 4:8.

LEARNING TO RIDE a bike was a challenge for me. In the first place, the family had only one bike to serve four children, so the competition was keen. And I, being the timid one, didn't fight for my rights.

In the second place, the bike was too big. Our parents couldn't afford a beginner's bike, if there was such a thing at the time, and then purchase more bikes as we matured. It was as though one bike, *large*, fit all. And learn if you can, or wait until you grow up.

Finally the day arrived for me to try my riding skills. I determined to be a winner on two wheels. With a sibling on either side supporting the bike until I climbed on, and amid commands of "Steady . . . Ready?" I put my feet into action. Before I had gone very far, there were shouts of "Turn right!" and "Turn left!" Predictably, the bike and I fell to the ground. My siblings eventually became tired of my failures and left me to figure out a way to maintain my balance.

With an I'll-show-you attitude, I carried a huge stump from the woodpile for a mounting post. Slowly I made some progress. Each attempt became a bit longer before I lost my balance and fell. Finally I knew how to ride.

How proud I was the day I put on a show for the family! Between the house and the barnyard was a slight hill. At the bottom of the hill was a gate, about a yard wide. I decided this looked like an interesting feat, to ride down the hill, through the open gate, and around the barnyard.

With all eyes focused on me, I mounted the bike and took off. I braked a bit as I descended the hill, but wanted to exhibit daring speed as well. As I neared the gate, the space between looked so narrow. I kept my eyes on the left post to make sure I'd miss it.

Poor gauging! The post and I collided head-on, and I went flying over the handlebars. That was the day I learned, "Look at where you want to go and not at what you want to miss!"

How like temptations! The best way to avoid evil is to turn away from sinful enticements. Concentrate on what is right, pure, kind, and holy. Keep *God,* not Satan's allurements, in sight. EDITH FITCH

(?) Thought: Philippians 4:8 gives a list of good things to aim for. You may want to memorize it.

Under the Tree

He himself went a day's journey into the desert. He came to a broom tree, sat down under it and prayed that he might die. "I have had enough, Lord," he said. "Take my life." 1 Kings 19:4, NIV.

I WOKE UP ONE MORNING feeling very bad. I was facing a separation and was spending some time in my parents' home. I felt insecure regarding the future, and all my plans were going wrong. Additionally, I had had to adapt to life in a family after so much time living another style of life. The final drop in the bucket took place on the weekend I had exhibited a selfish attitude toward one of my sisters, and I was remonstrating myself for this.

I began to think about all that I was experiencing, and I prayed that the Lord would take my life—I didn't see any more purpose to my life. I was useless and depressed; I was causing sadness for others; and I didn't even know how to live with my own family.

Then I remembered the story of Elijah. Elijah was a great prophet during the time of the kings of Israel. After redirecting the children of Israel to God on Mount Carmel and praying for rain, he was threatened by Jezebel, the wife of King Ahab. Suddenly fear overtook Elijah, and, forgetting all of the great things that he had accomplished on that day, he fled to the desert, where he sat down under a broom tree and asked God for death. Then he fell asleep. He was awakened by an angel who told him to eat and drink. When he looked to his side, he saw a cake of bread baked over hot coals and a jar of water. He ate, drank, and slept again. After some time the angel woke him again and ordered that he eat and drink, because he had a long way to go. He ate and drank, and walked 40 days and 40 nights until he reached Mount Horeb, where he met with God. After this episode Elijah carried out many marvelous tasks through the power of God.

Before Elijah could carry out other great things, he needed to sleep, eat, and drink in the solitude of the desert. Even though Elijah fled and then asked for death, God didn't abandon him; He fulfilled his basic needs. I felt like Elijah in the desert of loneliness and pain, feeling sorry for myself, and praying for death. Then I saw that God was continually sending food, refreshment, and rest through an understanding family, therapy, good books, and friends. During these moments under the tree I was being nurtured by God to accomplish His will in the future. IANI LAUER-LEITE

Oh, Yes, He Cares!

Casting all your cares upon him, for he careth for you. 1 Peter 5:7.

WHILE VISITING WITH MY dear friend Yvonne in Nova Scotia, we eagerly looked forward to and enjoyed immensely our frequent walks along the water's edge. This beautiful area on the outskirts of town had a beautiful lake that attracted many wild ducks, geese, and seagulls.

One day that seemed to be more beautiful than all the others is etched in my memory. The sun was shining very brightly, the little birds were singing—evident signs that spring was in the air. Two blue herons strutted proudly along the water's edge, seemingly unaware of our presence. However, as we approached the area where they stood, they exhibited a tone of nervousness and took their leave.

Continuing on our way, we rejoiced and were exceedingly glad to have been so very blessed to share so much nature. Seagulls soared high above the water and over our heads, and the little birds continued singing sweetly in the trees. Our hearts sang "How Great Thou Art."

Much too soon it was time to make our way back home, but we decided to rest for a while on a portion of an old wooden wharf lying on the grassy bank along the water's edge. Overhead a small, leafless tree displayed only half-opened buds. Soon those buds would miraculously burst forth. We lay flat on our backs, faces uplifted to the sky, as rays of sunshine found an inviting resting place. We engaged in some chitchat concerning the events of the day and of our lives, unaware that we were being watched.

Suddenly two little black-capped chickadees flitted from branch to branch, so close that we could almost reach out and touch them. Yvonne began conversing with them, and their immediate reaction was to approach both of us simultaneously, one perching on Yvonne's shoulder, the other on mine, and then to the tops of our heads, remaining for several seconds before taking their leave. We were both speechless as tears of joy and wonderment filled our eyes. We were once again reminded in a most unexpected and miraculous way of God's great love and care for us, as we are so special in His sight.

O Father, thank You for the many expressions of Your great love to us, and most of all for Jesus, the greatest expression of love this world will ever know.

VIRGINIA CASEY

The Unexpected Detour

Trust in the Lord with all your heart and lean not on your own understanding. Prov. 3:5, NIV.

THE BEAUTIFUL NEW ENGLAND spring day beckoned us outside. Spring fever afflicted both my students and me. When I announced my plan to take them on an afternoon walk, they were elated. By starting at the edge of the 600-acre school property, proceeding until we hit the back road, and making three left turns, I planned to end up on the road back to the school.

Our walk started with much anticipation. The beauties of nature gave us a sense of exhilaration and freedom. On and on we walked without encountering the back road. Nevertheless, we continued on.

With my poor sense of direction, taking them without first doing a dry run was really foolish. I feared weariness might overcome my younger students. I began to pray silently. Finally I told the children that we were lost. We prayed together for guidance.

At last we encountered a road going left, and we took it. Soon an isolated home came into view, and we stopped there. By this time I knew that to arrive back at school in time for the students to meet their parents was impossible. Getting permission from the woman of the house to use her phone, I called the school office to inform the secretary of our plight and asked her to notify the parents of our late return. I volunteered to take home students whose parents had time restraints that didn't allow them to wait.

The woman volunteered to drive us to the school, so all 12 of us jammed cozily into the back of her aged station wagon. At the school we showered her with many grateful thanks as we piled out and went our separate ways.

This experience left me feeling totally embarrassed and guilty. Though my leadership in this instance proved flawed, I claim the promise that when we allow Christ to be our guide He never leads us astray. Wrong courses and detours result from trusting in our own understanding. "God never leads His children otherwise than they would choose to be led, if they could see the end from the beginning" (*The Desire of Ages*, p. 224). This brings us into an intimate relationship with Him and, ultimately, to life with Him forever.

MARIAN M. HART

Building a Life

For God will bring every deed into judgment, including every hidden thing, whether it is good or evil. Eccl. 12:14, NIV.

ONE YEAR AGO CONSTRUCTION began on our new house. My husband, who concerned himself considerably with the foundation so that it was well built, closely followed each step of the construction. The land we were building on was sandy, and many other homes in the same area had developed large cracks in the brick construction. We didn't want our house to end up with cracks, so all measures were taken to avoid this. Now we are happy, because it seems that our construction effort resulted in a good, sturdy house.

A life can be compared to building a house. It begins when we are still small, being taught by our parents. If parents educate their children with love and care, avoiding the "law of the least amount of effort," this foundation will be sufficiently strong to support the weight of the construction. Each thought, act, and decision that I make is part of the construction of my life and will determine what type of building I am constructing. Even when I hide parts of the construction that were put together haphazardly, God knows the difference and will not allow that wall to remain standing. I have to keep in mind that each choice I make will help to determine how stable my house will be.

In the midst of life it would be good if we could stop from time to time to observe the beauty of a sunset. I now live in a wonderful place where I can enjoy the most beautiful sunsets that I've ever seen in my entire life. I'm enchanted by them! What a wise God we have who creates such marvels! And the mountains! So majestic and silent—their slopes and rocks speak to us of a strong God who never lost a battle, a God in whom we can always trust. The stars that dot the sky at night fill our heart with peace. Wherever we walk we see "His handiwork." When we guide our thoughts to heavenly things, we are strengthening the structure of our lives. Cracks will not appear, because with God we will be strong.

Loving Father, thank You for helping me to construct my life. Make my thoughts pure, my decisions correct, and my acts acceptable before You. Amen.

ANI KÖHLER BRAVO

Like Little Children

He called a little child and had him stand among them. And he said: "I tell you the truth, unless you change and become like little children, you will never enter the kingdom of heaven." Matt. 18:2, 3, NIV.

I WAS TALKING TO the man whose apartment we were renting in Mongolia. I remarked that he spoke very good English and that I could understand everything he said. He replied, "My daughter, though, speaks better than me."

One day this gentleman brought Tenggis, his 9-year-old daughter, to our place. She was a little shy at first, but soon began to talk. I was quite surprised at her fluent, flawless English. She was so prim and proper as well. After we chatted a while, she said, "Mrs. Christo, I want to ask you one question." I put my arms around her and asked what she wanted to know. "Mrs. Christo, do you believe in God?" I was dumbstruck to hear a question about God from a 9-year-old girl living in a godless land. I tightened my arms around her and answered, "I not only believe in God, but I also love Him very much." She replied, "Me too!" When leaving, she said, "Goodbye, Mrs. Christo. It was nice meeting you."

My thoughts centered on this child often. I became very close to her, and she came often to spend time with us. Tenggis was studying at the International School, which explained her perfect English. I learned that she lived with her father and grandmother, as her parents were separated and her mother was working in Korea. She expressed her sadness and desire to see her mother, whom she had not seen for a number of years. She would get very excited whenever her mother telephoned her. We talked much about Jesus and His love. She had a Bible that she read every day. I gave her books and stories to read, and I taught her three songs: "Jesus Loves Me," "Who Made the Beautiful Rainbow?" and "Whisper a Prayer." One day she asked if I wanted to go to heaven. The question was asked merely for the sake of starting a conversation about heaven, a place she looked forward to seeing.

I have often thought of this child, and I hope that God has watched over her through the years. I look forward to the day when I will meet her in heaven.

BIROL CHARLOTTE CHRISTO

?Thought: If you had a chance to influence the life of a child, what would you do?

A Tale of Two Lizards

The Lord is . . . not willing that any should perish, but that all should come to repentance. 2 Peter 3:9.

AT THE SOUND OF our glass back door opening, a pair of small black lizards sunning themselves on the warm cement path race for cover. We have to take care where we step lest we hurt one of them.

Yesterday I noticed a movement in the garden near the steps. A newly hatched black lizard was tangled in a spiderweb. Carefully I set the tiny fellow free and went off to my weeding. An hour later I returned to find the lizard curled up where I'd left it. Apparently the spider had injected its venom before I arrived.

This morning I carelessly left the screen door open for a minute while I dealt with a few weeds. The first thing I saw when I stepped back inside was another black lizard, a little bigger than the previous one, obviously bewildered by our tiled floor.

"Wait a moment, Lizzie," I said softly. "I'll take you back outside."

I quickly brought brush and dustpan and prepared to gently sweep the tiny creature into the pan and carry it outside. But the lizard had other ideas. No matter how carefully I approached, it skittered away, and as it had four legs and I only have two, I had to give up. The last I saw of the poor little thing it was dashing under the freezer, where it will no doubt perish.

Frustrated, I sat down to get my breath. "Lizzie, if only you had let me, I could have saved your life."

I wonder whether that is how God feels when He looks down at us earthlings rushing hither and yon, doing our own thing, falling in and out of trouble, and viewing His profferred helping hand as yet another frightening obstacle. No wonder Jesus said to Jerusalem, "How often I wanted to gather your children together, as a hen gathers her chicks under her wings, but you were not willing!" (Matt. 23:37, NKJV).

Dear Lord, please take away my lizard mentality. Give me faith to know that Your plan for my life is best. No matter what difficulties arise or temptations press, teach me to look to You for help. Thank You, Lord. Amen.

GOLDIE DOWN

Unexpected Help

I will not leave you as orphans; I will come to you. John 14:18, NIV.

IT'S MY OWN FAULT, I thought just after I closed the front door of my home and realized that I had locked myself out. There was no hidden key stashed away to let me into my own home. Trying all of the outside doors and finding each one securely locked, I noticed that a bathroom window was open. Although it provided only a small opening, I thought it might be possible to open it wider and squeeze myself through—if I could just remove the screen.

Alas, the screen was secure against removal from the outside, and any tools that might help were locked away in the garage. There seemed to be no way out of this predicament—or, I should say, no way in!

Just then I remembered how my neighbor Jeff had helped me once before with an emergency situation. I rang his doorbell and explained my embarrassing situation. He immediately came with me. Just as we neared the curb a family who are friends of Jeff's pulled up in a van. When their 4-year-old son jumped from the van, Jeff immediately grabbed him by his hand and without explaining anything to him or his parents said, "You are coming with us." The child's face lit up with both surprise and curiosity.

Jeff got out his pocketknife and easily removed the screen. He lifted the boy through the open window with instructions to go to the living room and open the front door. What a blessed relief! Gratefulness flowed straight from my heart to their ears as I profusely thanked them.

Was I surprised that help had been so quickly found? Not in the least. Once again God had provided for an 87-year-old widow at just the right moment. His angels came in the form of a kind and thoughtful neighbor and his little visitor.

Since my husband passed away several years ago, God has repeatedly sent help whenever it was needed, whether it was car problems, health problems, or home repair problems. Daily He extends His loving mercy and care. What a wonderful God and friend to send help at the exact moment of need. I'm reminded of the refrain from the hymn "Jesus, What a Friend for Sinners": "Hallelujah! what a Savior! Hallelujah! what a Friend! Saving, helping, keeping, loving, He is with me to the end."   ANNETTA M. JOERS

Spilled Grape Juice

This do in remembrance of me. Luke 22:19.

AS THE YEARS GO BY and the struggle with sin never leaves us, the sacrifice Jesus made in shedding His blood and dying on the cross has become very meaningful to me. In the service of Communion I feel a real sense of reverence in partaking of the bread and wine. The symbols remind me of the brokenness of body and spilled blood given by Jesus, not only for me personally but for all who will accept it.

In the church I attend quiet music is played throughout the whole Communion service. The atmosphere is one of stillness, reflection, and reverence as the story of the Last Supper is brought before the members and as the emblems are passed around the church for all to share. After partaking, everyone joins hands for prayer before singing the closing hymn.

As the organist, I'm not left out either, for after the hymn someone is delegated to come to the organ and share prayer while I too take the emblems. On one of these occasions (to the embarrassment of the elder serving me) the glass of wine was accidentally dropped, causing its contents to spill down over my clothes. The experience served a good purpose as I reflected on the reality of Jesus' sin-cleansing blood that washed over all of me, and not just this small, spilled glass of grape juice we were using as a symbol. Both of us grasped the significance of this meaningful object lesson and, with embarrassment gone, enjoyed a wonderful blessing together.

I've often thought about those times long ago when the little innocent lambs were slain for the sinner. How horrible it must have been, as one death was not a permanent cover for sin, and lamb after lamb had to pay the price. Never could they come to life again like the risen Lamb of God, the victorious Savior of humanity.

We can rejoice in the promise of John 3:16: "For God so loved the world, that he gave his only begotten Son, that whosoever believeth in him should not perish, but have everlasting life." This gives me wonderful hope, reassurance, and a guarantee of Calvary's gift, for when sin means death, Jesus gives life.

As I celebrate the Lord's Supper I want to remember Him and someday be able to say thank You to my Savior face to face. LYN WELK-SANDY

An Encounter With a Snake

"Because he loves me," says the Lord, "I will rescue him; I will protect him, for he acknowledges my name." Ps. 91:14, NIV.

THE WORD OF GOD tells us that Satan disguised himself as a serpent and deceived our first parents. God cursed the serpent and introduced enmity between the snake and the woman, between his offspring and hers. Her offspring would crush his head, God said, and the snake would strike His heel. This enmity has persisted, a continuous life-and-death struggle between man and woman and the snake.

I've always feared and dreaded snakes but hadn't had the ill fortune to encounter one until one beautiful Friday evening. I went to the bathroom to wash a few things out before going to sundown worship. As I stood in front of the tub, an object dropped from nowhere onto my head. Instinctively I bent down and used my hand to push the object into the bathtub. To my horror, it was a big green snake! My screams brought the security guard, who struggled with the snake that was now trying unsuccessfully to get out of the slippery bathtub. Its head was once again crushed in death.

That evening at the sundown service at church I told my story. The security man's testimony was "Sister, God loves you. That snake was a venomous one." A girl in the church added, "Aunty, God loves you. That was how my father was killed. The snake wound itself around his neck and choked and bit him to death."

Since that day I have not stopped thanking my God and my Savior for saving me from an untimely death. I was not aware that a snake was waiting to attack me, but Jesus knew all the enemy's devices and had provided a way of escape in accordance with His promise. He who has promised is faithful.

"Because he loves me," says the Lord, "I will rescue him." We cannot deliver ourselves; the enemy may be too much for us. Often his temptations are overpowering, but Christ offers us His power of deliverance. We must completely rely on and surrender to Him. Christ delivers us; with Christ and by Christ, we are completely set free.

I have vowed to serve Jesus as long as I live, for I owe my life to Him. What about you?

SAL OKWUBUNKA

The Comforter Did Come

And I will pray the Father, and he shall give you another Comforter, that he may abide with you for ever. John 14:16.

HAVE YOU EVER BEEN in a situation in which you couldn't seem to get enough air into your lungs? As a registered nurse I've seen situations like that. Several times I've assisted such patients, keeping their airways open, often administering oxygen to them. I've even experienced that specific breathing problem myself—twice. Not until you've experienced that undeniable "air hunger" can you really understand how it feels.

That's how it was recently when I again began developing a respiratory problem. For a few days I seemed to be dealing with it, but somehow nights seem to worsen whatever problem I had coped with during the day. One particular night I felt very tired, trying to complete all the everyday jobs at hand. Then the Holy Spirit impressed me to leave the tasks and retire to bed. I prepared for bed and lay down.

Not 10 minutes later I discovered that I was having difficulty, and the "air hunger" drove me to get up frequently, leaving me totally exhausted. I was about to cry when I sensed Jesus Himself bending over me. It seemed as if He was about to weep too. Then I heard the Comforter speak: "I am not the type of God who leaves when you are ill. I am with you; you will be all right. But tomorrow, go and see your doctor." Reassured, I settled down and fell asleep.

Before He departed from this earth Jesus promised His disciples that He would not leave them comfortless. He promised to send the third person of the Godhead—the Holy Spirit—as their Comforter. I know that Jesus' promise given 2,000 years ago is just as relevant and precious to His followers today. I know that it is relevant and precious to me!

Like Jesus Christ, I have to be dependent on the Father. He showed me that I have the Comforter.

I thank God for His Son, who gave up His omnipresence to come to earth for me. I thank Him for the example of His Son, who was solely dependent on His Father, and for the Holy Spirit's reassurance.

I praise You, Father, for Your comfort, even when I'm not distressed.

MADGE S. MAY

Furlough

In my Father's house are many mansions. . . . I go to prepare a place for you. John 14:2.

IMMEDIATELY FOLLOWING A WORLD church conference in 2005, my family and I returned home to Trinidad for a one-month furlough. Those of us who work for the church in a country other than our own are entitled to return home every year or two for furlough. It is a time to rest, recuperate, reconnect with family and old friends, and reflect on the calling that God has placed on our lives that took us away from our homes to a different land.

On this particular trip I had much to think about. I was taking on greater responsibilities in my job and was concerned about my ability to do all that God had placed on me. I remember lying on the white, sandy beach of Pigeon Point, Tobago, listening to the gentle waves wash the shore.

As I think of that memorable and joyful furlough, I see a parallel to heaven. Jesus has gone to prepare us a home in heaven. That is His promise to us. This earth is not our home, and we long for a better place. We Christians want to be where our Savior is, and that place is heaven.

Heaven has been prepared for God's children who have been working in a land that is not their home. God placed a calling on their lives to go and tell a world about a Savior who came and died so that all can receive salvation. But often we feel like strangers in a strange land. We wonder if we have the ability to do all that God has called us to do. We work hard and the journey is long, but we still have the hope of our unending heavenly furlough.

It will be a time of rest and recuperation. A time to reconnect with family and old friends. And yes, a time to reflect on God's goodness to us. When I think of that time, I know that with God's help I can work now in this strange land called earth. I know that I can do all things because He is giving me the strength. And I know that one day I'll lie on the sand near the sea of glass and bask in the joy of my Father's love.

HEATHER-DAWN SMALL

?Thought: Have you really thought about what you would like to do when you get to heaven? Are you looking forward to the mansions? to be reunited with loved ones who have passed away? to fly from planet to planet? Or are you just looking forward to being with Jesus?

He Cares for Me

Therefore do not worry about tomorrow, for tomorrow will worry about itself. Each day has enough trouble of its own. Matt. 6:34, NIV.

I CONDUCT SEMINARS with a team of young people from the western part of Nigeria, where we live. We were once invited to go to Umuahia, in the east, for a weekend seminar. Because of the distance, we had to go by air from Lagos to Port Harcourt, the nearest airport to our destination. We were late getting to the airport and had only 20 minutes to buy our tickets, tag our luggage, and board the plane. However, we made it, and after a 50-minute flight we arrived in Port Harcourt. At baggage claim we collected all our luggage—except my suitcase that contained everything I needed for the weekend, including my seminar papers. I was really troubled. How would I manage for the weekend, and how would I deliver my lectures?

We contacted the Lagos Airport authorities and requested that they help us look for the suitcase and to send it on to Port Harcourt. Friday and Sabbath came and went, and I managed to get through with the only dress I had on by doing a lot of washing and ironing through the weekend. I went to the market to buy another suit so as to have something to wear for Sabbath. I salvaged seminar materials from others and, with the Holy Spirit's help, managed to give my lectures.

We left for Lagos on Sunday without ever hearing anything about my suitcase. Oh, how hard I had prayed—as never before! Every time I thought about the contents of my suitcase I would sigh and pray. It was a real test of faith.

When we got back home, we learned that the suitcase had been found and sent to Port Harcourt, but we were assured that it would be brought back. I had to leave Lagos without the suitcase, but by Tuesday it arrived with all the contents intact.

God definitely kept a watchful eye over my untagged suitcase. There is no doubt about it: anybody could have picked it up and destroyed it if not satisfied with the contents. But because my Father who sent me loves me, He kept my suitcase safe. *Praise the Lord!* He cares for us and takes care of us.

BECKY DADA

? Thought: What can this story of unanswered prayer teach us about God?

May (6)

Saved!

He also brought me up out of a horrible pit, out of the miry clay, and set my feet upon a rock, and established my steps. Ps. 40:2, NKJV.

I SAVED THE YOUNG boy's life that day. But if I'd not been there, someone else would have saved him. Even so, it felt good.

It was spring, and my husband and I were visiting friends in the Canadian province of Saskatchewan. While the men were seeding the fields, the women took us and the kids to a lovely lake hidden among trees somewhere on that bald prairie. It was a peaceful spot. The pier had just been lifted up from below the lake's surface, and Blaine, my friend's 3-year-old boy, was standing on the far end, staring into the water. His mother cautioned him to be careful.

Suddenly his little body plunked into the deep water. We gasped in unison. My husband couldn't swim, and both women were cradling infants. So I dashed across the sand and onto the long pier. Miraculously, Blaine rose to the surface just off the end of the dock, and as I ran toward him, his little head was above the water, his arms outstretched. I prayed frantically that he'd stay there so that I wouldn't have to dive into the murky water to search for him.

As I attempted to slow down as I neared the end of the dock, I discovered why Blaine had fallen in—the wet boards were slicker than an ice rink. Fearing I'd slide right into the water and land on top of the terrified child, I dropped quickly to my knees, then flat on my stomach, and reached my long arms sideways to grab the edges of the pier. I ground to a halt with my chin at the end of the dock, eyeball to eyeball with little Blaine. Reaching forward, I plucked him out of the dark, cold water.

He shivered uncontrollably as we headed back toward shore and Mommy. I can still see his small arms, outstretched to me for salvation from his watery grave. I would have done anything humanly possible to get him out.

How much more desperately our heavenly Father wishes to pluck us out of the miry pit of sin! Are our arms outstretched to Him?

DAWNA BEAUSOLEIL

(?) Thought: If you feel as if you are sometimes still in the pit, meditate on Psalm 40.

Look Before You Leap

Then if any man shall say unto you, Lo, here is Christ, or there; believe it not. Matt. 24:23.

AS WE WERE GROWING UP, my brother, sister, and I often heard our parents say, "Look before you leap." The phrase still often comes to mind—I've seen, and heard, of many experiences of mistaken identity.

Having worked with children, I've experienced mistaken identities made by classmates over backpacks, lunch boxes, hats, and other things. The jacket of one of my first graders was taken home by someone else at the end of the school day, and the child didn't realize that it wasn't his until the next morning. I was greeted by two eager parents and two boys with look-alike jackets—same color, same style, but different sizes. There was a happy ending as I thought of my parents' favorite phrase: "Look before you leap."

I've been guilty of mistaken identification, too. I once left the shopping mall to go the parking lot where I had parked my car. As I walked toward the car and pressed the remote button I didn't hear the clicking sound. So I pressed the remote again. No success. Before panic set in I began repeating one of my favorite phrases (which my three grandchildren have become familiar with since their toddler years): "Lord, have mercy; give me strength." Before pressing the button a third time, I looked inside the car. I saw packages on the front seat. I hadn't left packages. I was trying to unlock a car that looked like mine—same color, same year—but wasn't mine. My car was two parking spaces over. A happy ending.

However, mistaken identity can have (and has often had) unhappy endings. Some persons wrongly identified have been killed, or incarcerated for years, only to be found innocent later. Life is a learning process, and I've learned that one cannot depend on outward appearance alone for identification purposes. I do thank God for His words in Matthew 24, and for the privilege of having connection with Him, the Good Shepherd, who knows His sheep, even to the number of hairs on my head. I pray that I will stay in close connection with Christ so that when He comes in the clouds with power and great glory there will be no mistaken identity. I'll know it is He, my Redeemer.

ANNIE B. BEST

Thought: What can we each do today to be certain we do know Christ?

Havre de Grace

Let us therefore come boldly to the throne of grace, that we may obtain mercy and find grace to help in time of need. Heb. 4:16, NKJV.

BABY SHOWERS ARE SUCH happy celebrations! We women love buying and giving those darling dresses with ruffles and matching bonnet, or those wee train conductor overalls. I always enjoy being asked to share a devotional thought, and to pray over the mother and baby.

One baby shower was different, though. Not because the baby modeled a head full of gorgeous red hair. Not because the mama delighted in the animal-sound toys more than her baby. No, this shower was different because the mother was also battling cancer.

Is it any wonder she named her baby Grace? Six months into her pregnancy Joyce was diagnosed with Hodgkin's disease, a cancer in the lymph system. The doctors promised the baby would be full-term and fine, but you know mothers—it's not always easy to shape worries into prayers. Baby Grace *was* born healthy and happy. What a gracious gift from God!

Bible verses, such as 2 Thessalonians 2:16, that include the word "grace" have special dual meaning for Joyce: "Our God and Father, who has loved us and given us everlasting consolation and good hope by grace" (NKJV).

Baby Grace continues to be a special and hope-filled gift from God. When Joyce comes home from a round of chemotherapy she is transported beyond nausea and fatigue as she cradles her baby. She even looks forward to nighttime feedings, another chance to caress and cuddle Baby Grace. It is a time of peace and quiet, a time to delight in the wonder of new life, a time to thank God for blessings.

I shared at the shower how this reminded me of the name Havre de Grace, a quiet city in Maryland on the Chesapeake Bay. It means Harbor of Grace, or Harbor of Mercy. For Joyce her baby is her harbor of grace, her haven, a place of peace and joy amid the rough storms of cancer treatments. Baby Grace is her reminder—a very tangible reminder—that God is her ultimate Havre de Grace, her Harbor of Mercy, her Haven amid the storms of life.

Let God be your Havre de Grace. He says, "My grace is sufficient for you, for My strength is made perfect in weakness" (2 Cor. 12:9, NKJV). "My power is strongest when you are weak" (CEV).   HEIDE FORD

Friends Forever

A friend loveth at all times. Prov. 17:17.

WHEN WE WERE GROWING UP in the South, my only sister, who was four years younger, used to really "get on my last nerve." She seemed like such a whiny, thumb-sucking baby, and the four years between us was like a chasm across which she could not understand anything I tried to explain. One benefit I recall, however, was that I would send her to ask Dear (which we affectionately call our mother) if we could do, or have, this or that when I feared she would turn me down. And it worked. She would make the request and get a yes more often than not. After all, she was the baby of a clan of four boys and us two girls. We never really played together, because she was "too young." I was older. She was such a kid.

Then something happened, almost unnoticed. She began to grow up, and those four years didn't seem like the huge gap that they used to be. First, she was a teenager; and then, somehow, she became an adult. It was during those teenage-into-adult years that we just kind of became friends—laughing, sharing, and really getting to know and appreciate each other on a more intimate level.

Today we are full-fledged adults, she in Ohio, and I in New York; I in my middle-age years, and she hot on my trail. Despite the miles that have separated us during our adult lives, we have managed to continue to nurture the friendship that began, it seems now, eons ago. Yes, she is one of my very best friends. We talk by phone at least four times a week and visit several times a year. I always look forward to the times I travel to Ohio to spend time alone with my sister. We don't really do much besides sit and talk about our children, the goodness of God, about our deceased mother, our "knucklehead" brothers, and yes, even those growing-up years in the South. But more than anything, it's just being with my sister, my precious friend, who I enjoy so immensely, making memories that we'll both cherish for years to come.

I thank God for my sister's friendship. It reminds me of a day when my Friend Jesus and I will sit down and just talk—about my struggles down here, about how often He rescued me from dangers, about how He gave me strength to overcome difficult temptations and trials. And yes, He'll remind me of His great love for me that made Him willing to give His life on Calvary. We'll just sit and talk and enjoy each other's company. What a day that's going to be!   GLORIA STELLA FELDER

Let Jesus Feed You

Come to Me, all you who labor and are heavy laden, and I will give you rest. Take My yoke upon you and learn from Me, for I am gentle and lowly in heart, and you will find rest for your souls. Matt. 11:28, NKJV.

IT OCCURRED IN THE early hours of one gray morning when the fishers of men had returned to their previous occupation of being fishers of fish. What else were they to do? Jesus was no longer a part of their lives. With their own eyes they had seen him nailed to a cross. They had witnessed that cross slammed into the ground high on a hill. They had heard his agonizing cries. They had watched his limp, lifeless body being lifted from the wooden beams and then hidden behind a heavy boulder.

Memories of miracles, snatches of conversation, comfortable laughter as they strolled through wheat fields, became blurred in their minds. They tried to remember the suppers they had shared, conflicts they had endured, starlit skies where they had watched the silhouette of Jesus praying as they snuggled down to sleep, but it brought them no comfort. How they longed for the presence of Jesus! With hearts full of despair they settled down to days without Jesus, days dusted with mediocrity, dullness, and predictability that seemed to have no beginning and certainly no end.

They had spent a whole night's fishing only to end up with an empty net to match their empty hearts. It was then that they had heard Jesus calling to them. As a result of His first call, their empty nets now became full. As a result of His second call, they became His breakfast guests.

The breakfast scene is a picture to ponder. Jesus Christ, the one who had just smashed the power of sin, sat before an open fire preparing a meal for those who needed Him. The newly scarred hands reached out to feed those who reached toward Him with open hands. He fed them with what they needed the most—His presence, assuring them that they would never be alone, and His power, assuring them that the Savior who conquered death could also conquer an empty fishing net.

Whether you have hearts filled with emptiness, sorrow, discouragement, anxiety, or hopelessness, remember that just as Jesus met the needs of those fishermen, He yearns to meet your needs, too. Jesus Christ is there to serve you, to minister to you, to feed you with the food you need to satisfy the hunger in your stomach and the hunger in your heart.

MARY BARRETT

A Mother's Bond

Before I formed thee in the belly I knew thee; and before thou camest forth out of the womb. Jer. 1:5.

AN ARTICLE IN A national magazine noted that women who have given birth carry the child's fetal cells throughout their lives. Conversely, a child carries random cells of its mother. These cells are exchanged through the placenta during pregnancy.

Because of this cell exchange, mothers have a tangible lifelong link with the children they bear. And the child, male or female, has a true link with their birth mother. This finding explains the "old wives' tales" about the almost psychic connections shared by mothers and their sons. This something is usually explained away by scientists as the "nurture/environment argument," rather than a true bond, a physical fact.

Psychologists and sociologists also often attribute the near-psychic relationship between mothers and their daughters as "shared female experience." While this may contribute to the phenomena, it begins at the molecular level in shared and exchanged cells.

Which helps explain why women who miscarry mourn the discharged fetus as though it were a completed person.

The fact that some men lack a firm identification with their children may also be explained by the fact that they have no lifelong, shared, exchanged cells with the offspring. And it is possible that the woman who is able to abandon or kill her children without remorse is a woman who somehow—possibly through antigen destruction of the fetal "invading cells"—does not have the exchanged cells in her system.

I marvel at how God left nothing to chance, at how thoroughly and completely every aspect of our being and life is taken into consideration and prepared for in the very cells of our being. Discoveries such as this one draw our eyes upward in love and worship of our loving, all-seeing God. Truly, "you created my inmost being; you knit me together in my mother's womb. I praise you because I am fearfully and wonderfully made; your works are wonderful" (Ps. 139:13, 14, NIV). "I was made in the secret place," and curiously wrought (verse 15, NIV).

DARLENEJOAN MCKIBBIN RHINE

Breaking New Ground

But I say to you who are listening, love your enemies. Do good to those who hate you, bless those who curse you, pray for those who are cruel to you. Luke 6:27, 28, NCV.

NOT LONG AGO I found myself in a situation that proved to be extremely uncomfortable. "I can't imagine that anyone would not like you," said a colleague, giving me a genuine compliment. Yet this was not the case. I had discovered that some of my colleagues did not like me, not because of any failing of my own as stated by my boss, but, simply put, because of jealousy. "Face it, Curry," he said to me one day, "you've willingly taken on major challenges and succeeded. Some folks don't like that. Besides," he added, "you're honest—and others don't like that!" Trying to win the popularity of others was not a goal, but genuinely wanting these ill feelings against me to stop was. So I talked to my Father. "What can I do differently?" I asked. "You put me here for a reason. It's not just about the work—I'm supposed to be Your ambassador. So show me what to do." Immediately the answer that is found in today's text came.

Mentally I argued, *How can I love people who want to hurt me?* In the quietness of the room His spirit spoke: "I interceded for you, even when you acted like the enemy. Can you do any less?" Without delay I listed three names in my journal and wrote out my petition for each.

After several months of continuous prayer I noticed a change in their behavior. Not that they were any nicer, but at least the personal attacks had ceased. One later complimented a portion of one of my projects, noting that she too would like to use it as a model for her project. As for me, I also experienced a change. In electing to pray for those who were hurting me, I had grown. God opened my eyes on an important life lesson that drew me closer to Him. My prayer for others also benefited me. It helped me to realize that He continues to intercede for me even when my actions hurt Him.

Father, thank You for helping me to pray that prayer. I know I've been Your enemy many times, but You continue to petition Your Father on my behalf. I do love You, and I'm glad You love me. Amen.

YVONNE CURRY SMALLWOOD

Thought: How do you do good to those who hate you? Is prayer the only solution?

Lessons From a Child

Let the little children come to Me, and do not forbid them; for of such is the kingdom of heaven. Matt. 19:14, NKJV.

KATIE WAS A HAPPY toddler who was at the informal afternoon church meeting because her parents were attending. Since she could be seen easily by her mother, she was allowed to move around freely as long as she didn't get into trouble or disturb the gathering. Up and down the aisles she wandered, occasionally stepping between the pews, then out into an aisle again.

Eventually she arrived at one end of the pew where I was sitting. She looked at me for a moment then ambled away. However, she seemed to be fascinated by that particular area, so returned to look at me several times, coming a little closer each time. I noticed she'd wait for a while, watching to see if I was going to stop her. Finally she got brave enough to stop beside me. Then she reached out with one of her baby-size fingers and touched my purse that was lying on the seat beside me. She whispered something I couldn't understand, but I nodded in agreement, hoping my response was the proper one for the situation. Deciding it was time for her to return to the safety of the aisle, she backed up, accidentally bumping her little head on the back of the pew behind her.

I felt so bad for her and attempted to distract her from what had just happened. But my efforts failed, and she solemnly walked away and headed to her mother. As soon as she reached her mother's knee she burst into tears. Her mother put her arms around her and picked her up, offering the comfort she so much needed. Soon Katie was her happy, busy self again.

I'm so glad God made babies, and I often find that in their innocence they can teach us such tender and beautiful lessons. We all get hurt from time to time. Sometimes the pain is physical; sometimes it is emotional, or even spiritual. At such times we can take the example of little children and hasten to take our problems to God, our heavenly Parent. He is so willing to put His loving arms around us.

Dear Jesus, please enfold us in Your arms today. Amen.

MILDRED C. WILLIAMS

? Thought: Do you hurt? Study Matthew 19:14 and consider how it applies to hurting adults. Whatever the pain, Jesus is waiting to enfold you in His arms.

Heaven-sent Shoes

Call unto me, and I will answer thee, and shew thee great and mighty things, which thou knowest not. Jer. 33:3.

MY YOUNGEST SON WAS going to graduate from high school, and I would accompany him to the graduation ceremony. I found a black dress with silver details, and I wanted a pair of silver shoes to match the dress. I'm a single mother with two children and earn very little, and after paying the graduation fees, I didn't have enough money to buy a pair of expensive shoes. Every time that I looked in a store the prices were so high that I had almost lost hope of finding a new pair of shoes. I asked the Lord to help me find something appropriate.

The day of graduation was approaching, and I hadn't found shoes at a price I could afford. One Sunday afternoon I asked my son to go with me to the mall near our home. As I went down the escalator, I noticed a shoe store. I took a quick look at the shoes and didn't see anything within my budget.

We window-shopped, but I found nothing after four hours looking, so we decided to go home. As we were leaving, there was that same shoe store again. My eyes caught sight of something in the window display—the perfect pair of shoes!

Even though I had no hope of buying them, I took a closer look. Then I asked my son to verify the price to see if I wasn't just dreaming because the price was exactly the amount of money that I had to spend. I entered the store and asked to try on a pair. Incredibly, there was only one pair left— and they were my size!

Certainly it was the Lord who reserved this pair of shoes for me.

Each day I depend more and more on God for everything. In the midst of so much pain I still see the hand of God helping me in the purchase of a simple pair of shoes. He truly does provide for all of our necessities. We can trust in Him in the minor things of daily life. It is in these things that we find a blessing that He has reserved for us, and the confirmation that He cares for His children when they give their whole heart to Him.

SÔNIA REGINA FRIEDRICH

(?) **Thought:** List other reasons God sometimes answers our needs and wants, and other times does not. Does our text give any clues?

My Way

If any man serve me, let him follow me; and where I am, there shall also my servant be: . . . him will my Father honor. John 12:26.

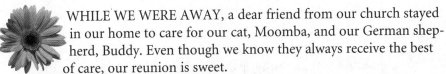

WHILE WE WERE AWAY, a dear friend from our church stayed in our home to care for our cat, Moomba, and our German shepherd, Buddy. Even though we know they always receive the best of care, our reunion is sweet.

After unpacking and putting some clothes in the washer, I decided to take Buddy for our usual two-mile walk down our country road. When I picked up his retractable leash, he came running, and we walked down the road for some much-needed exercise. As we walked I lustily sang praises to my Lord. While singing, I made two mistakes in judgment: I allowed the retractable leash to unwind to its full length, which gave me less control of Buddy; and Buddy, who was behind me, sniffed a wild animal scent. Just as I tightened my grip on the leash handle to gain better control of him, I felt myself spinning around. The leash was jerked from my hand by Buddy's sudden dash into the woods. Suddenly I hit the asphalt, facedown, with a moan.

My first thought was *I hope nobody saw this.* My second thought was *Did I break one of my nails?* And the third thought *How badly am I hurt?* As I lay there, checking to see if I could use my four extremities well enough to get up, Buddy came running out of the woods. He looked at me as if to say, "What are you doing down there?"

I sat up slowly, both hands skinned and bleeding. Then I stood up, knees skinned and bleeding. Every part of my body hurt. I started a very long quarter-mile trip home. My husband, who was in the driveway washing his truck, walked the short distance to meet me. In the privacy of our bathroom I began to access my injuries. Other than abrasions on both my hands and knees and two large bruises on my chest, I had sustained no serious injuries. I was very grateful to my dear Lord.

Whenever I think of this incident I am reminded of the gentle leash the Lord has on each of us—the instruction found in His Word. We sometimes yank the leash from His kind hand and run headlong to do our own thing while He sadly watches, knowing the sadness and disappointment we will face by refusing to accept His leading.　　　　　　Rose Neff Sikora

God Is Always Present

I praise you because I am fearfully and wonderfully made; your works are wonderful, I know that full well. Ps. 139:14, NIV.

IN THE MIDDLE OF MAY 1998 I was with my mother, who was gravely ill in Silvestre Seventh-day Adventist Hospital in Rio de Janeiro, Brazil. Since she was in a room with another patient, I couldn't stay there with her during the night. I sat on the stairs in front of the room so I could hear if she called me during the night. From this location I could see the entire room, and I took advantage of the time to read, write, and meditate almost the entire night.

Through the window that was in front of the stairs I could also see the illuminated *Cristo Redentor,* the giant statue of Christ (one of the tourist points in the city of Rio de Janeiro) with arms open wide. As I looked at the monument I thought of Jesus, who died on the cross with His arms opened wide for me and for everyone who was in the hospital and throughout the entire world.

As I read Psalm 139 I felt comfort in the certainty of a God who is so loving that He has been concerned with me since I was conceived in my mother's womb. "Your eyes saw my unformed body. All the days ordained for me were written in your book before one of them came to be" (verse 16, NIV). How marvelous is our God! With His blood He redeemed us from our sins, and He places us in His arms, which continue to be open, waiting for all who accept Him.

My mother passed away on June 22 that year, but hope in a loving and saving God remained with her until the end. Today I anxiously await the coming of the Lord Jesus. I want to be with Him for all eternity, and I also want to see my dear ones who have already died. I want my entire life to be made for Him.

NICÉIA TRIANDADE

Thought: In the hours of the night, when you have concern and worry on your mind, can you "see" Christ with arms open to you? Do you really feel that He has always been with you? What texts help you have assurance of His care? Read Psalm 139 to see what it has to say to you.

Miracle on the Highway

Before they call I will answer; while they are still speaking I will hear. Isa. 65:24, NIV.

AT THE END OF the school year my granddaughter, Jennifer, started driving home from Walla Walla College, in the state of Washington, to Michigan. She carefully mapped out her trip, then began heading across the northern United States, into the Upper Peninsula of Michigan. She needed to cross the Mackinac Bridge, and then continue on home to East Jordan.

She entered the Upper Peninsula and headed down Highway 2. She was in the middle of nowhere, and it was the middle of the night—no houses, no cars—when suddenly a tire blew. Taking all her gas cans out to get to the spare, she hunted for the wrench, then discovered it didn't work. What was she to do? There was only one thing to do—she prayed. She asked the Lord to send someone who could help her and not hurt her.

Soon she saw lights coming as a large tractor-trailer bore down on her. When the driver saw the car with the trunk up and all the gas cans lined up, he slammed on his brakes, bringing the rig to a stop. He got out and walked back to Jennifer and asked what her trouble was, thinking she was out of gas. After she explained about the flat tire, he went to his truck and found a wrench and changed the tire for her. They talked as he changed the tire. She explained she was a student in college in Washington, heading home.

"What college?" he asked.

She told him. Because Walla Walla College is a Seventh-day Adventist college, he asked if she was an Adventist. When she said she was, he told her he was as well. His home church was in Cadillac, Michigan. Jennifer explained that her dad was a pastor of three churches down that way. He then told her that this wasn't his regular night to drive, but his boss had called him in.

"Before they call, I will answer." It's such a comfort to know that God is in control and had worked this all out before Jennifer even called on Him in prayer.

The truck driver followed her to the bridge and called to tell her dad that his daughter was well on her way home. God's guiding hand was on her all the time!

We have a Father who cares for us in every situation. We must share this good news!

ANNE ELAINE NELSON

A Beetle Shares a Secret

We have this hope as an anchor for the soul. Heb. 6:19, NIV.

BEFORE MY NEIGHBOR installed a chain-link fence, a wooden fence separated our yards. In my yard I had a big oil drum that I used to burn yard waste.

One day I decided that the oil drum was too close to the fence, so I decided to move it. Tipping it toward me, I balanced it on its bottom rim and rolled it to a safer spot. Looking back at where the oil drum had been, I noticed that a group of assorted backyard residents that had been living under that drum. Thanks to me, they were now homeless. Guilt pierced my heart.

Sow bugs rolled up like ball bearings and pretended not to see me. A group of earthworms, all tangled in a knot, seemed to be looking for someone to untie them—but I wasn't the good Samaritan volunteer. I tried to ignore the spider—anything with eight legs had better be two chairs.

One creature, though, in a tiny housing unit especially caught my interest. In moving the oil drum, I had inadvertently upended a black beetle. That little fellow was jogging upside down as fast as his six little legs could go, not getting anywhere but making good time. I watched to see what he would do.

Beside him was a clod of sun-baked dirt, about the same size as the beetle. By chance, one of his feet hit that clod of dirt. It wasn't much, but he was able to anchor himself and, with some effort, turn himself right side up. I thought *Even a bug needs an anchor.*

I can identify with that little guy. When a problem or trial turns my life upside down, I often try to solve it in my own strength. Like that beetle, I make good time, but I don't get anywhere. I need to remember that Jesus has the ability and the desire to turn things right-side-up again. He's right beside me, waiting for me to reach out to Him.

Jesus is our certainty in our uncertain world. He is our anchor in the storms of life—the only anchor that will hold in today's chaotic world. We can never drift out of His reach or beyond His love.   MARCIA MOLLENKOPF

(?) Thought: God can certainly help those who feel like they are flat on their backs, but have you thought about the fact that He might want you to be a help in the process?

Hidden Lions

Because your adversary the devil, as a roaring lion, walketh about, seeking whom he may devour. 1 Peter 5:8.

IN 1980 WE LIVED in the city of Ongwediva, in the Owamboland region in Namibia. One long weekend we went with our children to visit the Etosha National Park near Tsumeb. In order to see a greater variety of wild animals, we drove to the "watering holes," small lakes, and streams where the animals came to drink.

At one of these watering holes, while we were observing wild pigs and giraffes, some small, curious animals came to our car, begging for food. My husband opened the car door and was giving them something to eat when a Land Rover, driven by park rangers, sped up to us.

"Close the door!" they yelled. "You cannot imagine the chances that you are taking with that door open!"

We smiled and answered that in front of us, by the watering hole, there were just some giraffes and wild pigs.

"Very well," stated one of the rangers, "but look to the right, near that high rock."

There was a pair of lions! We had not noticed!

"Now look toward those bushes to the left, a little nearer to us."

Another pair of lions! We could hardly believe what they were showing us. How could it be possible that we hadn't seen them?

The rangers added, "Park visitors cannot, under any circumstances, leave their vehicle—not even open the doors. The reason is there, right in front of you. Visitors can leave their vehicles only in protected locations."

Although we were camping within the park, the areas where we slept and ate meals and where the children swam and played was in a protected location.

In this park, the earth, where we live, we do not see the lion walking about. He acts like those lions in the park—invisible, hidden among the bushes and rocks of our concerns, our interests, our frustrations and longings, or our selfishness, which can give him easy access.

Beware of the "hidden lions"! MARIA COSTA SALES CARDOSA

Just Passing Through

In my Father's house are many mansions: if it were not so, I would have told you. I go to prepare a place for you. John 14:2.

ON A RECENT TRIP to Vienna, Austria, I became acquainted with a striking royal couple whose images were portrayed on nearly everything salable, from chocolate boxes to souvenir key chains. Upon inquiry, I learned that this couple was none other than Franz Joseph I and his wife, Empress Elisabeth, who was fondly known as Sisi. He was handsome, and she was beautiful; they had married when she was 16.

Their lives intrigued me, as their marriage was one of love, not merely an arrangement for political purposes. I imagined their lives to be romantically enchanting as I gazed with awe at their huge collection of silver, glass, and china, including massive table centerpieces, candelabra, and napkins folded into fanciful scrolls or accordion-shaped animals. Their apartments at the Hapsburg Palace, as well as the Schonbrunn Palace, are filled with family portraits and works of art. Their gardens delight visitors with lovely floral patterns, sculpture, and fountains.

However, amid all this splendor life was not blissful. Sisi did not get along with her mother-in-law, and hated the strict demands of palace life. She therefore traveled often and seldom saw her husband, though they had three children. She ate very little to maintain her very slim figure, and her actress-friend became her husband's concubine. I further learned that Franz Joseph lived the Spartan lifestyle of a soldier. After sleeping in an iron bed, he rose at 3:00 every morning to tend to the affairs of state. Being a disciplined person, he too ate very little and maintained a trim figure. He died at age 86, and she was assassinated by a madman at age 60 on one of her travels.

What did I learn from all of this? First of all, dysfunction can occur in any family. Whether one is rich or poor, Christian or non-Christian, sin is no respecter of persons. We all have faults and failures but, thanks be to God, He has overcome the world for us. We can take hope and can encourage others. This world is not our final home; we're just passing through. We need to keep focusing on Christ and the home He has prepared for us, which will be far more splendid than any palace on this earth.

AILEEN YOUNG

Of Crocodiles and Stars

The heavens declare the glory of God; and the firmament shows His handiwork. Day unto day utters speech, and night unto night reveals knowledge. Ps. 19:1, 2, NKJV.

"WHO WOULD LIKE TO GO crocodile spotting tonight?" Never one to miss a new experience, I quickly indicated my intention to fill a seat in the canoe. Evening found us waiting at the edge of a lagoon in the western Solomon Islands, anticipating the adventure to come. After we took our seats in the dugout canoe, our guide started the outboard motor, and we glided off across the glassy surface of the lagoon. The soft glow of the kerosene lanterns in the village slowly faded from sight as our canoe made its way toward the distant mangrove-fringed islands. Phosphorescence sparkled in our wake as the canoe cut through the water.

As we reached a channel through the mangroves, the motor was stopped, and we drifted silently toward the trees. Not wishing to capsize the canoe in the possible vicinity of crocodiles, we sat motionless as our guide shone his flashlight in sweeping arcs along the base of the mangroves. Soon we were rewarded by the sight of two glowing lights showing just above the water, the telltale sign of a crocodile. We made our way quietly through the maze of mangroves and spotted several crocodiles of various sizes. One small crocodile even gave some extra excitement by charging the canoe. It was an interesting experience to see these creatures at such close quarters.

As exciting as it was to see the crocodiles in their natural habitat, they weren't what impressed me most that night. Drifting quietly on the still surface of the lagoon, I looked up into the tropical night sky. Against the velvet blackness shone the jewels of the night. I was amazed to see stars glowing so brightly that they were reflected in the water below. The Milky Way, Orion, and the stars of our Australian flag—the Southern Cross— were on display, along with countless others. The words of the psalmist came to mind; we were there to witness that the heavens do indeed declare the glory of God, and in the night sky of a small South Pacific lagoon it was there for all to see just by looking up.

ANNE CRAM

Thought: Where else might you see His handiwork? What do these tell you about God's care for you?

The Coffee-colored Wallet

Look not every man on his own things, but every man also on the things of others. Phil. 2:4.

EARLY ONE SPRING MORNING my friend of more than 45 years and I decided to go walking. She was visiting from Seattle, Washington, and had come prepared with the appropriate attire. After some discussion we concluded that the best place to go walking would be the flea market grounds, located about 10 miles (16 kilometers) from my home. We climbed into my old 1982 Cadillac and set out for a happy adventure.

In a few minutes the soles of our shoes were on the rough pavement of the flea market grounds. We vigorously navigated the area, up one lane and down the next, until our aging bodies began to react to the effects of the hot Florida sun. This was only February, but the thermometer was registering in the high 70s, so we stopped to try out the ice-cold juice from the sugarcane machine. We strolled along as we quaffed the uniquely refreshing drink, delighted by every mouthful. All too soon we drained the last drops from the paper cup.

Before long we began to feel the heat again, so we stopped to rest in one of the food stalls. My friend noticed something on the floor—it was a wallet, a coffee-colored wallet with money inside.

We decided to wait and see if the owner would come back, looking for the wallet. After a few minutes, when no one came, we did something we should have thought of before—we prayed and asked God to send the owner. In less than five minutes a young woman appeared, intently scanning the very area where the wallet had been lying.

This was a direct answer to our prayer, the sign we had agreed upon. The young woman looked at us, and before she could say anything, I asked her, "¿Qué color?" (What color?)

"Café" [coffee], she replied. That was the identification we needed. I retrieved the wallet and placed it in the grateful hands of the owner. Moved with deep gratitude, she replied. "Gracias a dios!" [Thanks to God].

As we endeavor to live for Jesus, we realize that God engineers ministering opportunities for us wherever He chooses. So we must be prepared to render the most commonplace service wherever the need arises, even in the most commonplace surroundings. And as our prayers are answered, we too can exclaim, "Gracias a dios!"

QUILVIE G. MILLS

Plagues

These have power to shut heaven, . . . and to smite the earth with all plagues, as often as they will. Rev. 11:6.

IT SEEMS AS IF EVERY day we hear of some strange new disease. We've had the scare of HIV for some years, as well as anthrax, the West Nile virus, SARS, avian flu, and now something called monkeypox disease. It makes one wonder if these are part of the seven last plagues of Revelation.

It reminds me of what happened years ago while we lived in Connecticut. My husband repaired clocks and watches out of the second floor of our home; I taught a parochial school and kept his accounting books. We had no central air, but we did have a window air-conditioner. A bird decided that right beneath the air-conditioner was just the spot to build her nest. That was fine with me—I could watch her babies hatch.

At least it was fine with me until one particular night. I began to itch and scratch, and I wondered what I had caught or what I had wandered into, as I liked to hike in the woods. I finally figured it out: I was itching from bird lice that had managed to crawl from the nest, through the fine cracks in the window frame, and into the house, down the wall, and up to the desk where I was working. All of a sudden building a nest on that windowsill was certainly not all right. I didn't dare spray too close to the nest for fear of harming the babies. But I sprayed as much as I dared within the room. I felt, at that point, that I was experiencing one of the last plagues.

Eventually the birds left the nest. We opened the window, removed the nest, and sprayed well. We didn't plan on having bird lice again.

That is the way it is with our lives. Something good comes along, and then something happens to spoil the good. I think God permits episodes like the bird lice to happen so we won't get too comfortable down here on this earth; so we won't forget we are only visitors here for a short time. This spring it rained for eight consecutive days. When the sun finally shone, we were so happy to see its rays again. Dear reader, when bad things happen in your life, let the Son shine in and make it all worthwhile. Your home and mine, are waiting for us in heaven. LORAINE F. SWEETLAND

? **Thought:** If this event had happened to you, how would you apply I Thessalonians 5:17?

Asleep

They came to the house of the synagogue official; and He saw a commotion,
and people loudly weeping and wailing. And entering in, He said to them,
"Why make a commotion and weep? The child has not died, but is asleep."
Mark 5:38, 39, NASB.

I WAS TRANSFERRED TO a new position last spring, so I had to change offices. One of the parting gifts to me was a plant. I watered it each week, and it bore beautiful flowers, which I enjoyed all summer. In the fall I noticed that the leaves were drying up, one by one, until there was nothing but dirt visible in the pot. Convinced that the plant had died, I moved it from the table to a corner on the floor. Time passed, and I forgot the pot was there.

This spring, as I was reaching for a binder on the floor, I noticed a very tiny green spot in the pot. I had not watered the dirt all winter, but new life was springing up in the long-forgotten pot. I was excited and quickly repositioned the pot on the table in front of the window. I began watering it. The plant, which I thought was dead, was, in fact, alive. It had been only sleeping. It is now laden with buds, waiting to burst into beautiful flowers.

This reminds me of Jairus' daughter, whom everyone thought was dead. Death brings about a feeling of sadness, pain, grief, and loss. I felt those emotions at the passing of my parents, grandparents, and brother. It's as if a part of you becomes missing when a loved one dies. Nothing we can do will bring them back.

There is hope, as there is One greater than we who has the power to give life, and more abundantly. Jesus told Jairus not to be afraid but to believe. They went into the room where the girl lay. Jesus took her by the hand and called out her name, telling her to arise. Immediately she got up and began to walk.

A day is coming when those who have died in Christ will hear the trumpet sound. The dead in Christ shall rise. Oh, what a glorious day that will be when there will be no more death, no more sorrow, and no more pain! I find comfort in knowing that my family is not dead but asleep. I can't wait for the day when He will call their names, and they too will arise.

SHARON LONG (BROWN)

(?) Thought: Do you have loved ones you are looking forward to seeing again? What texts give you this hope? Be prepared to share them with someone else who needs this same hope.

Stuck in the Sand

Because of the Lord's great love we are not consumed, for his compassions never fail. They are new every morning; great is your faithfulness. Lam. 3:22, 23, NIV.

WE WERE ON VACATION on the southern coast of Brazil, and every day our family walked together on the beach. The weather was mild, the late-afternoon sun was not at its entire splendor, and the breeze that blew lightly in our faces made our walk very pleasant, something we looked forward to each day.

As we walked we found several aquatic creatures of different colors and shapes in the sand. Our children were fascinated and excited. I noticed that when the wave broke on the beach it cast little silver fish on the sand. They were left flipping on the shore until their death, or until the water reached them and took them back to sea again.

Observing that the water didn't always reach them in the coming and going of the waves, I called my two children to make them aware of the agonizing, life-threatening situation of those defenseless little fish. We decided that we would help these creatures return to the sea. We waited, and when they were left ashore, we returned as many as we could to the water. The sensation of saving the little fish by putting them back into their natural habitat was gratifying.

We human beings are washed ashore in the quicksand of sin. God has provided His Son to save us from eternal death. Our natural habitat is not here on this earth—we need to be returned to the restored Eden.

How many times we are in the midst of agony, immersed in a quagmire of problems, and Jesus kindly comes to our rescue, encouraging us and comforting us! He doesn't allow us to perish in this minuscule point of the universe. God has provided a means for us to be saved through His Son, the Lord Jesus.

If you are a woman who is experiencing difficulties, feeling suffocated by problems and by despair, cry out to the Lord, for you can be certain that He is always by your side, ready to save you.   LÍLIAN BORRELI DOS REIS

(?) Thought: This family couldn't save all the little silver fish, but they saved many. We can't reach out to every woman in need, but we can reach many. What might you do today, this week, to help someone floundering in sin?

The Olive Tree

But I am like a green olive tree in the house of God. Ps. 52:8.

A FEW YEARS AGO my husband bought two tiny olive plants. They looked so fragile. He tended them carefully and planted them near the entrance to our home. In the Mediterranean climate here in the Western Cape they grew well.

The olive tree has a twisted trunk and uneven pendulous branches. The leaves are small and oblong in shape. The dull-green, egg-shaped berries turn to black, and are bitter to the taste. To be edible, they must be cured in brine.

The olive tree is an ancient fruit and is often mentioned in the Bible. This tree, widespread in Palestine, yields much oil. The beautiful wood was used to make the doors, lintels, and posts of the Temple built by King Solomon, and also the two great cherubim in the Holy of Holies (1 Kings 6:23-32).

Some parents have named their daughters Olive, perhaps because they resembled cherubs when they were born. As Hosea says: "[Her] beauty shall be as the olive tree" (14:6).

In the story of Noah and the ark, Noah sent a raven, then a dove out twice. The second time the dove returned with an olive branch in her beak (Gen. 8:11). An olive branch is a symbol of peace, or an offer or desire for reconciliation.

Olive oil was one of Palestine's most valuable products and was used for medicinal, religious, and cosmetic purposes, among many others.

By nature the olive tree is wild. We are like the olive tree when we do not know the Lord. Our wildness may be permanently tamed through the knowledge that Christ decided in Gethsemane to die for us. All the pain and humiliation He suffered was so that we might be saved from sin. To stand as flourishing green olive trees in the Lord's court is our calling.

Like the wild olive tree, we can be grafted, contrary to nature, into a good olive tree (Rom. 11:24). We can be grafted into Christ and be enabled to bear the fruits of the Spirit. PRISCILLA E. ADONIS

Thought: Am I still a wild olive, or am I well-grafted and flourishing in Christ? What do I need to do today to make the difference?

Trust the Lord With Your Life

When you find me, you find life, real life, to say nothing of God's good pleasure. Prov. 8:35, Message.

"TILL DEATH DO US PART." We had been married more than 48 years. After three and a half years in a life-and-death struggle, the enemy won, and my dear husband breathed his last.

You always ask yourself, *Was there something more we could have done?* There were the exercise programs, medications, doctor visits, healthier eating habits, much prayer, and an anointing service.

Our prayers were that God's will be done. Years before, when our then 17-year-old son lay in the hospital, lingering between life and death because of an automobile accident, my husband and I had prayed that very difficult prayer for any parent to pray: "Thy will be done." God had answered our prayer with a "Yes," and our son's life was spared. But this time God didn't intervene and spare my husband's life. He now sleeps, awaiting Jesus' soon coming. What a wonderful day that will be!

Losing your life's companion is not easy, as many of you can affirm. Mr. Fix-It was no longer there. Shopping for plumbers, electricians, etc., was something new, and often frustrating for me (as well as expensive). Several items had to be replaced or repaired, one right after the other.

But that wasn't the part of my life that was most difficult—it was losing my soul mate, my best friend. How lonely life became at certain times! We had done everything together. How I missed worship times together, singing together, sitting in church together, and sharing meals together! Friday nights and Sabbaths were—and still are—the most difficult times. But I still had the Lord, and He has carried me through the lonely times. He continues to open doors for me to fill those times: getting more involved with church activities, beginning a women's prayer group in my home, invitations from friends to go out for lunch or to their homes for dinner. Then there are the phone calls from family and friends, and some travel.

The Lord has provided so abundantly! I thank Him every day. I encourage each of you who are widows, single women, divorced women, or married to men not of your church affiliation to put your life in His care and trust Him with your life. You will never regret it.

PATRICIA MULRANEY KOVALSKI

God's Garden

Hereby perceive we the love of God, because he laid down his life for us.
1 John 3:16.

CAREFULLY I PICK UP the heavy photograph album that has been part of my life for so long. I turn each page and thoughtfully reminisce over my life—childhood years, my own children, and finally retirement. Another page . . . My eyes fall on photos of a beautiful, peaceful garden. Memory takes me across serene green lawns, along pleasant valleys, and over rolling hills. Flowers are profuse, and trees bend their friendly branches in the cool morning breeze. An eternal flame stands in the center of this lovely expanse.

People who visit here come with a purpose. It is a place where tears are shed and hearts are emptied in sorrow. Rows of marble markers are garnished with love blossoms, wafting their fragrance into the paths along which we walk.

Loved ones, resting peacefully beneath these green carpets, are affectionately remembered. A young man, a schoolmate of my son's, sleeps on a nearby hill. A colleague rests close by. Other cherished friends lie here as well. Two markers carry the names of my precious parents, the two people who shaped my life and taught me by their Christlike example.

I try to imagine how much love rests beneath this living carpet of green, how much love is poured out upon those who sleep. I think of words written by the great songwriter Oscar Hammerstein. One evening just before the Broadway musical star Mary Martin was to go onstage in *South Pacific,* a note was handed to her. It was from her friend Oscar Hammerstein, who at that moment was on his deathbed. The short note simply said: *"Dear Mary, a bell's not a bell till you ring it. A song's not a song till you sing it. Love in your heart is not put there to stay. Love isn't love till you give it away."*

Then I think of another garden—Gethsemane—where the inestimable price of love for our redemption was paid by the Son of God. And not far distant, it was poured out to its fullest on that cross standing on a lonely hill.

Love given away! One day it will break the bands that have bound His children. It will push aside the heavy marble stones that carry their names, and new names will be given. All because of His love, given freely at the cross. "Love isn't love till it's given away." Truly!

LORRAINE HUDGINS-HIRSCH

Sitting at the Airport

"You are My Witnesses," says the Lord. Isa. 43:10, NKJV.

I'M SITTING AT THE AIRPORT. Many people pass by me—some hurrying, some wanting to but can't, their feet unable. I see people reading newspapers or interesting novels. Some scurry madly. There are people whose faces beam with smiles, obviously happy to meet their loved ones. Others wear harried looks, evidence of distress, seemingly unaware that God cares for them.

Sitting at the airport, I see tears flowing down a woman's cheek as she talks on the phone about her loved one who has passed away. I let an opportunity go by to share a word of comfort, to tell her God cares, that He understands her grief.

Sitting at the airport, I see pilots and flight attendants walking with hastened steps, and the young and carefree—I wonder if they ever think of what tomorrow may bring their way. There are those who are older; once young and strong, they are now frail and slow, tenderly trying to help each other along. There is luggage of all colors, shapes, sizes, and descriptions—some new, some torn and falling apart, some broken and patched. I am reminded of my past but am encouraged to know that although my life might be torn and tattered, I have a loving Savior who specializes in restoring broken lives and making them like new again.

Sitting at the airport, I hear the sweet laughter of little children. Nearby is an old blind man, waiting anxiously for someone to help him get the right electronic car to take him to the right gate. I watch as he checks his watch—not too much time left, it seems. I see people go swiftly by, no one caring about him sitting there and fretting about missing his flight. I wonder what will happen to him if he does miss it. Finally I go to the attendant at the counter and ask him to help. Brusquely he replies, "Someone will be with him shortly," but no one comes. I wait, then go again to tell him that the man's flight is scheduled to leave at 2:00 p.m. and that he is quite a distance from his gate. He is finally helped and on his way. I am so thankful that my Friend Jesus is never too busy to help me when I call on Him in my moments of despair.

Sitting at the airport, I see all kinds of people for whom Christ gave His life, but I failed to share a word of His love for them, or even a smile or greeting. Yes, so many precious moments passed by. *Please Lord, forgive me and help me to do better next time.*   SHIRLEY C. IHEANACHO

Voice of Youth

And we know that all things work together for good to them that love God, to them who are called according to his purpose. Rom. 8:28.

IT SEEMS TO BE a human tendency to question God's dealings with us. When favorable experiences come, we view them as blessings. But whenever tough times come, such as loss of loved ones, we opt to perceive it as a curse.

While at the university, I joined the Voice of Youth. This program gives students the opportunity to be involved in sharing the good news of the gospel with people in different places. When we arrived in our assigned territory, I received the heartbreaking news that my father was in serious condition. Without hesitation I left the group and the work that I had been assigned to do.

When I reached home, I was told that my father had already died. I cried bitterly because I didn't expect that the day I left home to serve God would be the last time I would see my father alive. I asked the Lord about it, why He had let this happen to His child, and especially to my father, who had worked actively for God.

I felt God's answer in the stillness of His presence, reminding me of His unfailing love—and even His purpose of letting me pass through this kind of experience. I also realized that when God closes the door of uncertainty, He opens windows of opportunity.

When my father died, I was afraid I wouldn't be able to continue my studies. But God had another plan that superseded what I had planned for myself. Though I'm not able to study the easy way, I believe He has a purpose. God is making a way for me to pursue my studies—the hard way—in order for me to know about the realities of life.

Ellen G. White wrote concerning today's text: "All our sufferings and sorrows, . . . all our persecutions and privations, in short, all things work together for our good" (*The Ministry of Healing*, p. 489).   DAISY B. PRINCESA

Thought: Have you found Romans 8:28 to be true in your life? Another translation reads: "We know that in all things God works for the good of those who love him" (NIV). Do you see a difference in emphasis? How do you think God is working for Daisy's good?

An Unexpected Spiritual Journey

The stones of the wall will cry out, and the beams of the woodwork will echo it. Hab. 2:11, NIV.

MY RECENT RETIREMENT gave me the time to travel to places I had only read about before. I settled for a relaxing week on the open seas and some interesting fun-filled side trips in Central America. But the Lord had something different to offer me—what I received was an unexpected spiritual journey by boat, bus, and ancient stone steps.

My destination was the Mayan ruins. After a short, bumpy ride, I stepped off the bus and stood in amazement. Before me loomed four tall Mayan temples, equally positioned around the perimeter of a large open square. White temple stones sparkled in the hot tropical sun. A well-informed guide gave riveting descriptions of the many ceremonies held at these temples. He spoke at length about the ancient Mayan people and their culture, dating the building of these structures long before the birth of Jesus, when "the craftsmen of Solomon and Hiram and the men of Gebal cut and prepared the timber and stone for the building of the temple" (1 Kings 5:18, NIV).

Old Testament people and their cities always intrigued me. Intelligent humans also peopled the Americas in Old Testament times. These perfectly built temples gave proof of that.

I eagerly approached one of the temples and started my climb up rough-hewn stone steps. I looked out over a vista of palm trees and antiquity. As I neared the top, I shivered, thinking about human sacrificial ceremonies the native guide had spoken about.

Loud shouts below jarred me back to reality. Two workmen shoveling dirt into a wheelbarrow yelled "Hello" (or the equivalent). I stared at these present-day men of Mayan descent. Suddenly I saw in my mind Old Testament pages flip forward to the cross. Jesus knew the builders of these temples. He died for them, also. How wrong of me—and how dare I dismiss these stone builders of ancient towers as undeserving! Truly "the stones of the wall will cry out, and the beams of the woodwork will echo it." While I continued to stand on rough stone steps, Jesus taught me that His love for all humanity—past, present, and future—never changes. I felt humbled and blessed that the Lord Jesus Christ directed my every step on an unexpected spiritual journey.

MARIANNE TOTH BAYLESS

I Have Hidden Your Word in My Heart

I have hidden your word in my heart that I might not sin against you.
Ps. 119:11, NIV.

"IF THE BIBLE WERE prohibited, would you have enough of the Word hidden in your heart to guide you through future crises?" This question asked by the speaker for a women's ministry meeting captured my attention. She explained that Christians during the Dark Ages cherished the Word, memorizing it, risking their lives and facing death rather than turning their backs on its truth. In courts of law some were required, on pain of death, to quote texts in support of their beliefs—without a Bible.

I longed to memorize Scripture. But how, and when, would I find the time? The speaker's words lingered with me: memorizing Scripture increases our knowledge of God, creates a way for God to speak to us, strengthens us against sin, reduces negative thinking, restores us to His will, and prepares us for ministry.

By now I was "almost persuaded" that this must become a priority in my life. But when I heard her quote Isaiah 55:6 from memory—"Seek the Lord while he may be found; call on him while he is near" (NIV), it was like water for a thirsty soul. I wanted to be able to hide words like that in my heart and quote them from memory. The four passages of Scripture conducive to memorization she handed out to get us started became treasures to me.

How could I make memorization happen in the midst of my busy lifestyle? The problem was quickly solved. It is my custom to pray during my "walk for health" every morning. I determined to devote half my prayer time to memorization. The next morning I made a copy of Isaiah 55 before leaving the house and tucked it in my pocket. While pounding the pavement on a foggy November morning, I switched from praying to memorizing. I plugged along, committing two to four lines a day to memory. The next day I added a couple of new lines and reviewed what I had learned the day before.

This began a year ago. I have now memorized all four passages, including Isaiah 55, Psalms 119:9-16, Proverbs 2, and Psalm 27. I learned that it is easier to memorize a complete passage than just one Scripture! Truly I can say that I have hidden His Word in my heart! Why not join me in this exciting venture?

NANCY VAN PELT

The Faith of a Little Child

The fundamental fact of existence is that this trust in God, this faith, is the firm foundation under everything that makes life worth living. It's our handle on what we can't see. Heb. 11:1, Message.

WE (MY PARENTS, SISTERS, and their families) were at family caravan camp in Scarborough, England. This was the perfect site for families. Some areas were laden with fossils for any would-be archaeologist to dig for; there was the pebbly beach to splash in, and the town's famous Victorian spa. We'd had a good time, but now it was time to leave. I paused in the sunshine before I walked into our caravan. Slipping a sweater into my suitcase, I felt a tug on the hem of my shirt. My 4-year-old nephew was insistent. "You have to pray now. I've lost something. God will help us find it."

I don't remember what the lost item was, though I do remember that it was very small. I also remember being humbled by young Louis's request. That he chose me to help him pray was heartening. But now I had a problem. What would happen to the little boy's faith if we didn't find his lost treasure?

Quietly I moved aside, bowed my head, and talked to my Savior: "Listen, Lord, this is for You to handle. Louis has put You to the test. This is between You and him. Let Your light shine upon us. Please help us now." I was as forceful as my little nephew had been, even though I knew that my faith was not as strong as his.

Then it was as if a gentle hand nudged my bowed head even further forward. Startled, I opened my eyes. Louis's treasure lay right before me. God had shown me where to look. Shocked at the immediacy of His answer, I thought about that father's faith in Gospel times (verse 24). He knew Jesus would solve his problem. "I believe. Help me with my doubts" (Mark 9:25, Message). I realized then what 4-year-old Louis already knew. I had no reason to doubt.

Humbled again, I praised God for giving me evidence of His divine character. I know I cannot doubt His word just because I don't understand the mysteries of God's providence. God has a handle on my problems.

Father, let the sunlight of Your truth shine forth into my reality. Scorch the seeds of doubt that remain in me, for the sake of Your Son, Jesus.

WINSOME DACRES

Quack Grass

Look after each other so that not one of you will fail to find God's best blessings. Watch out that no bitterness takes root among you, for as it springs up it causes deep trouble, hurting many in their spiritual lives. Heb. 12:15, TLB.

THE GREATEST BANE OF gardeners in my area is quack grass. Its very name suggests an impostor. The difference between it and lawn grass is seen not only in the different texture of the grass aboveground but even more so when we look underground. The roots of quack grass are coarse and long, reaching out in every direction from the mother plant. If even a short piece of root is left in the ground it has the potential to start another clump of quack grass. Quack grass grows quickly and forms its seed head, giving it the capability of also reproducing by seed.

Every spring I find an excessive amount of quack grass in my flower beds. Though I have carefully pulled the roots out of the soil the previous year, it seems there is always some left to sprout and reach for the light. Invading the perennials is the most frustrating. Then I must try to remove the quack grass roots without disturbing the flowers.

We can choose to allow the quack grass of negative habits, thoughts, and actions to proliferate in our lives. Gossip is allowed to spread like the roots of quack grass. We may think we have squelched the questionable stories when all of a sudden reports will appear in another area. Looking underground, we will find an individual who has felt he or she needed to perpetuate the gossip. Our feelings of suspicion and resentment find a place in our minds, and we dwell upon them until they grow and grow to infect those around us. Gossip often becomes lies, suspicion causes us to lose respect for others, and hate for others can grow into self-hate.

Naturally, we wouldn't choose to have our lives full of quack grass to destroy our Christian beauty. We may think they will only hurt someone else, but the greatest damage is done to our own soul. Quack grass is a bane in our gardens. So also the quack grass we allow to grow in our characters is a bane to our spiritual growth. We must work tirelessly to eradicate the roots of our personal quack grass. Thankfully, the Lord is ever present to help me as I dig out the roots of the negativism in my life. I need only to invite Him to come take control of my thoughts, words, and actions, and He will assist me as I struggle to remove the roots of my personal quack grass.

EVELYN GLASS

What's My Lie?

Speaking the truth in love, we will in all things grow up into him. Eph. 4:15, NIV.

I FINALLY DID IT. I started the next round of my education. It wasn't easy. I never thought going beyond my bachelor's degree was something for me to do. I loved learning but hated being a student. The added factor of using the Internet to learn was daunting.

On the first night of the communication and ethics class we had the usual get-to-know-each-other games. One of the games we played was "What's my lie?" Each of us was to tell about ourselves but insert something that was not true. Then, if we guessed what the lie was, it was our turn to tell our story.

I was so intimidated. First, what could I lie about? I had been brought up not to do that. Second, I had to pay attention to each participant and try to figure out what his or her lie was. It was interesting and a really unique way to get to know each other. I found that most of my classmates were military veterans or government workers, and they knew about as much as I knew about computers.

It was terrible trying to figure out what was right and what was wrong. Finally I guessed someone's lie simply by mistake! I was up next, and I still couldn't think of what to say. So I began "My name is Mary E. Dunkin, and I am a long-lost relative of the Dunkin' Donut family." I then continued with the rest of my story. To my amazement, nobody could figure out what was not true about me. I had stumped the class! They were pretty disappointed to find out that Dunkin' Donuts describes the act of dunking a doughnut into something—it was not started by a family named Dunkin! They were also disappointed that there would be no free doughnuts from me.

When we speak, are we "speaking the truth in love" as we are advised? It doesn't really matter whether it is with words, actions, or attitudes—we speak volumes about who lives in our hearts. We preach untold sermons to the world in what we do and say, as well as how we act.

Let's make sure that no little lies are laced throughout the message God wants us to deliver to the world. Let's make it 100 percent pure with God's love and truth. — MARY E. DUNKIN

Thought: Why not read Ephesians 4 for practical advice on daily living?

Lesson From the
Woman With the Issue

When she heard about Jesus, she came up behind him in the crowd and touched his cloak, because she thought, "If I just touch his clothes, I will be healed." Mark 5:27, 28, NIV.

THE WOMAN WITH THE ISSUE of blood—I imagine her often, that woman, bleeding for those 12 life-changing years. She travels from doctor to doctor, seeking a healing message. If she were a woman with a family she must have thought, *What will my husband's and children's lives be like without me?* If she were a single woman she might have thought, Lord, who will nurse me when I can no longer take care of myself? She is propelled to whisper a motivational mantra: *I have to find a way to stop this bleeding, because the life of the body is the blood. I-I-I am,* she stutters, *losing my life.* Weak, she travels to another doctor. I imagine the grief-stricken expression on her face as she is told yet again the spirit-draining message: "There is no human healing for your issue, woman!"

The woman continues her search for healing because she is trapped in a promise. She has a spiritual knowing that she will be healed. Why else would she have gone to so many doctors? Then she hears of Jesus, so she ventures out into the crowded streets that day, a desperate woman trapped in a healing promise. She senses that if she can just get outside, if she can just get close enough to the Messiah, if she can just touch the bottom of His robe, certainly she will be healed. And she does just that. I imagine her crawling about in the crowd. The woman with the issue gets close enough to the Healer to touch the *bottom of His robe,* and she is healed.

A woman with an issue. At times I too feel the desperate need to touch the hem of Jesus' garment in an effort to be healed from an issue that has no human relief. During these times I try to mirror the woman with the issue of blood. I drag myself out into the street. I meditate on the words of Jesus. I pray God's Word back to Him. I go to church to fellowship with the saints of God. I find faith in these activities, a kind of touching of Jesus' garment. Oh, how I love Jesus for making these modern-day touching activities available to me!

And like the woman with the issue of blood, I feel Jesus speaking to me: "Daughter, your faith has caused a healing in you." Amen, amen!

RAMONA L. HYMAN

Reflections of God's Love

Again [Jesus] began to teach beside the sea. Mark 4:1, RSV.

"OVER AND OVER, like a mighty sea, comes the love of Jesus rolling over me." The words of this old hymn ran through my mind and burst from my mouth as I gazed at the beautiful, powerful Pacific Ocean. I was taking one last walk at sunset the evening before our departure. We were on a family vacation in Hawaii, a once-in-a-lifetime experience that had been filled with happy hours, beautiful sunsets, lots of family time, along with unforgettable memories.

We experienced what we had anticipated—that a vacation in Hawaii revolves around the water. At least when you love it as our family does, and it's surrounding you. As we played in the ocean, walked on the beach, and gazed at the powerful waves and beautiful sunsets, I found many instances that reminded me of our Creator and His teachings.

While swimming and floating up and down on the rolling waves, I contemplated how we need to learn simply to roll with the troubles in life—not fight them—and trust Jesus, and we will come out on top. The daily ebb and flow of the tides reminded me of the high and low times in life. When the waves washed away our footprints and sand castles, I thought of how Jesus washes away our sins. When an unexpected wave doused me during a beachcombing walk, I reflected how important it is to be prepared for the trials of life. In my search for the "perfect" seashell I was reminded that nobody is perfect—not me, not my husband, not my family. And I never found a perfect shell, just many pretty ones. In the many sunsets I understood the inevitable ending of experiences and life as we now know it. During the frequent rain showers that stopped as quickly as they started I thought of being prepared for sorrow and washing in the cleansing showers of tears. The rain always brought with it rainbows, and in their brilliant colors I was reminded of God's promises to His children.

On the thought of leaving I reflected on another point. We don't have to be at the beach for the love of Jesus to wash over us—we can be anywhere. But we have to put ourselves in the presence of Jesus, where His love can wash over us. How? By daily spending time with God in His Word, getting to know Him, and learning to trust Him.

God, please show me how to feel Your love continuously flowing over me!

JUDY MUSGRAVE SHEWMAKE

Poison Ivy!

Bless the Lord, O my soul, and forget not all his benefits: Who forgiveth all thine iniquities; who healeth all thy diseases. Ps. 103:2, 3.

POISON IVY. ALMOST everyone has heard these words and knows, at least to some degree, the misery that the shiny green plant with the triclustered leaves can cause when people with sensitive skin get too close. I got poison ivy while cutting weeds in the small patch of woods behind our house. Poison ivy is no respecter of lawn borders. Berry bushes grow wild in our woods, and runners of canes from them had encroached into our backyard. The stickers from those canes and other greenery blew back against me, hitting my clothes and my skin.

I should have taken a bath in hot soapy water right away instead of waiting until I had finished other chores. Nothing seemed to help the resulting bout of poison ivy until the doctor administered a shot, and that came after three weeks of misery. From now on, I must always take extra care and protect myself as much as possible in order to keep from getting poison ivy.

Poison ivy is a lot like sin. I recognize and stay away from poison ivy vines and bushes. But my undoing was the little sprigs of it, camouflaged by other weeds and greenery. I didn't see it until all the weeds had been cut and I had already been in it. As Christians, we recoil in horror at the thought of committing the more obvious sins, such as killing someone, robbing a bank, or embezzling money. But it's easy to "brush against," or find ourselves entangled in, some of the more "respectable" sins before we even realize what's happening.

We can't stop sin from growing and spreading in our lives by our own power any more than I could stop the spread of my rash. Sin can leave permanent scars—just as my poison ivy left lasting effects upon me.

We need the help of Christ, the Great Physician—the shots of love and the forgiveness that He can give. Just as I need poison ivy protection, we Christians need the protection of the full armor of God—the regular study of His Word, much prayer, and the strength that can be gained by regular church attendance.

God helping us is the only way we can ever reach the point where we can recognize and avoid even the little "sprigs of sin" and achieve total victory.

BONNIE MOYERS

Seashore

They went away in a boat. . . . Now many . . . saw them . . . and ran . . .
and got there ahead [of those in the boat]. Mark 6:32, 33, Amplified.

I LOVE THE SEA because it brings a soothing feeling to my soul, and I like watching the waves building up and gradually disappearing. Morning manna at the seashore at Hartenbos was a blessing.

The urge in me for praying was great. As I walked to the beach, making my way with the rest of the women's ministries group, I was just keen to get to the shore and meet whoever would be joining my group. We formed a ring but remained quiet for a moment. As we looked at each other, one woman said, "We know why we are here." So we split into twos and began praying.

Somehow that morning I felt the presence of the Lord and had a strong feeling that He was speaking to me in His special way. After praying, we hugged each other, announcing, "God bless." Just those words made me feel warm in soul and spirit.

After a short introduction to each other, I turned around and looked at the sea. I saw a boat sailing away from the shore with people on board, but there was a prominent figure standing. It reminded me of Jesus as I often see the picture in religious books or picture rolls. In my imagination this person resembled Jesus, reminding me of the crowds watching Jesus leaving on the boat, and how they still longed to hear Him speak. His leaving did not hinder them from running from town to town to meet Him, and finally to arrive at His destination before He did, so thirsty were they for the Word of God.

I also felt I could have run to meet Him on the other side. I felt a longing in my heart for Jesus, to see His face. This simple scene was just what I needed. *Thank You, Lord, for the sea You created to remind me of how wonderful You are.*

I returned home with a revived desire to look for opportunities to do what I can for Him. I pray that I prepare myself to do as He would have me do in this world.   ETHEL D. MSUSENI

? Thought: If you could run or drive somewhere to meet Jesus, would you do it? Or would you be too busy? Do you meet with Jesus each day?

Locked Out!

You are blessed. . . . I will give you the keys of the Kingdom of Heaven. Matt. 16:17-19, NLT.

The door to heaven is narrow. . . . When the head of the house has locked the door, it will be too late. Luke 13:24, NLT.

I WAS FRUSTRATED and upset! The door to my basement apartment was locked, and there was no key. The house's owner had apparently changed the lock before I moved in, and had never given me the key. I had keys to the mailbox, my bedroom, and the outside door of the house. But I didn't have the key I needed, and I had never realized it.

I had never been locked out before without a way to get in—a spare key, a family member with a key, or somebody to let me in. I tried some extra keys that I had. One of them fit into the lock but wouldn't turn it. I pried, prodded, and poked with paper clips, nail files, and screw drivers. Still, the lock mechanism wouldn't budge.

Forty-five minutes later, in desperation, I finally called a locksmith. A little past the time he said he'd arrive he showed up with tools in hand. Within seconds he had given me the bad news: the lock was a "good one," and no amount of picking was going to get me in. He would need to drill through the keyhole to release the mechanism, then replace the cylinder with a new lock (another "good one") and two keys. The landlord was out of the country, and there was no other way I could think of to get the door open. I had no choice but to let him proceed.

The locksmith began working, and in less than 15 minutes the old lock was off, the door was open, and the new cylinder was installed. Total cost? An unbelievable $293. It would have been $29 more if I hadn't given him cash. I was extremely upset! This was not in my budget. I was relieved, nonetheless, to get back into my apartment after the afternoon's trauma.

Today I thought about that whole key situation again. Then I thought about how fortunate I am that I don't have to worry about paying ridiculous fees to get into heaven. I don't have to wait around for God to show up with the tools to unlock the door. There is no need to pry, prod, or poke around to gain entry. And I surely don't have to attempt to pick the lock. The Owner of heaven has given me the key, and all I have to do is insert it, unlock the door, and enter into everlasting life! *Thank You, Lord.*

IRIS L. STOVALL

Another Good Samaritan

But a certain Samaritan, as he journeyed, came where he was: and when he saw him, he had compassion on him. Luke 10:33.

RACHEL WALKED SLOWLY into the backyard where the loud, noisy high school graduation party was being held. She was dressed attractively in a beige suit and red blouse, with a gray wig finishing off the outfit. I noticed immediately the large bruises on her face, but I didn't want to ask. She had been suffering from cancer for many years. When Bob walked by, he asked about her accident. Then I learned the story.

She had taken her dog for a little walk on her street. Upon returning, she slipped and fell in the street. She didn't quite know what happened—maybe she tripped on the dog leash. It was a hard fall, and she had been weakened by years of her illness. In her pain she glanced up and saw a car coming up the hill. She heard the engine being gunned, and then the car zoomed off into the distance. She could not get up, but lay there in pain and with blood on her face. A second car came; it stopped, and the man came over and lifted her and helped her into her nearby house. He stayed with her while she called for help, and left only when he was sure she could manage until someone came.

This sounds somewhat like the story of the good Samaritan from the Bible. Jesus told this story to illustrate who was our neighbor. The man lay wounded and bleeding from the robber's attack on the road to Jerusalem. The priest and the Levite, whom we might think of as being the ones to teach love and caring, turned the other way. Perhaps they had an important committee meeting to attend, or new robes they didn't want to get soiled. The Samaritan, of a despised race, did not look to see if the man was of his ethnic group when he stopped to help him. He put him on his donkey and took him to an inn to recover. He paid for his care and even told the innkeeper, "If there are more expenses, I will reimburse you." The Samaritan was willing to give of his time and money for a stranger who was, in reality, his neighbor.

Today we can race our engines and hurry on—perhaps we have important things to do. We may think that someone else will stop and help the ones in need. Maybe there is one who has more free time than we have. As Christians, we first must love our God, and then our duty is to love our neighbor. *Stop and give a helping hand today and be another good Samaritan.*

DESSA WEISZ HARDIN

The Life-giver

He who testifies to these things says, "Surely I am coming quickly." Amen.
Even so, come, Lord Jesus! Rev. 22:20, NKJV.

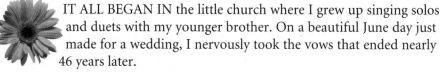

IT ALL BEGAN IN the little church where I grew up singing solos and duets with my younger brother. On a beautiful June day just made for a wedding, I nervously took the vows that ended nearly 46 years later.

We had a full life, Papa and I, blessed by five children and 16 grandchildren. We faced our own particular share of problems over the years, as most married people do. The last five years after we retired were the happiest ones but also the most stressful. We moved away from our roots, built a log house in the woods, and laughed together more than at any previous time. Until the last year. Papa had battled lymphoma for nearly 18 years, fought hard and prayed hard, but the cancer finally won. Now I live with memories and find I am a member of the widows' club.

The last year we spent every week at medical appointments of some type—chemotherapy, radiation, lab work, or doctor's offices. We went through surgeries, home medical treatments, and, finally, the hospital bed in the house. If ever anyone fought a war, it was the two of us against the dreaded enemy. But we gradually lost ground, and the enemy took him away from his beloved family four days before Christmas.

We had taken long drives around the beautiful countryside; we had long talks about our future in a better land, our heavenly country, after the resurrection. His faith seemed to grow right before my eyes, even as his body faded. After I had spent one long night of wrestling with God for assurance that Papa would indeed awake in the resurrection, God answered my prayers through him. He asked for a pencil and paper and had me write these words: "God is the Great Physician. You are my best nurse. So I leave my life in His hands." A great peace flooded me at God's assurance of Papa's eternal life; there would be an end to this pain forever.

It won't be long now; Jesus is coming soon. From a little country cemetery will come forth one vital, handsome, loving man, responding to the call of the Life-giver. We'll take up the rest of our lives in eternity together with our loved ones and the Great Physician. *"Even so, come, Lord Jesus!"*

BETTY R. BURNETT

Sammie

And he . . . said . . . , Peace, be still, . . . And there was a great calm. Mark 4:39.

SHE WAS CURLED UP in the only spot of sunshine in a pen containing three other dogs, a very thin, very young puppy at the city pound. However, as soon as we spoke to her, she got up and came toward us, wagging her tail. Instantly we were smitten. After completing formalities (paperwork and a payment), the puppy was ours. We named her Sammie. I wondered where she had come from, this little part-spaniel, part-Australian cattle dog. Who could have left such a darling animal in a street to fend for herself? Why had no one been out looking for her?

Sammie sat obediently when I put her lead on, obviously so happy to be out of the confines of her pen. When Jesus sets us free from sin, isn't it wonderful? No longer confined, we are in the full sunshine of His love.

For 13 years now Sammie has given us a lot of joy. I have often heard it said, "It doesn't matter what mood you come home in—good or bad—your dog is always pleased to see you." Similarly, it doesn't matter how we are feeling when we go to God in prayer. Our moods don't worry God; whether we are feeling sad or glad, God is always so pleased to spend time with us.

Every morning, very early, we are off for our walk with Sammie. She knows the routine and is always right at the garage door when we open it, faithfully waiting for us. I think about Jesus. He stands at the door to our heart, waiting for us to open it and let Him in. No matter what the time—early in the morning or late at night—Jesus is always there, just waiting.

The summer storms where we live come often but fortunately do not last long. Sammie, like most dogs, hates the thunder, and at the first clap she is looking up at the stairs. Her "safety zone" is beside our bed. And there she curls up quite calmly. Similarly, our "safety zone" in the storms of life is God. As we look up to Him, we can be reassured that the storm will not last long. Psalm 107:29 tells us, "He maketh the storm a calm."

LEONIE DONALD

(?) Thought: In Matthew 15:25-27 Jesus called a woman a dog. What was her response, and what was the blessing?

Almost Heaven

No eye has seen, no ear has heard, no mind has conceived what God has prepared for those who love him. 1 Cor. 2:9, NIV.

THE DAY WAS ABOUT as beautiful as a day could be this side of heaven. The sunlight scattered into myriads of diamonds as it touched the breeze-rippled ocean close to Flores Island, just west of Vancouver Island.

We were in a tiny power boat, skirting the tree-lined shores and heading out toward the Pacific Ocean. Suddenly our friend slowed the boat. "Gray whales!" Two huge gray whales, a mother and a calf, broke the surface, spouted, and turned, lifting their heads out of the water to look at us with large, dark eyes. Our tiny boat seemed very vulnerable to me next to these massive creatures.

"Do they ever tip the boats?" I asked, a little nervously.

"Oh, no," our friend assured me. "The whales just swim around the boats the way we walk around a room without bumping into the furniture."

I wasn't totally at peace—I often bump into furniture!

But he was right. At that moment the whale calf swam under the front of our boat. The water was so clear that we could see the barnacles on his back. Without even nudging our boat, he turned around and came alongside us, so close we could have reached out and touched him.

The whales swam around us for a while, then slipped away. We turned the boat back out to sea. "Look! Orca!" yelled one of the children. Three black-and-white orca swam in synchrony through the sun-sparkled waves, surfacing and diving, as we tried to guess where they would show up next. Behind the orca the island gently rose from a sandy beach sheltered by pine trees. A bald eagle swooped down to catch a fish. It was a day we wanted to hold on to forever.

It had been an awesome day; "Like being in heaven," said our children. But perhaps in heaven we would be swimming all day with the whales and the orca, diving and rising, without getting cold or tired. Perhaps we would be flying with the eagle, and not just watching it.

I remember someone telling me that our lives were sometimes tough on earth so that we would long for heaven, but it's not just the hard things in life that make me wish for heaven—the beautiful moments do too.

KAREN HOLFORD

(?) Thought: What makes you long for heaven?

The Torture Glove

Then some began to spit at him; they blindfolded him, struck him with their fists, and said, "Prophesy!" And the guards took him and beat him. Mark 14:65, NIV.

But he had Jesus flogged, and handed him over to be crucified. Matt. 27:26, NIV.

IT WAS AN EXPERIENCE I shall never forget! I was in the back of our Ford Club Wagon with both hands full, moving items from the white van to our red Windstar, preparatory to making a trip.

Somehow I missed the step and crashed to the asphalt driveway on my left hand and arm. The pain was excruciating, and I immediately screamed for my husband while I lay on the ground, clutching my arm. Since he was inside the house listening to the news on TV, he couldn't hear my cries.

Finally I struggled to my feet and got to the door, where he met me. At first he thought I was having a heart attack; then he saw my arm. He immediately put me in the van and rushed me to Parkridge Hospital in Chattanooga, near where we live. After seeing the seriousness of my injury, they moved me to the Memorial Hospital, where Dr. Brian Smith operated.

The metal device he used to hold the pins in my arm was very heavy, and I quickly learned what a blessing it was that the Lord made us with two arms. Life is very difficult with one arm. After several weeks the metal device was removed, and then therapy began to help me regain the use of my stiff fingers.

One of the therapies involved a glove with Velcro attachments to stretch my fingers. I was to wear it for 20 minutes three times daily. It was somewhat painful during the time I wore it, but oh, what excruciating pain when the tension was released and I took the glove off!

Each time I used this glove I was reminded of my Savior's pain and suffering. I read again the account of the treatment given Jesus by Pilate in John 19:1. In the King James Version it is called scourging. In *The Desire of Ages* we're told that Jesus "was taken, faint with weariness and covered with wounds, and scourged in the sight of the multitude" (p. 734).

And it was for me! What a wonderful Savior is Jesus my Lord!

RUBYE SUE

(?) Thought: It is painful even to think of what Jesus suffered for us. But was it the pain and cruelty He endured that killed Him, or was it our sin? Which was the most painful to Him?

The Cherry Tree

Blessed be the Lord, who daily loadeth us with benefits, even the God of our salvation. Ps. 68:19.

WE NURTURED IT. We pruned it. We watered and fertilized it. We even threatened to chop it down. But nothing that we did to the cherry tree in our yard helped it to bear any fruit. We secretly envied other cherry trees that had been planted about the same time as our tree. Our cherry tree refused to give us the mouthwatering fruit that we anticipated.

The following year the pleading was repeated. We felt desperate and concluded that the tree was not a fruit-bearing one, and that maybe we should cut it down and plant another one. But we had planted it and cared for it. I just couldn't cut it down. Even though we were disappointed with the tree, we decide to leave it. The birds had fun perching on it and enjoyed hopping from branch to branch.

One spring I noticed blossoms on the orange trees. Mostly out of curiosity, I walked over to the cherry tree—and there they were! It had proudly displayed an adorning of tiny pink blossoms. It was bearing its first fruits. We almost apologized for threatening to cut it down. That summer we feasted on red, juicy cherries, many more than we could manage. As soon as we picked, the next hour there were more cherries to be picked. We distributed them to friends and invited passersby to come and pick as many as they wanted.

Then we started to complain that we had too many cherries. What would we do with so many cherries? *OK, cherry tree, we can't handle all the cherries that you're giving us; you can stop now!* But the cherry tree continued to produce more and more cherries. Some days the ground under the tree looked like a red carpet. *We just had too many cherries!*

My experience with God makes me think of the cherry tree. I plead with God for so many things—and even become impatient with Him for not answering my prayer requests immediately. But when He begins to pour out His blessings, I don't have room enough to receive all that He is willing to give. It's too much. And that reminds me of a popular saying: "Be careful what you ask God for, because He will give it to you."

What is your request? Can you handle it? He will give it to you.

GLORIA GREGORY

No Plan B Needed!

You are the God of miracles and power. Ps. 77:14, Clear Word.

MY FRIEND HAD JUST called to tell me that she didn't want to be a bearer of bad news but had I heard the weather forecast for Sunday? Storms, high wind, and, most likely, severe weather. Not unusual for spring in Oklahoma, but my heart sank. My only daughter (out of four children), Stephanie Jean, was getting married on Sunday evening, and it was to be an outdoor wedding. We had been planning this wonderful event for many months. Stephanie Jean had chosen to have the ceremony at a beautiful country club that overlooked a lake surrounded by beautiful trees, a little touch of heaven on earth.

And now the bad weather could ruin everything. What should we do? We needed a "plan B." Should we rent tents? The wedding coordinator at the golf club advised that the high winds would probably blow them down. We could have it inside the clubhouse where the reception would be held, but it wouldn't be the same.

I told my daughter, "We must pray." And pray we did! I asked all my friends, family, and everyone involved with the wedding (as well as everyone I came in contact with) to please pray! The forecast remained the same for five days straight. When I started to doubt, a small voice would say, "Oh, thee of little faith."

In the middle of Saturday night the storms arrived in full force. Tornados were all around the area, and Stephanie Jean and her bridesmaids were huddled in closets with pillows over their heads. But, to our delight, we awoke Sunday morning to the most beautiful day. The weather was perfect—not a cloud in the sky and no wind.

That evening as I sat among 250 guests, watching my daughter and her wonderful new husband say "I do," I was praising God for answering my prayers. My wedding coordinator said she would like to be on my prayer chain.

God, You are so awesome! Help me not to doubt You, because You truly care. I will always thank You for keeping us from having to use a plan B.

JOYCE BOHANNON CARLILE

Thought: How do you decide when you should just pray in faith, or when you should be a good planner and have a backup plan as well? Is not having a plan B faith or presumption?

The Slightest Breeze

But the Lord was not in the wind. After the wind there was an earthquake, but the Lord was not in the earthquake. After the earthquake came a fire, but the Lord was not in the fire. And after the fire came a gentle whisper. 1 Kings 19:11, 12, NIV.

THE NATIONAL NEWS BROADCAST concluded with a story about a special garden that had been inaugurated in the São Paulo Botanical Gardens. Perhaps the inauguration of a garden does not seem to be a newsworthy story, but this particular garden was planned for a very select group of individuals—those who were visually impaired.

The reporter explained how the plants had been carefully chosen because of their textures and the scents they emit. The pathway throughout the garden was even specially constructed with a slightly elevated concrete border to assist those who can't see so that they can find their way through the garden with greater ease.

But the most touching part of the news story was the joy and appreciation of those who visited the garden. One woman commented that visiting the garden was as though she had regained her sight. Each statement by those who were able to enjoy the beauty of this strategically planned project seemed to shout a message to my heart, a reminder of the many times I take things for granted, especially the wonderful scenes in nature that God has provided for me.

I consider myself to be blessed with the lovely nature that surrounds our home. There are stately pine trees, and almost every afternoon I observe hummingbirds visiting the pink and red hibiscus. Our backyard contains several fruit trees that help me grasp a new insight into how our heavenly Father greatly desires to communicate with His children through nature.

In the middle of that newly inaugurated garden a woman who had lost her sight mentioned how she was pleased to be able to touch the leaves and smell the flowers and plants, concluding, "We can hear the slightest breeze moving among the plants, something that perhaps those who see cannot perceive."

Dear Lord, Thank You for Your fantastic natural gifts that offer us a glimpse of what You are. Today, please help me to observe more closely the nature that surrounds me so that I may gain a greater insight into the wonders of Your love.
BETH VOLLMER CHAGAS

My Passport

For by grace are ye saved through faith; and that not of yourselves: it is the gift of God. Eph. 2:8.

ON MAY 26 I DREW a picture of my passport in my prayer journal. Beside it I wrote, "Urgent Request." My prayer that morning was *Please, Lord, I need to get my passport renewed quickly. It would be a disaster if I missed the Zimbabwe Women's Congress, where I am the guest speaker. The advertisement has gone out. They are counting on me. I need my passport before June 25.*

In the days that followed, the need for a new passport filled my mind. I woke up sweating, imagining that the passport had not arrived in time. I mentally kicked myself for my delay in making the application. My passport actually didn't expire until October, so I thought that I had lots of time. When I ordered my ticket to Zimbabwe, I discovered I'd have to have a passport valid for six months in order to get a visa and then to reenter India, where we lived.

I also was mistaken in thinking that I could simply go to the nearest American consulate and hand over an application and my old passport and get a new one the same day, as I had done before. Now the procedure was much more complicated because of the World Trade Center disaster. The application had to be made in person. Then it would be sent to the United States, and then it would come back to the consulate. We were instructed to allow at least six weeks for this transaction, but I barely had one month. I had a problem.

That passport arrived the very last day I could pick it up before leaving the country! A close call, but God was good. I could now travel with assurance because I had a valid passport.

I have another journey planned, and it is much more important than my trip to beautiful Zimbabwe. My trip of a lifetime will take me through space to my heavenly home. However, to get admittance into that land I need a passport. I have already applied for it. The fee has already been paid on Calvary. The life and death of Jesus is my passport to eternity.

Thank You, Precious Lord and Savior, for dying for my sins and offering me a passport to heaven. I accept Your gift. By faith I have the passport in hand. I live each day with assurance because of the gift that You have given that gives me entrance to Your kingdom. DOROTHY EATON WATTS

Who, Me?

The Lord will fulfill his purpose for me. Ps. 138:8, NIV.

I do not consider myself yet to have taken hold of it. But one thing I do: forgetting what is behind and straining toward what is ahead. Phil 3:13, NIV.

AS I SAT IN THE LOBBY of the Grand Hotel in Cape May, New Jersey, waving goodbye to the last couple, I had to smile to myself. After a whole year of planning, the marriage retreat was over. It had been a success—God had blessed us beyond our expectations. More important, God had used me, something I never thought possible. My mind drifted back over the years to my many failures and many uncompleted tasks. It seemed that I never finished anything I started. After a while, this became a way of life for me. No one expected any more, or less, from me, so it was comfortable just to give up and give in when things got difficult. Little did I know that God had a plan for me, a plan to bring out the best in me. God's Word says that the Lord will perfect all that concerns me (Ps. 138:8).

My friend Laurie had asked me to help her plan a marriage retreat. We had always wanted to give one, and I had always said no, but reluctantly I said yes this time. After all, I could always quit if things got harder than what I thought I could handle. But God was going to break that cycle in me. As the months went by and the deadline came and went, I had learned to pray about everything, to seek God's will, and to trust Him with the biggest to the smallest of matters. We had a very small budget, and we couldn't meet the demands of our expenses—the hotel, speaker, so many costs. So we began to pray and trust God. And God began to open doors.

The deadline for the retreat drew near, and we didn't have one couple signed up. Our plans were looking impossible. But I was hooked—I had come this far trusting in God, and I was not going to give up!

God did bless us with the couples we needed, and the speaker, who was a well-known author who lectured on family and marriages. I've learned that I can do all things through Christ, who strengthens me.

AVIS M. JACKSON

?Thought: Each of us has at least one character flaw that God can help us correct so we can enjoy more success in our life. Have you thought of taking this need to God in prayer?

The Fragrance of Christ

But thanks be to God, who always leads us in triumphal procession in Christ and through us spreads everywhere the fragrance of the knowledge of him. 2 Cor. 2:14, NIV.

I'VE ALWAYS LOVED PERFUME. In fact, it seems that every time I go shopping some unseen force pulls me straight to the perfume aisle. I love looking at the different shapes of containers and find myself compelled to do more then just look.

I glance around; there aren't many people in the aisle, the clerks are busy helping others, and I have lots of time on my hands. *Why not?* I tell myself. *There might be a new fragrance since the last time I was here.* And so the fun begins—one spray per perfume. Soon I have scented polka dots up and down my arms, on the backs of my hands, and on my neck. And if it weren't for all those women who have nothing better to do than stare at someone testing perfume I probably would be able to try every perfume on the shelf, but I carefully put the perfume back in its box and gracefully move to another aisle.

The best thing is that all the fragrances I sprayed on my body go with me, even after I leave the perfume aisle. They are now a part of me, the tiny oils embracing my skin, leaving their scent with me for hours.

What is it that seems to draw us to a fragrance? Is it just the way that we were created?

I like to think of Christ as a "fragrance." Maybe a perfume, all packaged up in a store, waiting to be purchased. He's not in a beautiful glass bottle—actually it's really quite plain. Nothing from the outer appearance seems to be extremely attractive, but I decide to try it anyway. Once I test it, I will never be the same. The perfume permeates the air around me; its gentle droplets touch my skin and seem to melt away, leaving a fragrance that is heavenly.

Even when I set the bottle down and leave, the fragrance stays with me. Others are attracted to me not because of what is visible to the eye, but because of the unseen. There is something addictive about it, and I find myself daily reapplying the perfume to my entire body.

Do you have the "Fragrance of Christ" on your dresser? Do you spray it on yourself daily? Are others attracted to you because of "Christ Fragrance"? Why not start every day with His fragrance surrounding you?

KIM DEWITT

Care for the Other

But ask now the beasts, and they shall teach thee; and the fowls of the air, and they shall tell thee. Job 12:7.

THERE ARE A COUPLE of large trees that grow at the back of the library where I worked for months. They are gifted neither with beautiful flowers nor delicious fruits. There is no fragrance from the flowers, and not much nectar, either. So they don't attract many birds or insects. The rare visitors are the monkeys from the neighboring woods. They jump from branch to branch and swing and play. It's fun to watch them.

But one of the blessings of these trees is that they provide plenty of shade from the hot summer sun for a variety of birds on the branches. They come, rest for a while, and then depart. No birds stay for long. So it was strange when one day I saw a pair of black ravens perching on the branch for quite some time. The more I watched them from the window, the more curious I became. One of the pair was trying to keep the other one happy, or so it looked to me. It was putting its beak through the soft feathers around the neck of the other one, making a strange noise all the while. They were crooning and fluttering their wings. They were there when I went for lunch, and still there when I came back. I watched them with more interest, surprised at the way they were expressing their feelings.

The following day I opened the window, as usual, and what I saw was totally unexpected: a dead raven on the ground beneath the tree. I didn't know the reason for its death (maybe sickness or wounds) but one thing I did know: the other raven knew it was sick and tried to cheer it up, and did all that it could to keep its peer in good spirits and happiness till the very end.

How much more are we humans, supposedly having more understanding and blessing, expected to care for each other! "Love one another; as I have loved you" (John 13:34) is one of the commandments of our Lord. Are we not obliged to heed that command? I asked God for many things that I might enjoy my life; God said no, and He has His own reasons. I asked Him to help me love others as much as He loves me. God said, "Ah, finally you have the idea." MARGARET TITO

(?) Thought: Jesus seemed to be able to sense when someone was in need, then He reached out to meet that need. How do you suppose we can/should become more like Him?

Reunion

Now about brotherly love we do not need to write to you, for you yourselves have been taught by God to love each other. 1 Thess. 4:9, NIV.

RECENTLY I ATTENDED MY high school reunion. It was great to connect with people I hadn't seen in years. I have other friends I've always stayed in touch with. One of the best things about having a longtime friend is the memories you share. Some of my friends date back to grade school days. Knowing someone for a long time means that you're free to be yourself. You don't have to worry about impressing someone who remembers you falling flat on your rear in gym class!

Sharing memories means that you always have someone to fill in the blanks when you tell a story—except that that person may remember things a little differently than you do. There are other advantages, too. When a friend of mine was upset over the fact that she didn't have any photos of a beloved cat, I remembered that I had once taken a picture of her holding the cat and was able to surprise her with a copy.

Later on, when my elderly dog died, it was the same friend who came up with a funny story that comforted me. She recalled the time she had taken my dog and me on a trip to the mountains to play in the snow. At one point as we drove along on the winding roads, I asked her to stop because we were going to be sick. She did, and my dog and I both threw up. She said that she thought that when I used the word we I was talking like a nurse who'd say, "Now it's time for our bath." She thought it was amazing that we were so in sync that we were actually sick together.

I love my friend, but there's Someone who knows me even better—Jesus Christ. I like to think that going to heaven will be like visiting with a childhood friend. Jesus remembers things about us that we, with our imperfect memories, don't remember about ourselves. We can relax and be ourselves with Him. I have old friends I'm longing to see in heaven, but the friend I most long to connect with is my Savior. What a reunion that will be!

GINA LEE

?Thought: Our text for today talks about brotherly love. How much more special is sisterly love! As the author shows, women do have a special connection. Read 1 Thessalonians 4 in any modern version and think about your friendships. How can they be even better in Christ?

A Journey Through Time

From the fullness of his grace we have all received one blessing after another.
John 1:16, NIV.

WAS IT ONLY A FEW days ago—or weeks, months, and years? The experience has become timeless, as if it had happened at my birth, or my death. When I came to my senses I saw that according to the calendar only a week had passed.

I was faced with a strange curriculum. It was willful, pert, impatient, despondent, small and great, and in spite of all, lovingly and confidently placed in my heart—His personal handwriting.

This hadn't always been the case. How many times had I fought with my God! Many days, piled-up years. But this day it was not as easy. This time I couldn't defer things. My doctor had presented me with the fact, crisply and clearly: "You have breast cancer!"

My Creator and Supporter came closer and closer to me. Deep under my skin my fear lurked. *God, where are You? Can I speak with You? Can You hear me? What should I do?* Had I become dull?

On the first day after this news I had to find my way about, a definition of my whereabouts.

On the second day of the long week my situation became clearer, like a fog that starts clearing away. Only God could save me; His grace determined my life.

On the third day I became calmer. It was as if God had spread His coat over me. Light and warmth surrounded me.

On the fourth day I lay protected on a summer meadow, the butterflies dancing around me, the wings of the dragon-fly sparkling in the daylight, clinging to a narrow blade.

The next day I laid my hands into the great and almighty hands of my loving Father.

On the sixth day I was told that no metastases had been found in my body. I do not yet know how things will turn out. In the meantime, the operation and radiology treatments lie in the past, but what does the future hold for me? For now, God's grace, kindness, and love cover me.

I have never before felt so secure. Whatever will come, I am in God's hands, and His grace will give me everlasting life.   CHRISTEL MEY

Yearning

But may all who seek you rejoice and be glad in you. Ps. 40:16, NIV.

I GREW UP WITH one sister, three years my junior, and we were about as different as any two sisters could be. We didn't look alike—she's a blond and I'm a brunette—nor did we have any interests in common. We were never really close. Even when we both married and started raising our families, the distance was still there, not just emotionally but physically—my husband and I in Africa, Carole and her family in the United Kingdom.

Dad's death brought us closer because Mom went to live with her, and we visited often. But it wasn't until Mom died in 1996 that we really started to draw together. Carole and her husband started taking holidays near to us, and we'd have good times together. When we visited the UK we'd make the trip to Wales and spend time together. We talked regularly on the phone. Over time we got to know each other. We've grown very close. With our parents dead, we only have each other, and I cherish her and her friendship so much. I'm always so relaxed when she's around, and it's such a joy to visit together. I love being in her company, and I find myself, from time to time, just longing to be with her. What a pity it didn't all happen sooner!

A few days ago I talked to someone about my family and described my current relationship with my sister. When I told him that I actually yearn to see her, my eyes filled with tears.

Later that day I was reliving the conversation while taking a shower. As I got to the bit about yearning to be in her company I was brought up sharply with a very distinct thought. I could just imagine God listening in on my conversation with myself and interrupting me with this question: "Do you yearn to be in My company as much as you yearn to be in the company of your sister? Do your eyes fill with tears at the mere thought of being with Me, talking to Me and hearing My voice?' Actually, no. Serious stuff. I have to ask myself why I feel the separation from my sister more acutely than I feel my need to be in company with God. Maybe I don't know Him well enough to know what I'm missing.

God is calling me into the same intimate relationship with Him as I have with my sister. There are many texts in the Bible asserting that if I seek Him, I will find Him. I think I'll spend some time with Him now.

VALERIE FIDELIA

He Gave the Best

Lord, you have assigned me my portion and my cup; you have made my lot secure. Ps. 16:5, NIV.

AS OUR BANK BALANCE was a bit lower than normal, I thought it necessary to find a temporary job in the summer. I prayed about it and left it in God's able hands. For my part, I phoned some job agencies in the advertising columns; and I waited with hope for weeks.

Even though nothing came up for a while, I never gave up hope. Finally one agency called me for an interview. After the interview I was told that I would be called to let me know when to start work. I went home with joy, praises, and thanks to God.

Still delighted about my success, I was met by my daughter. "The agency where you had an interview called," she told me.

"What did they want?"

"They said they were sorry but the position had been filled."

How could that be? What about the assurance they had given me? I was very disturbed; but as I sat there in disappointment a little voice told me, "He is the Lord; let him do what is good in his eyes" (1 Sam. 3.18, NIV), even though I only had 10 weeks left for work. I kept waiting with hope till God gave me a better job through a friend. That job had better conditions and more money than I had anticipated. Truly, God is good!

The Lord knows what is good for His children, and He has apportioned each person's blessings which He gives at the right time. We just have to wait patiently for Him, as it says in Habakkuk 2:3: "Though it linger, wait for it; it will certainly come and will not delay" (NIV).

Some of us can't wait. After asking God for help, we still rush and do things our own way. Most of us often mess up things or get into more problems and learn the hard way before we try to come back to God with our disappointments. Let's try to wait and hope in the Lord, for those who hope in the Lord will renew their strength.

Please, Father, bless me with the patience that will help me to hope in You and wait on You, as did the people of old—Job, Noah, and Hannah. Help me to realize that You have assigned me my portion and my cup; and You have made my lot secure. MABEL KWEI

Sparrows

Are not two sparrows sold for a penny? Yet not one of them will fall to the ground apart from the will of your Father. . . . So don't be afraid; you are worth more than many sparrows. Matt. 10:29-31, NIV.

IN OUR GARDEN IS a nesting box made by one of our grand-daughters. It stands on a pole so that we can see it from our windows. Last year sparrows built a nest and raised a family in it.

This year we watched as a couple of sparrows came to inspect it and started to build a nest. One day a couple of starlings were seen swooping down at the sparrows. Then no birds came. A week passed with no sign of the sparrows. I was sure the starlings had frightened off our feathered friends. Another week passed, and still no sparrows. I wondered if the starlings had killed or injured the smaller birds. I prayed, *Lord, I know this is a small thing, but You did say that even the sparrows are in Your care. Please let "our" sparrows come back safely.*

A few days later, to my delight, I saw a sparrow sitting on the nest box, and later we saw the mate flying around. We were sure they were our sparrows!

We watched in fascination as they brought "bedding" for their nest. Then we thought the female must be sitting on the eggs. We assumed the eggs had hatched when Mama and Papa Sparrow were frequently busy bringing something in their beaks to the nest. Then how happy we were to see—and hear—at least two noisy little birds in the opening of the nest box and watch the parents very involved in feeding them. Soon the young ones left the nest, and now adolescent sparrows sat and cried for food on the branches of nearby bushes.

A few weeks later I stood at the window again. "Oh, come look!" I called. "It looks like Mama and Papa are rearing another family!"

Sure enough, the whole process was repeated as they raised another batch of chicks. And we enjoyed watching the whole process of feeding and rearing once again.

I thanked God for this evidence of His care of even the sparrows. And I found comfort that He would care for me, no matter what troubles come my way.

RUTH LENNOX

The Pond

Wash away all my iniquity and cleanse me from my sin. Ps. 51:2, NIV.

LAST YEAR WE WERE transferred to a new district just north of Atlanta, Georgia. We purchased a house on two and a half wooded acres of land in a subdivision on a mountain. The house has a sun room and a large deck overlooking a koi pond in a garden setting at the edge of the woods. We were excited about our new home. The house had been vacant for more than a year, and the pond had not received any attention.

The pond has two sections, a smaller section higher up, with a waterfall emptying into the larger pond below. Both sections were filled with so many rotting leaves and debris that you could see only small pools of water on top. Hundreds of frogs called it home. They made their music every evening and would quickly disappear under the leaves when they saw us or our dog approaching.

I would go outdoors with my dog and longingly look at the pond, eagerly anticipating the day we could clean it out and restore it to its beauty and function. We talked about it for months, but never found the time to clean it.

This summer three of our sons and their families came to visit us. It was such fun to be surrounded by family, laughter, and young children! I relished every moment!

One morning two of our sons decided to clean the pond with shovels and rakes. When my husband returned from an errand and saw the progress, he became enthusiastic and began helping them. They worked all day until they finally finished cleaning and got the pump running again. We filled the pond with water and got some water plants and fish.

Many times as I sit on our bench enjoying the sound of the water falling over the rocks I'm reminded of the transforming power of God. How often, because of our busy schedules and routines, we put off coming to God so that He can clean out our spiritual ponds. I'm so thankful that He is patient with us and waits for us to come, to be cleansed, and to be filled with His Holy Spirit, and made beautiful again.   CELIA MEJIA CRUZ

(?) Thought: For an interesting exercise, list the ways that God cleans up your spiritual pond. Then thank Him and enjoy the beauty!

Ride in the Chariot

See, the Lord is coming with fire, and his chariots are like a whirlwind; he will bring down his anger with fury, and his rebuke with flames of fire. Isa. 66:15, NIV.

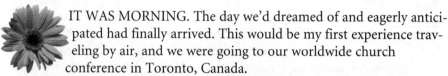

IT WAS MORNING. The day we'd dreamed of and eagerly antici-pated had finally arrived. This would be my first experience trav-eling by air, and we were going to our worldwide church conference in Toronto, Canada.

We checked in and waited with bated breath for the boarding call. Finally it came, and after the usual maneuvers, the plane took off on its four-hour flight. I was a bag of nerves. Although I had a window seat, I was too scared to look outside, so I kept the blinds down until I had adjusted to all the movements and sounds on the plane. When I regained my compo-sure, I eventually raised the blinds and stared outside. The sight was such a beauty, one I could never have imagined! Here I was in the sky, looking down at clouds and space. The scene was awe-inspiring!

As I viewed God's marvelous creation I reflected on the return of our Savior Jesus Christ, the One who will come in the clouds of glory, riding in His chariot. "Every eye will see Him" (Rev 1:7, NIV), and those who are watching and waiting for Him will be caught up to meet Him in the air (1 Thess. 4:17). There, with God the Father, Jesus His Son, the Holy Spirit, and the heavenly hosts, we will listen attentively as the mysteries of earth are explained.

Booking and check-in time is now. Announcements of this eternal flight have been made. "No one knows about that day or hour" (Mark 13:32, NIV, and Matt. 24:36, NIV), but it's almost time.

A church conference session is an exciting and inspiring event, and I'm happy that I have attended one. However, no church convocation can com-pare with this rendezvous in the sky. Are we anticipating Christ's return?

Let's be prepared as we wait for that flight, riding in a chariot over clouds, through space to our heavenly mansions. Jesus Himself will be our pilot. Our journey will take a week, and we'll celebrate and praise our Redeemer and King along the way as we travel to glory land. All our fears will be over, and we will live forever!

Lord, help us prepare for this chariot ride in the morning.

BULA ROSE HAUGHTON THOMPSON

The Petunia

The Lord will guide you continually . . . and you will be like a well-watered garden. Isa. 58:11, TLB.

I WAS RUNNING LATE, as usual. My daughters, Lillian, age 7, and Cassandra, age 2, were preparing to spend the summer with my parents in Florida. Although this was an annual occurrence, somehow it had sneaked up on me, and now I had too much to do. In the middle of the frantic searching, washing, mending, and packing, I was notified that my New York driver's license was about to expire. As I read, my mind made a mental note to write and mail a check. But the final sentence read, "A vision test is mandatory upon renewal." Now what was I going to do? I couldn't just write a check, as I hadn't had a vision test in almost two years. Now with time as short as it was, I would have to find the time. The next day my girlfriend Margarita and I, with the girls in tow, arrived at the Department of Motor Vehicles.

We got off to a late start, and it was already hazy, hot, and humid, so we decided to walk in the shade to enter the building. Halfway up the ramp, I saw it—a pure-white petunia growing in a small crack in the cement walkway. I stopped short and showed my daughters this beautiful flower. I asked, "Lillian, does this flower belong here?"

She replied, "No, Mom; it should be in a garden."

I replied, "Really? Do all flowers grow in gardens?" When she agreed that all flowers do not grow in gardens but would probably be better off there, I said, "You know, you are probably right. It would be better for the flower if it were in a safe place with other flowers. It would be watered when the others were watered and have a larger place to grow. But does this flower look beautiful to you? If it were in the garden with the other flowers, we would not have seen it. It would not have made us stop and talk about it, especially when we were pressed for time. After all, although flowers are pretty in a garden, we expect to see them there. We don't expect to see one in the middle of the walkway!"

All day I thought about that flower and about how God plants each of us in a different place. Some places are well watered and in a place where the growing is easy. In other places life can be a challenge and we have to struggle to exist, much less bloom. Thankfully, God continues to water us and shade us in His love as we grow more into His likeness each day. I pray that we can all be a well-watered, fragrant blossom for Christ, no matter where we are planted!

TAMARA MARQUEZ DE SMITH

Fistfight With a Dust Ruffle

So let's agree to use all our energy in getting along with each other. Help others with encouraging words; don't drag them down by finding fault. Rom. 14:19, Message.

WE'RE MAKING THE BED, my husband and I. It's a big, heavy mattress, hard to tug and coerce. And today I'm unwrapping my latest bargain, a shrink-wrapped bed ensemble. I'm good at bargains. And bedmaking? My specialty. It's what I do.

And so on this bright summer morning we're standing six paces apart. Well, it seems so anyway, like master duelists going for the competency award. That is, I am. He, on the other hand, has never given the art of bed-making much thought. Until now.

On the other side of the bed he's bent double, face red and contorted, a corner of the mattress propped on his knee. He's muttering deprecations. To whom, I'm not sure. Surely not to me. The mutters and peeps are ominous. No self-respecting dust ruffle should dare to challenge his domestic skills. He's stuffing, poking, and now jamming sheets, blanket, and yes, the dust ruffle—up—up and under the mattress. He lets go, straightens up, surveys the wad, and erupts.

My side is smooth and neat. I suppress a chortle at his ineptitude and unholy huff. In my most righteous tone I say, "No need to get into a fistfight with the dust ruffle."

The little episode hangs in the air like a cloud of pesky mosquitoes. My spiritual "aha" is still a few days away. Sometimes God just lets things simmer a while until the stew is right.

Summer means serious lawn mowing around our house. So I'm doing the weekly requirement of powering around on the lawn tractor. Now, I've never given lawn mowing much thought. A job to be done, no great skill needed, right? Rounding a corner toward the patio, where my husband happens to be standing, I think I have more lawn than mower and sail by, neatly taking a corner of the cedar deck with me.

The motor roar cancels out his exclamation, but I bet it isn't the doxology. Suddenly it seems wise to head out and mow a far corner of the back field. The solitude gives me a chance to reflect on how I've treated his minor infractions and what I deserve. But for the rest of the day, with much more mercy and grace than I had offered him, he didn't say a word. — Marilyn Joyce Applegate

What's in Your Hand?

And the Lord said unto him [Moses], What is that in thine hand? And he said, A rod. Ex. 4:2.

MOST OF US ARE FAMILIAR with the story of God calling Moses to lead the children of Israel out of Egypt. Of all the questions that God asks Moses in Exodus 3 and 4, I believe the most significant is the one found in our text for today: "What is that in thine hand?"

Everywhere I travel I meet women who tell me they don't know what to do for God. They can think of many talented women whom God has used, but can find nothing in themselves that God can use. Some of these women secretly wish they could be like their more "talented" sisters. Others are glad that they seemingly have no talents—then God cannot expect too much of them.

My reply to them has been to tell them the story of Moses by the burning bush. When God asked Moses to be the deliverer of His people, Moses had a list of excuses. In Exodus 4:1 Moses tells of the possible unbelief of the elders and leaders when he would approach them. But Moses is really talking about his lack of belief in himself. When he looked at his life, he could see nothing that God could use.

God has given us all at least one talent (Matt. 25:14-30). Today God asks us the same question he asked Moses: "What is that in thine hand?" What God-given talent do you possess on which you have placed little or no value? Look again. God sees a woman of worth, and He's waiting for you to surrender your "rod" into His care so that He can change it—and you—into something great for Him.

God looked at Moses' rod and saw potential. He saw what Moses did not see. God saw a rod with the ability to become a snake, but only if given into God's divine care. What does God see when He looks at your life? No, He doesn't see our mistakes, our weaknesses, our inabilities. He sees only potential. He sees what we could become if we surrender ourselves into His divine care.

God calls each of us to minister to others, and He has given us all we need. Just give it to Him and watch with awe and wonder as He uses your life to bring praise and glory to His name.   HEATHER-DAWN SMALL

(?) Thought: So what is in your hand? And what are you going to do with it?

Rooted and Grounded

A sower went forth to sow; . . . some seeds fell . . . where they had not much earth: . . . and because they had no root, they withered away. Matt. 13:3-6.

THE WIND WAS FIERCE and often changed directions, which we were afraid was bad news for the corn in our garden. It had happened a few years earlier as well, so we knew what to expect. When we checked, we found that about a third of the corn lay flattened on the ground. We'd been told that sunshine would pull the stalks up, but it hadn't happened. My husband set to work straightening them up, but the roots were near the surface of the ground, so in spite of his efforts some corn was lost.

Winter brought a heavy, wet snowstorm one night. In the morning I looked out and thought I was seeing the weeping cherry tree, and then realized it was in the wrong place! No, the cherry tree hadn't moved—it was our tall, beautiful weeping willow that had been uprooted by the combination of wind, snow, and wet ground. Unlike the corn, there was no way to try to save it. Its roots were not deep enough to withstand the storm.

This summer some of our corn again fell when the strong winds blew. We considered not planting corn next year until we mentioned our frustration to a friend, who told us what to do. Next year we'll try it. We'll dig a trench several inches deep, plant the corn, and cover it as usual. As it grows, we'll gradually fill in the trench, burying the roots deeper in the soil, which should make the stalks strong enough to resist any but the most violent winds.

I began checking in our gardening books to see what they recommend, and do you know what? I found the same advice our friend had given us! It was there all the time, but we hadn't read it, causing us to waste hours of work and lose part of our corn crop because of the shallow roots.

As I think about the lesson we learned about gardening, I realize that I too can have shallow roots if I fail to read and follow the instructions in the Book that tells me how to be safe from the fierce winds Satan sends my way. Unlike the willow tree and the corn, if we are rooted and grounded in truth we can stand in the storms of life and bring forth fruit for the Master Gardener to claim as His own.   MARY JANE GRAVES

The Bird Who Came for Help

Remember that God never loses sight of you. Look at the sparrows and see how little they're valued, and yet not one of them dies without God noticing it. Matt. 10:29, Clear Word.

ONE OF MY FAVORITE camping spots is at a seaside town on the coast of York Peninsular. I enjoy fishing, and one day, while watching the people on the jetty toss their lines, my attention was drawn to a cormorant swimming strangely around the bay. It appeared to be lopsided and had problems swimming straight. It eventually came closer, and I could see that it had somehow entangled itself in fishing line and was surely doomed.

I watched as it awkwardly swam away again far out into the bay, but something inside of me wanted to free the poor creature. I knew the possibility of this was highly unlikely, as the water was deep, the banks rocky, and the bird wild. I began thinking of the song "God sees the little sparrow fall," and found myself uttering a silent prayer that this bird would come to where I could help it.

To my utter amazement, it started to swim back around the bay and headed for the boat ramp. My heart raced as I walked ever so slowly to where it sat bobbing at the side of the ramp. Then quickly bending over, I grabbed it and could see that the line had pulled one of its wings tightly to its side.

My friend, seeing the situation, grabbed some tools from the car, and together we freed the bird from its burden. Strangely, it didn't resist much as we carefully cut the line away; however, it wasted no time in swimming away to freedom once again.

God cares for His creatures, and He certainly answered my simple prayer. This bird yielded to the temptation on a hook and would never have had freedom again if it had not been rescued.

We too get caught in the hooks of sin and need to be rescued. I'm glad Christ came to be my loving and caring Savior, aren't you?

LYN WELK-SANDY

(?) Thought: Sin comes in many guises, just as someone fishing uses different types of bait. What can you do today to ensure that what you latch on to is not harmful?

Sharing His Glory
on the Fourth of July

In my distress I called to the Lord; I cried to my God for help. From His temple He heard my voice. Ps.18:6, NIV.

In the day of my trouble I will call to you, for you will answer me. Ps. 86:7, NIV.

I LOVE CELEBRATING the Fourth of July—Independence Day in the United States. I love patriotic music, hearing bands and orchestras play it, choirs sing it, bells ring it, and singing and playing it myself.

For several years I've been music director for a little country Methodist church. For Sunday, July 4, I chose several appropriate musical selections. The choir had been practicing for weeks, but we still had some work to do before we were ready. We met early that Sunday morning to finish working on our music. One piece, "The Battle Hymn of the Republic," had been practiced, but we still hadn't gotten it right.

Concerned that it wasn't coming together, I went to my car and called Melanie, a friend from my church family, and asked her to pray with me. I explained how we had been practicing, and everything had gone well except for four measures in "The Battle Hymn of the Republic." Nearly every time we got to those four measures, we just didn't get the timing right, and it sounded terrible. We were all frustrated and didn't know what to do.

After praying together, I felt peace in my heart. I went back into the church where I met my pianist. He told me that all through Sunday school class he kept asking God to help him. All at once he had a solution! He would play something different, a few runs or broken chords, during those four measures. He said, "God put this idea into my mind." We were so thankful for this immediate answer to our prayers in the distress we were experiencing.

The choir began to sing "Mine eyes have seen the glory of the coming of the Lord . . ." The music was sung well, and the changed accompaniment fit perfectly. It was a gift from God. He cared that the song declare His glory and not detract from it! As we continued singing, "Glory! glory! Hallelujah! His truth is marching on," I humbly realized how God cared about our choir, and we were able to share His glory without the distraction.

Thank You, heavenly Father, for hearing the voices of Your children in their time of trouble, and for giving a clear solution that glorified Your name.

SHARON FOLLETT

Modern Miracles

If ye abide in me, and my words abide in you, ye shall ask what ye will, and it shall be done unto you. John 15:7.

MY GRANDMOTHER SUFFERED serious headaches, so she always kept pain relief medication on the little table by her bed. Her headaches began early in the morning and lasted the entire day. Unfortunately, my mother inherited these same headaches, and I was also afflicted with the same condition. The problem was hereditary, but I didn't know it. I have taken medications my entire life to relieve my headaches. I went to many physicians, but it was of no use. One of these doctors even told me that only a miracle of God could cure me.

On one occasion we went to California and visited a beautiful park. I realized that a headache was beginning and became concerned because I hadn't remembered to bring my medication with me. I began to look in my purse, hoping against hope there might be some medication forgotten in a corner of my purse. Fortunately, I found a capsule that I had brought from Brazil. I took it at the first water fountain that I found and was able to enjoy the rest of the trip in the company of my friends.

Because I had taken medication for so many years, I began to feel that my stomach and my heart were beginning to indicate the excess of caffeine. I felt that I had to stop the medications or I would end up being stopped by them. But how?

One day I began to feel worse than I ever had before. My head felt as if it was going to explode; my arms felt as though they were being stuck all over with needles. In despair, I fell to my knees on the floor and prayed. With faith in Jesus I implored that, if it were His will, He would perform a miracle for me, right there. Aware that the Lord had preformed so many miracles in the past, I began to mention all of them out loud as they came to my mind. I cried before God! To my surprise and joy, I was heard, and my prayer was answered. Two years have gone by, and I no longer have the terrible headaches. Praise the Lord!

We have to ask in faith, trusting, without doubt, to be answered. We must give Him our burden and rest in His promises.   HERCILIA M. COELHO

More Than a Speedy Answer

When I am in trouble, don't turn away. . . . Answer me quickly when I call!
Ps. 102:2, TEV.

THE SUN SHONE BEHIND me as I drove along that beautiful July 6 morning. I was on my way to be with my older sister, who lived alone. She was under the weather, and I promised to be with her that day. Suddenly my car started jerking left to right. I kept repeating, "Lord, help me!" while trying to steady it, when forcefully it veered to the right. "Lord, save me!" I cried aloud in my distress. The car struck the guardrail and flipped over, and the engine stopped. I tried to open the passenger door—it didn't budge. I moved to the driver's side, rolled down the window, and climbed out over the guardrail. A man arrived first. "Please take me to the hospital," I begged. Soon two men joined him. They said they were calling for an ambulance.

Shortly a woman appeared, waving her hand. "Let me take care of her," she told the men. "Come," she said, leading me to her car. "Can't let you bleed while waiting for an ambulance." After getting in, she draped a clean towel over my forehead. "I happened to bring this," she said. "Hope it'll help stop the bleeding."

The emergency room team took over my care, but my angel stayed on. Only after the senior state trooper arrived did she start to leave. Again, I thanked her profusely, repeating she was my heaven-sent angel, and asked her to write her name on a piece of paper.

"Julie Johnston," she wrote. Under her name she wrote her telephone number. "Call me when you're feeling better," she said. On the phone the next day, she asked, "Did you know that only a little tree kept you from hurtling down the precipice?" Of course, I didn't. Later I called the tow truck office to ask what I owed. The tow truck operator said they had to use two wreckers to pull my car out. It was "a total—beyond repair."

My heart overflowed with praises to God for His deliverance and all the human kindness I received that day. I wrote a letter to the editor of the local paper, applauding the exceptionally caring people in our area, mentioning the names of all the angels who dispensed tender loving care, concluding it with "The angel of the Lord encampeth round them that fear him, and delivereth them" (Ps. 34:7). CONSUELO RODA JACKSON

Six Hundred for Starters

He who offers a sacrifice of thanksgiving honors Me; And to him who orders his way aright I shall show the salvation of God. Ps. 50:23, NASB.

WHILE THE ORTHOPEDIST examined my feet prior to casting plaster molds for my new arch supports, I described and indicated exactly where my pain was. "I worked with my husband for many years as a drywall applicator, and considering that this body has been used as a human forklift, I think that it's in pretty good shape. I did what I did, without regrets, to help make a living and a home for my precious family," I explained. Having done some construction himself, the doctor could appreciate what I was saying.

Then, looking at my shoes, he inquired if they were 4 or 5 years old. "No, they're only a year old," I replied. Pointing to the worn-out soles, he informed me that I definitely needed new footwear. "Your shoes look as if you've put 600 miles on them," he said.

I smiled and shared with this caring young man about my special-needs son, Sonny. He is 16 years old, but he'll always require the supervision you'd give a 3-year-old. For the past several years we've walked together along the roadways in our community, picking up cans and bottles for recycling. I told the doctor how very proud I am of my son. *Besides,* I thought, *I wear my dress shoes to church on the weekends. Six hundred miles? It's no wonder my feet sometimes hurt!*

Personally, I feel that Sonny and I are unofficially active members of DeBolt's Volunteer Beautification Committee. We could easily have walked 600 miles this past year, climbing in and out of the ditches.

Vehicles slow down to pass us, and our friends and neighbors take the time to smile and wave. I sincerely appreciate this gesture of love and understanding. No matter where we are or what we are doing, people are always watching Sonny and me. I continually pray that we be used for God's glory.

Dear Jesus, please give others the desire to establish a wholesome and pleasant home environment for their family, a home where Your Spirit resides, a place of unconditional love and acceptance, a place where hearts are filled with thanksgiving. O Jesus, You've gone to prepare such a home for us, a place we call heaven. Thank You. DEBORAH SANDERS

Your Passport, Please!

Not every one that saith unto me, Lord, Lord, shall enter into the kingdom of heaven; but he that doeth the will of my Father which is in heaven. Matt. 7:21.

FOR MORE THAN EIGHT months my husband, Richard, and I worked, saved, planned, and talked about nothing other than the Caribbean cruise we would take during the summer vacation of the following year.

The long-looked-for day finally arrived. After saying goodbye to our daughter and her family in Miami, we took a cab to the pier where the ship was docked. While we waited our turn in the immigration lines, I heard the official say something to the passenger in front of me that caused my heart to feel as if it literally moved from its place: "May I have your passport, please?" I turned to my husband. "Honey, we have a problem."

When we bought our tickets for the cruise, the travel agent had given us a brochure with a description of all the exotic places we would visit, as well as all the necessary requirements for the trip. I had read and reread the brochure many times, but somehow I had failed to notice that a current passport was one of the requirements. Therefore, our passports were at home. Two very disappointed tourists did not board the *Sensation* for the Caribbean cruise.

As I watched passengers who had fulfilled the requirements happily take their places on the ship, tears filled my eyes. I envisioned another trip that I have been preparing for throughout my entire life. I prayed, *Dear Lord, please help me to have my passport ready for an entrance into Your kingdom.*

The promoters of the Caribbean tours were cooperative with us and made arrangements for us to go at a later date, even though it caused us more expense and inconvenience. In our trip to heaven, however, there will be no later date, no second chance. I must do the will of God now in order to enter into heaven.

When the divine mandate is pronounced, my eternal destiny will be forever sealed: "He that is unjust, let him be unjust still" (Rev. 22:11). God grant that we will be found with our passport stamped as holy and righteous, ready to enter into that kingdom of glory.

OLGA I. CORBIN DE LINDO

No More Worries

Casting all your care upon Him, for He cares for you. 1 Peter 5:7, NKJV.

I WAS 16, ENERGETIC, and eager to please. As a counselor in training at a Christian camp, I was ready to handle any situation that came my way—or so I thought. I soon became frustrated and overwhelmed with the problems and disagreements of the 10-year-old girls in my charge. I began to think that maybe I wasn't equipped to handle it all.

Nearing the end of my rope, I decided to turn to the counselor in charge of the cabin for help. I poured out all the problems that I'd been trying to hide from her, from homesickness to hurt feelings, and almost immediately every situation was easily resolved. "Lori," she said, "it's my job to handle the problems—not yours. If you let me know when issues arise, I will take care of them."

I was not at all comforted by these words. Rather, I begin to feel self-doubt. Did the counselor think that I was unable to take care of the campers? How could she expect me just to turn over even the smallest of problems? Despite my misgivings, I decided to follow her instructions, and to my surprise, the once-stressful job became carefree and enjoyable. I found relief in saying, "The counselor will handle this," or "We'll talk to the counselor about it." I wondered why I hadn't gone to her in the first place. Work was so much easier with someone to guide me and handle those things that were too big for me.

So it is in our relationship with Christ. We women address issues ranging from children to money to personal needs and desires, and we soon discover that we don't have all the answers. Rather than talking to Jesus first, we exhaust ourselves through every avenue imaginable, usually creating more problems than we solve. Then, when the stress of handling these difficulties overwhelms us, we cry out to God for help, sometimes even blaming Him for not rescuing us sooner. In response to our distress our Savior gently says to us, "I love you, and I will handle all of your problems; but first you must give them to Me." Once we surrender to Him we wonder, as I did many years ago, why we had waited so long. When we finally let go and let God, we know the peace that comes from having no more worries.

LORIAN LENISE BRIDGEFORTH

Miracle Lunch

I have been young, and now am old; yet have I not seen the righteous forsaken, nor his seed begging bread. Ps. 37:25.

THE MUCH-AWAITED JULY vacation had arrived. We could hardly wait to change our routine of work and college classes. During vacation we were going to do a different type of work—selling books on health and religious topics. The income from the book sales was going to support us during the following semester and would allow us to pay the tuition for the theology degree that my husband was working on.

One Sunday we were invited to go to a neighboring city and have a delicious lunch prepared by friends. Before leaving, my husband decided to deliver some books that he'd sold. He was late getting back, and we missed the bus. And now? We needed to eat lunch.

We had only a little money—not enough for the two of us to eat lunch. Even so, we decided to go to a restaurant that sold food by the kilo. My husband said that we should be content to eat just a little, because we had just a little money!

We put the food on our plates and went to weigh it. When my husband placed his plate on the electronic scales, the weight's reading began to flicker rapidly, and then went off.

"You won! You won!" shouted the clerk. "Didn't you read the notice?"

"No," my husband responded.

The girl explained that whoever had exactly 500 grams of food on their plate would have the right to one kilo (2.2 pounds) of food without paying!

That day we felt God's presence because once more we were certain that God never abandons His children. He had reserved that prize for us at a time when we really needed it. Perhaps today you're not in need of food or money. Perhaps it's not clothing you need; but whatever it may be, you can be certain that Jesus knows and is ready to give you what you really need. Just take your request to Him.

My prayer is that you may always find refuge in Jesus each day, always having more certainty that He can resolve all of your problems.

WALKÍRIA VESPA S. S. MOREIRA

? Thought: Have you seen the righteous forsaken? What does it mean to be forsaken?

Under His Wings

He that dwelleth in the secret place of the most High shall abide under the shadow of the Almighty. Ps. 91:1.

AFTER MANY YEARS our class decided to hold a reunion at the boarding school so we could remember the good times and see each other again. It was touching to meet old classmates, to offer a strong embrace, and to tell each other how our lives had changed. Within this group were some who practiced religion, and others who didn't profess any faith. Délia belonged to the latter group. She always smiled as she saw our "innocence" because we believe in God. But her life had been very different from ours. Her marriage had fallen apart, and it was very difficult for her to bring up two children alone.

While we ate together and looked at the rest of the group she asked me to tell what each one did and what their life was like. For Délia, the success of the majority of her classmates who were "deceived with their beliefs" was revealing. What was the secret that she couldn't see?

"Donald is a physician, Roberto is a professor, Susy is the wife of the current boarding school director . . ." And so I continued, mentioning each one. I told her, "They've placed their lives in service to God, and they don't wander away from Him."

"So you believe that if I had followed the Christian guidance given at the religious boarding school on how to follow God, I would be as blessed as all of you?"

"Well," I answered, "if your motives had been correct, I'm certain this would be true." Délia remained silent and began to look at other things.

"Sincerely," said Délia before we left, "I think that you are right. All of you always lived hand in hand with God, and you entrusted your lives to His care. However, I don't believe that the same would have happened to me."

I tried to encourage her and give her proof of God's care, asking her to give Him her life. She gave me a small smile and thanked me.

I haven't had news from Délia, except for some cards that she sends me at Christmas, telling me that everything remains the same. However, I do know of the great blessings and the care God has for His children who shelter themselves under His wings.

Dear Father, do not allow anything to separate me from You, and may I always be thankful.   LENI URÍA DE ZAMORANO

Steven

I tell you the truth, unless you change and become like little children, you will never enter the kingdom of heaven. Therefore, whoever humbles himself like this child is the greatest in the kingdom of heaven. Matt. 18:3, 4, NIV.

HE WAS A 7-YEAR-OLD returning home after spending a few weeks with grandparents and cousins. After the last hugs and kisses, they saw him safely on the plane. Now he was alone.

He had the window seat, and I had the middle seat. As the plane taxied down the runway, I heard sniffles and saw tears, so I became a parent to Steven. He was a cute little blond-haired lad. As he was an only child, I recalled our son's flight alone at a younger age.

I offered Steven a tissue, a pillow, and my lap. "Why the tears?"

"Because I don't want to go, and I was watching them put luggage on the plane, but I didn't see mine. All my Beanie Babies except these three are in my luggage."

I convinced him that his luggage was indeed on the plane, and that his mother would be happy to see him again. The tears dried. We became friends. He began singing a tune he had learned in Maryland: "Before the beginning, before there was time . . . God loves me, God loves you." He sang all three verses about 10 times, and each time he got to the phrase "God loves you" he would point to me. I taught him "Deep and wide; there's a fountain flowing deep and wide" using hand motions.

He loved birds and showed me his book with pictures of those he had seen. The closer we got to Denver the more eager Steven became about seeing his mother and his dog. He looked forward to seeing friends also. Before we landed I asked him to sing his song. He did—three more times. I asked him to tell his mom that she had a well-mannered, intelligent son. He responded by saying that he would tell her about me. My last words to Steven were "Never forget your song, and as long as you live, remember that God really does love you."

Because of time constraints with our connecting flight, I didn't meet his mother. I never saw him again. Even today I wonder how he's doing.

The day is coming when our loved ones will meet us in the air with Jesus, never to part again. Meet me in heaven where we'll sing songs together. Let's meet at the Savior's side. Pray that we all will be there.

MARIE H. SEARD

The Broom Handle

Every good gift and every perfect gift is from above. James 1:17.

"COULD YOU PLEASE CLEAN the parking lot, Charlotte? There are a lot of cigarette butts in the corner areas that need to be picked up," my boss at the post office asked. I had seen them, but often time gets away from me when doing other jobs.

I hurried outside with the big push broom and started sweeping eagerly—maybe too eagerly, as the broom handle broke in half. I apologized, and told the boss that I would buy a new broom handle. He said, "Don't worry about it; we'll get one later."

Three or four months later, no broom handle had been purchased yet, and every time I saw the broom in the supply closet I felt a pang of guilt. Then one day, coming home from the third post office that I cleaned, I thought I saw a broom handle lying beside the road. *Was that a broom handle?* I thought as I went by. Then I thought that maybe I'd been thinking about the broom handle too much lately. I talked to God quickly in my hurry to pick the kids up from school: "God, if that is a broom handle that would fit my broom in Gentry, please let it stay there for two more days until I return to this town again to clean."

On Friday I returned once again to clean the third post office. There it was, the same stick lying beside the road. Again I was in a hurry, so I said I would stop and check on it when I returned. Then I went a different route to get my kids and forgot about the handle.

I thought about the little talk I'd had with God and felt guilty that I hadn't taken the time to stop. On Tuesday, six days after I'd first seen it, I saw the handle again as we came home. I started slowing, then turned around in the closest driveway.

"What'cha doing, Mama?" my kids asked.

"I saw something alongside the road. I need to check on it." And there was a dirty, brown, wooden handle, one that would fit my broom exactly. I was thrilled!

I told the children how God had saved this handle just for me. I had the chance to get it earlier, but in my haste, I had avoided stopping. However, I felt I needed to do my part for God—He had held up His part of the deal. I told my coworkers how God had given us the broom handle, and they agreed with me! All good gifts do come from above. CHARLOTTE ROBINSON

Ocean Enough for Everyone!

To him who is thirsty I will give to drink without cost from the spring of the water of life. Rev. 21:6, NIV.

I LIKE TO WALK along the sandy beach, receiving reinvigorating energy from the salt water and the hot rays of the sun. I observe the attitudes of people, and see that everyone could make use of this natural source of relaxation.

The ocean makes no distinction among people. It is not concerned with who you are—little or big, ugly or beautiful, rich or poor, young or old. Before its immensity everyone is the same and will receive its benefits in their own special way. Each one takes advantage of the ocean as they desire. Some are brave and swim without fear, facing the noisy waves. Others play in the shallow water, allowing their imagination to run free as they build castles in the sand. There are also the somewhat fearful, who just observe from afar. Some sleep, protected by their colorful beach umbrellas, listening to the sweet murmur of the water at a distance. However, the ocean is there, waiting for each one who desires to receive abundantly of what it has to offer.

Jesus, too, always has His arms open wide, waiting for us. What we receive from Him depends on us, on our availability.

Through daily communion with Him we can grow deeply in our spiritual life. We can receive a shower, or only drops of blessings—it depends on us and the time we dedicate to our personal, daily relationship with Jesus. If we stand still, just observing others, we will have superficial spirituality.

One assurance we can have: He is always waiting for us, day and night, regardless of who we are. He is ready to give us countless blessings, because His love is greater than the ocean. EDIT FONSECA

(?)Thought: The Psalms contain many promises and assurances from our God regarding the sea. Here are a few texts that you will enjoy looking up—especially if you're at the seashore (or wish you were): Psalms 33:7; 72:8; 93:4; 95:5, 6; 96:11-13; 98:7; 104:25-27; 107:23 and following; 139:9 and following.

The Perfect Dress

But my God shall supply all of your need according to his riches in glory by Christ Jesus. Phil. 4:19.

WHAT WAS I GOING to do? The first of my four daughters was to be married in the summer. The previous year had been one of the most traumatic years of my life. My husband had unexpectedly left me for another woman. He met me in the driveway, took 10 minutes to tell me he was leaving, and then moved into his girlfriend's house that same night. A very bitter divorce followed. To make matters worse, I was now being sued for a large amount of money with no hope of insurance covering my portion of the suit. Not knowing where it would all stop, I was afraid to spend any money. My daughter was even paying for a large portion of her own wedding. I needed a dress to for the wedding, but I knew I couldn't afford the typical mother-of-the-bride dress.

I spoke with Tami, my close friend and spiritual mentor, about this. She asked me how much I thought I could afford. I told her I could spend $50, but knew that wouldn't buy much of a dress. Tami answered, "You will find a dress for that amount, because we are going to pray that you do."

We both prayed about it for several weeks. The wedding was now only a week and a half away. I knew I couldn't put this purchase off any longer. So my mother and I went shopping together, after Tami and I prayed once more. My mother suggested we go into an upscale store at the mall "just to look." She knew my circumstances—I couldn't believe she was even suggesting such a thing, but I had no energy to argue.

There weren't many size 2 dresses, so it didn't take long to look though the rack. Then—there it was. A beautiful dress! The perfect dress for the mother of the bride! Before I turned the price tag over I sent up a silent prayer. Holding my breath, I finally mustered the courage to look. To my amazement, this dress, originally $250, was marked way down. I walked out of the store with this perfect dress for $50, including tax.

"Before they call, I will answer; and while they are yet speaking, I will hear" (Isa. 65:24).

SUSAN BERRIDGE

(?)Thought: Have you ever thanked God for the blessing of finding a bargain—whether you prayed for it or not?

Is My Name Written There?

A good name is rather to be chosen than great riches. Prov. 22:1.

SEVERAL YEARS AGO I conducted a Vacation Bible School in my home for the children in my neighborhood. Among those who attended were my neighbor's two children: David, who was 8, and Barbara, who was 7.

One evening when David and his sister arrived he noticed a beautiful family Bible on a table. Curiosity caused him to open the sacred book and turn the pages in a random manner. Unexpectedly he saw the name David in the book of Psalms. Suddenly David exclaimed in surprise to his little sister, "Baba! Baba! My name is in the Bible!"

The lad continued to turn the pages of the Bible very cautiously, as though he was looking for treasures. Lo, and behold! He saw so many Davids he could not contain himself. With a smile on his face and intensity in his voice, he said, "Look Baba! Baba, look! My name is all over the Bible! I must be very important, Baba!"

As far as David knew, the Bible had been personalized just for him. And guess what? I didn't tell him that he wasn't that David, because I didn't want to change his strong childish belief. Probably David went home that evening feeling very important because his name was in the Bible.

Mary Ann Kidder, author of a familiar hymn, wants us to think about this vital question: "Is my name written there, on the page white and fair? In the book of Thy kingdom, is my name written there?"

Heavenly Father, help us each day to do Thy will, so that our names will be written in the book of Thy kingdom. CECELIA LEWIS

(?) Thought: Many people have Bible names. Is yours a Bible name? Even if your name isn't found in the Bible, you can personalize texts with your name. An excellent text to begin with is Jeremiah 29:11: "'For I know the plans I have for [supply your name],' declares the Lord, 'plans to prosper [your name]'" (NIV). Try it with other texts, as well—because you are in the Bible!

Satan Lost Another Battle!

Let us therefore come boldly to the throne of grace, that we may obtain mercy and find grace to help in time of need. Heb. 4:16, NKJV.

IT WAS GLADSTONE CAMP meeting time in Oregon, and for any of you who have ever attended such a camp meeting, you will understand why we were excited to be going. Not only would my husband and I be receiving the blessing of the meetings, but a woman who had been attending our Bible study group was going to go to all the evening meetings with us and planned to spend the entire day there on Sabbath.

The opening meeting on Tuesday evening was just wonderful! We were all filled with joy as we left that evening and were already looking forward to the next night. But Satan had other plans.

Around 3:30 the next morning my husband woke me up and asked if I would take him to the emergency room. He'd been in excruciating pain since midnight but hated to wake me, thinking it would go away. We hurried to the hospital where, after four hours, it was declared that he had a big kidney stone, and there was nothing they could do but give him pain relievers and send him home. The doctor suggested I get him to a urologist as soon as possible. Fortunately, I was able to do so that very day. He was given a prescription to break down the stone and told to rest until it passed.

In the meantime I had decided I'd take our friend to the meeting that evening, even though my husband couldn't attend, but we got a message that she was extremely ill with the stomach flu. Somehow we sensed that Satan did not want us to attend the meeting that night—or any of the remaining meetings. We prayed for God's deliverance from pain and illness that we might not miss any more of the spiritual feast He had planned for us.

That very evening my husband began passing the broken-down stone, and by morning he was feeling wonderful. Our friend sent an e-mail that she was feeling so much better that she was planning to go with us that evening. We didn't miss any more meetings, and we just praise God that He answered our prayers for healing so quickly. And our friend made a commitment to follow the Lord that weekend! Once again, Satan was defeated.

ANNA MAY RADKE WATERS

Sarah's Journey

Commit thy way unto the Lord; trust also in him; and he shall bring it to pass. Ps. 37:5.

WHILE A TYPIST FOR the Los Angeles *Times* in 1974, I did many stories about the Alaska pipeline and the plans to extend it to Seattle, Washington. In those stories I saw an opportunity for the strong, ambitious, and imaginative person who was also single and unencumbered.

I was excited about these visions and yearned to exploit them, but I didn't have the freedom to do so. I was the sole support of both my son, who has a disability, and my mother, who is in poor health.

God saw me set aside these dreams because I wasn't inclined to abandon my love—or responsibilities—to my family. He stood beside me and guided me in the battle I waged on my family's behalf. He also saw to it I had a rich, fulfilling life, personally and spiritually. And He watched as my dreams of adventure in the Northwest dimmed, then disappeared—totally forgotten.

Twenty-eight years passed. My mother laid down her earthly burdens. My son grew up and claimed his independence. Soon all my youthful responsibilities and bills were discharged.

Inexplicably, my life was then thrown into chaos by a myriad of bewildering events that totally changed my life. Suddenly I was retired early, and I was called to help a friend in Washington State for six months. When that task was completed, I established my own home on an island in Puget Sound.

Now, more than 30 years after dreaming of adventure in the Northwest, I find myself in a very definite adventure in the State of Washington. Oh, it isn't the experience of excitement and riches I dreamed of as a young woman. This, too, was Sarah's adventure in the Bible. I, in my senior years, have journeyed to a land other than the one I was raised in, where I must rely on God for everything. The excitement I deal with is the exhilaration of learning how personal, specific, and individual is God's caring and love for me. Every day something new and wonderful about Him is revealed to me.

God saw my yearning for adventures in the Northwest. When I was finally free of myself-imposed responsibilities, He brought me to the state of which I had so long ago dreamed. He has given me an exciting, wonderful adventure of faith. He can be trusted. Darlenejoan McKibbin Rhine

Chicks

Hide me in the shadow of your wings. Ps. 17:8, NIV.

IT WAS SUMMER, AND unusually stormy and rather cold. We'd had a lot of rain. There were puddles all over the place, so we had to skirt the holes in the village roads carefully. In the middle of this Ukrainian village was a village common with luscious green grass and many shady trees. Cows, sheep, ducks, geese, and hens spent their days there. Even a donkey had been tied to a post.

I was fascinated by a hen that had covered her chicks with her wings. Maybe it was too cold for them, and she wanted to keep them warm. You could see only their legs from under the hen's wings. Then one of the chicks, more curious than the rest, poked its head out. Still protected by the hen's wing, it could observe what was happening in the world outside.

Unfortunately, I didn't have my camera with me, and every time we passed the village common I looked for this hen and chicks. But there was no second chance to take the picture.

Even without a photo I can still see this chick, and it reminds me so much of how I often act. I too want to enjoy God's protection and let Him, as it were, cover me with His wings. But I find it hard to stay completely covered by His protecting wings—I want to be able to see the world in which I live. So I poke out my head between His breast and wing so I can look out.

God protects even such chicks as I. He is not a harsh father who says, "If you don't trust Me completely you'd better take care of yourself alone," and thrusts me from His warm lap.

On the other hand, I could be spared a lot of worries if I could just relax in the dark warmth of His wings. God doesn't want us to worry unnecessarily. He wants to care for us. I want to learn to trust in Him completely. Will you join me today in trusting in His protection, even if we can't see where He is leading us?   HANNELE OTTSCHOFSKI

? Thought: There are many texts that speak of God's hiding us under His wings. Look up and enjoy as many as you can. In Ruth 2:12 Boaz tells Ruth, "May the Lord repay you for what you have done. May you be richly rewarded by the Lord, the God of Israel under whose wings you have come to take refuge" (NIV).

Precious Little Stones

For you are a people holy to the Lord your God. The Lord your God has chosen you. . . . The Lord did not set his affection on you and choose you because you were more numerous than other peoples, for you were the fewest of all peoples. But it was because the Lord loved you. Deut. 7:6-8, NIV.

OUR FAMILY WAS ENJOYING a mini-vacation in the country. On a certain Saturday afternoon I decided to go for a walk by myself. From the top of a high mountain I wanted to observe the earth that embraced the vast sea. The view was so inviting that I couldn't resist climbing down the steep incline that separated me from the ocean. When I reached the shoreline, I touched the hot sand that from my mountain vantage point I could see had been marked by the footprints of the unknown people who had walked along the beach. Sifting through that fine sand, I discovered little shells, periwinkles, and other "archaeological finds," which from up above had looked like nothing but sand. All of those objects had been fashioned by the hand of the Creator of the heavens and the sea. I couldn't resist taking these precious pieces with me to decorate my house.

From above, in infinite space, what is this world to the eyes of a mighty God and Creator? Only a tiny grain of sand, compared to all of the galaxies, the sun, and the moon that surround us. However, the entire heavens were emptied of the most precious Being that it had, the beloved Son of God, the only One willing to come down to the abyss that separated us, because He wanted to save you and me!

He did all of this because He simply could not resist loving us until death, death on the cross, to restore in us the value that had been lost. How can we repay this great love? There is no way to do this, but we can always give thanks to God because He loved us and chose us to be little precious stones in the crown of Christ and in the home that He went to prepare for us for all eternity.

"This day I call heaven and earth as witnesses against you that I have set before you life and death. . . . Now choose life, so that . . . you may love the Lord your God, listen to his voice, and hold fast to him. For the Lord is your life, and he will give you many years in the land" (Deut. 30:19, 20, NIV).

Dear Lord, thank You for Your wondrous creation and for caring enough to come down from on high to our small world and give Your life to save us.

IRINA JEANETE PIRES ALMADA

The Long Road Home

And the woman conceived, and bare a son: and when she saw him that he was a goodly child, she hid him three months. And when she could no longer hide him, she took for him an ark of bulrushes, and daubed it with slime and with pitch, and put the child therein; and she laid it in the flags by the river's brink. Ex. 2:2, 3.

THE MORNING SUN HANGS as low as her spirit. The summer's haze, like a blanket, already covers the freshness of the morning. Today she will go home alone. What has to be done has to be done in a hurry. She nurses her son for the last time, places him in a tiny ark, and lays it by the river's bank. Then she turns and walks away, away from her most precious possession. The sound of her rapid footsteps pounds the dusty path like the drum of her heartbeat.

She hesitates—pressed to turn back, reluctant to move forward; stuck in the quicksand of her own thoughts. The road home is a long one for her. She reflects on the baby's birth, how she hid him for three months, and how she nursed him to keep him from crying. After three months she could no longer hide him, for he had taken on a life of his own.

Come with me to the river's edge. We are not standing here by accident. We have come for a purpose, for each of us carries something close to our breast that we have been nursing far too long. And we can't hide it anymore. For some of us it may be our children crying out for independence. For others it may be corrosive relationships that have eaten our heartstrings. For some it may be pain, grief, hurt, bitterness, habits, or abuse that you have managed to hide and nurse in some secret place where no one can see or hear. For some it may be spiritual emptiness that you've nursed to keep it from crying out to be filled. You can't hide it any longer.

Christ is our ark of safety. He's calling you and whatever you've been nursing to come to the river of life and by faith place your burdens in His hands. Then turn and walk away. The road home will be a long one, but you'll not journey alone.   AMY SMITH MAPP

(?) Thought: Another promise to claim as you lay your burden down is Matthew 11:28-30; you will want to memorize this. The wonderful thing is that you can leave your burden behind, but you never have to walk alone.

The Alphabet Prayer

You alone know the hearts of all. 1 Kings 8:39, NIV.

SQUEAKY CLEAN AND SMELLING of rose petals, Melissa snuggled down under the comforter in the big guest room bed, where she was visiting while her parents were away for the weekend. It had been a wonderful day, from feeding dried bread to the migrating ducks at the estuary to finishing her first crochet lesson. How we had laughed and joked about the little crochet hook having a mind of its own. "You say your good-night prayer first," Melissa suggested, her words accompanied by a huge yawn.

I began with "Dear heavenly Parent," expressing thanks for a number of things, including the fact that Melissa and I had three whole days to spend with each other. I ended my prayer with "Amen."

Silence. I opened one eye. Melissa was lying quietly in bed, hugging her teddy bear tightly. More silence. Believing that prayer is a very personal and private activity, I didn't want to prompt her. Just about the time I had decided to let my prayer serve for both of us, her sweet voice broke the stillness.

"A, b, c, d, e, f, g . . ." The sound of her voice went on clearly and deliberately through the entire alphabet and ended with "Thank You, Amen."

What in the wide, wide world was that all about? I wondered. Aloud I asked, "Was that a new type of prayer, Melissa? Prayer without words?"

"Not really," she replied serenely. "But my heart is so full that I didn't know what words to say." Pause. Sometimes I find it difficult to be patient and wait for the answer in her own time. "Mom says God always knows what's in my heart," Melissa added, after what seemed an interminable wait. I nodded encouragingly. "So," she continued, "I just gave God the letters—to make the right words. The words my heart can't say," she added with a little smile. And with that she closed her eyes and was asleep in seconds.

I kissed her on both cheeks, turned on the night-light, and left the room. Sitting by the fire, I pondered my lesson for the day, provided by the insight of my young teacher, Melissa. I'm not always right. Older isn't always wiser. God knows the words my heart can't say. ARLENE TAYLOR

The Lord Will Go Before You

A man's heart deviseth his way: but the Lord directeth his steps. Prov. 16:9.

A BIT GRUDGINGLY I was giving my neighbor a ride as my mother and I set off for a weekend trip to my cousin's wedding in New York City. He said it would be on the way, but Mr. Jefferies didn't seem sure of himself as he directed me off the highway and farther into the city. One hour and at least 35 miles later, we dropped him at his destination. I was polite but quite irritated that he took us so far out of the way.

Once we arrived we went about taking care of things for the wedding, scheduled for midday on Sunday. Although I had lived in New York for 18 years, I got lost getting to the church. I must have added at least 10 miles to the trip. I was furious with myself, but we finally arrived at the church in time for the ceremony.

After the wedding reception, I easily found my way to where we were staying. When we were about 10 minutes away, I stopped at a red light. When the light turned green, I moved, but the car slowed down, then stopped, and wouldn't restart. We were in the middle of a crowded intersection. Cars blew their horns behind me, and a group of young men sitting on a stoop, listening to music, took notice. One with long dreadlocks approached to help. Not being able to start the car, he began pushing it to the side of the road with the help of his friend.

Suddenly I heard someone call my name. It was a friend who also lived in Maryland and who also was originally from New York City. He was visiting his family, and it turned out that the young man helping with my car was his brother. His mother's next-door neighbor of many years was their trusted mechanic.

I realized that because of all the extra driving I had done (which had frustrated me) I ended up at the best place for my car to stop. I left the car there overnight, and my friend's mechanic was able to repair it the next morning. I realized that the Lord had been with me all along.

Father God, forgive me when I allow anger to overcome me when things don't go the way I'd like them to. Help me trust that You are with me through all situations, and that You have a plan for things to turn out for my good. Thank You for Your continued guidance. MIRLÈNE ANDRÉ

You Are the Light of the World

You are the light of the world. A city on a hill cannot be hidden. Matt. 5:14, NIV.

IT HAD BEEN A VERY stressful week, and I could hardly wait for the weekend. A plumber, scheduled to come to my apartment to clean the hot water tank in the bathroom, was supposed to come during my lunch break. So I got home by 12:00. As soon as the young man arrived I apologized for not being there three days before, when he was originally scheduled to come. With all the stress I was going through, I had completely forgotten about the appointment. He told me that he wasn't too happy about my absence but added, "Well, we are here to forgive." Suddenly, I had the impression that this man was open to the leading of the Holy Spirit and that I should give him a religious book.

After he finished his work we talked a little bit, and all of a sudden he started preaching at me. I was astonished, as I hadn't expected this of him. I didn't agree with everything he said, but I let him speak, expressing my opinion about what he was telling me. Finally, I gave him the book, which he promised to read.

I don't know what has happened to his life since then, but a seed has been planted. This is only one example of the various opportunities we have to tell somebody of our Christian faith every day, whether it's through a book or through our words and deeds—even when under stress! But are we really taking advantage of all the possibilities we so often encounter?

In the movie *Schindler's List,* there's a scene in which Oskar Schindler, a wealthy young man who lived during World War II and invested a lot of his money to employ Jews in his Eastern European companies to save them from the Holocaust, is standing before many Jews who are expressing their thankfulness and gratitude for what he has done for them. Little by little he becomes aware that he could have invested even more of his wealth and thereby saved more Jews. He is overwhelmed, and as in a fit cries out, "I could have saved more!"

Dear Lord, I don't want to repeat Mr. Schindler's words of despair when I one day stand before You. Please help me today to recognize any opportunity to witness about Your love, and please make me sensitive to Your leading in this regard.

DANIELA WEICHHOLD

(?) Thought: Read Matthew 9:37 and 38 and meditate on what it might mean to you personally.

He Hears Us

*I love the Lord, because he hath heard my voice and my supplications.
Because he hath inclined his ear unto me, therefore will I call upon him as
long as I live. Ps. 116:1, 2.*

I WOKE UP TO A beautiful summer morning and dressed quickly. I was late for meeting my ride to the university. I waited at the customary meeting place for a while, but soon it became apparent that the person who was to give me a ride that day had already gone by. Praying silently, I asked Jesus to send me another ride, or I'd be late for class and run the risk of not passing the semester because my number of possible absences had already reached the limit. An error had occurred in counting the number of absences, and the professor refused to correct them. So I had to adapt to the situation—and I could not miss any more classes.

I began to walk as fast as I could to where it would be easier to find someone passing by. I prayed anxiously that Jesus would provide a way for me to reach the university in time for the beginning of class. With a knot in my stomach and a feeling of despair, I looked back, hoping a car would be coming in my direction. But no car appeared. I prayed again: *Lord, You know about my situation. Please help me!*

My legs could no longer walk so fast. *I cannot withstand any more, Lord; I have reached my limit!*

Then, to my surprise, I heard the sound of a car. I looked back to check, and saw that God had sent not one but two cars. I thanked Him in silence, feeling His marvelous hand helping me. I understood in a very practical way that God leaves to our care that which we are capable of doing, and what is not possible for us to do He provides and acts in our favor. At the time of necessity, He operates in favor of His children.

Thank You, dear Jesus, for allowing us to know that when our strength goes the Lord is at our side to give us His hand and to lift us up and help us. Thank You for hearing our prayers. ADRIANA AZEVEDO DA COSTA

(?) **Thought:** If God does not answer our prayer the way we ask, does it mean He hasn't heard us?

Be Ready at All Times

Therefore you also be ready, for the Son of Man is coming at an hour you do not expect. Matt. 24:44, NKJV.

OUR FRIENDS THE HALLS come every year to visit us. Pioneers of our church work in Laos, they now live in Oregon. They make a trip to California yearly, and they never fail to stop to see us. We always enjoy these visits and reminisce about the time when we were all working together in Laos.

They called us recently to say they would like to stop and see us again, if we were going to be home. We told our friends that we would certainly meet them at our home and would make every effort to spend some time with them. On this particular day we began doing the laundry, then left to try to finish our errands. We had also decided to introduce a young man to a couple who were receiving Bible studies, because we were planning to move soon.

In the middle of our visit with the elderly couple, we got a phone call from the Halls saying they were already at our place. But in between the visit and going home we decided to stop at the supermarket to pick up some fruit, lettuce, and tomatoes for making some sandwiches for our supper.

When we finally arrived home, our daughter was there with her two girls, her mother-in-law, and another couple. I welcomed all of them to our humble home, only to be greeted by the unfolded clothes on the sofa in the family room and the stack of mail I had been sorting on the kitchen table. How could I have been so careless? I cringed while I hurriedly gathered up the clothes and the pile of letters and junk mail and began to prepare the evening meal. What a lesson!

Someday our Savior will appear in the clouds to take home the redeemed. What a glorious day that will be! But will I be ready, or will I be running here and there, unprepared? Oh, may that never happen! Dear God, please help me to be ready to meet You then.   OFELIA A. PANGAN

Thought: Read Matthew 24:43 and 44. What are the differences between Ofelia's experience and the experience of the homeowner in Matthew? What are the implications for you?

The Wrong Cat

Wherefore, beloved, seeing that ye look for such things, be diligent. 2 Peter 3:14.

IT WAS THURSDAY. My church's Pathfinder group was selling cookie dough as a fund-raiser so that we could go to the international camporee at Oshkosh, Wisconsin, and the order had just arrived. There were 27 boxes to unload, each weighing 25 pounds. After we transferred all the boxes to another truck, it was time for another move. Luke, one of the Pathfinder counselors, had offered his freezers for storage. He had to go back to work, however; so he left us a house key so that we could finish organizing and putting the cookie dough away. Just before leaving, he warned us, "Watch out for the cat. He's very skittish."

As I worked I kept a watchful eye on Simon, the cat. After about an hour the backbreaking work was done. All the boxes that wouldn't fit in Luke's freezers were transferred into our car. I was so thankful that the job was over that I didn't even check to see where Simon was.

We didn't return to Luke's house until later that evening when people came to pick up their orders. After everyone had gone, my sister, Briana, and I started looking for Simon. Then panic struck! Simon wasn't there. We searched everywhere, but had no luck. Disheartened, we were driving down the road when suddenly Briana yelled, "There he is!" Immediately my mom made a U-turn and stopped the car. Briana and I ran out and tried to catch the cat. He was having none of it. We prayed, but still he wouldn't come to us.

Finally Luke's sister, Heather, showed up and tried to help us catch Simon. But no matter how softly she cooed and called, the cat wouldn't come near her. At last we gave up and sadly made our way home.

When I saw Heather the next day, I asked if she and Luke had ever caught Simon. Chuckling softly, she replied, "It was the wrong cat. Simon was in the house all along." God had answered our prayer when the wrong cat wouldn't come to us—and I didn't even know it.

Dear Jesus, I thank You for answering my prayer in Your way.

TAKARA GREENE

?Thought: When was the last time God saved you from making a mistake? Have you thanked Him?

Heavy Bags

Carry each other's burdens, and in this way you will fulfill the law of Christ. Gal. 6:2, NIV.

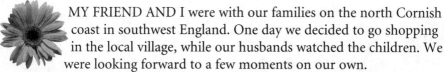 MY FRIEND AND I were with our families on the north Cornish coast in southwest England. One day we decided to go shopping in the local village, while our husbands watched the children. We were looking forward to a few moments on our own.

We had planned only to wander around the craft galleries and have our special treat of black currant tea, with Devonshire scones, Cornish clotted cream, and raspberry jam. But as we passed the tiny grocery store, we each remembered some things we needed for supper. Then we thought about dinner for the next day. We needed juice for picnics, and tins of soup—and by the time we had done our shopping, our bags were quite heavy.

We tried calling our husbands on our cell phones, but we had forgotten that we were in a place where there aren't any phone signals. It had only been a short walk down to the village, but now we were returning up the steep hill. The sun was hot, and our bags felt very heavy. We had both begun complaining about our groceries when suddenly we had an idea. Why not swap bags so that we were carrying each other's shopping? It was a slightly crazy idea, because the bags were about the same weight. But it worked! It somehow felt much better to carry my friend's groceries than it had been to carry my own.

Since then I've thought about how much happier life tends to be when we share burdens. I hate cleaning windows, but it feels better if I do it with my husband. Tidying their room is not high on my children's list of fun things to do, but if I help them the job seems to go much faster, the children learn "tidy" skills, and we chat, tell funny stories, and listen to lively music. Working together makes the job feel much more manageable.

Is there someone close to you who needs some burden sharing today? Is there a task you have to do that you could invite someone to share with you? Perhaps you could help clean your friend's home, and then she could come and help clean yours, and the load would be lighter.

But the best news of all is that even when I think I am all alone and struggling, Jesus shares my burdens. And in the same way I used to help my mom carry the bags home from market, I think He carries most of the weight.

KAREN HOLFORD

Thief in the Night

He who watches over you will not slumber. . . . The Lord will keep you from all harm—he will watch over your life. Ps. 121:3-7, NIV.

IT WAS ONE OF THOSE hot summer days when nothing relieves the scorching heat. The fan only circulates the stifling air, food loses its temptation, and children whine and get irritated easily. Everyone at home was feeling on edge.

Just before supper we all went out to make the beds. In those days, during the summer, we often slept outside. The beds were soon made, the mosquito nets tied securely, and a bucket of water placed nearby in case we needed to sprinkle the nets to help cool down.

By evening a gentle breeze was blowing, and the sheets were cool to lie down on. In no time the children were asleep. My husband was away, so it took me longer to drift off to sleep. I hadn't been asleep long when my mosquito net was pulled from under me. It had suddenly become very windy, and it wasn't long before all the nets were flying like sails. Then I heard peals of thunder. I jumped from my bed, shouting, "Children, get up; it's going to rain!" All of them were like logs. I had to pull them up, one by one. Eventually we got all the bedding inside.

The next thing I knew, I heard a loud banging on the door. I opened my eyes and saw that it was morning. I unlocked the door, and there stood the watchman and two of the Hapur School staff members. One of them said, "Mrs. Christo, you were sleeping away while a thief was trying to get into your house through this door!"

The watchman had seen a man fiddling with our door. When the thief heard the footsteps, he ran quickly over to one of the rope beds near the door and pretended to be asleep. The watchman, a neighbor, and some others tied him to a papaya tree. We learned that he had just been released from prison the day before. The prospective thief was sent back into jail.

God sent the storm so that we would get inside, where it was safer. We had heard of instances of thieves assaulting the people sleeping outside, demanding the keys, and then robbing the house. God was looking after His own, and I thank Him for watching over us that night. God always keeps His promises.

BIROL CHARLOTTE CHRISTO

Angels in Human Form

For he shall give his angels charge over thee, to keep thee in all thy ways. Ps. 91:11.

WE WERE ON THE WAY to our new work location, 800 miles (1,300 kilometers) away from our previous work. We had already traveled almost 600 miles (1,000 kilometers) when the car hit a large hole in the asphalt, and we lost control. The car fell into a deep ravine and flipped three times before landing in a small river. I fell with my head in the water. I heard my husband shout for help, but at that location on the highway, who would come to help us? It seemed that the last moments of my life were passing.

My husband tells how within a few minutes God sent four angels in human form, workers who cut the weeds along the highway. With their sharp sickles they cut the seat belts that held us in the car seats, and pulled us out. They improvised a stretcher to take me up to the road. A pickup was already waiting for us, and they placed me in it to take me to a hospital.

What a pity I didn't have the opportunity to see the faces of these human angels! But I would have another opportunity to meet angels—the doctors and nurses. After four hours of losing blood and with an open fracture of the femur, I needed surgery. But the anesthesiologist said he wouldn't risk this because my body would not support the surgery.

At this moment I felt my strength ending. Certainly my time to leave this earth had arrived. I silently offered a prayer: *Lord, I place myself in Your hands!* A nurse took me by the hand and whispered Psalm 23 very slowly in my ear. The next morning one of the physicians entered my room. He took my hand and asked me to squeeze his hand. With a deep sigh he told me, "I thought that you would not make it through the night!"

If I could have spoken I would have told him, "I am alive because this marvelous God once again placed angels in human form in my path to help me and save my life!"

God is wonderful! We just need to give ourselves to Him daily without reserve, and He will work wonders in our life.

Thank You, Lord, for Your immense care in keeping us from dangers, and for the angels who minister in our favor!　　　ARLETE FRANCISCO LEÃO

Songs in the Night

"For I know the plans I have for you," declares the Lord, "plans to prosper you and not to harm you, plans to give you hope and a future." Jer. 29:11, NIV.

I'VE ALWAYS LOVED BEING with a group of young people in worship, singing around a campfire with a guitar as our only accompaniment. No songbooks. Which sometimes leads to the occasional ad lib. I loved the rousing songs from "Do Lord" and "When the Roll Is Called Up Yonder" to the sweet songs of "El Shaddai" and "Side by Side." I also enjoyed listening to the wind whistle through the trees as the speaker tried to lead us into a closer walk with God. Somehow, in the valley or on a mountaintop, it has always been easier for me to truly open my heart and soul to worship God. There's just something about worshiping God in nature that makes Him seem closer and more real. That is what touches me the most.

Several times I remember stopping at the edge of a clearing, or looking out over a lake and staring at the stars. Most times I would revel in the wonder that the God who made all loved me and accepted my worship. There were a few times (usually when something was bothering me) that I wondered if I was really all that important, or if I was just some animated speck of cosmic dust.

One day when I was really frustrated the Lord showed me that I was important. He helped me to realize that He, the God of all creation, had taken time to give me my basic character, special gifts, and the potential to do great things for Him.

I remember very clearly a time in junior high when I really seriously wished I had been born about a hundred years earlier. I so loved stories of the wild West and life on the frontier that I wanted to be there. Now, however, I know that God knew all along exactly when He wanted me and why. You see, I finally learned that God has always had a plan, and He even has backup plans for those times I foil so many of His.

Now, whenever I stand on the side of a mountain or on a lakeshore, gazing up at the stars with a campfire burning behind me, I remember that I am where—and when—God wants me to be. I also remember that of all the things that God created with just the sound of His voice, He created our bodies with His hands and our souls with His heart. JULI BLOOD

Power in the Blood

These are they who have come out of the great tribulation; they have washed
their robes and made them white in the blood of the Lamb. Rev. 7:14, NIV.

IT WAS ONLY ONE flight of stairs, and I was carrying only one carry-on suitcase, but when I reached the top I knew I was about to pass out. I also knew why I was faint: a loss of blood. After a few minutes my mind began to clear, and I felt I could walk on. I needed to get to the gate to catch my plane home to see the doctor and find out what was going on.

The Charles de Gaulle Airport in Paris is huge, and as I walked on I became incredibly thirsty. I stopped at a kiosk. "How much is the water?" The price seemed exorbitant, but I gladly shelled out the euros. Later I learned I was so thirsty because I was going into shock.

I'd been on an overnight flight to Africa when I suddenly began to hemorrhage massive amounts of blood. When the plane landed in Johannesburg I aborted my itinerary and sought medical help. After checking out treatment alternatives, I decided to try to get home. But that was not easy, and by the time I reached Paris more than 35 hours had passed, and my colon was still bleeding. I kept drinking water and orange juice and felt sure God would help me make it home.

And I did. But I had to be hospitalized in the intensive-care unit and receive seven units of blood before I could walk around again. And oh, I appreciated blood so much more!

Scripture tells us that without blood there can be no life, no eternal life, or hope. That lesson begins in the Garden of Eden with the killing of the first lamb. The shedding of blood continued on through Abel and Abraham and on to the sanctuary service in the wilderness. The services in the sanctuary and the temples built by Solomon and Herod were places of blood. Blood everywhere! Millions of goats, sheep, bulls, and doves sacrificed until the system culminated in the death of Jesus. He shed His blood for me. For you.

Oh, I am so thankful for blood—the blood others gave for my transfusions and, more important, for Jesus' blood! It is by the blood of the Lamb that we can overcome and survive each day (Rev. 12:11, NIV); and it is by the blood of the Lamb that our sins are forgiven and we are redeemed (Rev. 5:9). "There is pow'r, pow'r, wonder-working pow'r in the precious blood of the Lamb."

ARDIS DICK STENBAKKEN

Treasure

For where your treasure is, there your heart will be also. Luke 12:34, NIV.

MY HOLIDAY WAS A wonderful experience, but that experience was badly shattered when I came home to discover that my home had been broken into and almost everything taken. I called the police but nothing could be done except to take fingerprints and report what items were stolen.

Days went by; my heart was aching when I thought of all the things I had to buy for the second time. Strangely, not one item had been stolen from my church clothing. I prayed hard for a miracle, but days passed by and nothing happening. Several other houses at Bethel College were also broken into. Then two of the thieves came back onto the campus to sell some items they had stolen, and were caught by the security. I had been taking an afternoon nap when I heard a crowd of students and other people coming to my house with these two men so that they could demonstrate how they got in and where they took the stuff. A few hours later the police arrived. Not all the items were recovered, but we were glad for what was.

A few days earlier I had been walking on the road in a place called Zizamele, and a teenage boy had approached me and asked for my cell phone. When I refused, he threatened to kill me. Two weeks later, when I went to the police station to make a written statement regarding my stolen goods, I passed by the reception and saw a familiar face. I quickly remembered that face and immediately called the police and told them that I'd seen the boy who had taken my cell phone standing in front of the reception. With the policeman beside me, I looked the boy in the eye and said, "You took my cell phone a few weeks back at Zizamele." He was so shocked that he simply admitted it. Even though I didn't get my cell phone back, the satisfaction I got from facing that boy was enough. I only hope that he learned that crime does not pay.

Sometimes as we journey in life we lose things. Some can be replaced; some cannot. But the most important thing to remember is the source of everything in our lives. When we have the Savior, we have everything. Our faith should not be based on material things which are here today and gone tomorrow. When we go on vacation, it is wise to make sure that all the security systems are in place, but the most important thing we can do is to place our lives in the hands of the One who does not sleep or slumber.

DEBORAH MATSHAYA

My Star-filled Sky

And I saw a new heaven and a new earth: for the first heaven and the first earth were passed away. Rev. 21:1.

FROM THE TIME I was young, the sky—and especially the stars—have always enchanted me. I still have stick-on stars on the ceiling of my room that represent shining constellations and planets. I like to look at them as they glow in the dark. Better yet are the real stars I always look at before going to sleep. On those nights when the sky is clear and there are no clouds, there's always a star I like to look at until my eyes close. This star is my "pet star."

In August 2003 I was very happy to learn that the planet Mars would come near Earth and could be seen without the use of a telescope or any other special instrument. It would appear to be like a second moon, but with a reddish tone.

I couldn't wait for this day to come! Then a while before Mars reached its nearest approximation, it began to rain. The rain continued for several days. I didn't want it to rain on this day! But it rained, the sky was dark, and the stars were covered by clouds. When I said my prayers before going to sleep, I insisted (even though the clouds were still covering the stars), "Lord, You know how much I want to see Mars. Please open the clouds and clear the sky. Amen!" My alarm rang at midnight, the best time to observe Mars. I woke up and looked at the sky again. To my amazement, the sky was clear—not even one cloud!

Even though the sky was clear I couldn't see Mars, perhaps because of the position of the building where I live. But I was certain that God had heard my prayer. A few nights later, when the planet was farther away and appeared to be small, I was able to see it from the veranda.

Lord, You created all the planets, stars, galaxies, and everything that exists in this infinite universe! Thank You for filling the sky with stars. Thank You, Lord, for letting me know that one day I can live with You and hear You say the name of my "pet star." This lets me know that You are with me each night, because You know each star by name, just as You know each one of us by Your name. Thank You for allowing me to continue seeing planets and stars until the day that I will be living with You in my new home in heaven!

THAÍS RAINHA DE SOUZA

Come, Run With Me

How beautiful upon the mountains are the feet of him that bringeth good tidings, that publisheth peace. Isa. 52:7.

THE YEAR 2004 WILL always be remembered in Greece as a celebration year, for in August the Olympic Games came home to the country that gave them birth. Though many thought that Greece would never be ready in time, "Olympic fever" spread rapidly, and preparations were completed before the very impressive inauguration ceremony in Athens.

Earlier, in January, announcements appeared asking for volunteers to carry the Olympic torch throughout Greece's major cities and important archaeological sites. This fired my imagination, and hopes of being a torchbearer rose when I saw that there were few age requirements.

I rushed to post the application form, already dreaming of being chosen. But I had to get ready. Rain or shine, in the early morning darkness of winter, I ran three or four times a week. Willingly, I watched my diet.

Weeks passed. When I made it to the short list, I intensified my effort. Then one day came the bitter disappointment of rejection. I had not been chosen.

The Olympic Games have come and gone. For every athlete who received well-deserved recognition there were many others who did not. It is sad, but that's life.

There's a training program for an event far more exciting than running with the Olympic torch and, praise God, all who apply are accepted. There is no age limit, nor are there any time restrictions, though you may sometimes have to train under adverse circumstances or even deny yourself some creature comforts. You must also finish the course if you want to be a winner.

Come, run with me, and we'll carry the torch of the everlasting gospel. We'll hold it joyously today, tomorrow, and every day until we reach that great opening ceremony before which every other celebration fades into insignificance. The music of angel choirs and golden trumpets, light beyond imagination, and sound so intense that it penetrates the ears of every sleeping saint—all these herald Jesus' glorious return.

Our victors' crowns will be far more beautiful than the simple wreath of olive leaves with which Olympic winners are crowned, and we shall have the unspeakable privilege of laying them at Jesus' feet, because they are really His. We are victors only by His grace. REVEL PAPAIOANNOU

Roses and Thorns

A gentle answer turns away wrath, but a harsh word stirs up anger. Prov. 15:1, NIV.

I'VE BEEN WORKING A LOT with roses lately, which is lovely because they are one of my favorite flowers. Invariably, when I work with flowers I am reminded of people. Roses are very beautiful, and there are varieties these days that are bred so that they have no thorns. Their stems are straight and smooth. On the other hand, some have small prickly thorns, while still others have large barbs that tear the hands and inflict sharp pain.

Years ago most flower arrangers owned a little instrument that could be dragged down the stem of a rose and tear off all thorns, leaving the stem smooth and easy to work with. Unfortunately, it was discovered that tearing the thorns off damaged the flower and shortened its life. Nowadays we're advised just to snip the end of the thorn. That way, while the thorn remains, the sharp edge is removed, the flower is undamaged, it can be handled more easily, and its beauty can be enjoyed. Similarly, we were advised to hammer woody stems so that they would take water more easily. Now it's been proved that such treatment was too harsh and the stems were damaged.

Sometimes we meet people who are prickly and hard to work with. We may have children who give us a hard time. The temptation is to try to change them, to "rip away" the parts that we find difficult. Sometimes harsh discipline seems the only way to get some people to listen. The problem is that in the process we may damage their essential core. Instead of making the situation better, we make it worse. Perhaps we should take a lesson from the rose and try to soften the sharp edges while at the same time retaining their unique attributes. Instead of "hammering" them, we should make a smooth, clean cut.

As the wise man advises, using kind words instead of harsh ones will deflect anger, and by using gentle discipline we will invariably bring out the best in people. We are all flowers in God's garden. He has often had to remove thorns from my life, but always it has been done smoothly and with love. So if you meet a "rose" with thorns today, handle gently!

AUDREY BALDERSTONE

His Mysterious Ways

Because you are my help, I sing in the shadow of your wings. Ps. 63:7, NIV.

I HAD NEVER THOUGHT about God having such a refined sense of humor. One simple event made me think about God's sense of humor and kindness toward me. I was studying for a qualification test as a master's degree candidate. My mind was going a mile a minute, considering that I was applying in an area different from my bachelor's degree and that I had no idea how many people were applying for that one vacancy. I desperately wanted to enter that master's program. A few days before, I had gone to the university to get information regarding the selection process. While there I met a girl who was already in the master's program. She gave me several hints about the test, the obligatory preproject, and what the course would be like. Also, she gave me her telephone number and her e-mail address.

Three weeks later I had an idea about the subject that I would approach in my preproject, and I wanted to contact her. Where was the paper on which I'd written her telephone number? To my complete despair, that was the day the cleaning woman had come to do her weekly cleaning in my apartment while I was at work. I imagined her throwing away the little slip of paper with the telephone number on it. I searched for this paper for two days, but I didn't find it.

Feeling that time was running out, one night I prayed, "Lord, You know that I need this piece of paper. Show me where it is." I waited for Him to show me through my memory where the paper with the telephone number was. I thought I remembered where I had left it. I went to look, but it wasn't there. I gave up!

After some time I decided to go to bed. Then I looked at the night stand beside my bed, and there I saw a folded piece of paper on top of my devotional book. I recognized it immediately and smiled as I thought of the creative ways that God has to answer our prayers.

I thought that the cleaning woman could have found the piece of paper and left it in that location. How had I not seen it before? Was it really there before? One thing I know: I felt the kindness of God—as well as His sense of humor—very close to me.   IANI LAUER LEITE

? **Thought:** Do you suppose Iani would have found her paper earlier if she had read her devotional book? What might this teach us?

Love That Grows

May the Lord make your love increase and overflow for each other and for everyone else, just as ours does for you. 1 Thess. 3:12, NIV.

EACH TIME I USE my shampoo I squeeze a little dab on the palm of my hand and work it through my hair. That little dab saturates my whole head, covering it with a foamy lather that cleans every hair. Likewise, a little dab of conditioner makes my hair soft and shiny. With a single press of my finger my mousse swells out of its canister in a volume sufficient to make my hair more manageable. My toothpaste lasts far beyond my expectation. From outward appearances the tube contains only enough toothpaste for one more use, so I squeeze enough out for that time then and three or four more times before the supply is finally completely depleted.

God's love works in a similar manner. It grows in my heart as I continually partake of Bible study, prayer, Christian friends, and authors until my heart is overflowing and I can't help sharing with others. Many times the ones I share with in turn testify of how His love has affected their lives, and unlike my toiletries, which eventually run out, it continues on and on.

Because His love is unconditional, it's available to every human being without exception. Sometimes they need someone like me to make them aware of it. Just as my shampoo cleanses every hair on my head, His love cleanses me from the filth of my unrighteousness. My hair keeps getting dirty, and I have to shampoo it again and again. No matter how many times I slip back into my old sinful ways, dirtying my soul, I can go to Him in repentance and ask for forgiveness, and His love washes me clean again. It is always waiting for me to accept and to share with others.

The shampoo, conditioner, mousse, and toothpaste do no good sitting on the shelf. To experience the desired result, I must put forth the necessary effort to use them. So it is with God's love. It is always available, but I must make a conscious decision to accept it and allow it to cleanse, fashion, and mold me in order for me to reflect His love effectively.

Dear God, Lover of my soul, cleanse me from all unrighteousness, and fill my heart to overflowing with Your love, empowering me to share it with others.

MARIAN M. HART

The Gulls

Be not hasty in thy spirit to be angry: for anger resteth in the bosom of fools.
Eccl. 7:9.

I climbed the little rise overlooking Harrisville Harbor one day to watch the gulls as they frolicked near the parkway below. I could see one of the birds chewing on what appeared to be pieces of fish, apparently tossed from one of the boats moored at the nearby marina. The gull continued to eat, and was soon joined by a second bird, then another, and still another, until within just a few seconds a dozen or more hungry gulls were vying for the three morsels of food lying on the pavement.

A quiet lunch by a lone bird suddenly erupted into a noisy free-for-all by a flock of unruly gulls as they attempted to crash the private party.

What hotheaded little creatures you are! I thought, as it seemed that a certain few were not satisfied with having just their place at the table—they wanted the entire buffet. Screeching full blast, they flew head-on toward the one gull eating nearby.

When they finished with that invasion, they proceeded to their next victim, going through the same noisy ritual, seemingly bent on taking out any bird that got in their way. The loud squawking continued for some time; then I noticed the three spots that had been gull lunch were fading, and no doubt soon would be gone completely. Only then did the gulls decide to call it quits and fly away to some other haunts—some to the top of the high harbor light poles, others to ride the gentle waves of Lake Huron, and the rest to soar with the wind.

I asked myself, *What just happened here?* Then it hit me. I had seen some of myself and other humans in those birds—tempers flaring, pushing, and shoving to get what we wanted. I had to admit it wasn't a pretty sight. When at last the final gull had flown away, all that was left in its wake were three dirty spots on the road.

Lord, help me always to rise above that anger or other behavior that may exist in my life so that Jesus can always shine through.

CLAREEN COLCLESSER

(?) Thought: What do I leave behind after I've displayed my impatience and anger? Is there something I can do so that I don't get to this point of anger? What does Scripture have to say about this?

A Promised Blessing

Fear not, for I am with you; be not dismayed, for I am your God. I will strengthen you, yes, I will help you. I will uphold you with My righteous right hand. Isa. 41:10, NKJV.

WHEN MY DAUGHTER, IRYTTA, was enrolled in a Christian boarding high school, God led her to join the student magabook program, in which students sell religious books and magazines. After being away at school all year, I had wanted her to spend the summer at home, but God reminded me that she is His child first. I wondered how, with her shy personality, she would be able to sell books. I knew God is big enough to protect and help, and I tried to trust my girl to His care, but I missed her so much.

In church one Sabbath I requested special prayer for Irytta, longing to ask for prayer for myself as well. I struggled with fears and loneliness. My request was brushed off. No one seemed interested in my soul's longings. Everyone had their own concerns. The service that day wasn't meeting my needs, so I opened my Bible and sought a message from God. He knew my heart's need, and like the loving God He is, He reached out to meet it.

I "just happened" to open my Bible to Isaiah 44 and read these words: "For I will pour water upon him that is thirsty, and floods upon the dry ground: I will pour my spirit upon thy seed, and my blessing upon thine offspring" (verse 3). Hungrily, I read on. "Fear ye not, neither be afraid: have not I told thee from that time, and have declared it? ye are even my witnesses. Is there a God beside me? yea, there is no God; I know not any" (verse 8). God was caring for my daughter, pouring out His Spirit on her, enabling her to be His witness. Besides that, He would satisfy my thirsty soul, and I could be assured that He is God. Peace poured into my heart as I thanked God for His loving assurances.

During our phone conversations and personal visits on two occasions during the summer, Irytta shared many of her experiences of God's working and blessing. Miracle stories. God sold book after book. At the summer's end she had the top sales for their group. God abundantly fulfilled His promise to me in blessing my girl and keeping her safe. It was not an easy summer for either of us, but we grew in the Lord and, looking back, I see that it was a rich experience. God's promises and prayer are powerful!

BARBARA ANN KAY

Code Blue

Pray one for another, that ye may be healed. James 5:16.

"Code blue, room 373. Code blue, room 373." Those words are terrible to hear, especially if you are the mother of the patient in room 373. Our 6-day-old baby boy was dying. My husband and I had brought him to the emergency room late the night before with symptoms of rapid breathing and a rising fever. After hours of being poked and prodded and tested, he was placed in room 373.

Now I held Baby Elijah as he slowly stopped breathing. This is a mother's worst nightmare. Being a nurse myself, I knew by education and the look on my baby's face that this was very bad. I had no doubt in my mind during those few minutes that we had just lost our baby.

Moments after the code blue call, the staff nurse rushed back into the room and laid our Elijah in his bed. I was at his side, but didn't know whether I should start rescue breathing or let the staff take charge. Seconds later about 15 people barged in, bringing life-saving equipment.

My husband and I were pushed to a corner, where we clung together. I started pleading with God: "O God, help him; please, help him," I wailed. The nursing staff then placed us near a phone so that we could make phone calls. The words I spoke next I hope to never repeat.

"Mom?" I fumbled for words as the call went through: "Call everyone you can. Start praying. Elijah's dying." My husband called his mother with a similar message.

As the minutes passed, the nurses updated us on his condition. Slowly, before our very eyes, a beautiful, wonderful miracle was performed. Our baby Elijah slowly started to pull out of his respiratory failure. Before any major interventions could be done, our loving heavenly Father had answered so many of our prayers. What a caring God!

Elijah remained in the hospital for five nights—the longest nights and days of my life. Today Elijah is a healthy and happy baby boy. Each time I look at him—and my other children—there is no doubt in my mind that God loves them more than I can ever imagine.

Thank You for loving the babies of this world. I know that You love them more than any mother or father could ever imagine, and for that I am so thankful. You are the best parent that anyone could ever ask for.

MANDY LaFAVE-VOGLER

No Eye Has Seen

No eye has seen, no ear has heard, no mind has conceived what God has prepared for those who love him. 1 Cor. 2:9, NIV.

IT HAD BEEN A BUSY and stressful week—grape juice to make, a meeting to attend in the city, preparing for a camping trip my husband had long looked forward to.

Finally we were on our way—then our pickup truck, which had always been reliable, began to overheat, and we barely made it to the city where we had planned to spend the first night. We phoned our daughter, who was planning to join us, and told her the camping trip was off. She too was disappointed, since she had taken time off from work, but she immediately began to make other plans.

We met her at the airport with a more reliable vehicle and were off on a day trip to visit some museums. As the day passed quickly, we saw that there were more places in the area we wanted to visit, and we really weren't ready to go home. Our daughter disappeared and soon came back with good news. She had been on the phone looking for a place for us to spend the night. She had found a room and made a reservation at a nearby motel.

That was good news, as I was getting very tired. But our hearts sank as we saw the motel—a row of boxlike rooms on a barren hillside above a busy street. One look at the two shabby beds and a whiff of the stale air, and our daughter said, "No way!" In spite of the room, I collapsed on one of the beds while she and my husband went to look for a better place to stay.

I was awakened by my daughter saying, "Come and see the beautiful place we found!" Only a few miles away were the most charming little cottages among the tall pines, and my husband was already relaxing on the front porch as we drove up. What a tranquil place to stay, and such a contrast to the first place that we had almost settled for!

At times it is so easy to become satisfied with the things we have here on earth—beautiful houses, nice cars, so many things. Even as I was almost ready to settle for the inferior motel, sometimes it seems that we aren't really looking forward to heaven and the things we will see there.

Thank You, Father, for the promise of a place far better than we can even imagine. Help me to focus my thoughts on the home prepared for me in heaven instead of being satisfied with things here below. BETTY J. ADAMS

Experience God's Love

The Lord hath appeared of old unto me, saying, Yea, I have loved thee with an everlasting love: therefore with lovingkindness have I drawn thee. Jer. 31:3.

OUR 3-YEAR-OLD NEPHEW, Caleb, loves spending time at our place. He often asks us if he can sleep over. At first it puzzled me, because there are no children his age to play with and no toys to play with either. But he enjoys it when we sit and read to him. His favorite words are "Tell me a story!"

One evening I bathed Caleb, read him a story, made sure he said his prayers, and gave him a hug. I tucked him into bed, but he would not sleep. Eventually I asked, "Caleb, why are you so restless?"

He answered, "But you didn't tell me."

"Tell you what Caleb?"

He just kept on saying, "You didn't tell me." Eventually I figured out that often I would tell him that he is special and that we love him. It was only after I had told him that he is special and how much we loved him that he fell asleep.

So often we forget to tell—and show—our families, friends, and others how much we love them and how much we appreciate them. We lead such busy lives that we take each other for granted; we brush past each other without realizing what the other person might be feeling deep down. Everybody wants to be loved, accepted, and valued.

As we go to bed, do we take time to listen to our Creator's voice saying, "I love you—you are special. Can we spend time together reading 'My Story Book'—the Bible? There are so many treasures and promises that I would love to share with you. Remember, I love you so much that I gave My life for you so that we can spend eternity together." Our Father is waiting patiently to tell us how much He loves us, and wants to give us the assurance that He is always there for us. He assures us, day after day, that we are special because there is no one in the world just like us. We are special because the God of the universe gave Himself for us. We are special because God loves us with His whole heart. God invites us to have an intimate friendship with Him. He wants us to trust Him implicitly and to give our lives over to Him.

Today, appreciate the magnificent and generous gift of God's love.

CORDELL LIEBRANDT

The Payment

Freely you have received, freely give. Matt. 10:8, NIV.

SINCE I MET JESUS I assumed a commitment to Him to help others come to know Him. This commitment has lasted 10 years with good results. Praise the Lord!

Among the many people with whom I have studied the Word of God is Paulo. Paulo was a young military police sergeant who, because of his perfectionism, had a difficult temperament and many times was not nice to various individuals.

When I met him I saw the challenge that was ahead. Paulo was a strict and hard man. We began the studies, and soon I realized that each time we met he was more eager for knowledge of the Bible. At first the studies were once a week, but soon we were meeting three times each week. Even so, this did not keep him from coming to my house in his police car to ask about some point in the Bible that he didn't understand. I strongly disliked the police, and it bothered me to see that police car stopped at my door.

Then the studies began to take place daily, and more and more Paulo demonstrated evidence of visible change. His wife and daughter were happy to have a new man by their side. When the studies had finished, Paulo surprised me by asking: "What is your price? Tell me quickly, because if I cannot pay the amount all at one time I will pay you in several installments."

I had studied the Bible with various people before, and never had anyone asked me such a question. Surprised, I answered, "Freely you received, freely give."

Now Paulo was the one who was surprised. "You are telling me that you aren't going to charge me anything? You came here, changed my life, taught me how to live correctly, and you are not going to charge me anything for this?" I then told him that the One who had transformed his life, gave all for love, and did not charge for anything was Jesus alone. He wanted only Paulo's surrender without any reservation.

This helped Paulo to make his decision to follow Jesus. He was baptized, together with his wife, and today they are happily serving God's church in the Brazilian state of Bahia. His motto is "Freely you received, freely give." Could that be ours as well?   EDILEUZA NASCIMENTO RAMOS

Lesson From a Child

"For I know the plans I have for you," declares the Lord, "plans to prosper you and not to harm you, plans to give you hope and a future." Jer. 29:11, NIV.

ONE DAY A FRIEND shared an experience she'd had with her little daughter. The day was so hot that they decided to get some ice cream. As they arrived at the ice-cream shop she asked her daughter to choose a flavor of ice cream. She reminded her to get the ice cream in a cup rather than in a cone, as it holds more ice cream. But the daughter said, "Mommy, I want my ice cream on the cone so that I can see the ice cream while I eat it." Her mother tried again to convince her, but still she refused to change her mind. So the mother bought one ice cream in a cone for the daughter, and one ice cream in a cup for herself.

As they walked to the car, the girl started to eat her ice cream and had finished it within a very short time. When they arrived home a few minutes later, the mother began to eat her own ice cream. As the little girl saw her mom eating the ice cream, she said, "Mommy, I want some of your ice cream."

"No, honey," her mother said. "You've finished yours, and I told you to get your ice cream in a cup, but you refused. So now you don't have any more ice cream."

The little girl said, "Mommy, I am so sorry. Yes, I made a mistake not to follow you. I just chose the ice cream on the cone because it looked more interesting to me. I am sorry, Mommy."

As I listened to this story, my eyes were opened. This little girl reflects us. How many times do we make a decision simply because it looks more appealing to our eyes? We tend to forget that God has prepared something that is more beautiful and perfect for us. We know that He always has the best plan for us, as His promise in today's verse says.

How sweet and comforting to know that God is always leading us every step of our lives. Always ask for His wisdom in making decisions. "I keep asking that the God of our Lord Jesus Christ, the glorious Father, may give you the Spirit of wisdom and revelation, so that you may know him better" (Eph. 1:17, NIV).

LANNY LYDIA PONGILATAN

Learning to Trust

The Lord will fulfill his purpose for me; your love, O Lord, endures forever—
do not abandon the works of your hands. Ps. 138:8, NIV.

SHE RETURNED HOME IN a sea of tears. It didn't seem possible that after having placed all of her plans in God's hand that the visa to the United States had been denied! My 21-year-old daughter, Estefania, was to help an American family with their children, study at a university, and, of course, practice her English.

She had felt that God had given her a green light. We had received clear signs, and doors opened in a providential manner; but now it was all going downhill. She had gone to the United States consulate to obtain her visa with a positive attitude, and she happily paid the fees. Now she had lost her money, and her dreams were gone too.

We had prayed many times for God's will to be done. I attempted to console her. "Don't cry, dear. If God wants you to go, even if everything seems to be going wrong, you will go! If you do not receive the visa, it is because God is saying that you should not go." Estefania agreed and, wiping away the tears, went on with her activities.

Two days later the telephone rang. On the other end of the line a voice speaking Portuguese with an American accent asked for Estefania. "This is she," my daughter answered.

"Please, tomorrow morning at 10:00 come to the American consulate; you have an interview with the consul regarding your visa. It will not be necessary to pay the visa fee again."

Estefania hung up the telephone. Jumping with joy, she ran to tell me the news.

The following day the consul was waiting for her and stated, "I believe that a miracle has happened for you. Come with me!" And after a 10-minute conversation she was granted the visa.

Estefania spent a year filled with blessings. The Lord used her to care for rebellious teens who were under her responsibility. She depended constantly on God in the same way she had since she was a child. However, during this time far from home it seemed more tangible because things are not easy when one is in a foreign country. She learned to place her trust in God daily. Now my daughter is certain of His existence and knows that there is nothing better than putting her plans in the hands of our loving Savior.

RÓCIO ORTIZ

Miniature Wisdom

*This is the day which the Lord hath made; we will rejoice and be glad in it.
Ps. 118:24.*

SEVERAL DAYS AGO MY HUSBAND offered to mail a fistful of letters for me. He spotted them perched on the kitchen counter as he dashed out the door with a birthday package he was mailing to his mom. At supper that evening he remarked that the package cost was $5. I thought little of it at the time, but later I inquired if the cost included the stamps to mail my letters. "Oops!" he said. "I didn't notice they needed stamps." The next day all eight envelopes were in my mailbox.

This little episode prompted a return trip to the post office the following day with eight carefully stamped envelopes. Lisa pulled into the parking lot next to me. She is known to be a hurrying soul with a constant agenda. She quickly released her little granddaughter, Katie, from the car seat and hipped her with a quick stride to the post office service counter. Katie chatted freely all the way.

A few minutes of chatting with Lisa would be a treat before we both started our day. Little Katie sat perched on the counter, snowmen stamps in one hand and letters in the other, still chatting. The commute to the parochial school is a long one each morning for Lisa, her three gradeschool children, and the 2-year-old granddaughter. As she and Katie stamped their envelopes with snowmen, Lisa began to chuckle as she told me of the early-morning shuttle to school. The children had been talking loudly and fussing among themselves. Katie suddenly raised her tiny hands and said, "OK, just calm down. I said, *just calm down.*" The kids began to laugh, and the mood was quickly transformed.

"The past few days Katie has been full of happy energy, but it has been a little overwhelming!" Lisa exclaimed. The previous night she had been exceptionally busy. Lisa had cupped Katie's tiny face in her hands, telling her she needed to slow down. Again in her miniature wisdom Katie responded, "I need to slow down; I know what I need to do; I need to slow down."

Too often we hurry and scurry with overwhelming energy, planning for tomorrow, next week, or next month. We borrow from tomorrow its troubles and anxieties. Like Katie, we know what we need to do. We need to slow down. This day is new, a gift from God. Treasure its moments.

JUDY GOOD SILVER

The Miracle Is Operated Through Faith

Your grief will turn to joy. John 16:20, NIV.

WHEN MY DAUGHTER-IN-LAW was expecting her second child, she had prenatal examinations done. The laboratory found that she had contracted rubella. If rubella is contracted during the first months of pregnancy, it is capable of producing irreversible effects on the fetus. The laboratory requested that she repeat the examination. To our dismay, the disease was confirmed.

We panicked, not knowing what to do. We began to pray and place the life of that child in the hands of God.

Some friends joined us in prayer. But in spite of the fact that we were praying, many times depressing thoughts came to our mind through people who had experienced living with children affected by the disease. However, in spite of her suffering, my daughter-in-law decided not to end the pregnancy and to allow God to act as He so desired.

The months that followed seemed like years, such was our anxiety. Within our hearts there was pain, and in our minds a question that we did not have the courage to express in words: Why did this have to happen? We didn't know what to do other than to ask God for a miracle.

Finally the long-awaited day arrived. Although we had hope that everything would be fine, doubt remained in our minds. That day we asked God that the baby would be normal and healthy.

God is infinitely merciful! He had already preformed the miracle in the mother's womb. Today this child is 11 years old, an intelligent and healthy boy. He knows that his name, Raphael, was chosen because of its meaning: "God cured him."

Thank You, Lord, because my sadness was transformed into joy. Thank You that I can feel Your presence as I see You each morning.

NICÉIA TRIANDADE

(?) Thought: One of the hardest challenges a parent can face is to have a baby born with physical or mental problems. They too may have prayed for a healthy baby. If you meet or know someone to whom this has happened, what could you say to them? Would today's text comfort? How?

Summer

If we confess our sins, he is faithful and just to forgive us our sins and to cleanse us from all unrighteousness. 1 John 1:9, NKJV.

SUMMER IS MY FAVORITE time of the year. I love going on a vacation! Through the years my husband and I have been fortunate to go on some fun vacations—some alone, and some with our children. My favorite vacations are trips to a beach. My first vacation (when I was a small girl) was to the ocean with my parents. I guess that's what started my love of the ocean and beaches. I love hearing the waves as the tide comes in and goes out. I love the white sand as it sifts through my toes as I walk. I love looking for shells, feeling the cool breeze, seeing the tropical birds and the palm trees. I'm so thankful to God for creating these beautiful places that my husband and I can get away to once in a while to enjoy His wonderful handiwork.

One of our favorite places to go is Mexico, where we stay at a resort on the beach. Every morning we get up early, have our devotional, and then head to the beach to walk. It's so beautiful early in the morning, watching the sun come up. During the night the waves have brought up dark-brown seaweed, and all along the ocean edge is an ugly dark line. Before long large tractors come down the beach with big shovels that pick up the seaweed and put it in large dump trucks and carry it away. When the tractors are finished, we can see the beautiful white sand again.

One morning as I was walking I thought that this ugly dark seaweed is a lot like the sins in our lives. It's so wonderful that we have a loving, caring, and forgiving Father who, if we ask, will come and take those ugly sins away.

Father in heaven, thank You for the oceans, for the beautiful beaches, for providing a way to clean them, and for providing a way to clean our hearts as well!

JOYCE BOHANNON CARLILE

(?) Thought: Newly cleared beaches are beautiful. Have you ever thought of the idea that it is sin that makes us ugly and dirty, and that Jesus' blood cleans us up and makes us beautiful again? Read Psalm 51 and note how David asks God to clean him up—can you imagine that the process makes him beautiful inside as well as outside? Read also the lovely picture found in Psalm 45:13.

Desert Spectacular

And after the earthquake, a fire; but the Lord was not in the fire: and after the fire a still small voice. 1 Kings 19:12.

THE NIGHTLY NEWS IS AN unlikely travel guide. The focus of the beautiful anchor people is rarely pleasant. I guess that's why I was so attracted to the news story. All of the elements in nature had coalesced that year to provide the perfect conditions to bring the desert into full bloom. The parched earth had received just the right amount of rain to cajole the ancient seeds into activity. The weather forecaster had promised a once-in-a-lifetime spectacular display of brilliant color against the dusty California earth tones. The local newspaper had followed up with a story and close-up pictures of cactus in bloom to whet my appetite. The writer had provided detailed directions along Interstate 15, heading toward Nevada. As the weekend approached, several of us planned a day's journey to take in the sights.

In the early-morning hours I began to imagine beautiful blooms on cactus, like the roses that sit atop thorned rosebushes. As we whizzed along the gradually inclining highway, the terrain slowly changed from green lawns and shade trees to tall pines and shrubs, from housing developments to undeveloped land.

Finally we began to descend into a valley spotted with sand dunes that marked the beginning of the desert. Excited, we scanned the landscape in search of the promised explosion of color. We decelerated as we searched for anything other than the muted beige-and-olive tones that blurred the landscape. We saw nothing—until we stopped and walked out onto the desert floor. Only then did we find that the desert floor was covered with tiny plants and grasses. Nestled within each little mound of foliage were sprinkles of beautiful miniature flowers.

In today's text Elijah had to learn the same lesson. Living in the well-watered city, I'd become so accustomed to the big, bold displays in the Exposition Park Rose Garden and the overpowering fragrance of Hawaiian plumeria tree blossoms that I nearly missed the still small beauty of the desert floor. Sometimes we look for God as we run, and all He wants us to do is stop and listen for that still small voice.

SHIRLEY KIEMBROUGH GREAR

Human Impossibility

And it shall come to pass, that before they call, I will answer; and while they are yet speaking, I will hear. Isa. 65:24.

MY SISTER WAS RETURNING from a trip with some friends. After lunch, as she was sleeping in the back seat of the car, it was suddenly hit by a piece of tire that crashed through the windshield, hit the shoulder of the passenger beside the driver, hit my sister's forehead, took out the headrest, and passed through the back window before disappearing along the highway—all in a matter of seconds.

Soon the travelers were given emergency assistance and taken to a nearby city. My sister had to be moved to a larger city, where the hospital was better equipped to do the surgery her serious injuries required. This transfer took place because of the intervention of a Christian nurse who offered the first care of her injuries and directed my sister's case to another hospital.

The medical team was amazed that my sister had survived her injuries, and during the surgery the physicians simply called her "the patient" because they didn't want to pronounce her name, Obida, because it reminded them of the word óbito ("deceased" in Portuguese). After 10 hours they were able to close up her skull and said there was nothing more to be done. If we had faith, they said, this would be the time to ask our God to act with mercy toward my sister.

That day a great chain of prayer extended throughout Brazil, as well as abroad. The medical staff predicted that she would remain in the intensive-care unit for three months, and then spend six more months in the hospital. Only at this point would we learn what complications would remain. We would have to learn how to care for her.

But the Lord had other plans. Five days later she left the intensive-care unit, and two days later the physicians came to say goodbye to her because she was being discharged from the hospital. The manner in which they looked at her and smiled joyfully made us realize that they really felt they were looking at a miracle. We brought her home to São Paulo, and after one month of rest she returned to work.

We have the joy of serving a marvelous God!   ODNAR LIMA DOS REIS

You Can Go Back

His father saw him, and had compassion, and ran, and fell on his neck, and kissed him. Luke 15:20.

IT WAS DURING THE SUMMER of 2000 that I traveled from Canada to Laurel, Maryland, and decided to visit my family in Rochester, New York. At the station in Canada I was told that I would have to change my ticket in the United States. The next stop was Buffalo, New York. While my sister and I were changing our tickets, the bus going to Rochester left, so we had to wait in the station for about two hours for another bus.

When I travel from place to place I enjoy meeting people, but on this day I was tired and really didn't want to talk to anyone. A voice coming from behind me said, "Where are you going?" I turned, saw a pleasant-looking woman, and replied that I was going to Rochester and was waiting for the next bus. When I asked where she was headed, she replied, "Chicago." Her daughter, who was a doctor, would be meeting her at the bus station.

Then I told her I had been attending religious meetings in Toronto and that Christians from all over the world had been there. She told me that she knew about those meetings. "You see," she continued, "I used to go to that church from the time I was very young. But when I was older I wanted to do things that the church did not approve of. I didn't want church members to look at me with a disapproving look every time I would come to church—so I left the church. I have not returned to that church since."

I listened to her story, and when she finished I told her, "You can go back. The members will receive you and be happy to see you again. Most of all, Jesus will welcome you. It doesn't matter why you left the church or what you are doing right now. You can go back."

She promised that she would. We talked about other things, but as we parted that day I reminded her of the promise she had made to go back to visit the church she left.

If you have left your church for whatever reason, you can go back. Jesus will welcome you, and Christlike people will receive you. The prodigal son came back and was received with open arms by his father. It is not too late. You *can* go back.

MILDRED ELLEN MOORE

The Ants

This day I call heaven and earth as witnesses against you that I have set before you life and death, blessings and curses. Now choose life, so that you and your children may live. Deut. 30:19, NIV.

IT WAS SUMMERTIME, and we were going on a long-antici-pated and much-deserved weeklong vacation. We cleaned and packed our motor home and headed out for the Georgia Veterans State Park in Cordele, Georgia. Two hours later we pulled into our campsite in the shade of stately trees overlooking a beautiful lake, reflecting a beautiful blue sky, and kissed by a gentle breeze. The view was so lovely and tranquil that it looked like one you'd find on a postcard.

We set up camp, ate our lunch, and took our dog for a walk. Later that evening, when we went back inside our motor home, I discovered tiny black ants marching along the kitchen countertop. I quickly wiped them up with a wet paper towel as I followed their trail. I searched all around inside and outside, looking for the place they were entering, but couldn't find it.

The next day I went to the camp store and bought bait traps for ants and put them around, but the ants continued to come in. For the next week I battled the ants, determined to get rid of them and keep them out.

When we unhooked the electricity to pack up and go home, we finally found where the ants were getting in. They were marching up the power cord connected to the breaker box on the ground next to the motor home.

The ants remind me of the devil. He is constantly looking for any little hole we leave unguarded to enter our hearts. I remember hearing a sermon in which the speaker said that the devil never takes us from a spiritual high to a sinful low in one large step. He always does it a little bit at a time so that we don't notice where he's taking us.

I always appreciate the patience of the Lord. He is always so willing to help me plug up the holes in my life that are left open because I keep mak-ing the wrong choices.

Thank You, Lord, for the eternal life You offer each one of us.

CELIA MEJIA CRUZ

(?) Thought: The writer speaks of unguarded holes in our hearts. What do you think those might be in your life? What is the best way to plug the holes? Effort, prayer, or Scripture?

Playing Bodyguard

The Lord watches over you—the Lord is your shade at your right hand. Ps. 121:5, NIV.

IT WAS SO HOT as my brother and I played "grocery store" in our backyard for hours. I was the customer and my brother was the clerk. Without great concern about us, Grandmother prepared lunch while a helper cleaned the house. Grandmother never needed to be greatly concerned with us, because we were always well-behaved children. However, one day things were different. I almost gave her a heart attack when I decided to go out into the neighborhood to collect some things for our grocery store. Grandmother thought I had disappeared.

While the helper took care of my brother, Grandmother began to look for me around the house, then on our street, and finally throughout the neighborhood. "Have you seen a little girl with blond hair and green eyes, who's about 4 years old?" she asked the people who lived in the neighborhood. The more no's she received as an answer, the more upset Grandmother became. It was getting late, and I did not appear.

As Grandmother reached the beach that was about 1,600 feet (about 500 meters) from our house, a young man, seeing Grandmother's state, promptly decided to help her. She went looking in one direction, and he went in the opposite. But neither of them found me.

Grandmother was in extreme despair; the only thing left to do was to wait for my grandfather to arrive or notify the police. She thanked the kind young man and returned home. I can only imagine the expression on her face, the joy and relief that overtook her, as she opened the door and saw me inside the house. When she asked me what had happened, I simply answered, "I went to get yeast for our grocery store."

I can imagine Grandmother giving me a big hug and drying the tears that mixed together on our faces. Certainly she must have offered a prayer of thanksgiving to God, because He had led some friends of the family to find me, lost on the street, and take me back to my grandparents' home.

In an almost childlike language I like to say that Jesus "plays bodyguard" because He is always at our side, offering us His loving protection. We don't need to be afraid to walk along the highways of life, because He is ready to extend His hand and offer His pleasant company.

CAROLINA KUNTZE SILVEIRA

To Love Mercy

He hath shewed thee, O man, what is good; and what doth the Lord require of thee, but to do justly, and to love mercy, and to walk humbly with thy God? Micah 6:8.

MICAH 6:8 WAS MY father's favorite text. Often he would repeat it to me. He was merciful and always tried to help the poor find jobs or even win court cases.

One day he observed an old woman being mistreated by her own children. He took note of the meager bedding in the corner where she was made to sleep on the cold floor. He noted that she even had to eat alone and wash the plate herself. My father asked if I would cooperate with him to help this old woman. I promised I would try. So he bought a blanket and asked me to deliver it to her. I wasn't too sure if this would help or just insult the family, as they were well off. But in good faith, I went. As I gave her the blanket, all I heard was an order from the granddaughter that she should thank me. I was relieved and left for home. This is the way my father taught me to help others.

Now, as a mother, my heart rejoices as I see my own children offering a helping hand to others. Once, one of my children was severely injured in an accident because of the carelessness of others. His vehicle was damaged and needed repair, and he was confined to bed with multiple cuts and stitches. When the police told him the fine on the offender he said, "Let's dismiss the case; the man is too poor to pay."

When Moses asked God to show him His glory, God could have shown him His majestic form, the splendor of heaven, His mighty armies of angels, or even the numerous galaxies of stars and unfallen worlds. But no, God preferred to reveal His mercy. As He passed before Moses he proclaimed: "The Lord, The Lord God, merciful and gracious, longsuffering, and abundant in goodness and truth" (Ex. 34:6).

As a sinner I deserve a death sentence, but Jesus has taken that penalty for me and set me free. Yet how many times do I judge others without any mercy? I fight for my rights. I demand justice. James 2:13 says if we show no mercy to others, even God will judge us without mercy. Jesus says, "Blessed are the merciful: for they shall obtain mercy" (Matt. 5:7). I certainly need to obtain that precious mercy from my Savior.   BIRDIE PODDAR

It Doesn't Have to Be Green to Be Beautiful

He has made everything beautiful in its time. He has also set eternity in the hearts of men; yet they cannot fathom what God has done from beginning to end. I know that there is nothing better for men than to be happy and do good while they live. Eccl. 3:11, 12, NIV.

I WAS DRIVING MY RENTAL car across the desert of southern California. It was mid-August, and the temperature gauge on the car was registering 108°F (42°C). As I looked to the right, to the left, to the front and back, it all looked the same—brown! Brown sand stretched away on both sides of the highway, and a crescent of majestic but brown mountains rose high to the sky on my left. No signs of life anywhere. I thought, *This has to be the ugliest country I've ever seen.* What a contrast to Tennessee—beautiful, green Tennessee with its green trees, green grass, winding rivers, and beautiful hills! There each peak is so different, covered with green foliage, wildflowers, and towering trees.

When I arrived in Palm Springs, my destination, I found it to be no different. Everything around me was still brown sand. The only changes were those human beings had made: hotels and resort areas had been carefully landscaped and watered to create a small illusion of greenery.

One of my daughters, who had spent several years in the area while in college, said to me, "Wasn't it a nice drive? And weren't the mountains beautiful?"

I could not believe her remarks. "No," I said, "It is all so ugly—everything is brown."

"Mom," she said, "everything does not have to be green to be beautiful. Did you not notice how the sand looks so smooth, like a rolled-out carpet? And the mountains turn all shades of brown and gold, as though they're shimmering in the sun? In the evening the mountains go from tan to all shades of lavender and purple when the sun begins to set." No, I really hadn't noticed any of that. I was looking only for green.

We sometimes go though life like that, missing the small yellow cactus flower or the purple-hued mountain because we think we can find beauty only in the bigger, more common, green experiences of life. We can truly find beauty in our surroundings, in our individual life circumstances, if we learn to appreciate the blessings that are there in each everyday experience we have.

BARBARA SMITH MORRIS

245

E-mail Friends

A man that hath friends must shew himself friendly. Prov. 18:24.

I BEGAN LEARNING COMPUTERS in 1983. At that time we worked with something called DOS. We didn't have Windows 3.1, or even 95 or 98. It was much harder to run programs, spreadsheets, or word processing. I never took computer classes, but I read manuals and asked those who knew. I then worked my computer. It helped to take workshops in my library work. Next came the e-mail capability.

The first e-mail capabilities were like the old model T Ford. Our e-mail world today has evolved into something unique. I can now e-mail relatives and friends in Vermont, Washington, Florida, Michigan, California, Africa, and other places, and receive replies almost instantly. I still correspond with former students from the 1960s and 1970s. It doesn't matter where they live; if they have a computer and Internet access, I can "talk" with them by e-mail.

One of my hobbies is genealogy. When researching family lines, I often find others who are working on different areas of the same family line. It is a big help to correspond with that person and compare notes. Together we progress faster than either one of us could alone. Without my e-mail capabilities, my work would go very slowly. I believe God helps me, even in genealogy; otherwise, the Bible wouldn't have all those "begats."

Some of my e-mails to these people are brief, and I may correspond only once or twice. E-mail friends are those with whom I develop a real friendship and wish to meet. We often share, not only notes on ancestors but pictures of our family, our pets, our philosophies, and ourselves.

E-mail friends can become very close, just as with everyday friends, even though we have never met. Some people ask about my faith in God, "How can you believe in someone you can't see or talk with?" If I can become friends with people via e-mail, how much easier is it to become friends with the God of heaven, who created me, my world, all without whom I would not have my modern conveniences, including my computer? And even if e-mail is quick, God is even quicker. He answers *before* we call.

LORAINE F. SWEETLAND

(?) Thought: Loraine makes a good point regarding e-mail friends and God. What does one have to do to make a correspondent into a friend? Does that apply to God as well?

My Unruly Garden

Thou shalt be like a watered garden. Isa. 58:11.

WELL, I CAN'T REALLY put all the blame on the garden. After all, except for the weeds, we planted it. Things just have a way of straying from their original locations. The marigolds have wandered into the strawberry patch, and the strawberries have invaded the onions and asparagus bed. Although it was planted only once, years ago, the dill reigns over one end of the garden, as well as sprigs here and there in the strawberries. This year I planted a few pumpkin seeds between rows of corn, and the vines now stretch for yards in different directions, headed toward the squash and beans. One year I accidentally planted flower seeds where I had already planted okra, but it wasn't unpleasant to pick okra from among cheery blossoms! Another year the cucumber vines climbed the cornstalks. Then there was the time I had run out of space in the garden and planted watermelons in the rose bed. Again, this year tomato plants form a ring around the strawberries.

Truthfully, with an overabundance of rain this spring and early summer, our garden is almost a solid carpet, with little or no space between rows, making it almost impossible to get through without squashing the squash!

We had a brother-in-law who was a family physician by profession but a farmer at heart. Although his children hated working in the garden, the oldest son is now a master gardener who would be appalled at our jungle. His garden, no matter how big or small, is picture perfect, carefully tended and cared for, and beautiful to see. In spite of the regular weeding my husband and I do together, we can't keep the whole garden free from those pesky weeds.

I have another garden, and it also needs regular inspection, weeding, and cultivating: the garden of my heart and mind. The enemy plants seeds of sin and doubt and the cares of this world. Try as I might, I'm unable to get rid of all the thorns, thistles, and weeds. It's such an overwhelming task that I despair that this garden will ever be beautiful and weedfree. Then I remember that there is a Master Gardener who is standing by, ready to use His special tools to uproot the unwanted plants and replace them with something beautiful. He longs to do the same for everyone.

If you haven't already done so, won't you invite Him into your heart's garden today? MARY JANE GRAVES

Unexpected Treasures

The kingdom of heaven is like treasure hidden in a field. Matt. 13:44, NIV.

WE HAD PURCHASED MORE than an acre of land and built our house on the ridge where we could see beautiful Lake Macquarie and enjoy the summer breezes. Bit by bit we tamed the land, planting gardens and fruit trees, but down the hill the natural Australian bush flourished.

It was lovely to look out on different species of eucalyptus trees and watch the multicolored lorikeets swoop down in a cloud to feast on the nectar of gum blossoms. Then there were the wonderful little balls of yellow fluff all massed together when the wattle bloomed.

But the birds were always there to bring us delight—brilliantly-colored eastern rosellas, king parrots, galahs, kookaburras, magpies, butcherbirds, and countless others were constantly flying among our trees.

My husband decided to tidy up the bush area; the undergrowth was so prolific that it could be a real danger in summer when fires took hold. It was hard and dirty work, especially since a nasty morning glory vine covered about half the area and had obviously been growing vigorously for many years. It took weeks to fight the enemy, but his determination won out.

One morning as he was cutting and digging, he found a very strange thing. He thought he must be imagining it, but it seemed like a branch of a mulberry tree very low to the ground. Fascinated, he worked on, and there it was, a mulberry tree stunted by the weight and binding arms of the morning glory, but a mulberry tree it was.

He raced up the hill as fast as he could climb to tell me about the amazing mulberry tree. My husband loves mulberries, and we had planted a tree, but now he had two, and you can be sure that the second one would have special care and attention.

The symbolism was not lost on me. It was indeed a parable in my own yard. No matter how burdened down I am—I might feel as though I have disappeared under the weight of the rubbish of this world—the Savior is willing to get rid of all that nasty stuff and give me the best possible opportunity to grow into what He planned for me to be. I need His care and attention to survive.

He even considers me a treasure worth rescuing. The enemy cannot keep me down.

URSULA M. HEDGES

God's Gifts

It is I who made the earth, and created man upon it. I stretched out the heaven with My hands and I ordained all their host. Isa. 45:12, NASB.

THE WAVES RUSHED RESTLESSLY up the beach. The tide was coming in this midday in August. The weather was warm as the sun shone around the scattered dark clouds. All sorts of people filled the beach, in groups or alone. Some read the last great book of summer; little children were busy making castles, tunnels, or whatever they imagined in the wet sand. Others collected the usual shells washed up on the shore, and even a baseball game was in progress.

I too had come to the beach to enjoy a good read with the added joy of sun and the sound of the endless breaking of the waves. I lived here year-round, but I also wanted to partake of this great pleasure that brings so many people from all over our country and from around the world.

At last I put my book aside and went for my walk. I often walk this beach to enjoy the coolness of the water. This is the Atlantic Ocean, and we are too far north for the ocean water to get really warm. After a few steps it feels just right to me, and I delight in the splashing of the water and the on-going, endless looking for shells—for that one great find.

The clouds floated splendidly in the sky above me, changing shapes and colors. I am always fascinated with the beauty of them whatever time of day or evening it is. They make me think of the majesty of God up there so high above, and often I find myself in prayer. I want to thank Him again and again for the beauty of His creation. The great beauty in sight and sound of this ocean constantly in motion, the sky's parade of colors and shapes, and the towering trees in the distance on the shore all attest to His greatness in creating this all for our joy.

A young girl ran toward me, her hands cupped over something special. She stopped before me and cautiously lifted up one finger to show me. "It's a monarch." We smiled as we enjoyed the beauty of the monarch butterfly, one more of God's special creations. I returned to my beach chair and packed up my belongings. I have been so blessed again with this special time in God's creation.

Truly God's love is shown to us in all our surroundings as we pass on life's way. Let us not forget to thank Him again and again.

DESSA WEISZ HARDIN

My Tree Garden

On either side of the river, is the tree of life. . . ; and the leaves of the tree are for the healing of the nations. Rev. 22:2, NRSV.

LIFE DIDN'T START OUT this way for the plum tree that sits at the edge of my garden. As a sapling it held much promise for the sweet and juicy plums we would one day enjoy from its lovely branches. In its first year of maturity it produced a profusion of beautiful white blossoms. These heightened our anticipation. To date, however, our plum tree has failed to retain and develop its fruit to maturity. While I'm not a horticulturist, I would hazard a guess that the lack of sufficient cross-pollination is at the root of its problems.

In my typical style I suggested quite strongly to my husband that if the tree would not produce fruit as it is supposed to, then it must go. Thoughts of a gorgeous, flowering magnolia as its replacement swirled around in my head. Fortunately for me—and the tree—Leon believes in giving second and third chances to the deadest-looking plant, let alone a living tree. He decided that the tree's location was the perfect spot on which to hang a bird feeder. We could now see the birds from every window at the rear of our house. He subsequently added hanging baskets of flowers to the tree. I liked the idea so much that I have now joined him in hanging my own baskets of flowers on the tree. Seeing the tree in the splendor of color, I wonder if this was not its intended purpose. The tree is not very high. Its branches are wide and low, which makes it easy for maintenance of the flower baskets. On a hot summer's day our grandchildren enjoy the shade it gives.

Dear sisters, aren't you glad that only God can be God? When we fail to live up to our God-given potential, He doesn't cut us down and destroy us, as I would have done with my plum tree. Instead, our heavenly Father picks up the broken pieces of our lives, and remolds and reshapes us into a thing of beauty. He gives us another chance to be the perfectly finished person He would have us be.

Help me, dear God, to be in the earth made new, where I will be able to sit under the tree of life and talk with You face to face. AVIS MAE RODNEY

? Thought: Have you ever felt like cutting a person down? How would today's text influence you?

Tidewater

Thank you, Lord for helping me. My confidence in You is strengthened. My faith is fixed. I will sing your praises and give thanks. Ps. 57:7, Clear Word.

MY SON, DON, AND I were doing some island hopping in the Philippines. Our last stop was fabulous and exciting, and the reception by old friends, who were key staff at the local hospital, was unforgettable. To make sure that we were comfortable, they had us stay overnight in the air-conditioned intensive-care unit. While we ate a delicious and healthful breakfast, the head nurse asked us what we would like them to do to make our day even more pleasant.

Don was hoping to experience deep-sea diving off the famous Mactan Island. We had no idea how to find transportation to get there or where to get the paraphernalia we would need. One of the women facilitated our wish when she spoke to Dr. Cruz, who asked her son to take us to the island. The son asked his wife, who is also a diver, to come along. Mrs. Cruz quickly prepared lunch for the family and us. Mr. Cruz checked the van and made sure that we had fuel; then away we went to the beach, arriving at lunch time. After a great picnic, Don and Mr. Cruz found an equipment shop where they fitted themselves with the diving suits and other equipment and headed to the deep portion of the sea.

The children were swimming at the beach, supervised by their mother, so I drifted toward the breakwater. The close-up view of the coral, colorful rockfish, sea anemones, and waving seaweeds fascinated me. I enjoyed the feeling of the passing current against my skin but didn't realize that I had entered the tideway area. The current was getting stronger, and I thought that was exciting. Little did I know that it could quickly sweep me away.

Just then Don saw me. He screamed, "Mom, what are you doing?" At that very moment I realized that the raging current was upon me and would be insurmountable in only a few seconds. Don extended his strong hand, and I hung on tight. He pulled me up, and I was saved from disaster.

Many times we wander aimlessly, leisurely, unaware of the dangerous lures of life. Our attention is diverted, and we find ourselves in danger. Our Father, who looks after us with love and compassion, will never let us fall into a pit of sin if we reach out to Him.

Thank You, Lord, for putting Your strong and loving arm around us.

ESPERANZA AQUINO MOPERA

Is It Really Greener on the Other Side?

Yahweh is my shepherd, I lack nothing. In meadows of green grass he lets me lie. To the waters of repose he leads me; there he revives my soul. He guides me by paths of virtue for the sake of his name. Ps. 23:1-3, Jerusalem.

The fruit of righteousness will be peace; the effect of righteousness will be quietness and confidence forever. Isa. 32:17, NIV.

DURING THE SUMMER OF 2004 I had the privilege of spending eight weeks in central London while participating in a study-abroad internship. My weekdays were taken up with my internship, but on the weekends I loved seeing and exploring the English countryside via train. Looking out the windows at the constantly changing landscape was a true joy—I wanted to see every bit of the countryside that I could.

Again and again I noticed that no matter which side of the train I sat on, half the time I would start to think that the other side would have been a better choice, for the view looked better. As a result, I'd wish I had chosen to sit on the other side. My side would have an exquisite view, and then it would become mediocre. Then I'd start to look to the other side.

During one of these moments I realized a spiritual lesson. In my spiritual walk my experiences are sometimes exquisite; I'm happy and content with my life. Then come the mediocre moments when I feel tired and alone. My eyes begin to wander to others' lives and their happiness. I want their experience and wish that I were over there, not where I am.

One thing I took away from my musings on this phenomenon is that the view is constantly changing. I began to understand that I have to be happy in the moment where I am. Maybe others do have it better than I; however, if I am patient the landscape will change, and brighter views will again open before me. The feeling that things are greener on the other side doesn't produce contentment or happiness. The other side may look more appealing, yet God desires me to be content with what He has chosen for me. On my train rides the other side would lose its appeal after a while, and I would turn back again and see a glorious view appear before my eyes.

O Lord, teach us to be content where we each are. May our contentment be in You and not in our changing experiences and circumstances.

RISA STORLIE

How Great Thou Art!

When I consider the heavens, the work of thy fingers, the moon and the stars, which thou hast ordained; what is man, that thou art mindful of him? and the son of man, that thou visitest him? Ps. 8:3, 4.

EARLY ONE MORNING as my husband and I sat on my sister's front porch studying our Bible study guide, we were fascinated by the beautiful sunrise and the majestic white fluffy clouds gliding across the azure-blue sky. This splendid display of God's creative handiwork captivated our attention. I said to my husband, "It's difficult to understand how anyone can doubt there's a God when evidences of His magnificent work are visible everywhere." He agreed.

A few hours earlier we had awakened to the crowing of roosters, which caused me to reflect on Jesus' telling Peter that before the cock would crow twice he would deny Him three times. There have been numerous times that I too have denied my Savior by my uncaring attitude or my too-busy schedule to talk to Him. Somehow He never forsakes me.

Midafternoon we watched as the roosters and hens gathered in my mom's front yard. The chickens came around the same time each day for Mom to feed them. No one had to call them. Yesterday's food wasn't enough to last for the next day. Just as these creatures come daily for a fresh supply of food, I need to come daily for my fresh supply of spiritual nourishment, to feed on His holy Word, to talk to Him, and to listen as He talks to me.

On another occasion we observed a mother hen as she taught her two little chicks how to search for food. When they strayed too far, she made clucking sounds, and without hesitation the chicks ran to her. I wish I were as obedient when my Master calls.

Just before nightfall I watched as the hens flew up to the branches of a tall tree to hide among the thick foliage. I wondered how the little chicks would make it to the top. Then I heard their mother clucking, and one by one, branch by branch, these little chicks reached her at the top of the tree. The mother spread her wings and covered her chicks to keep them safe. I too want to be sheltered under my Father's strong, powerful wings, secure from the master predator, Satan.

So many spiritual lessons I experienced sitting on my sister's front porch!

Thank You, Jesus, for these refreshing glimpses of what a great and mighty God You are. SHIRLEY C. IHEANACHO

Before You Call

I will bless the Lord at all times: his praise shall continually be in my mouth. Ps. 34:1.

ONE MORNING AS I prepared for the fall session at the community college where I served as an instructor, I turned to the Bible and read the promise found in 2 Chronicles 20:17: "Ye shall not need to fight in this battle: set yourselves, stand ye still, and see the salvation of the Lord with you."

I put the Bible down and reflected on the phrase "ye shall not need to fight." The significance of these words arrested my consciousness for the moment, but as the day wore on, other thoughts and ideas claimed my immediate attention. School reopened with the usual pressures: unresolved curriculum problems, unsettled or unsatisfactory schedules, and oversubscribed courses. The teaching schedule my department chair placed in my hand indicated a split schedule. This necessitated my presence at school as early as 6:30 a.m. and as late as 9:45 p.m. That was fine! I adjusted to that arrangement, and things even brightened a bit when another instructor asked me to trade two courses with her because this permitted me to continue my studies at the university.

However, a second look at the schedule brought me face to face with a shocking realization. I had been assigned a course that met on Wednesday nights. I would thus be forced to miss the weekly prayer meeting. My heart gave a sudden lurch. Just then the words "ye shall not need to fight" flooded my vision. I felt immediate relief.

I discussed my problem with no one. As I approached the secretary's desk the next day I encountered one of my colleagues. "How would you like to take my Tuesday night class and give me your Wednesday night?"

I could hardly believe what I was hearing! Of course I gladly accepted the offer, and in a short planning session we made the adjustments necessary for the proper presentation of the courses. I expressed my gratitude to my colleague and raised joyful thanks to God.

Dear Lord, my faithful friend, thank You for meeting my every need. Help me to trust You completely. Thank You for going to battle for me and winning the fight.   QUILVIE G. MILLS

Come and Be Clean

Wash me throughly from mine iniquity, and cleanse me from my sin. Ps. 51:2.

I SAT DOWN TO ENJOY a leisurely cup of tea in the quiet of late morning. My children, Lillian, age 7, and Cassandra, age 2, were in Florida for the summer with my parents. I thought about all the projects I had planned for while they were gone. Thinking that the dining room was probably the best place to start, as it needed very little work, I took a look around the room. My eye caught something strange on the far wall. On closer inspection I realized that the specks were food, and the streaks were some kind of liquid behind the place where my 2-year-old ate. Sighing, I reached for a cleaning cloth and some cleanser. I started rubbing gently so that only the dirt—not the paint—would come off. I had no intention of painting if I didn't really have to. After a few careful wipes and a few not-so-gentle rubs, I realized I was in trouble. There was no way I could get the walls clean without taking off the paint.

After a moment I remembered a commercial I'd seen for a new product that came with the promise that would remove dirt with only a gentle wipe. Having nothing to lose, I rushed to the supermarket, located the product, purchased it, and raced home. I read the directions, wet the sponge, and, with a little trepidation, gently wiped the first streak. I was pleasantly surprised— the streak came off immediately! So I tried it on the dried food, and it wiped off with just a few gentle wipes. Now I was excited! I ran from room to room, looking for dirt to clean. I wiped off pen marks in the hallway, crayon in the kitchen, tape residue on the countertops, and black scuff marks from the wall. Everything became clean immediately! I called my friends and gave them testimonials. I even purchased a few bottles to give away!

Sometimes I go through life completely oblivious to the dirt in my life until something points it out. Then I try to clean it myself, making excuses or apologies, trying to rectify the situation. Eventually God gently reminds me that only He can resolve the problem of sin in my life, and without His help I only create spots that look as if someone tried to clean but wasn't able to get the job done. Once I read my manual, the Bible, and follow the directions and let God take control, I am actually clean. Praise God!

TAMARA MARQUEZ DE SMITH

I Am So Lost

I will instruct thee and teach thee in the way which thou shalt go: I will guide thee with mine eye. Ps. 32:8.

MY YOUNGEST GRANDSON, Grant, had just started kindergarten, and I planned to pick him up after school to spend some one-on-one grandmother time with him.

I allowed myself 35 minutes to drive the 25 miles to his school. When I turned onto Highway 191 I was making good time. Then everything seemed to slow me down—two motorcyclists who were enjoying the lovely day, each looking frequently at the roadside scenery; and then a pickup truck that had a single sheet of plywood in the truck bed and was driving very slowly to keep it from blowing out. I began to realize that I truly was going to be late.

I saw a rural road off to the left that I remembered was a shortcut I had taken several years ago when picking up Grant's older brother at the same school. I drove on for several miles without seeing anything familiar. I soon realized that I needed to ask for directions. Finally I saw a service station and pulled in quickly. I noticed a car with a young mother and her son. *They will know where the school is,* I thought. I carefully followed their directions only to find myself at a dead-end drive in a trailer park. I quickly retraced my way back to the main road. A feeling of hopelessness came over me, and the tears began to flow. I kept saying again and again, "I am so lost! I am so lost!"

When I came to a rock business I stopped and sadly spilled out my dilemma to the man working there. He took a piece of paper from his pocket and calmly said, "Ma'am, you need to calm down. I will draw you a map to the school."

I took a deep breath and thanked him. I arrived 10 minutes late to find a very hot, sweaty little boy standing on the curb, accompanied by a school attendant. I apologized to both of them. "I got lost, Grant, and I'm sorry. I would never forget to come get you!" I blurted out. He smiled sweetly while wiping the sweat from his little forehead. "I know" was his forgiving reply.

While lying in bed later that night, I began to think over my trip to the school. I determined to allow myself extra time when I picked him up again. But the thought that kept haunting me was this: Am I lost—really lost—while trying to take shortcuts in certain areas in my life?

ROSE NEFF SIKORA

Picture ID Time

By this all will know that you are My disciples, if you have love for one another. John 13:35, NKJV.

IT WAS THE BEGINNING of another school year, and we were reminded to have our pictures taken for our new school identification badges, which we were advised to wear every school day. Each year we had to have a new picture taken. We had to stop what we were doing and rush over to the modular building where the cameras were set up to take all faculty and staff pictures. *What's the big deal?* I thought. *We're too busy to stand in line for this. We haven't changed that much. And all of us know each other. Why can't this be done every two years?*

Nevertheless, there were physical changes in all of us. For most they were minute and sometimes imperceptible, but evident when pictures were compared from year to year. Also, there were a few newcomers.

It made me think about Christ. Does He require His followers to wear an ID badge that says "Christian"? Not in the literal sense. But He does expect us to be recognized as His followers. How are we to know what our badges should have on them? His Word describes His followers.

Do we have to update our Christian badge each year? No—we should update it daily. We are changing every day, every minute, and every second. For most of my adult life I didn't feel worthy of wearing His badge. But He gently kept reminding me to come to Him as I was, and He would make the changes. He's given me His badge. He updates it when I ask Him and when I spend time with Him—wherever I am or whatever I'm doing. If I don't do this daily, my badge isn't current and isn't a true reflection of the changes that my heavenly Father wants others to see in me.

Thank You, heavenly Father, for giving me Your badge to wear in humble submission to Your cause and will. Please give me Your strength to come to You daily so that the changes in my life will always reflect You, and my ID badge can stay updated. SHARON M. THOMAS

?Thought: What do you think are elements of the Christian badge the author writes about? Can the badge be internal, or must it be external?

Act Immediately

And straightway he called them. Mark 1:20.

EVERY TIME I READ the Gospel of Mark in the King James Version I am struck by the decisiveness of his reports. The first chapter tells about John preaching and baptizing in the Jordan River, and how Jesus came to be baptized: "And straightway coming up out of the water" (Mark 1:10). The 40 days fasting and the triple temptation in the wilderness are dealt with in two verses, Mark 1:12 and 13: "Immediately the Spirit driveth him into the wilderness. And he was there in the wilderness forty days, tempted of Satan."

Then Mark moves on to Jesus calling His disciples. As Jesus walked by the Sea of Galilee He saw Simon and Andrew fishing and invited them to come with Him and fish for men. "Straightway they forsook their nets, and followed him" (verse 18). Verse 20 says, "Straightway he called them" (referring to James and John, who were working with their father and his servants), and they too left everything and followed Him. And "straightway on the sabbath day He entered into the synagogue, and taught" (verse 21).

Then for a short time Mark substitutes the word "immediately." Verse 28 says: "Immediately his fame spread abroad." "Forthwith" is another adverb used to describe how Jesus left the synagogue and went to the house where Peter's mother-in-law was sick with a fever. Jesus took her hand, and immediately she was healed (verses 29 and 31).

By verse 42 Jesus was back with the throng when a leper, who came to Him, was cleansed immediately. Going on to Mark 2, we have "straightway" (verse 2) and "immediately" (verses 8 and 12). In Mark 3: "straightway" (verse 6).

Mark is using these words as terse transitions, but I feel that there is a message here for me. I've not always reacted "immediately" or been eager to follow my Lord's directives. Nowadays, if I think of something helpful that I can do for someone I try to do it "straightway." Too often, if I hesitate, the opportunity passes or I forget or the idea grows stale. If I have doubts about it, a quick call to my Father will tell me whether the time is opportune. Seldom is it not opportune to do or say something kind and pleasant.

GOLDIE DOWN

At the Top of the Mountain

So do not throw away your confidence; it will be richly rewarded. . . . For in just a very little while, "He who is coming will come and will not delay." Heb. 10:35-37, NIV.

I ALWAYS ENJOYED HELPING the young people in the Pathfinder Club, and considering that Ribeira, a city in the interior of the state of São Paulo, Brazil, is a city rich in natural beauty, we decided to organize a long hike. Our goal was to reach the top of one of the mountains. The mountain wasn't high, nor was the climb steep; we'd be able to climb without any equipment and would take just one water canteen along with first-aid supplies. We really wanted to reach the top of the mountain and discover its beauty.

Within the first 975 feet (300 meters) we began to realize that some of the hikers were already exhausted, perspiration running down their faces. I was just about to give up along with this group when I thought, *Is it really worth it?* But I also said to myself, *Go on, Walkíria—you can do it. Look how far we have come!* The top seemed so far away.

When we were halfway up, I slipped and slid down several meters. I thought it would be best to give up, but again I looked up and realized we were almost there. I cried; my strength was gone. *Go on, Walkíria—you can do it!* a voice seemed to encourage me again. I looked up, wiped the tears, and climbed so fast that I overtook many who were ahead of me. Soon I was on top of the mountain.

How marvelous! I stood up, raised my arms, turned to admire the beautiful scenery that surrounded me, and inhaled the fragrance of the lovely wildflowers. The river flowing down below now seemed to be full of crystal-clear water. What peace! What a comforting sensation!

And now I want to reach the top of another mountain where our eternal mansion is prepared! How many times we slip! So many tears! Such struggles! It seems that we work and work but appear to stay in the same place. We can be certain that after so much struggling the reward is certain for those who do not turn back or give up on the goal.

Lord, today do not let us give up on receiving the reward that Jesus has gone to prepare. His coming is much closer than we think!

WALKÍRIA VESPA S. S. MOREIRA

God Really Cares

Not even a sparrow, worth only half a penny, can fall to the ground without your Father knowing it. And the very hairs on your head are all numbered. So don't be afraid; you are more valuable to him than a whole flock of sparrows. Matt. 10:29, 30, NLT.

DO YOU EVER ASK YOURSELF, "Does God really care about me? Does He really protect me?" I was shopping the other day for our annual Kids' Day where I work. We can have as many as 500 kids visit our store on that day. My coworker and I had almost finished filling a large shopping cart with the necessary supplies when we both thought of one more item. So after parking our basket in one of the main aisles in the store, off we went in different directions.

I returned to our shopping cart before she did, and my eye fell on my purse—on the top of the basket, in plain sight! My heart sank as I realized the foolish mistake I'd made, leaving it there unattended. I thanked the Lord immediately for watching over my purse. He was watching out for me more than I was! Isn't God good?

My husband and I just returned from vacation, traveling nearly 1,200 miles (1,900 kilometers) by car. We drove through some of the rain from Hurricane Gaston, which had recently hit the United States. One section of the road we traveled was closed shortly thereafter because of terrible flooding. We reached our destination safely, but we kept a close eye on the weather reports as another hurricane threatened that area. However, that whole week the weather was nice, and we were able to return home on the day planned. Later we called some friends who lived in the area where we had vacationed. They told us that that area was hit hard by Hurricane Frances two days after we left. The Lord had been so good to give us that window of time between storms to relax on the beach.

When I think that Jesus says our very hairs are numbered—that would mean every time one fell out He would know which number that was—I am humbled and amazed that He would care that much for me! My mind can hardly comprehend that concept. All I can say is "Wow! What an awesome God!"

LOUISE DRIVER

Thought: Recount some special-care blessing you've received, and spend some time in praise to God.

The Test

Examine yourselves to see whether you are in the faith; test yourselves. Do you not realize that Christ Jesus is in you—unless, of course, you fail the test? 2 Cor. 13:5, NIV.

TESTS IN SCHOOL are one thing—but tests in adulthood are another matter. Take my test as a grandmother, for example. My granddaughters—Tami, 6, and Kimi, 4—were spending the afternoon with me. I enjoyed their chatter and play as they helped me in the kitchen. "Grandma," Tami suddenly asked, "how is it that you never yell or get mad?"

Startled, yet pleased that my granddaughter could see that I revealed Christ in my daily life, I smiled and prepared to answer her. I was just about to say something pious, like "Well, when you have Jesus in your heart you don't yell or get mad" when Kimi spoke up.

"Grandma," she said, "I've heard you whine around sometimes."

Astonished, I laughed ruefully. It's true—anger and yelling are not my besetting sins, but complaining is. Even a 4-year-old recognized this.

Another test. One Friday afternoon my granddaughters were with me as I hurriedly prepared for Sabbath. I talked briefly with one of our church members on the phone in the kitchen, replaced the phone, and rushed to complete my tasks. My granddaughters, desiring my full attention, were not very happy. Finally I sat Tami down hard on the kitchen counter, speaking quite firmly (crossly, I'm afraid), telling her that I must get the Sabbath cooking finished, and I expected her to amuse herself until I finished my kitchen tasks.

The next day at church the very woman I had talked to on the telephone the afternoon before approached me. It seems I hadn't replaced the phone properly, and our lines had stayed connected. She had heard my dialogue with my granddaughter and was shocked that her pastor's wife would speak so crossly to a grandchild.

I didn't pass that test. I'm afraid I often don't. These little pop quizzes come up now and then to show me where I'm weak and those areas in which I need to surrender more completely to Him. God's promise, however, is that if I remain faithful to Him I will pass my final test.

"Being confident of this, that he who began a good work in you will carry it to completion until the day of Christ Jesus" (Phil. 1:6, NIV).

CARROL JOHNSON SHEWMAKE

My Raggedy Ann Doll

For the Son of man is not come to destroy men's lives, but to save them.
Luke 9:56.

MY RAGGEDY ANN DOLL is 74 years old. She doesn't look like those seen in stores today. Nor do the modern Raggedy Ann dolls look like the one in the book. I wonder if my father ever realized how cherished his creation would be. I was 10 years old when he cut and stitched and painted her for me. He had even sewn her printed cotton calico dress, white pinafore, and pantaloons, just like the picture on the cover of that book. And then he was gone, and there was little else to remember him by beyond memories.

I read and reread the Raggedy Ann book that came with my doll until the pages were dog-eared and the back binding tattered and loose. And the doll itself was worn and tattered with so much hugging and loving. Since my father was an artist, he had painted the doll's exposed arms, legs, face, and features with oil paints. When the paint dried and flaked over time, her head fell off, and her clothing has had to be replaced through the years. I grew too, and outgrew dolls, but couldn't bear to throw my precious doll away, even though the years had taken their toll on her physical appearance. What does one do with a ragged doll when dolls have no more meaning? I'm so glad I didn't toss her into a trash barrel. One of my daughters is sentimental and saw the treasure in my Raggedy Ann doll.

Ardie took her to a place to be carefully restored. Her parting words to the doll hospital were that this was a very special doll with a very special heritage. And she was treated as such. Today my repaired and restored doll is enclosed in a shadow box, along with the tattered, well-read book of Raggedy Ann's adventures. A small brass label tells her story, along with the pertinent dates. Because my Raggedy Ann doll meant so much to me as a child, it will always be a reminder to my daughter of how much that doll meant to her mother in the early years. The shadow box is displayed on a wall in her home and is a conversation piece to all who visit her. And Raggedy Ann continues to smile, happy in her new position.

I wonder if sometimes humanity is like a cherished doll to God. Every one of us is worth saving—and the love of Jesus made saving possible. Actually, we have so much more value, and Jesus' sacrifice to save us was so great!

Thank You, Lord God.   Laurie Dixon-McClanahan

Miracle

Praise the Lord, O my soul, and forget not all his benefits—who forgives all your sins and heals all your diseases. Ps. 103:2, 3, NIV.

I WAS ALREADY AT my work location in the laboratory when I received a telephone call from my husband stating that our youngest daughter had suffered an accident. I could hardly believe it—only an hour before I had seen her and she was fine, getting ready for work, too. I advised a work colleague that I was leaving and rushed to the location that my husband had indicated.

When I arrived, I saw my daughter lying on the ground. The firefighters and paramedics were already immobilizing her. Her eyes were closed, and her head was bleeding profusely. I was unable to utter a single word—the only thing I could do was cry and pray. Then she called to me and said, "Mom, don't cry—everything is fine!"

Amazed by the faith that she was demonstrating, I thanked God that she was confident and conscious. We entered the ambulance and sped to the hospital. The rest of the day was spent in radiology, taking X-rays and CAT scans that revealed a concussion, swelling in the brain, and a cut to the scalp, which was soon stitched by the physicians.

The neurologist transferred her to the intensive-care unit, and I went with her as far as the door, where I had to say goodbye. I felt totally helpless, and as the door closed I felt desolate. I knelt right there in the hallway of the hospital and cried out to the Lord for my daughter's life. When I arrived home, I learned that there was a vigil at our church. Many prayers were offered on behalf of our daughter.

Very early on Saturday morning we received a phone call from the hospital informing us that she had been taken out of the intensive-care unit and was now in a regular hospital room. I praised the Lord and immediately went to the hospital. When I entered the room, I saw that beautiful young girl seated on the bed. She smiled and told me that she was ready to go home.

The following day my daughter was released from the hospital and continues her recovery at home. Miracles cannot be explained—they must be accepted. She had no aftereffects, not even a headache. Our God is marvelous!

MARIA CLEUZA RODIGUES DA SILVA

The Lost Key
That Was Not Lost

Do not think of yourself more highly than you ought, but rather think of yourself with sober judgment, in accordance with the measure of faith God has given you. Rom. 12:3, NIV.

ON A BEAUTIFUL SUNNY afternoon I was busy trying to get my chores done—going to the bank, doing some shopping, and buying groceries. After my third stop I decided to leave my shopping bags in the car before going on to the grocery store. Just before leaving the last store, I looked for my car key in my handbag but couldn't find it. I emptied my handbag—it wasn't there. I asked the salesclerk to help me see if I had dropped it in the store somewhere, but it wasn't to be found. By now I was earnestly praying that God would help me find that key, but I was calm and felt that I would find it. I had a spare key in my bag, so there was no need to panic.

Since I had no idea where the key had fallen, I checked in every store I had visited and gave them my home and office telephone numbers in case they found it. Finally I used the spare key, put the bags in the trunk, and went on to the grocery store.

After I got home I checked my handbag and the shopping bags again but didn't find the key. I didn't allow the loss to dampen my spirit, and went about my daily duties and had a pleasant night.

After a few days the thought of my lost car key slowly faded, and life was back to normal. But three weeks later I was looking for something in my storeroom, going through the shopping bags, and in one of those bags I found the car key! Apparently I had missed checking one of the shopping bags.

I thanked God for keeping my key safe. It could have fallen out in the parking lot or in one of the stores, but God made it fall into my shopping bag. It amazes me to think that the God of the universe cares for us humans even in such trivial matters as a lost key! I'm very encouraged by these verses: "Fear ye not therefore, ye are of more value than many sparrows" (Matt. 10:31). STELLA THOMAS

(?) Thought: It's hard for many women—even Christians—to appreciate their value in God's eyes. Think about incidents when God has shown His special love for you, and take another look at your value in Him.

Early Snowfall

Hast thou entered into the treasures of the snow? Or hast thou seen the treasures of the hail, which I have reserved against the time of trouble, against the day of battle and war? Job 38:22, 23.

THE FIRST THING I DO every morning upon arising is look out the window to determine what kind of day it will be. I don't rely completely on the weather forecast. The outdoor thermometer on the patio helps me decide what to wear for the day.

September 14 should have been an ordinary late-summer day—a brisk, cool morning dispelled by warm 10:00 sunshine. But alas! Snow covered the ground. You can imagine my disappointment about signs of winter so soon. Of course, I knew it was unlikely that the snow would stay long, but just the same I wasn't eager for winter to come.

As I prepared to go to my volunteer job, I removed my winter coat from its protective plastic bag, fresh from the dry cleaners. I had to admit it would be cozy warm, so my spirits lifted. Since the snow wasn't deep, I wouldn't need to don winter boots. That was another plus.

My car is in a heated garage, so there was no snow to sweep off or frosty windshield to scrape. Maybe this winter thing wasn't too bad after all! The sun was making an effort to break through the clouds. *H'mmm,* I thought, *I'm trying to look on the positive side of a wintry, dull day, too.*

When I reached the side door of the administration building that leads to the archives where I revel in historical information, I stopped short and paused a long moment. To the left of the door hardy pink petunias with their cream centers peeped through a thin blanket of snow. How I wished I had a camera to capture this beautiful sight for future reminders that whatever harsh circumstances I find myself going through, I can still find something good on which to concentrate.

To my amazement, when the snow disappeared the next day the petunias still retained their bright colors. And even the grass remained its springtime green. Again, the lesson to be grateful for all things was reinforced.

Lord, help me to cultivate a positive outlook on life today and every day.

EDITH FITCH

Beauty for Ashes

To all who mourn in Israel he will give beauty for ashes, joy instead of mourning, praise instead of despair. For the Lord has planted them like strong and graceful oaks for his own glory. Isa. 61:3, NLT.

ALTHOUGH I APPRECIATE most growing things, I've never managed to develop "green fingers." If I agree to care for someone else's potted plants while they're away, I make it clear that it is a case of "all care, no responsibility." That is, I'll do my best, but don't blame me if something doesn't survive.

In the plant world there are some species that are very temperamental and prone to succumb to the slightest experience of adversity in their environment. There are other plants and trees, however, that seem almost impossible to kill. Take eucalyptus, for example. Many times I've seen a eucalyptus forest that has been ravaged by bushfire. With all their foliage and smaller branches burned away, leaving only stark, blackened trunks, the trees look lifeless and hopeless. But given a little time and a little rain, a small miracle occurs. Leaves begin to sprout all along the trunks and remaining limbs, hiding the blackness behind a veil of living green. They may look misshapen for some seasons to come, but the trees begin to reach heavenward again.

Not long ago a tall eucalyptus was cut down in our front garden because it had some large dead limbs that were dangerously close to the house. When the fallen tree had been cleared away, there was no visible stump. Apart from some sawdust in the grass, there was nothing to show where the tree had been. But some of its root remained in the ground, unseen. Within a few weeks young leaves began shooting from the spot where the tree had stood. It was clear that the old root was setting out to become a tree again.

The persistent tree is a God-given promise of hope in a daunting world. The very same illustration also appears in Scripture as a promise of salvation in Jesus. Isaiah predicted, "A shoot will come up from the stump of Jesse; from his roots a Branch will bear fruit" (Isa. 11:1, NIV). And though sometimes it seems impossible, God's will for this world will prevail.

JENNIFER M. BALDWIN

Not My Way but His Way

Now to him who by the power at work within us is able to accomplish abundantly far more than all we can ask or imagine, to him be glory . . . forever and ever. Amen. Eph. 3:20, NRSV.

EVER SINCE I WAS 3 my passion was to become a teacher, and the good Lord opened the way for me to do just that. Every year of teaching brought more excitement and meaning to my life. My spiritual gifts and choice of vocation were matched perfectly. What better way to serve the Lord than to fully develop the natural gifts He has given! How narrow a view I found this to be further down the road of faith that God led me on.

As I was working on my master's degree, through a questionnaire I found out that I was weak in administration. I devoted my energies to developing teaching approaches and strategies, exploring how the teaching-learning process could be improved from year to year. No administrator role for me, as I had no natural gifts for it.

In the mid-1990s, however, I found myself slowly but surely moving in that direction. I resisted it, but God wouldn't leave me alone. Finally I relented, and even though the questionnaire indicated that I had no aptitude for administration, God supplied the gifts necessary for me to do the task. It wasn't easy—it felt as if I had jumped from the frying pan into the fire. The learning curve was steep and difficult. Time and time again I felt pushed into a corner, not knowing what to do, with no one to turn to for help. In the corner I learned to look up to God, to find comfort in His Word. In the process, through all the tears, I learned to depend on Him and not on my own abilities.

Hebrews 13:21 became very real as I grasped the hand of a God who has promised that He will "equip you in every good thing to do His will, working in us that which is pleasing in His sight, through Jesus Christ, to whom be the glory forever and ever. Amen" (NASB). Instead of depending on our natural gifts, we should trust God to supply the gifts necessary for the work He calls us to do.

Nothing is impossible with our God—in Him the weak can be strong; the foolish can be wise (1 Cor. 1:27). Yes, we can be more than what we have ever imagined to be, because God is working through us so long as we fully submit to His will.

SALLY LAM-PHOON

Kitty Pity

Look at the birds of the air; they do not sow or reap or store away in barns, and yet your heavenly Father feeds them. Are you not much more valuable than they? Matt. 6:26, NIV.

HE WAS THE SIZE and color of a chocolate bar, with huge, bright eyes that seemed too big for his little fuzzy face. Pulako, who was named after a favorite chocolate store, was found dehydrated and hungry by my friends Rhonda and Steve on the median of an interstate highway near our home. The young kitten had apparently been hit by a car, and his left foreleg hung limp, flattened and useless. The vet said that even though it didn't seem to be causing him pain, it would have to come off at the shoulder. He insisted that the little guy would experience a more complete recovery if the leg was removed at the shoulder rather than leaving a stump, because he wouldn't try to walk on it. The tough decision was made, and the surgery was performed.

Two days after the surgery, Rhonda brought Pulako to my house for a visit. His little neck and belly were shaved, and he had an incision from the middle of the back of his neck to the middle of his chest. The amazing thing was that after all of that, he wanted to play. Forty-eight hours after having an entire limb removed, he was pulling himself across the carpet with his good leg, rearing up like a stallion, and batting at string just like any kitten. He even ran around and jumped up on the couch! Today he is a huge, affectionate, gorgeous, three-legged cat, happily living with Rhonda and Steve.

This courageous little kitten taught me that it is possible to recover from devastating injuries—sometimes quickly. That even though someone has a "disability," it doesn't mean they are disabled. That sometimes, even if we don't realize that something is hurting us and even if the process to remove it may be painful, we will be infinitely better off in the long run if it is taken out of our lives. I know that God cares about every aspect of our lives. If He will take care of a little kitten and see that he gets a good home and medical care, just think what He will do for you and me!

VICKI MACOMBER REDDEN

(?) Thought: Do you think of disabilities as impossibilities, or as challenges to be overcome? How does God help meet these challenges in your life?

The Angel of the Lord

For the angel of the Lord guards all who fear him, and he rescues them. Ps. 34:7, NLT.

WE HAD JUST COMPLETED supper at the kitchen bar, and my family had moved into the living room. I finished cleaning up in the kitchen and joined them. We enjoyed the brilliant flashes and loud crashes of a late-summer thunderstorm displaying the power and brilliance of nature.

Suddenly, right on top of us, was the loudest boom-splintering sound we'd ever heard. Outside the window we could see smoke and knew something close by had been struck by lightning. Seeing no fire, we moved through the house. To our dismay, we discovered that it looked as if a bomb had exploded inside our kitchen—a corner cabinet was shattered. Shredded cookbooks, broken glass from measuring cups, splinters of wood from cabinets, a twisted metal recipe box I'd kept from high school home economics class, electronic and plastic parts of a telephone, and other kitchen paraphernalia were scattered everywhere.

After everyone calmed down and the storm moved on its way, we went back into the kitchen, took some pictures to remember our experience, and started to clean up the mess. As reality and the extent of destruction set in, we were awed at the evidence of God's protecting hand.

There were shards of glass and wood where we had enjoyed supper only 15 minutes before. A three-foot piece of cabinet had been thrown the length of the bar and landed 10 feet away, right where my son had been sitting. Across the room, above the range, exactly at my head level was a five-inch-long gash in the wall made by part of a glass measuring cup. The telephone wire was charred with burn marks on numerous places throughout the house. After the kitchen had been cleaned up, my husband discovered that there was more damage—everything electronic in the house had been blown out.

Though I can't even open it, I've kept the twisted metal recipe box in my new kitchen because it reminds me of God's protection and love. In telling and retelling this story, we always come back to the fact that it was only things that were destroyed. Indeed, the angels of the Lord both guarded and rescued us!

JUDY MUSGRAVE SHEWMAKE

Great Is Thy Faithfulness

The eyes of the Lord are upon the righteous, and his ears are open unto their cry. Ps. 34:15.

IT WAS EXACTLY 4:11 when the train that I take every day came to an abrupt stop. The conductor announced over the loudspeaker that there had been a power failure, but that we should be moving shortly. After an hour and a half of sitting in a dark, hot subway two gentlemen announced that we were about a mile from the nearest station, and they would help all of the women who wanted to get off to walk the subway tracks to the station.

I immediately stood up, and was assisted along the tracks and up to the platform. Upon emerging from the subway tunnel into daylight, I asked a group of individuals what had happened. They explained that there had been a power failure across the entire Northeast and that no transportation that used electricity was running.

I began to walk and to pray to the Lord. Finally, after walking about 20 blocks, I saw a bench and sat down. People came and went, all in the same predicament—no way to get home. As night began to fall I told the Lord, *I can't stay here, but I don't know what to do or where to go.* The taxis were all full. The few buses that were making an attempt to run weren't traveling the way I needed to go, and they were packed to capacity and weren't stopping.

A voice said to me, "Walk to that corner where all the people are." I did exactly that. As I neared the corner, I saw literally hundreds of people walking over the Williamsburg Bridge into Brooklyn. In the midst of those people I spied my two coworkers, Reuben and Mike. Was I ever glad to see them! After I loudly yelled Reuben's name for some time, he finally turned and saw me.

On the other side of the bridge we were met by Reuben's father, who drove us to my car, which was parked in Queens. Although the roads were completely dark, my heavenly Father guided me all the way, and I was able to drive my coworkers to their homes. A routine trip home that usually takes two hours had turned into a 10-hour experience.

Thank You, Lord, for Your watchcare and protection. Great is thy faithfulness!

DARLENE SIMMONDS

Thought: Read 1 Thessalonians 5:18 and see how Darlene applies this verse to a harrowing experience. Could you do the same?

Do Not Be Anxious

Who of you by worrying can add a single hour to his life? Matt. 6:27, NIV.

SOME TIME AGO IN BRAZIL when a child finished the fourth grade, he or she could go directly to middle school, or could take an intermediate course that prepared them to face middle school. When I finished the fourth grade the majority of my classmates went directly to middle school. I wanted to continue with them. The idea of staying behind didn't please me. My classmates were my friends, and I wanted to stay with them.

My parents, however, already had their minds made up about this. They felt that it would be better for their daughter to spend one year better preparing herself to face what was ahead.

I became very sad and frustrated. I tried to convince them in every way possible to let me skip that year along with my classmates. But there was no way to change their minds. I cried a lot, but had to accept how things would be. My very understanding mother prayed with me, asking God to give me patience so that I wouldn't worry so much about the fact that my classmates would graduate before I would.

The years passed. When I finished the seventh grade, I knew that only one classmate, Noemi, would graduate at the end of that year ahead of me. All of my other classmates had either quit school or had not passed and were already back in my class. At the graduation worship service on Friday night, someone told me that Noemi's grades hadn't been good enough to pass, and that she would not graduate. So we graduated together the following year. Not one of those students who had skipped directly to middle school was able to graduate before I did!

At times we become impatient and anxious about things that happen to us. We want things to be our way and want them to take place within the time frame that we stipulate.

I've learned that I should remain calm, because God knows what is best for me. As I entrust my life to God I can be peaceful and have certainty that the best for me will take place.

Thank You, Father, for giving me patience. Help me not to be anxious but to remain calm, awaiting events of Your planning.   Ani Köhler Bravo

The Making of a Mother

Behold, every one that useth proverbs shall use this proverb against thee, saying, As is the mother, so is her daughter. Eze. 16:44.

HAVING A FAMILY, a career, and not enough time in a week can put a lot of pressure on a person. I experienced this stress, especially after having two children. I'd always been focused on my career and goals to further my education.

The stress of trying to manage home and work became too much, so I decided to approach my supervisor about changing to part-time status. She agreed. But a few weeks after meeting with her I felt impressed to be a stay-at-home mom. I struggled with this for several months. I prayed about it and told the Lord that if He wanted me to make this change He would have to change me. Changing meant looking at what really mattered. In the meantime, I was buckling under the pressure of trying to manage both home and work. Trying to juggle everything was taking its toll on me, mentally and physically.

My day would start off with preparing breakfast, making lunches, doing laundry, and other tasks. Then, rushing off to work, I would deal with the mental challenges there. When I returned home, I would be on my feet in or near the kitchen for more than three hours. This would occur nightly—even with my husband's help and my efforts to better manage my time.

I didn't have a problem with the work, but while I spent my time maintaining the home I was not maintaining my relationships with my family and God. I realized I was running on empty. I turned to the Lord and prayed to be able to love my children more than I had been. The answer came that they needed to be my main focus.

Things have changed a great deal since then. I became a stay-at-home mom, and a lot of the stress has been alleviated. I thanked the Lord for His patience with me and His guidance.

Do I have all the answers, and is my life perfect? Certainly not! But I do have a better focus on what is important and have a lot less self-induced stress in my life. It's hard to believe how much better a relationship is when it is full-time—whether with family or the Lord.

MARY J. WAGONER ANGELIN

God's Precious Promises

Praise be to the Lord. . . . Not one word has failed of all the good promises he gave. 1 Kings 8:56, NIV.

IT IS AN AUTUMN DAY at the lake. Only three female mallards come for their early-morning breakfast of bread crumbs, and I notice that they are daily becoming more restive. A mysterious call from some distant land is luring them away, and soon they will be winging their journey to a new feeding ground.

I'll miss them. They were raised on our lake this year—six small ducklings following their mother around in the water. Their antics and struggles to become adults were engaging to watch.

One especially was a clown. He would arch his little back and spraddle his tiny webbed feet horizontally when searching for food on the bottom of the lake, turning himself almost completely over when his head went under the water! I wondered if he would ever learn to dive properly.

A mother loon and her two older youngsters were encircling and searching the lake also this morning. Their "Where are you?" call was a welcome sound indeed. Soon they too will be leaving.

My dog, Blackie, and I took a walk this afternoon through the young birch tree grove at the back of our cabin. We explored a deer path that meandered through the center of it and found that the deer have made a soft bed in there from various weeds and pine needles. The sun streaming through the canopy of the branches of the tall pine trees makes a warm haven for them. It was a walk that restored the soul!

Living among God's beautiful creatures has taught me many things. They have been good neighbors, but winter is nigh and new horizons beckon to them. I have the hope that spring will return as a result of God's ageless and unchanging promise to each of us, and once again the cycle of life will begin, and we will meet again at the lake.

Even more precious is God's golden promise of hope that Jesus will soon be coming again, and we will meet with Him in the air and be on our way to heaven.

Praises to the Lord!

ROSEMARY BAKER

Logo or Logos?

She will give birth to a son, and you are to give him the name Jesus, because he will save his people from their sins. Matt. 1:21, NIV.

WE LIVE IN AN AGE obsessed by packaging, titles, and appearances. Every name conjures up an idea. We know that certain names mean cheap or poor-quality goods, while others receive kudos. Before the average child can talk, he or she will be able to recognize the symbol that has become synonymous with fast food and ease of service—all packaged in the letter M. As our children grow older, the names of stores that we used to know will no longer mean anything to them. A present is of little or no value unless it has a certain name attached to it—usually Armani, Rolex, Gucci, or Nike. We call these name brands, tags, or logos, from the Greek *logos*, which means "word." So what's in a name?

In the book of Matthew we have mention of the greatest name: "She will give birth to a son, and you are to give him the name Jesus, because he will save his people from their sins."

In the book of John we read, "In the beginning was the Word, and the Word was with God, and the Word was God. He was in the beginning with God. All things came into being through Him, and apart from Him nothing came into being that has come into being. In Him was life, and the life was the Light of men. The Light shines in the darkness, and the darkness did not comprehend it" (John 1:1-5, NASB).

This might as well read, "In the beginning was the Logos, and the Logos was with God." As we study the book of John, we will meet again and again with the Logos. As we journey through life we will meet constantly with Logos. We know that ultimately our destination will depend on our relationship with Christ, the living Word/Name/Logos, because "God highly exalted Him, and bestowed on Him the name which is above every name, so that at the name of Jesus every knee will bow, of those who are in heaven and on earth and under the earth, and that every tongue will confess that Jesus Christ is Lord, to the glory of God the Father" (Phil. 2:9-11, NASB).

Armani, Gucci, Mercedes—all logos. Christ is the living Logos. *What will it be for you—logos or Logos?*   JUDITH PURKISS

Butterscotch and the Bear

The cow and the bear shall graze; their young ones shall lie down together; and the lion shall eat straw like the ox. Isa. 11:7, NKJV.

ONE FOGGY EVENING my husband and I went out to call our cattle into the corral for the evening feeding and lockup. "Come on, babies!" Jim called toward the pasture where they'd been grazing. We heard their moos as they made their way toward the hay barn. One by one they emerged out of the wet fog and into the light beaming down into the corral area from high atop a tall pole. "They seem jumpy tonight," Jim observed. "Maybe something out there spooked them."

"Like what?" I asked.

"Like a mountain lion—or a bear," he answered, forking hay into the feeding troughs.

I counted again. "All four mamas are here," I reported to Jim. "And there's little Calvin . . . and Larry Boy . . . and Goo-goo. But I don't see Butterscotch!"

Jim said we'd better go look for her. So I settled on the ATV seat behind him, and he put a wide-beam flashlight in one of my hands and a pistol in the other. "If that neighborhood bear or a big cat comes out of the darkness at us, you point and pull the trigger."

Cautiously we circled the big pasture in the thick fog, barely able to see ahead of our vehicle. The dense mist moistened and chilled our faces. Back and forth the beam of my flashlight sliced through the fog. Jim intermittently shut off the engine so we could call Butterscotch and then listen for any response. The resulting periods of silence were excruciating.

Finally we saw them through the mist—the reflection of our headlamp shining in two bright-yellow eyes. At last we made out the form of an upright Butterscotch, safe but terrified. Speaking calmly and advancing slowly, we maneuvered her into the corral and locked the gate.

Isaiah describes a not-so-distant time when a calf can graze fearlessly between a bear and a mountain lion. In that happy place no one will pack a pistol. Why would they, in a land of no terrorism, no abuse, no atrocities, no grief, no loneliness, no tears?

Thank You, loving Father, for preparing an earth made new where we will know only safety . . . only peace . . . only joy . . . only Jesus.

CAROLYN RATHBUN SUTTON

Moments of Grace

He mocks proud mockers but gives grace to the humble. Prov. 3:34, NIV.

THIS SUMMER I HAD to say goodbye to two of my cats, Gilley and Gilah. They were 16 and 15, and we had had a good life together. But I was still unprepared when I lost them to cancer less than three weeks apart. Because of their advanced ages, surgery was not an option. Basically all I could do was make them comfortable so that the time left would be as happy as possible.

Naturally I asked God why two such loving creatures would get cancer. I had to accept what I couldn't understand and ended up euthanizing them to spare them their final agony. But in the midst of my anxiety over the months of battling cancer, I did know moments of grace.

Gilah never complained but purred every time I picked her up, even when she was having trouble breathing. Half of her face was disfigured with tumors in her mouth and nose, and it spread to her lungs.

One day I lay down beside her. She rolled over with only the normal side of her face showing. I rubbed her belly and listened to her purr; it was like going back in time, to before the cancer. After she turned I could see the tumors were still there, but I had a few minutes of relief.

Gilley had cancer in one lung, but even as he grew weaker he still clung to me for attention. One of our favorite activities was sharing a bag of popcorn and watching TV together. Eating popcorn with Gilley took a really long time. Because I was afraid of him choking, I had to break off tiny pieces so he wouldn't get any hulls. It was well worth the trouble watching the little guy still enjoy life, even though he was so sick.

More grace came when I made arrangements to have Gilah buried at the local pet cemetery. I had buried my two dogs there 10 years earlier, and since whole sections had been added to the park I assumed Gilah would be buried a distance away. It turned out there was a plot right next to my dogs' grave. Gilah and Gilley were buried next to their doggy brothers.

It's hard losing our loved ones, even those with four legs and a tail. But God grieves with us. The Creator, who sees a little sparrow fall and clothes the lilies of the field, must have a special place in His heart for my cats, who taught me the meaning of grace.

GINA LEE

He Knows Our Necessities

And they that know thy name will put their trust in thee: for thou, Lord, hast not forsaken them that seek thee. Ps. 9:10.

IT WAS A FRIDAY AFTERNOON. I got a cart at the supermarket and began to place some things in it, mentally adding up how much I was spending. The money that I had would be enough to pay for the groceries, and I would still have enough for the bus ticket to go to church on Sabbath morning.

Then I remembered the offering that the children should take to church. I have twin boys who were 3 years old at that time, and a girl who was 14. I looked again at the basket to see what I could take out. The tube of toothpaste and the cookies would go. Now I'd have enough money left for the children's offering.

When I arrived home, I found a note from my sister: "I went to Madureira with the children." I thought this was strange; she never goes out on Fridays, especially in the afternoon.

About an hour later they returned. The children were euphoric. My sister said, "You cannot imagine what happened! As soon as we arrived in Madureira there was a group of students who were with the health department. They applied fluoride to the children's teeth and gave them each a tube of toothpaste and a toothbrush. When we were walking home, we passed in front of the cookie factory, and the security guard called the children and gave them so many cookies that they ate cookies as we walked, and there are still several packages in the bag. We will have cookies for several days!"

I could hardly believe what she was saying! The children had gotten exactly what I had taken out of the grocery cart. However, there was one difference. They had received much more than what I would have brought home. They also received the fluoride treatments and the toothbrushes! And there was money enough for their offering at church besides.

"His bread will be supplied, and water will not fail him" (Isa. 33:16, NIV). This is the promise that the Lord makes to us, and He fulfills this promise in an incomparably better way.

God never lets us down when we trust in Him and do His will. Everything that we attempt to give to Him He returns in much greater blessings.

ISABEL CRISTINA DE ALMEIDA MACHADO

The Football

Incline your ear, and come to me; hear, that your soul may live; and I will make with you an everlasting covenant. Isa. 55:3, RSV.

OUR FAMILY OF FOUR was about to become five, and we enjoyed working together to get ready. My husband painted the dresser. My son and daughter helped me put the crib together and fill the dresser drawers with little boy clothes. We filled a basket with toys that the older children had picked out.

After the arrival of Jeremiah, I noticed that one particular toy kept finding its way from the toy basket to the crib. Each day I would toss the stuffed football back into the toy basket, and each night it would appear again in the baby's crib. After several days of this pattern I asked my 11-year-old football-loving son if he knew anything about this. He was, he said, putting the football in the baby's crib because someday he wanted Jeremiah to grow up to be a great football player, maybe even a quarterback.

I teased my son a bit about this, asking if he really thought such a prop would accomplish football greatness. We had a laugh together at the silliness of the mere presence of a football in a crib turning a baby into a great sportsman. No need to work hard, study football plays, be a member of a team, or follow the coach's instructions—just instant football greatness from the presence of a stuffed toy!

Exhausted from the duties of motherhood, I started to climb into bed when the irony of the situation struck me. Beside my bed, on the night table, sits my Bible. I try to faithfully read the Word of God, but to be honest, there are mornings and nights when I feel too tired or too busy or too distracted to open the Holy Book that sits next to my bedside lamp. The object lesson suddenly became so plain to me. Have I set my "prop" beside the bed, somehow thinking that having a Bible sitting there would turn me into a great Christian? Do I really think that a Bible collecting dust beside my bed can help me know God and live for Him if I haven't even studied His instruction for me today? God can use the smallest daily events to turn us toward Him so that we might "incline our ears" and be saved through the everlasting covenant He promises.

How thankful I am that God can use something as small as a stuffed football to remind me of the importance of my connection with my heavenly Coach! SANDRA SIMANTON

The Comfort of the Rainbow

Whenever I bring clouds over the earth and the rainbow appears in the clouds, I will remember my covenant between me and you and all living creatures of every kind. Never again will the waters become a flood to destroy all life. Gen. 9:14, 15, NIV.

I KNEW THE HURRICANE was coming. I also knew that the large shutterless windows in my house were unprotected. The TV newscasters, reporting on the long lines at the hardware stores, noted that there was very little plywood to be had anywhere. People were battening down in earnest, but I knew I couldn't put shutters up by myself.

On the morning before the storm I sat down to breakfast. Looking out at the western sky, I saw a pale, seven-colored arch, incomplete yet distinct. I took it for what it was—God's message to me. "I want to remind you that never again will I destroy the earth by a flood. This rainbow is a sign of the promise between you and Me. You will be safe. I am protecting you."

In awesome wonder, I relaxed. Everything would be all right. Then the doorbell rang. My brother-in-law had brought plywood from my son and a friend, whose windows he had just finished protecting. He measured and cut and pounded, laboriously crafting shutters for each of my windows. Finally we were ready to face the storm.

Hurricane Frances came, ripping off roofs and smashing windows, but we were safe. Then three weeks later another more vengeful storm raged over our heads. When morning finally came, we ventured out cautiously. We had been taken care of again. My youngest granddaughter, aching to be outdoors, opened the garage door. Her exclamation of wonder sent everyone scurrying to see what had made her so joyful. Another rainbow glowed in the eastern sky. God's promises had held.

I praised God for the rainbows from both directions—east and west—before and after the storm. I thanked Him for the visual promises with which He bracketed the storms.

The aftermath of the storms reminded me that we can experience the calm that is so badly needed in this stressed-out world if only we will do our part and leave the rest to the Lord. Oh, if only we would trust Him.

Thank You, dear God, for Your assurance and protection. I know Your covenant is sure. CAROL JOY GREENE

Washer Gone Bad

He that is our God is the God of Salvation. Ps. 68:20.

SUNDAY IS THE DAY that I usually work at getting some chores done around the house, including laundry. This particular day I wrote my to-do list, set my schedule, and proceeded to check the items off, one by one. I started the first load of laundry, then went on to do some other things. About 45 minutes later I went down to start the second load when, to my horror, I found the clothes in the washer sitting there, wet and unspun. This would throw off my nicely set schedule since I would now have to take the clothes to the Laundromat and wait for them to finish. I was being inconvenienced and became very annoyed.

My husband contacted a washing machine repairman the next day. When we checked the warranty, we discovered that it had recently expired. When the repairman came three days later, he found that because of overloading the washer too often, a "little box" had cracked, causing the agitator and the spinning mechanisms not to function. He explained that this little box had cracked to keep the motor from going out. If it had not cracked, we would have to go to greater expense to repair the washer—or need to replace it altogether. Including parts and labor, the cost of the repair was a little more than $100.

As I pondered the ordeal that caused me such inconvenience, I thought about how sometimes God allows us to be inconvenienced or even annoyed by various trials and challenges that we face. His reasons are always for our best good, though we may not understand, or see clearly from our vantage point. At times He allows a plan to go awry for the saving of our souls. Sometimes He lets us become disappointed, detoured, or derailed because He knows that otherwise He could not save us. At times God allows us to be cracked or hurt or bruised to get our attention and help us set our priorities straight because He wants to save us from further disaster. Ultimately, though, He just plain wants to save us because He love us so much.

GLORIA STELLA FELDER

(?) Thought: Some trials come just because of sin, not because God wants, or even allows, them in our lives. Read I Peter 5:7 and Isaiah 26:3 for promises of His care.

Declaration of Love

And now abideth faith, hope, charity, these three; but the greatest of these is charity. 1 Cor. 13:13.

ALL YEAR I ANXIOUSLY await the months of October or November for a very special reason: during three or four days of the year I can see the most beautiful and sweet declaration of God's love for me.

In this season, as I leave my home for work, I look attentively from inside the bus to find this declaration—a beautiful, yellow, flowering ipê tree *(Tabebuia ochracea)*, which is a national symbol of Brazil.

It is spring in the Southern Hemisphere, and between the months of October and November we see these trees, which are totally covered with flowers. Not even one green leaf is to be seen—just flowers. The yellow blooms last only three or four days, but the majestic view of their spectacular golden color is well worthwhile, especially when observed in contrast with the blue sky and the green trees around it. These three colors together—green, blue, and yellow—under the splendorous sunlight fill us with a feeling of patriotism in Brazil because these colors represent our national flag.

I get impatient to touch these flowers, to feel nearer to the love of God for me, and I then continue on, comforted. In the future I will see another tree, beautiful and flowering in the same manner. I will feel as though I am being touched by marvelous and indescribable love.

Just as the flowers of these trees grow and rapidly bloom each year and disappear just as quickly, our lives also go through abrupt changes and difficult times. However, soon we will have the glorious blossoming of eternity! In contrast to the beautiful yellow flowers, eternity will not pass away, and we will live forever with the One who created us and who helps us to remember His love in the simple but marvelous beauty of the flowers He created. And while I await the arrival of the first yellow flowers opening on the ipê tree, I attempt to remember that His love goes with me each day.

Thank You, Lord, for giving us so many examples and proof of Your great love for us!   TÂNIA MICOL S. BARTALINI

New Beginnings

Behold I make all things new. Rev. 21:5.

Therefore if any man be in Christ, he is a new creature: old things are passed away; behold, all things are become new. 2 Cor. 5:17.

THE WARMTH OF THE October sun felt good as I walked in a nearby park. The gentle breeze made the weather seem perfect and refreshing as I soaked in nature's abundance. With each lap I smiled as I felt the hardened brown leaves under my feet, each making a unique crunching sound. Very soon these leaves, which looked so fragile and lifeless, would be replaced by the new, green, lively leaves of spring.

New beginnings. Those who don't have a relationship with Christ come to mind. They too seem hardened, fragile, and as lifeless as the brown leaves of fall. They too are often stepped upon by the weight of our uncaring, unloving, and lack of acceptance, or, as one pastor stated, the weight of our "long memories"—our unwillingness to forgive and forget mistakes of the past. They are often treated like the brown leaves we gather and disregard because there is no use for something in which we see no potential. Yet Jesus commissions us to love unconditionally and see the good, the potential, in others. We should see others through His eyes, who knows that failures are never final! He always wants us, no matter how fragile or lifeless. He wants us, and as His ambassadors we must follow His example. We must gather into our arms those without a relationship with Him, and provide a covering, a shelter of safety, love, and acceptance.

A special friend reminds me daily of how such a covering can aid in rebuilding and reconciliation. Many have seen him as a failure because of past mistakes made before he had a committed walk with God. But now he has a circle of Christian friends who love and accept him just as he is, no strings attached. He has friends who believe in the God of second chances, the God of new beginnings. Although it's fall and the leaves of nature are brown, fragile, and lifeless, in the life of my precious friend it's spring!

I'm smiling again and walking with a more rapid stride, my eyes filled with tears of joy as I witness God's gift of restoration and reconciliation. What an awesome privilege to have been chosen to be a part of such an experience! My friend is becoming a new creature in Christ! I marvel at God's gift of a new beginning.

TERRIE RUFF

Double Bagged

I delight greatly in the Lord; my soul rejoices in my God. For He has clothed me with garments of salvation and arrayed me in a robe of righteousness. Isa. 61:10, NIV.

THE WEATHER FORECAST was gloomy. Hurricane Frances, though a category 4 storm with wind gusts of 140 miles per hour, was predicted to move sluggishly through our state, leaving fallen trees, demolished houses, and broken power lines in its wake. Anticipating the worst, we hunkered down in my mother-in-law's comfortable house so that the family could be together. Our brief stay became a sojourn of several days when we were without electricity at the height of the storm.

At breakfast one morning I noticed a steady stream of tiny, almost transparent, brown ants marching determinedly toward the cereal boxes. I tried to push them away. They came back. I tried to scrub them away. They came back. My mother-in-law sprayed them. They came back.

The next morning there they were again. These tiny ants, commonly known as sugar ants, are one of the petty but annoying irritants of living south of the frost line. Relentlessly and without a sound, they advance toward their goal: obtaining nourishment for their colony.

Knowing that the grocery shelves would be bare in the aftermath of the storm, I determined to protect the last box of my favorite cereal from the tiny marauders. I firmly bagged it in a clean, dry plastic bag, using not only one but two very tightly tied knots. My supportive family declared me the winner of the ant versus human encounter. Our subsequent breakfasts found only fruit and soymilk floating in the Cheerios.

As we pondered the significance of double bagging, we saw two powerful connections with our spiritual life. The cereal didn't have a choice—we do. We can fight battles on our own, but how much more effective and certain our victory when we allow ourselves to be double bagged, as it were, with God's grace, protection, and assurance. Choosing daily to be double bagged with the Holy Spirit also protects us from negative influences and temptations that nibble away at our spiritual core.

Dear God, let Your presence shut out life's minor irritants just as the barrier bag shut out the sugar ants. Help me, after accepting Christ's redeeming and sanctifying love, to enclose myself in His robe of righteousness.

JANET M. GREENE

The Bitter Cold

Here I am! I stand at the door and knock. If anyone hears my voice and opens the door, I will come in and eat with him, and he with me. Rev. 3:20, NIV.

I LOOK OUTSIDE the window and catch a glimpse of our neighbor's beautiful maple, shaking in the wind. Some of its leaves have already turned a deep red and bright yellow. This, and the rain that is hammering on the tin roof above my head, don't leave any room for doubt—fall is here. I love every season, and fall is always special when I stay inside after having been outside a lot during summer. Lighting a candle and cuddling up with a cup of tea and a good book when the weather is really rough outside is one of the best things I know, given the fact that it is cozy and warm inside.

But that's exactly what it isn't right now. I already wear a scarf and an extra pair of socks, and I have a blanket wrapped around me—and still I'm not really feeling warm. My fingers get cold working on the computer. I have to ask my landlord to turn on the heating system. I have been thinking this for at least two weeks but didn't want to trouble him, always thinking, *He will turn it on when he feels cold himself. Don't be such a softy!* I decide to look at the valves of my radiators—they used to get stuck during summer. With a screwdriver and a hammer I work on the first radiator, feeling a little proud that I know how to do this myself. I hear a gurgling noise—warm water is flowing into the radiator! The second radiator isn't even blocked—I just have to turn it on.

How stupid can one human being be? Here I have been sitting, freezing, when all I had to do was turn the radiator on! The warmth has been there all the time, but I didn't let it in.

Isn't this one of the biggest dilemmas of our lives? We shiver in this cold world when all we have to do is let God's love come into our hearts. It's not enough to know that it is there—we have to take away everything that blocks His love from flowing into our hearts. God's love will make us feel warm, even though it's a cold world outside. SONJA KALMBACH

Thought: We don't have a spiritual radiator, so how do we let God's love flow into our lives? How do we warm others who may be cold? Do you have some favorite texts you can share with someone who is cold spiritually?

God's Hand in the Storm

If you make the Most High your dwelling—even the Lord, who is my refuge—then no harm will befall you, no disaster will come near your tent. Ps. 91:9, 10, NIV.

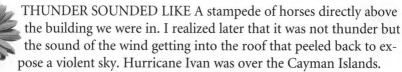 THUNDER SOUNDED LIKE A stampede of horses directly above the building we were in. I realized later that it was not thunder but the sound of the wind getting into the roof that peeled back to expose a violent sky. Hurricane Ivan was over the Cayman Islands.

The medical team hurried to get the more vulnerable people in the shelter to a safer area. Elderly people who had difficulty walking, children with disabilities, and pregnant women were all helped into the cramped bathrooms that seemed relatively safe. Everyone else pressed as close as possible to the end of the hall where the roof still held.

It seemed that death was certain. Winds raged at 165 miles (265 kilometers) an hour. Torrential rain drove down. I knew that this was my last day on this earth. I remembered the passage I had read in my devotional time earlier that morning: "He who dwells in the shelter of the Most High will rest in the shadow of the Almighty" (Ps. 91:1, NIV).

The remainder of that chapter gives assurance to God's people that no harm will come to them when they rest in His love. At that moment in the storm, when things were so uncertain, I had an incredible feeling of calm. God would be with me, even to death!

The occupants of the shelter were finally able to get into a more secure area of the building. We waited out the storm, cramped together and singing praises to the Lord! God had spared us from death, even though we had looked it in the face. As the storm slowly passed, prayers of thanksgiving rose among those gathered.

When we were rescued from the shelter late in the day, it was obvious from the widespread devastation that a divine hand had been protecting us. Buildings and cars everywhere were damaged, and yet none among us was injured.

God is still God. The same God who protected the Israelites in the times of the Old Testament, the same God who calmed the storm in the times of the New Testament, is still alive and working. I praise Him that He still cares for His children and protects us in all the storms of our lives.

ABIGAIL BLAKE PARCHMENT

The Family of God

His unchanging plan has always been to adopt us into his own family by bringing us to himself through Jesus Christ. And this gave him great pleasure. Eph. 1:5, NLT.

IT WAS THE FALL OF 1986 when we received our monthly newsletter from International Children's Care. Each issue had a photo of a child who needed a sponsor to help defray the cost of raising him or her in their Guatemalan orphanage. This particular issue had the cutest picture of a toddler sitting on a rocking horse, and immediately I wanted to sponsor him. Thus began a long relationship with a boy as he grew up many miles away from our Michigan home.

After having adopted a baby girl a couple years after we were married, we tried unsuccessfully to adopt a boy for several years. So when we started sponsoring 2½-year-old Elio, the spot for another child was partially filled. As he got old enough to write to us himself, we received letters and handmade cards at holidays. Every six months we got an updated photo and an official report on his progress in school, health, and social life. Little did he know that we had tried to adopt him but had run into legal difficulties.

In his late teens he started opening up more to us, telling us what he'd like to do with his life, and his frustrations at not having a family to call his own. Throughout his childhood he had trouble accepting the fact that he was an orphan, and he wanted to be adopted. Soon he was 20, and would be graduating from a vocational school with emphasis in computers. His dream was to have us come to his graduation. It didn't seem likely, and we gave him no hope of it happening, even though it was my wish too.

Two months before his graduation I discovered that after my last international flight I had enough frequent flyer miles to make the trip to Guatemala and surprise him. And surprise him I did! He hadn't planned to march because there was no family to see him, but now he scurried around to get things lined up to march because "family" had arrived. His biggest wish had always been to belong to someone.

I wonder: Is it our greatest desire to be adopted into the family of God? We are all orphans until we are born again and received into His family. It's my prayer that you and I will be part of that heavenly family.

DONNA MEYER VOTH

Apples of Gold

A word fitly spoken is like apples of gold in pictures of silver. Prov. 25:11.

TODAY BEGAN AS A "GOLDEN" day. The tall maple tree outside my window wears a crown of golden-red leaves. When the morning sun touches those lovely leaves even the air that surrounds them takes on a golden color. It slowly spreads until the firs have a golden cast. I almost think I can reach through the window and take a handful of golden air in my fingers. I want to breathe this golden air and assimilate it into my body so that I can radiate it back into the atmosphere. Perhaps my face will be golden and shining when I breathe it in and the words I speak will be golden.

Yes, it is a bit of fancy, I know, but when the air looks like this in the fall I always think of this scripture in Proverbs, "apples of gold in pictures of silver." Can't you just see that in your mind? A "word fitly spoken"—many words "fitly spoken"—how beautiful! Where do they come from, these fitly spoken words? From watching television, from gossiping with my neighbor, from reading the latest magazines? I think not. I rather think they come from the Word, His Word.

Sometimes our words rush so quickly from us that it is evident that we have not given much thought to their effect on others. Proverbs 10:20 says, "The tongue of the just is as choice silver." There it is again—the encouragement to have words emanating from our tongues as choice jewels.

The Word has promised us in 2 Timothy 4:8 that "there is laid up for me a crown of righteousness, which the Lord, the righteous judge, shall give me at that day: and not to me only, but unto all them also that love his appearing."

A crown of gold, of silver, of jewels? I pray that this golden day will create within me a kinder tongue with golden and silver words for others so that I may be able to wear the crown being prepared for those who love Him.

BETTY R. BURNETT

? Thought: James 3 also talks about the effect of our words, our tongues. If you want "fitly spoken" words, you might want to study and memorize all the texts referred to today. Fall is a good season for working on golden words.

Miraculous Escape

The Lord is my light and my salvation; whom shall I fear? the Lord is the strength of my life; of whom shall I be afraid? Ps. 27:1.

THIS OCTOBER NIGHT WAS as usual as any other night for the Singh family. Before retiring to our beds, we sat together as a family and studied the Word of God and our Bible study guide. After prayers we said good night to each other and settled in our beds.

About 2:00 a.m. my husband jerked out of bed, suddenly hearing the sound of things falling to the floor. Immediately he rushed to the kitchen to see if rats or other pests had been at their business. To his surprise, there were none. Then he went to the children's bedroom, where he saw various things thrown on the floor. Lotion and body spray containers were scattered around. Our elder son woke and got up; he had dreamed that somebody was throwing his things. He was surprised to see his dad in his room, bending over near the dresser. As he watched, he saw a snake weaving back and forth in front of the mirror. Quietly he alerted his dad. Getting the signal, his dad went out of the room slowly to fetch a stick to kill the snake. By then our sons were out of bed to help their father smash the so-called Satan.

It was a king cobra, measuring about six feet (two meters). By the time the episode ended, it was dawn. My husband and sons dragged the snake outside. Hearing the commotion from our house, some neighbors woke up. When they saw the dead snake hanging on the stick held by my husband, they demanded, "Oh, why did you kill it? It's a god. It's a garland of Lord Shiva."

Our younger son retorted, "What a god you worship, who bites people and they die!"

That night something drastic could have happened. We really thanked God for sparing the lives of my husband and our two sons.

Truly, that night we had been saved miraculously. We thank the Master from the bottom of our hearts for holding us together as a family where God dwells.

TARAMANI NOREEN SINGH

Thought: What kind of picture of God do you have? Someone who waits in darkness to zap people, or the God who protects His children from harm? Many people are afraid of God. Should they be? And if they are, what can you say to them?

The Key Chain

Call to me and I will answer you. Jer. 33:3, NIV.

I WAS WALKING ALONG a dirt road by tall eucalyptus trees. On the ground, beds of leaves had formed, and as I walked along, distracted, I had my key chain in my hand. A playful dog, wanting me to play with her, jumped up, pulled the key chain out of my hand, and took off running and jumping. I began to run after her, hoping to recover my key chain before she lost it.

By the time I reached her, she no longer had the key chain in her mouth. I began to search for it, returning several times to the places she had been, but I found nothing. I began to shuffle the leaves with a stick, thinking that the key chain could have fallen among them. Nothing! The sun began to hide, and I had to call off my search until morning. I returned to my house, but the only way to get in was to go through the kitchen window.

The next day I remembered that I had lost the key chain, so I asked my son to come with me on my search, certain that with two of us looking for it we would soon find it. But this did not happen. Already concerned with the late hour, I said to him, "Billy, let's pray!"

We knelt, and I told the Lord that if it had been another day I could dedicate more time to the search. But since it was a Friday, the preparation day, I had many things to do before Sabbath. So I trusted that He would help us quickly find the key chain.

When we finished with "amen" and opened our eyes, without even moving from our position I exclaimed, "Billy, the key chain!" There in front of us, in a pile of leaves we had moved several times, were the keys, sparkling as the rays of sun hit them.

Billy retrieved the key chain, and we again prayed, now thankful to God for His infinite love.

"Ask and it will be given to you" (Matt. 7:7, NIV).

CLARA HORNUS DE FERREYRO

? Thought: If God is willing to help us find small things such as key chains, how eager do you suppose He is to help His children find eternal life? Are you praying that He will help you find this vitally important item?

Well Equipped

Now, may the God of peace, who brought again from the dead our Lord Jesus, equip you with all you need for doing his will. May he produce in you, through the power of Jesus Christ, all that is pleasing to him. Jesus is the great Shepherd of the sheep by an everlasting covenant, signed with his blood. To him be glory forever and ever. Amen. Heb. 13:20, 21, NLT.

IT WAS MIDMORNING, a time when normal traffic is low. But this particular day was different—cars stretched as far in front and behind as I could see. I thought it wasn't so bad, because traffic kept flowing smoothly forward. But just when I began to feel it was OK, the woman in the car in front of me in the right lane had her left turn signal on, but no one seemed to want to let her into the left lane.

I decided to let her in ahead of me, thinking that she may need to turn left at the next street, and I wanted to help her. I was wrong. As soon as she moved her car in front of my car she slowed down and started putting makeup on, unaware that the traffic ahead of her had moved on, and the cars behind me kept piling up. Then she started fixing her hair.

At first I was irritated; then I remembered my prayer before I left the house. I had prayed for traveling mercies and that I would honor His name in everything I did. How could I honor His name at that moment if I allowed myself to be irritated by this little incident? I began thinking about how often I put myself first, not realizing the effect on others. Seeing this woman driving without consideration of others in traffic made me wonder, *How often do I hinder others spiritually by blocking them from going forward because of my wrong actions or bad attitude?*

I have the assurance of God, who equipped me with all I need to do His will. Let me—let us—learn from every incident that has happened in the past, as well as circumstances to come, to use what God has equipped us with and overcome any stumbling blocks in our path.

Lord, help me recognize what selfish ways I need to overcome that I will be able to honor Your holy name, for I have assurance that You have equipped me with all I need to do Your will. EUNICE URBANY

(?) Thought: Does this text mean that we should never become irritated? How should we handle such situations?

The Fun of Being You

And who then is willing to consecrate [his or her] service this day unto the Lord? 1 Chron. 29:5.

I WON MANY ART CONTESTS in high school. After graduation I was contacted as a candidate for a mechanical drawing job, preparing important blueprints for a national company. Though my mathematical skills were poor, I took the test anyway. I failed. I remember thinking that if the work was as hard as the lengthy four-hour test I'd have been miserable with the job anyway. Certainly I wouldn't have had the fun of being me. Mechanical drawing and I didn't mix.

After I became a writer, I noted this quote by Wally Amos, the man who created the Famous Amos chocolate-chip cookies: "The Lord gives us all a special way of getting pleasure, something that connects the brain and the hands and the personality. You should never miss out on your calling, or the fun of being you."

Along the way I've had some "day jobs" that weren't me, either. I've learned from each one to appreciate the special talent God reserved for me. In my late 30s I asked God to allow me to do something special for Him. I prayed for three years before I knew there was a writer inside me. I soon learned that God designed me for a purpose, "that I may publish with the voice of thanksgiving, and tell of all thy wondrous works" (Ps. 26:7).

God used a church nominating committee to answer my prayer. I was asked to serve as press secretary and started writing press releases. Soon I was offered a job with a local newspaper as a stringer. Voilà! A journalistic career and many thousands of published words followed.

I also didn't know that God would plant and replant my husband and me across the United States, equipping me with much writing fodder. God allowed me rare opportunities to witness to people of renown, people I would never have met except as a writer. Thus, I discovered how God can take a very common woman and allow her to do uncommon things.

If you haven't prayed such a prayer of service because you think God can't use you, think again! Don't pass up the chance to have the fun of being you. Just be willing.

I wasn't meant to draw blueprints to glorify God, but maybe He designed you for that purpose—or perhaps something altogether different. Why not pray about it right now?   BETTY KOSSICK

October 11

God Cares

Casting all your care upon him; for he careth for you. 1 Peter 5:7.

OFTEN MY MORNING DEVOTIONAL reading is exactly what I need for that particular day. Three instances remind me of the mighty God we serve.

I was one of those teenagers who had to have a tan. Every summer I spent hours sunbathing, getting browner and browner. Skin cancer was something I'd never heard of 40 years ago. But now, suddenly in the space of less than a year, I've had three malignant skin cancers removed. The first and second were very painful, and I was relieved when the stitches came out. In time the bruising disappeared. So when I was told about the third, it was a case of "Oh no; do I have to go through it all again?" I was full of self-pity. Then I read the morning's devotional. The text jumped out at me: "But the very hairs of your head are all numbered. Fear ye not therefore, ye are of more value than many sparrows" (Matt. 10:30, 31). God was looking after me, looking out for me, taking care of me.

The second promise was when my father was very old and frail and could talk only in a whisper. Dad had been a farmer, strong and fit, and like all farmers worked from dawn to dusk—all of which added to the anguish I was then feeling. The circle of life had turned. Now I was the one feeding my father mashed food at his meals. One day as I sat by his bed, stroking his sparse, white hair, the tears came. The text for that day? "And God shall wipe away all tears from their eyes; and there shall be no more death" (Rev. 21:4).

The third devotional that was heaven-sent occurred when we were in the middle of our preparations for our move from Australia back to New Zealand after 16 years. What a stressful time! My husband and I were getting only a few hours of sleep night after night as our brains worked overtime going over and over the many things still to be done. Early one morning, as the packing mess seemed to be closing in on me, I asked God, *How am I going to get through this day?* And He told me in my devotional reading, "I will never leave thee, nor forsake thee" (Heb. 13:5).

I can only repeat, What a mighty God we serve!

LEONIE DONALD

The Children's Day Present

Train up a child in the way he should go: . . . he will not depart from it.
Prov. 22:6.

CHILDREN'S DAY IS CELEBRATED on October 12 in Brazil. On this day in 1974 I received a baby doll as a present. I was 21 years of age at the time, and my baby doll was beautiful. She had very bright blue eyes, and the most incredible thing about my baby doll was that she not only cried; she moved her arms and legs, smiled, and—breathed!

When I arrived home from the hospital with my "present" in a little bundle, I was curious and wanted to open the package and verify the contents. She was a perfect doll! I took her in my arms, knelt down, and lifted her up to heaven, thanking God for His perfect present. I then asked Him for wisdom, strength, and patience to lead her in His ways. My wish was that she would grow and live to serve this wonderful God.

My doll began to grow, walk, and talk. She was intelligent, lively, and also impetuous and independent. She went through all the stages of childhood and adolescence full of health and joy. When she turned 18, she decided to go out into the world. I felt like the father of the prodigal son, waiting each day for her return.

And one day she returned.

We dream of many things for our children, attempting to accomplish in them our perfect dreams. When these dreams do not come true in our children, we feel frustrated, trying to imagine where we failed or why our children chose to do exactly what we didn't want them to do, and we're not able to accept the way that they chose to go. We turn our face from reality, and we lie to ourselves. We forget that Christ accepts us and loves us as we are, with all of our imperfections and with our defective character, because it is in this context that He accomplishes His work in us.

Our children are presents from God. It is through them that we are able to understand better the infinite love that our God has for us, always giving us one more chance. When we ask Him for forgiveness, He opens His eternal arms of love to receive us with joy.

Thank You, Lord, because You are the Father who receives the prodigal son or daughter with open arms. Thank You, Lord, for giving me patience to know, to wait, and to see Your promise fulfilled in my beautiful blue-eyed baby doll.

Maria de Lourdes Fernandes

My U.S. Visa

In all thy ways acknowledge him, and he shall direct thy paths. Prov. 3:6.

MY FAMILY AND I had been in Canada for almost 30 years, and I had come to love my adopted country in spite of the cold winters. It is a very peaceful country. Then my mom petitioned me to come and join her in sunny California. It was only last year that we received mail from the U.S. embassy regarding retiring in the States. We had our ample pensions to live on.

We were required to apply for our visas in the city of Montreal in Quebec. This city has a complicated subway and autobus system, and the French Canadians do not seem to communicate to anyone except in French. So we needed someone to guide us.

I was sure that the Lord would send us someone who knew Montreal to help us. My daughter-in-law, Myrna, volunteered to accompany us since she had a cousin, Cherry, whom she hadn't seen for 10 years. She contacted her, and she willingly consented to accommodate and help us find where we ought to go. She even took a day off and had the tickets for the subways ready. Not only that, but she treated us royally with sumptuous meals and a very comfortable place to rest.

Cherry took us to the U.S. embassy and left us for the interview while she went shopping with Myrna. The interview was short and quick, with just a very few simple questions, and they said our visas would be ready in a half hour. The half hour turned into an hour, and then two hours, with no call. Finally we were called. The woman was very apologetic—somebody had made a mistake and stamped my visa in my husband's passport.

The mistake was not a big deal. I praised the Lord and thanked Him for sending Myrna and Cherry to help us. What would have been a difficult situation for us turned into a blessing for each one of us.

Someday I will be needing my last visa on my homeward journey, and Jesus will be there to make sure things go well. Nobody will make any mistakes when we are faithful to Him.   EMRALINA PANGAN IMPERIO

(?) Thought: Consider how you might be able to help someone obtain her heavenly visa. What would you consider a visa for heaven to be? What are the similarities and differences between a heavenly visa and a visa to another country? And how do we obtain a visa for heaven?

One Moment in Time

I can do all things through Christ who strengthens me. Phil. 4:13, NKJV.

FOR YEARS I'VE BATTLED with seasonal lymphedema. My legs swell in the summer, and not in the winter. Last October my right leg began to swell, while the left leg remained normal. Every day my right leg was consistently larger than the left. For years I've gone to one doctor after the other without any real treatment that helped my legs. I tried natural remedies, such as raw foods and herbs. You name it, I've tried it.

In an attempt to get a quick fix, my last and final move was to go to a vascular surgeon. I wanted him to give his expert advice on my lymphedema. I was sure that he'd offer a dream come true. I visualized myself walking down the street on two good legs, golden as the sun rays with a mango hue.

The doctor appeared very unassuming. He spoke carefully to me. I wondered if I was in the right place. His manner almost seemed angelic to me. I began to wonder if I'd been "had" by the Lord. His delivery and poise reminded me of God.

He asked me what I was looking for in terms of my leg. I said emphatically, "I am looking for a cure; I want my old legs back!"

He said, "You can have your old legs back, but you must adjust your lifestyle."

This is where I sat up. (I had been lying back on the examination table.) He went on to say that my life would be about constant choices. He explained how change in lifestyle choices could enhance the quality of life for my legs.

It was at this point—one moment in time—that I realized that God had been trying to speak to me all along. I never really wanted to be a part of my healing over time. I would have rather opted for spontaneous healing, quick microwave healing. I realized I must choose the abundance of life rather than the quick fix of death, changes such as drinking water instead of juice, eating to live instead of living to eat.

As I continue on this journey I thank God for His divine providence in leading me to make better choices than I made the day before. And isn't that the Christian life? Making daily right choices? MADEIA JACOBS

The Hidden Word

Your word is a lamp to my feet and a light to my path. Ps. 119:105, NKJV.

IN MY TEENAGE YEARS reciting memory verses was a regular part of our youth meetings, and we diligently memorized sizable portions of Scripture during the course of a year. Even today some of these verses come readily to mind.

Why should we learn scriptures and store them in our memory banks? Is there any benefit to us even years after they were committed to memory?

During a time of severe stress I was worn down physically. One day as I worried over my situation a scripture came into my mind: "Trust in the Lord with all thine heart; and lean not unto thine own understanding" (Prov. 3:5). It reminded me that although I couldn't see a way through the problem, God could. Just what I needed at that time.

Attending a women's retreat for the first time, I was asked to give a short talk on mission trips I'd been involved in. After breakfast, as I sat quietly gathering my thoughts, the butterflies in my stomach started to flap their wings. I prayed for help to calm me down and sort out my thoughts. Immediately came to my mind the words "In quietness and in confidence shall be your strength" (Isa. 30:15). Reflecting on this later, I couldn't recall ever actually learning this verse, and in fact I had to use a concordance to find the reference, but at the time it was just what I needed. Since that day, any time I have to speak before a crowd of people this verse calms my thoughts and my knocking knees.

Even hymns and songs of praise can provide just the help we need at times. I recently traveled by plane with my daughter-in-law and her three children as they returned to their home in Fiji. After the routine safety instructions my imagination started working overtime. If we had to evacuate the plane midocean, how were we going to manage with a newborn baby and his two sisters depending on us? I was busy constructing this desperate scene in my mind when the words from an old song cut short my thoughts: "Fear thou not, for I am with thee, I will still thy Pilot be." I sang the words over in my mind for a while and then settled back to enjoy the flight.

Yes, there is value in time spent storing messages from God's Word in our memory banks.   ANNE CRAM

Daddy!

And ye shall know the truth, and the truth shall make you free. John 8:32.

AS DADDIES DO, my dad liked to tell us stories. We surely did like to listen to his stories, too. One story he'd tell often was the one about the day he was born, October 16, 1902. He claimed to remember it very well. As we grew older, we got a little wiser and doubted he really knew what happened on that day. But our doubts never deterred him from telling the story.

Finally I got a chance to talk to my aunt Ruth about Daddy telling tales about his day of birth. She said that all the things he said were true. She knew the facts just as he did. Now I really thought both of them were pulling my leg, because Aunt Ruth was born exactly one year and a day after Dad was born! After Aunt Ruth got her fill of teasing me about it, she did tell me that all of the kids knew about the day they were born. The family would tell the story again and again until it was so etched in their memories it was as if they would remember what happened.

Then she asked about the day I was born. It dawned on me halfway through my telling the story that I too remembered all of the events of the day I was born. I remembered how my parents told me the story many times. It was my favorite bedtime, naptime, anytime story. I was always so thrilled to hear how Dad called Mom to tell her that they had their little girl. I'm adopted—that's why Dad had to call Mom to tell her they had a daughter.

Knowing the truth takes that again-and-again telling. It takes that amount of "telling it again and again" to weave it into a remembered part of your life. God's love and the work He has for us to do not only brings glory to Him but also gives meaning to our lives as we tell it again and again.

My prayer is that we will all tell ourselves—and each other—the story of Jesus' love for all of us, not only in our studying His Word but in living it out in our daily lives. It isn't just in knowing what God's message is and the lives we should live; it is living it as it is really meant to be lived—in words and actions, as well as knowing.   MARY E. DUNKIN

Thought: Wouldn't it be wonderful if we all delighted in telling about our born-again birth, and how we were loved and wanted (and still are)? So many people need to hear this story so they can share it too!

Great Is His Faithfulness!

Because of the Lord's great love we are not consumed, for His compassions never fail. They are new every morning; great is Your faithfulness. Lam. 3:22, 23, NIV.

MY HUSBAND AND I became convicted to start a soup kitchen. We wanted to reach people the way Jesus did—sharing the gospel after first meeting their physical needs. Our church couldn't afford the building we looked at, so our members started feeding people on the beach. We would offer food to the homeless, then invite them to worship with us. After eight months God put us in touch with the right people. The same building was still vacant, and God set up a wonderful partnership between the Homeless Coalition and the members of our church. We invited area churches to get involved so that we could have enough volunteers. We now have a multidenominational soup kitchen.

We struggled to get volunteers to help while we were on vacation. We placed an ad in our church bulletin for four weeks, and God sent 14 volunteers to cover. Then our restaurant pickup person quit a few days before we were scheduled to leave on vacation. I took it to the Lord in prayer, as I didn't have time to place another ad. We were due to leave on Friday. On Wednesday one of our members said, "God has spoken your name four times to me, telling me that there is something you need me to pick up for you." I left church on a high, recognizing that God loved me so much that He spoke my name in prayer to get my needs met.

However, on the day we returned, our soup kitchen burned down. I walked through it in tears. But again I saw God's hand in my life. We had a temporary location within one day. Four months later we were in a new building that God had provided.

God's love has shown through all this, increasing my faith tremendously. He has shown me that if He calls you, He will equip you! He cares about your availability, not about your ability. He wants His children to go forward in faith to do whatever He calls them to do. The Lord has shown again and again that He is faithful!

Jesus, please help each of us to realize that nothing touches us that has not gone through Your hands first and to learn to praise You through all circumstances.

DONNA M. DUNBAR

Just a Breath Away

Where can I go from Your Spirit? Or where can I flee from Your presence? If I ascend into heaven, You are there; if I make my bed in hell, behold, You are there. If I take the wings of the morning, and dwell in the uttermost parts of the sea, even there Your hand shall lead me, and Your right hand shall hold me. Ps. 139:7-10, NKJV.

"OH, HOW I NEED THIS, God!" I sit back and exhale. It's finally here—my church's fall retreat for women. The location is by a lake in the hills, where the scenery is breathtaking. The autumn leaves are brilliant, and the water sparkles through the trees. I've grown to look forward to this weekend with great anticipation each year. One of my favorite parts of this annual delight is finding moments alone when I can just "be," just me with my Creator and creation all around.

I, and the group of women I came with, have settled into our cabin located on the side of a hill at the edge of the woods. We stayed up a bit late last night (but no later than I had expected), talking and laughing and just enjoying each other's company.

Now it's just me, in this moment of solitude I've longed for. In the driver's seat of my parked car with the window down, I sit enjoying the autumn breeze and the sunshine. Gazing into the forest, I soak up the warm colors of red, gold, and brown. The only sound I hear is the gentle rustling of leaves, and I know that my Father is near. "In the rustling grass I hear Him pass, He speaks to me everywhere." I sing that beloved hymn inside my mind, because I dare not interrupt the beauty of silence. Does He notice me here as I sense His Spirit go by?

Suddenly I'm aware of a crisp brown leaf floating toward me on the wind. My eyes cross as I follow it through the open window to my face, where, to my surprise, it gently thumps me dead center with a tiny crunch before tumbling into my lap. Cocking my head to one side, I hold up the curious leaf, study it for a moment, and laugh. "Here I am," He seems to whisper on the breeze. "I was just waiting for you to notice Me. I am always with You, just a breath away."

The weekend is over now, and I'm back to my usual daily routines. But that dried-up oak leaf is still sitting in the console of my car. Each time I look at it I am reminded. My Father is always just a breath away.

KELLY PICENO

Love Others While There's Time

If it is possible, as much as depends on you, live peaceably with all men. Rom. 12:18, NKJV.

MY MOTHER-IN-LAW AND I had the most complicated relationship. She felt that my husband had betrayed her by converting to my faith, and I felt rejected. Over the years we had more than our fair share of miscommunications and misunderstandings. To protect my feelings, I built a wall around my heart. I kept our conversation about my children short; I seldom spoke about personal matters and rarely visited. I consoled myself by bringing to mind every single offense and every tiny slight and hurt that she had imposed on me. Yet I was hurting, because the woman I had so much against had raised one of the most giving, wonderful, compassionate people that I know—my husband.

I wanted to tell her that I saw my husband in her. She too was very giving. While I thanked her for every gift to us, I wanted to write her a note to let her know that I truly loved and admired her. I wanted to list all the things we had in common, and I wanted to let her know they are the reasons my husband chose me as his wife. I never did. My pride wouldn't let me.

One day my husband announced that his mom had had a stroke. Suddenly life was taking an unexpected turn. I had no control over time after all. What I had failed to do in a long time I would have to do in a trying time. I rushed to the hospital, praying, *Please, God, stay near my mother-in-law; grant her Your peace and forgiveness.* While I prayed I hoped that I had enough time to be kinder, to forgive and be forgiven, and to love unconditionally.

During the next two weeks I prayed and sang with her. She had lost her language, and her speech was childlike, but she hummed the songs while I sang. One song we sang together was "Down by the Riverside." I would go when no one was there, hold her hands, and pray. I thanked God for her life and begged for forgiveness for wasting time focusing on the hurt instead of the good in my mother-in-law. When she died, I was overcome with grief and loss, but I was thankful for the short time that God had allowed me to care for her.

Dear God, please help me to see the good in others, and as much as it is in me, please help me to live peaceably with others. Rose Thomas

YME

My God, my God, why have you forsaken me? Mark 15:34, NIV.

WHEN I SEE THE LETTERS YME, along with numbers on car license plates, I chuckle, because to me they sound like "Why me?" Many years ago I heard of a couple who had several small children. At one point problems and more problems began. The only one I recall was about their little girl of 7 or 8, who fell out of an upper bunk bed and broke her arm. The family's reaction to the many problems was not "Why me [or us]?" but "God must love us very much to send trials to test our love and faith in Him." By now those children are grown and have families of their own. I imagine their attitude remains the same.

In my 70-plus years I've had plenty of opportunities to ask "Why me?" I used to say not "Why me?" but "Why not me? I'm no better than other people."

Then several years ago something very drastic caused me to change my attitude. I was unable to sleep. The day's events were milling around in my mind, and yes, I had many "why" questions. "Why did it happen, Lord? Why didn't Angie [my angel] warn me? What are You trying to teach me, Lord?" and on and on.

More recently something else happened—not as drastic, but bad enough. Strangely, for some reason, the "why" questions never entered my mind. I don't understand the difference.

In 2004 several of the many devastating hurricanes came close enough to my little corner of Virginia to cause a night of heavy rain. The first one caused part of the shingled roof of my rented home to leak. Water dripped down through the attic crawl space and seeped through the ceilings. It didn't drip onto the carpet and furniture, but the water stains needed repairing. I was grateful because what are a few water stains compared to losing everything?

"Why me?" is a very common way to feel. Even Jesus asked that heart-wrenching "Why?" in His cry "My God, My God, why have You forsaken Me?"

Now, when I see those three letters YME, I smile and think, *OK, my precious Big Brother, You had a "why" question, so I guess I can have some too! Thank You for being with me always. I love You!*

PATSY MURDOCH MEEKER

Jesus, Get in Our Car

But they urged him strongly, "Stay with us, for it is nearly evening; the day is almost over." Luke 24:29, NIV.

AS WE LEFT OUR APARTMENT one day to go to a clinic specializing in hydrotherapy for treatment of a neurological problem in my right foot, my husband and I prayed, as we always do, asking for God's guidance in our lives.

As we opened the door to the car, my husband said, "Jesus, get in the car and go with us!" The seat belts were adjusted, the day was beautiful, traffic was calm, everything was normal. Little did we know, however, what awaited us five minutes down the road.

As we passed through an intersection the engine of our car died. There was enough space for the oncoming vehicle to get by, but the driver was young and inexperienced, and he was unable to swerve or even brake, and he hit our car violently. The two doors on the driver's side were smashed in, and the impact threw our car against a wall, damaging the vehicle even more.

Passersby came to our rescue, thinking that our injuries must be serious. However, when we were able to get out of our car seats, my husband and I—and the other motorist—discovered that we had no injuries, not even a scratch.

After an evaluation of the vehicles by the insurance company, we were informed that our car had been totaled. We then understood that our special Guest had accepted our invitation to accompany us and had kept us from sudden death.

After a long talk, the two travelers who were going to Emmaus didn't know who had approached them and accompanied them. They also realized that the day was coming to an end and were concerned about what could happen to this Traveler if He were to go on alone on the dark and deserted road. Kindly they asked Him to stay with them. The Man accepted the invitation, entered the house of His fellow travelers, and accepted the meal they offered. Only then did they understand that Jesus was the one who had walked with them.

Now when I stop and think, I can understand how wonderful it was to invite Jesus to get in the car with us. He is always willing to answer when our request is sincere and made in faith. MARIA BELLEZI GUILHÉM

Extreme Makeover

Therefore if any [woman] be in Christ [she] is a new creature: old things are passed away; behold, all things are become new. 2 Cor. 5:17.

I'M NOT INTO REALITY TV shows, but one caught my eye the other night. Women were chosen to have a total makeover so that they could be transformed from "ugly ducklings" into "swans." I watched as some got nose jobs, breast implants, liposuction, new hairdos, new wardrobes, body sculpting, and much more. They went through many painful, agonizing weeks and waited with great anticipation for bandages to be taken off so that they could see their new look.

Family and friends eagerly awaited the day they would be reunited with their loved ones and see the transformation at the great unveiling. There were a lot of tears, laughter, hugs, and kisses when the new woman was revealed. Husbands didn't recognize their wives or children their mothers. I wondered why some women feel the need to go through such an experience. We don't seem to be satisfied with what we have been blessed with. Is it because society has brainwashed us into thinking that beauty lies in what we see in magazines and on billboards?

Those women may look different after surgery, but that is all—their personalities and characters remain untouched. After the hype and excitement is over and the tummy begins to sag and the age lines return by their eyes, one can only wonder if it was worth it.

All of us need extreme makeovers because we are born in sin and shaped in iniquity. There is only one Person I know who can truly transform us, and that is Jesus. There are many examples in the Bible that show us the transforming power of God through His Son Jesus Christ. Take the Samaritan woman at the well, for instance. Read the story in John 4. People ridiculed her, as they knew her lifestyle. One day she had an encounter with Jesus, and that transformed her. He revealed her life story to her, and she marveled at Him, for He had told her everything she had done. He offered her what no man had ever offered her before—a new life. She ran from the well testifying of Christ, never to be the same again.

We all need an encounter with Christ if we are to be transformed. Have you had an encounter with Him?

SHARON LONG (BROWN)

Don't Forget Your Umbrella

Therefore be ye also ready: for in such an hour as ye think not the Son of man cometh. Matt. 24:44.

IT HAD RAINED MOST of the night, but by morning the sun had managed to peek through the clouds, offering faint hope for a sunny day. As my daughter and I drove into the city I mentioned that the possibility of more storms was still a reality since they seemed to come regularly during the evening. "Don't forget your umbrella," I said to Alicia.

She smiled. "Don't worry, Mom; it's not going to rain."

Certain that she was wrong, I waited until we reached her place of work and again offered the umbrella. "Alicia, I really think you should take the umbrella," I suggested again.

"Mom, I don't think it's going to rain," she responded. "But if you insist, I'll take the umbrella." Feeling a bit more at ease, I continued on to my destination and the day's activities.

By midafternoon the first storm cloud appeared. In a very short time another rolled into place, blocking the sun and turning what had been a sunny day into an afternoon of premature darkness. Then the rains came fast and furious, soaking everything in their path. I thought of Alicia and immediately felt at ease because she had accepted the offer of an umbrella, even when no storm seemed apparent.

God told Noah that it was going to rain and to warn the people. Unfortunately, only eight people accepted the offer of cover. I've often wondered whether I would have heeded Noah's warning. Would I have understood? But an even greater question looms today. God has given us many warnings as to what will happen in the future, and the critical question I ask myself is Am I heeding this warning? Am I ready for His return?

My friend, this is a question that must be asked daily. Our Father has warned that the end is coming and to be ready. It's not His desire that any be lost. According to His Word, it won't be water that destroys, but fire. He loves us so much that He tells us kindly, "Be ready."

My sisters, let's promise that we are going to meet Him in peace. Let's do all we can to be ready.

Come quickly and take us there. Amen. YVONNE CURRY SMALLWOOD

Follow Him; He Knows the Way

But he knows the way that I take; when he has tested me, I will come forth as gold. Job 23:10, NIV.

IT WAS THE SECOND TIME I had called my girlfriends, Clelia and Linda, to invite them to lunch. The other week I had called them, but Linda had said she had already packed her lunch for the day. Clelia had said yes, but later on changed her mind because there was not enough time. Today my husband and I decided to invite them again. Clelia enthusiastically said yes, but Linda again said, "I have already packed my lunch!" I told her that she could reserve her lunch for the next day, but she was flying out the next morning. "Why not take your lunch on your trip?" I asked.

"Or I'll just give my lunch to somebody today," she replied.

Many times we argue with the Lord, giving Him so many excuses. "Lord, everything is already planned; I can't back off." I thought I had it all planned to go to England. I'd seen good fares on the Internet, and my heart was set for it. However, God came up with a better plan: to visit Luda and the boys. Luda is my younger sister, who lives in Fresno, California, with her three boys. Yes, I do visit her, but haven't really spent time enough to make memories.

I really didn't toy with the idea of going to Fresno until one day my husband announced, "I got your ticket to Fresno; it's my birthday gift to you!" However, I reasoned with the Lord, "If it's a birthday gift, can't I choose? How about England?"

I followed the Lord's leading, though, and went to Fresno, and I'll never trade the time I spent with my sister and the boys, because I saw the joy I brought to them. We did gardening, we painted, we played, we shopped—we did so many things together. Not only that, but I was doubly blessed myself because God gave me a bonus—He sent my daughters to join us that weekend.

Linda was willing to pass up a free lunch. God's invitation to us is also free: "Come to me, all you who are weary and burdened, and I will give you rest" (Matt. 11:28, NIV).

Let's start our day by accepting God's invitation. We can be sure that He has something wonderful waiting for us!

JEMIMA D. ORILLOSA

Saying Thank You

And one of them, when he saw that he was healed, turned back, and with a loud voice glorified God. Luke 17:15.

"THANK YOU SO MUCH," my pastor's wife said over the phone. "It meant so much to me!"

Teresa had called me to thank me for the handmade birthday card I'd sent. I told her she was very welcome and that I was glad she had liked it. "I send out lots of cards," I told her, "but very few people acknowledge them or remember to say thank you." I often wondered if my card made any difference in their day or week. It was nice to hear words of appreciation.

Compared to the 10 to 20 note cards that I send out each month, I receive a low response to my correspondence. Of course, I don't send cards for the sole purpose of feedback, but at times I wonder if I should even continue this mini-ministry.

After talking with Teresa, I thought again of how nice it was to hear thank you. I began to feel a little sorry for myself. *How much does it take to acknowledge a letter or note?* I thought.

Then a Bible story flashed into my mind: Jesus and the 10 lepers. When Jesus had commanded the 10 to show themselves to the priests, they all left Jesus quicker than you can say "unclean" to do His bidding. They all were ready to go back to their homes, their lives, and their families. They had places to go and people to see.

But there was one grateful soul. One leper had the presence of mind to come back and humbly, praisefully, respectfully, give thanks to his Healer.

And Jesus' response? "Were there not ten cleansed? But where are the nine?" (Luke 17:17). Jesus was happy that this man, a Samaritan, had returned to give thanks. But Jesus was also very aware of the remaining nine who had not acknowledged His help, His healing. His heart must have hurt to think that only one deemed it important enough to come back and give thanks.

I began to wonder how many times I, as His child, forget to give thanks. I know how glad I am when I am appreciated. I feel loved, supported, and cared for. Shouldn't I give Jesus the same courtesy—no, *more* courtesy—by praising Him every time I lift my voice up in prayer?

TRICIA WILLIAMS

Striving for the Mastery

Abide in me, and I in you. John 15:4.

WALKING IS JUST ONE STEP away from falling. That's why venturing out on two unsteady legs can be frightening to a very young child. Yet children keep at it until walking becomes second nature. This is similar to the walk of the Christian: we put our faith into practice, one step at a time.

Growth involves pain. Ever heard of growing pains? Could it be that the fiery trials that we encounter on our Christian journey are our growing pains?

A severe trial is sometimes called an acid test.

One person prayed, "Dear Lord, why are You allowing this to happen? I don't understand why it is that as I endeavor to live for You, everything seems to be falling apart!" Some years later that prayer changed. "Lord, I thank You for the trials You allowed. You are not an arsonist; You are a refiner."

Are you struggling in your Christian growth? Do you need help?

The story is told of a man who took home a cocoon so that he could watch the emperor moth emerge. As the moth struggled to get through the tiny opening, the man looked on in pity. Feeling sorry for the creature, he enlarged the opening of the cocoon with a merciful snip of his scissors. The moth emerged easily—but its wings were shriveled. It crawled around slowly until it died. It was never able to fly. The struggle through the narrow opening is God's way to force fluid from its body and into its wings to make them ready for flight. The merciful snip, in reality, was cruel.

Hebrews 12 describes the Christian life as an effort that involves discipline, correction, and training in righteousness. Surely such a race could not be run without a holy striving against self and sin. Sometimes the struggle is exactly what we need for us to soar on spiritual wings.

For believers to grow spiritually, the old habits and desires and ways of thinking have to die. As the old things are put to death, we automatically make room for Jesus. JACKIE HOPE HOSHING-CLARKE

(?) Thought: Invite Jesus to abide with you in your struggles today. By the end of the day you'll find that you have grown.

Does He Care?

Behold, the Lord's hand is not shortened, that it cannot save; neither his ear heavy, that it cannot hear. Isa. 59:1.

WALKING BACK HOME after work, I bumped into the campus gardener. He told me, "Your dog has met with an accident at 11 Hailey Road."

Brownie was lying on the road with a broken spine. I lifted up her head and called her name. She looked at me and seemed to say, "Please take care of my nine puppies." Across the road her puppies were whining away. I couldn't help weeping. My poor stray dog!

I couldn't find anyone who could help me. Disappointed, I paced the floor at home, pleading with my Father. With tears in my eyes I said, "Father, You have given this dog to be my joy, to accompany me every morning on my walk. Now she is dying. What will happen to her nine puppies? Please do something to save Brownie and her puppies."

Just at that moment I heard urgent honking outside my house. When I looked out, I saw a man on a scooter. Seeing me, he asked, "May I see the Christian lady who needs help for her dog?"

When I told him that I was the one, he stepped into my house and wrote on a piece of paper, "Prevention of Cruelty to Animals Society, New Delhi." He handed the paper to me, saying, "Go to this place. The society will take care of your dog and puppies and will charge nothing."

I thanked him, but as he left, I asked, "Sir, how did you know that I needed help for my dog?" He paused for a moment. Then he said, "Something very unusual happened. I was driving on Bara Khamba Road on my way to the office when I heard inside me a voice saying, 'Turn to Hailey Road.' Automatically I turned to Hailey Road. Then a guard at the Iran Embassy gate stopped me and said, 'Sir, please go to the next apartment at 11 Hailey Road to help a Christian lady who needs help for her dog.' So that was it, lady!" He smiled and left.

With wet eyes I whispered, "Thank You, Father. If You care for a stray dog, how much more You care for me!"

"Behold, the Lord's hand is not shortened, that it cannot save, neither his ear heavy, that it cannot hear."

ANNIE M. KUJUR

Sunset

The heavens declare the glory of God; the skies proclaim the work of his hands. Ps. 19:1, NIV.

WE WERE RETURNING HOME in a small plane from Portland, Oregon, to Vancouver, British Columbia, Canada. It was almost sunset as we lifted off, and below us the mighty Columbia River was winding its last few miles to the Pacific Ocean. I thought of other parts of this river I had seen on its long journey from the hills of British Columbia (which gets its name from the river) down through Washington State, near Walla Walla College, and then westward through the Columbia Gorge to the sea. What dramatic differences in God's creation this river sees as it makes this journey.

When the plane reached cruising altitude, a tremendous kaleidoscope of landscapes passed beneath us. The river, the fertile fields and orchards of Washington State, the irregular coastline, the small islands, and, in the distance, the mountains of the Olympic Peninsula. Above them the evening sun was just touching the clouds with splashes of pink and purple.

As we traveled and the sun got lower, the colors intensified. Now the Olympic Mountains were in bold relief against the setting sun, and the sky was a vivid orange. As we got nearer to the border, just across the narrow strip of water, the lights of the city of Victoria, British Columbia, began to twinkle.

The picture from my window seat in the plane was fascinating, always changing, and by far the most impressive sunset I have ever seen. Now the plane began its descent into Vancouver. Below there appeared to be pink candy floss all along the coast. What was this strange phenomenon? As we lost altitude it became obvious what this pink floss actually was—a strip of low cloud, or fog, along the coast around the city, and the color came from the pinkness of the sky from the setting sun. All too soon we were in the candy floss and on the runway at the airport. I was reminded that God is a God of beauty, and that He delights in demonstrating His art across a wide expanse of sea and sky and land.

I thanked God not only for a safe trip but also for allowing us to see His majestic glory in His works of art. RUTH LENNOX

(?) Thought: The heavens declare the glory of God. Do you? How?

My Spot

Does God realize what is going on? they ask. Ps. 73:11, NLT.

I WAS RUSHING AGAIN. I had planned to leave early, but I'm one of those rare people who can run late no matter how early I begin to get ready. I've been in situations in which I was actually an hour ahead of schedule only to dillydally until—you guessed it—I found myself running late.

On this particular day I had volunteered to help out at a special event at my son Brandon's school, and I definitely needed to be on time. Each volunteer had been given a time slot, and the switchoff as one shift left and the other came on duty was critical. The kids needed to be adequately supervised at all times—and I was running late.

I was doing a low flight down the highway, praying selfishly that I would not be worthy of police notice. (After all, couldn't the term *speed limit* be left to one's interpretation?) I was already working on my defense strategy, just in case.

Thank You, God, I whispered as I checked my watch. I had a whole five minutes to go, and the school was in sight. As I pulled into the already-crowded parking lot, I spoke out loud: "I need a parking spot now, Lord." As I rounded the corner I spied an opening. It would be tight, but I should just be able to *squeeeeeeeeeezzze* my car into it. I aligned the car for this parallel parking feat. I got out and did an initial visual lineup, then got back in and proceeded to park. Once, twice, three times. No go. "Come on, Lord, You know I'm early; don't bring me this far to make me late," I muttered, quite annoyed. I smarted as I pulled out to look for another spot.

Glancing at my watch, I realized that I was down to two minutes and counting, and I still had to find the kids. I went to the far end of the multibuilding complex and came around the back. With a "Thank You, Lord" on my lips, I stared in wide-eyed amazement. Although the area was filled beyond capacity, with cars parked in every which angle, there was a parking spot waiting just for me. And to add to that blessing, there was my son's class that I would be supervising right across from it!

In life, Lord, help us to realize that You have a "spot" for each of us to fill. Help us each to be faithful to Your direction. MAXINE WILLIAMS ALLEN

Be Careful Whom You Trust!

Casting all your care upon him; for he careth for you. 1 Peter 5:7.

EACH OF US HAS MANY experiences that will never be forgotten, experiences that teach us a lesson. One of my unforgettable experiences occurred during my second year of college. My sister, Carol, decided that we must go to the market to buy something we needed.

While we were waiting for a ride a man came near us. He told us that there would be a Halloween party that night on the Sison Plaza, and that many of our acquaintances from school would attend. It would start around 7:00 p.m. and end at 9:00.

My sister and I were excited; we wanted to join the party, and we promised him that we'd go. I told my friends, Sharon and Rowell, about the event. Then I was really happy because the four of us would go together. But I worried, too, because our parents didn't allow us to go to that type of party. So we never told them.

Around 8:00 in the evening the man came to get us. We were still nervous because we were going to the party, even though our parents didn't know about it, and I prayed that God would lead us even though we didn't have their consent. My heart beat faster—I felt so different because we were on our way to the Halloween party. Then we stopped at the market in Sison and picked up some really rough boys. The four of us felt so nervous, not knowing what to do now. All we could do was pray to God for guidance.

We began thinking about this stranger who had invited us. I've seen such men with guns, bombs, and knives. Then Carol felt in a bag in the vehicle, and there was a gun! I saw with my two eyes a knife in the hand of one guy. I prayed and prayed, "God, please help us!"

It's a miracle, but my classmate Jim came, and we got away. We certainly learned a lesson! We must ask God to help us make good decisions, as well as to save us.

Lord, You know that I'm afraid sometimes. Please be really close today and help me to remember to be confident in You. Jesus, thank You for saving us, even though it cost You so much. Thank You for showing us in such a real way how we can trust You to take care of us, no matter what Satan tries to do to us. Amen.   SAMYLINE P. SAMAILLANO

Promises

Praise be to the Lord. . . . Not one word has failed of all the good promises he gave. 1 Kings 8:56, NIV.

ECHOES OF THE LOON are drifting hauntingly over the misty blue hills this morning, and soon they'll be gone on their mysterious pilgrimage.

The quiet lake water in front of our cabin is now finger-numbing cold, and there is a rim of ice along the shore. As the brisk west wind skims across the lake, I can hear the pleasing sound of nature's win chimes—the tinkle of the ice as it breaks against the sand and the reeds.

Each tree is ablaze with color today. The red and orange maples, the yellow birch, and the golden aspen are beautiful to behold. It's as if each tree has its own inner light bulb and God has plugged them in simultaneously, lighting the world with His reflected glory!

Everywhere the forests are busily scattering their leaves profusely as they patiently design their colorful patchwork quilt in which the earth and the animals will snuggle cozily during the long winter months.

Yesterday I saw two flocks of Canada geese flying overhead, their V formations pointing southward. Their plaintive honking sounded as a signal for everyone to follow.

As I walked along our lane to our mailbox recently I found a few wild berries left on the bushes and some blue wildflowers still blooming on the hillside. When I neared the top of our driveway, a doe and her two fawns were standing silently among the tall pine trees, watching me. As I proceeded, three large partridge flew up from the grass before me. One day after a rain I noticed that a medium-sized bear had left his paw prints behind mine as he followed my previous footprints up our pathway. Occasionally I can still glimpse a white rabbit or a hawk as I take my daily walk, and it's comforting to know that a few of our wildlife friends are still with us.

The days are shorter now, and I savor each one. I find myself yearning to hold on to October with both hands, pleading with it to linger just a little longer. Fall is an all-too-short breathing space between the busy, hot days of summer and the many cold days of winter. But I have the hope that spring will return—green and gentle and generous—as a result of God's ageless and unchanging promise to each of us, and once again the cycle of life will begin.

ROSEMARY BAKER

This Way Up

Those who hope in the Lord will renew their strength. Isa. 40:31, NIV.

IT WAS JUST AN ORDINARY cardboard box, probably picked up in a supermarket and used to transport books and odds and ends in our move to Wales. I think it sat on an open top shelf opposite my bed all the 14 years since we retired here. As far as I was concerned it was always there, just part of the furniture—until one morning in early October.

More than a year before my husband had suffered a major stroke, and after seven months in the stroke rehabilitation ward of our local hospital he came home, thanks to our excellent health service, which had provided necessary equipment and four-times-a-day care helpers. After an initial improvement he had gradually declined, and the months had been long and distressing.

As I woke from a very spasmodic sleep I kept my eyes shut as I prayed, "Lord, I don't think I can do today." I said it out loud, and then lapsed into silence, reviewing the last heartbreaking weeks. He tells us to cast all our care upon Him, and I knew He would answer, because He always has.

"Open your eyes" seemed to be the instruction. I didn't want to because it meant admitting another day into my consciousness. But God had said it. So I did it.

And there, right in front of me, was the cardboard box with three words clearly printed on the side of it that faced me. THIS WAY UP ↑ it said, and it seemed the arrow was for emphasis. "This way up"—there was only one source of help, only one place to go to ask and receive it, and the cardboard box said it all.

I gazed at it for a few long minutes, and I knew God had spoken to me directly. I felt new strength within me. I threw back the bedclothes with the words of an old song echoing in my mind: "Keep looking up, thy God is still the same today. Keep looking up, He will not fail thee come what may."

PEGGY MASON

(?) Thought: Psalm 121 is a good psalm to memorize for those times when we need to be reminded to look up. The ancient Israelites were going to the high places to worship, and even thought the gods of the hills could help them, but David says that his "help cometh from the Lord."

One Mother's Godly Advice

Honor your father and mother, that your days may be long upon the land which the Lord your God is giving you. Ex. 20:12, NKJV.

IT WAS THE END of the first nine weeks of my freshman year in college. I had just received my first quarter grades and was not pleased with some of them. They were not the A's that I'd been receiving during my four years in the parochial boarding high school I had attended. So I decided that college was not for me. I would give up college and my plans to become a teacher. I would get a job and go to work.

My roommate and I had recently received letters from a department of the federal government to come to work for them. They would train us and pay us well, and stated that there were many opportunities for advancement. Our plans were to go to work, save our money, and go to a youth congress in Paris, France, the next summer. Oh, the naïveté of teenagers!

So letters and phone calls went back and forth to my mother and her parents. But they would not be convinced. Mother didn't have a car, she worked full-time, was a single parent, and couldn't make the trip herself. So she enlisted the aid of a wonderful Christian mother in our church to have a visit with me when she came to visit her daughter. This caring woman took me shopping and gave me an encouraging pep talk. She advised me to give college another chance. I'm sure many prayers were offered on our behalf by our parents. So we remained in college. My roommate became a secretary, and I became an elementary school teacher. Both of us worked for the church.

I completed not only my B.A. in elementary education but also my M.A. in administration and supervision. For 38 years I taught, and for a number of years I was an administrator in several church-related schools, working with hundreds of young people and teaching them about the Lord. Had I dropped out of college, what a blessing I would have missed!

As I reflect on those college days I am thankful that my mother had the long-range vision and the wisdom to insist that I continue my college program.

How thankful I am for the advice and sacrifices of a faithful, godly mother and for her insightful counsel through the many years that followed my college days.

PATRICIA MULRANEY KOVALSKI

Lessons From Cleaning the Barn

He answered and said, Whether he be a sinner or no, I know not: one thing I know, that, whereas I was blind, now I see. John 9:25.

MY HUSBAND AND I decided to clean the barn. I knew that meant taking out all the leftover hay, twine from the used bales, feed sacks, scattered bits of grain and sawdust, and horse manure. We had done this many times before. But this time my husband suggested I take a broom and sweep the dusty cobwebs from the stall fronts and tack room walls. So I did.

As I swept I suddenly felt embarrassed. I was the one who always wanted us to keep the barn floor cleaner, yet I hadn't even noticed the cobwebs! There were layers of them all over the walls that had been accumulating for years. Was I blind?

Whenever I went into the barn I always looked at the floor, noticing if it were clean or not, and at the horses and their water buckets and grain trays and hayracks. But I hadn't looked up at the walls. The Holy Spirit began to teach me an object lesson. He reminded me of Jesus' work of cleansing my mind of sin. There are many sins I don't even notice. It's as if I'm blind.

Jesus sees all my sins, but He can't sweep them away unless I know they are there and ask Him to. He gently points them out to me, one at a time, so that I'll become conscious of them. It could be embarrassing that there are so many that I've never even seen, but He so tactfully teaches me and gives me the courage I need to be willing to see them with Him. When I see as He sees and give Him permission, He will sweep them away.

While I was sweeping the walls of the barn I saw some spiders scurrying into the cracks and dark corners. I knew that that very night they would begin making cobwebs again. When Jesus takes away my sins, my carnal nature may seem to hide, but if I don't keep watch, the same sins will begin to show up in my life again.

Once Jesus has made me aware of them I see them, even if I pretend I'm not looking. Jesus promises that if I will let Him, when He shows me the last sin—the last little strand that is maybe almost invisible—and I let Him sweep it away, He will kill the spider, and I'll be free from sin forever.

LANA FLETCHER

? Thought: What can we each do to be certain that we are no longer blind?

Little Feet

By love serve one another. Gal. 5:13.

OUR CHURCH PRACTICES the ordinance of foot washing four times a year. And four times a year a little voice would urge me, *Skip church today.*

But one beautiful Saturday I experienced the service with new meaning. As I handed out basins of water and towels to participants, I felt blessed by simply being there. My mind went to that upper room and the last night that Jesus would be with his friends. They were stolidly averting their gazes, unwilling to acknowledge the water basin, towel, or a roomful of dusty, dirty feet. Custom dictated that before they could eat, a servant would appear and proceed with the lowly duty. Only no servant appeared. Then their Lord bent down and graciously washed 12 pairs of dirty feet. It's hard for proud hearts to understand such willingness to bend below our perceived status to serve one another.

Waiting in line was a young mother with her small son in tow. "Do you need a partner?" I asked as I handed her a pan and towel.

"Oh," she said brightly, "I thought it would be just Ryan and me today."

Ryan? I thought. *He is only a child.* When I was a child the service was only for grown-ups.

Today I saw a young mother take her son to a quiet corner, hold him on her lap, and speak quietly to him. His eyes mirrored his reverence as I imagined her telling him about Jesus becoming a servant, and why we were doing this. Then she nodded toward the pan, and the little boy hopped down and solemnly sloshed his mother's feet.

A moment later Ryan sat on the floor, his tiny feet swallowed in the adult-sized pan as Mom scooped warm water over his feet. How many times his mother had cleansed him! But this was different. A new understanding was dawning upon him—and me.

His joy and abandon infected the whole occasion. A child had broken down the walls and showed us how much joy there is in becoming a servant. I don't think the Lord minded at all that Ryan's tinkling laughter disrupted the grave silence of the room now ringed with joyous smiles.

MARILYN JOYCE APPLEGATE

We Are Not Alone

For the Lord thy God, he it is that doth go with thee; he will not fail thee, nor forsake thee. Deut. 31:6.

I WAKE UP EARLY every morning to take my husband, who is a nurse, to the hospital where he works. We have the privilege of living in a city that is part of the Mato Grosso Pantanal in Brazil, and this area offers much natural beauty. On one of these sunny mornings I was contemplating nature as I returned home.

This day I saw some macaws flying in pairs in the sky. While I observed those beautiful birds I thought of the care that our heavenly Father has for us, and how His love is so wonderful. As David said in admiration: "What is man, that thou art mindful of him?" (Ps. 8:4). He not only remembers us but promises to be with us always, and we can count on Him in all situations. What is more surprising is that He invites us to give all our cares and necessities to Him.

God, who is a loving Father, also gives us the privilege of angel protection. This angel is always at our side from the time we are born, and when the day of our rest comes, this angel will mark our grave. When Jesus returns to this earth, the first thing that we will see will be our angel.

After spending some time here on this earth, Jesus did not want us to feel abandoned after He returned to heaven. He was concerned about us; He didn't to leave us as orphans. So He sent us the Holy Spirit to always intercede for us.

It's wonderful to know that we have angels and the Holy Spirit available to us, to know that we need only to ask for and accept His protection, and He puts all that we need within our reach.

Thank You for nature and that You speak to me by using such simple things to show me how much You love me, and that I am considered as Your special child. May I always have a sense of Your presence in my life, even when concerns want to take the sunshine away from me, or when life does not smile on me.

AUCELY CORRÊA FERNANDES CHAGAS

(?) Thought: It really is amazing that God even notices us, to say nothing of protecting and caring for us. Read all of Psalm 8 and note the status that God gives to men and women.

God Was There Before

The Lord himself goes before you and will be with you; he will never leave you nor forsake you. Deut. 31:8, NIV.

BEING MARRIED TO A DOCTOR in the military means that we move a lot. This time we moved to Okinawa, Japan—a long, long way from home and family. In fact, it's on the other side of the world, which I found out when we flew here. I think I was on a plane for about 14 hours.

As we got ready to leave and we packed, sold our house and cars, I began to pray my usual prayers: That God would keep us safe. That my girls would find good Christian friends. That my husband would enjoy his new command. That we would enjoy the new culture and people. But God knows that I always have a special prayer—that He will find me a special Christian friend, one who will be a soul mate. Also, that He will give me a mission to serve Him. In my heart of hearts I am a missionary. I need to feel that I have a purpose from God.

Sometimes my purpose has been taking care of my family. Home schooling is a wonderful mission. Other times it is working through Sabbath school and small, sweet children. I have even been given the great job of having fun with other women in women's ministry. And there's been a lot more. So God and I have had interesting conversations.

After about two weeks in Okinawa we were already in our little bunker house and having Christmas early. Unpacking—what a lot of fun! I was also looking for a school, Christian if possible, and I found one. I called then went for an interview. When they found that I was a teacher, I was given a job teaching first grade.

I shouldn't have been surprised. But I was. God was there way before me. You see, our next-door neighbor was a chaplain's wife who knew the principal at the school. So when I walked in, they already knew my name. That was the miracle that started all the other amazing things that happened in the next months.

I hope that I'll always remember that I need to rely on God to go before me.

SUSEN MATTISON MOLÉ

Grace

For it is by grace you have been saved, through faith—and this not from yourselves, it is the gift of God. Eph. 2:8, NIV.

MY HUSBAND AND I sit around the dinner table each evening, candidly sharing the day's happenings with each other. One evening he told me that one of his students was in dire distress over having to take his class. You see, the student's first language isn't English, and my husband is a speech and communications professor.

To ease the poor student's distress, my husband told her that the grade she would get in his class would not be based on what she deserved. Rather, it would be based on her hard work. I can only imagine the sigh of relief that young woman breathed.

As I listened to that story a new concept of grace flooded my mind. Every morning I wake up because of God's grace, an unmerited favor toward me. Grace fills each day with promise.

Grace is what Jacob found while traveling alone in the desert after he had tricked his brother by stealing the birthright. Instead of meeting him in the arid wasteland with a reproach, God came to him with promises. Jacob did nothing to be granted those promises, and he certainly didn't deserve them. Just like Jacob, we don't deserve grace, and unlike my husband's student, our works will certainly not make us worthy of it.

Grace is our stairway to heaven. Recently I came across some thoughts expressed by Robyn Sarah in her book *A Day's Grace*. It underlines the blessings of His grace: "To be given a day's grace is to be granted an extension, a brief stay of a deadline—one last chance to make good what has been left unfinished. But a day's grace is also the grace that any day brings—its ordinary gifts that are so easily missed in the crush of a day's business."

Those thoughts, added to my daily experience, have led me to formulate the following acrostic, which is a constant reminder of God's love for us: Grace is (G)od's (R)econciling (A)gent to save His (C)hildren for (E)ternity!

Dear God, please help me to meditate on Your gift of undeserved love and salvation. Help me to share it with others, even in the crush of today's business.

REBECCA L. USOROH

Could It Have Been an Angel?

Be not forgetful to entertain strangers: for thereby some have entertained angels unawares. Heb. 13:2.

AFTER THE CHURCH SERVICE on a beautiful Sabbath day my husband and I and a friend decided it would be cooler near the beach. And it would be so wonderfully relaxing after a busy week. We packed a picnic lunch into the car, along with some blankets and books, and started down the road in eager anticipation. The hour's ride was soon behind us, and we found our favorite spot.

As we set up our camping table many people walked by, all involved in their own interests. One man stopped by, briefly looked over our assortment of food, and asked very softly if he might have some of our chips. When we completely ignored him, he stood there for a brief moment and then said, "Thank you anyway," and continued on his way. We looked at each other without speaking, wondering if we had just turned away an angel or passed up a golden opportunity to witness for Jesus. The remorse we each felt for not giving him the whole bag was soon evident on our faces, but he was gone, and we were in a very somber mood. We wished that we could have another chance to show ourselves to be friendly and generous.

Many years later, in another city with my daughter-in-law, a man stepped in front of us in front of some little shops and asked for some money because he was very hungry. Having a policy of not just handing out money, I told him that I would happily purchase some food for him. He indicated that there was a fast-food shop a block down the street, so we headed there. I wasn't about to make the same mistake I had made those many years before. When we got to the order desk and he placed his order, he asked for a medium size. I told the cashier to give him a large order. The man said that he ordered medium because he wanted to save me some money. I paid for the order, he graciously thanked us, and we went on our way. The Bible admonishes us to help those in need. HILDA McCLURE

(?) Thought: Have you thought of Hebrews 13:2 as applying to people asking for a handout? Who are the strangers that we are to entertain, and how can we do this in a way that glorifies God?

A Peaceful Valley?

"A snake on the ground will not hurt anyone. They will not hurt or destroy each other on all my holy mountain," says the Lord. Isa. 65:25, NCV.

I STOOD ON THE BROW of a hill and looked down on a peaceful, serene valley. Hat Creek widened into Baum Lake, which was bordered by green meadows and framed by towering pine trees. White pelicans and Canada geese peacefully fed and floated on the edge of the lake.

The next day I felt compelled to drive into this valley. As I set out to explore the trail, I noticed a kestrel, or sparrow hawk, harassing his much larger cousin, the red-tailed hawk. The red tail, tired of dodging this pest in the air, flew to the top of a nearby pine. The tormentor still didn't stop, so I hastened on.

As I neared a multistoried birdhouse, suddenly I too was pestered by dive-bombing birds. It wasn't until I spotted the fledgling tree swallows perched on top of the birdhouse that I realized why I was unwanted.

Next, an oak tree full of beautiful but agitated birds caught my attention. I trained my binoculars on the trunk of the tree and became painfully aware of the cause of these birds' trauma. An enormous gopher snake, with most of its body draped over a broken limb, had its head inside a hole in the tree. Mother and father house wren were attacking the snake with their tiny beaks. On impact, the snake would shiver and shake, but nothing would deter it from continuing its destructive feeding. It was painfully obvious by the bulges in the snake's body that the entire furor was a mission in futility.

Farther along the trail I heard a whooshing sound above. A majestic bald eagle had soared off a towering pine tree. A few minutes later I witnessed an aerial dogfight between the bald eagle and an osprey, both attempting to maintain control over their lakeside fishing rights. It was a vicious battle, but ended in a draw, each bird retreating to its former territory.

How could so many traumas exist in my peaceful valley? I wondered. How I long for the day when my Lord and I can walk through His holy mountains and look down on peaceful valleys that are truly free of every taint of sin and suffering.   DONNA LEE SHARP

Mapquest

There is a way that seems right to a person, but its end is the way to death.
Prov. 14:12, NRSV.

IT'S ONE THING TO GET lost during the day, but getting lost at night is more stressful. In certain situations it can cost you your life. During our carefully planned summer vacation we became lost in one of the big cities in the United States. With our limited navigation skills, we thought we were following exactly the directions we had printed from Mapquest.com. But for some reason we were taking a lot more time and resources than what we had budgeted to reach our destination.

Becoming more and more frustrated, we decided to stop at a local gas station and ask and check the map to determine where we were. To our disappointment, we were miles from our destination and headed in the wrong direction. In panic, we offer prayers for help and assurance. We then started driving back the way we had come so that we could connect with the correct highway that would lead us home. The drive back was long and painful, long enough to calm us down. Yes, it took us hours more than we had anticipated, but a lesson was embedded in all this.

The devil is out there waiting for us so he can drive us off track. He is ever ready to lure us into easy exits that may seem right for a long while. He lets us get so comfortable and makes everything seem perfect, but in the end we face great regret. Missing a single exit can lead us to deeper sinful lives. Thank God for His accurate Mapquest—the Bible—that will give directions that are always on course. They never change and are forever precise. In it there are the perfect signals to follow which lead into the arms of our waiting Savior.

We are all blessed to have a loving Father who is always ready to welcome us when we have strayed. Through prayer and supplication you can depend on the heavenly Mapquest, and you will never lose your direction—whether it's night or day. Thank God for His Word!

You are so wonderful and awesome, Lord God. Help us not to lose our focus.
Help us to make the right choices that will lead us back to You for eternity.

SIBUSISIWE NCUBE

? Thought: Is simply reading the Bible enough? Or is there something more we need so that we are sure we understand the directions?

Veterans Day

Yes, and I ask you also, my loyal companion, help these women, for they have struggled beside me in the work of the gospel, together with . . . the rest of my coworkers, whose names are in the book of life. Phil. 4:3, NRSV.

VETERANS DAY. SINCE MY husband served as a chaplain in the U.S. Army for almost 24 years and worked with military chaplains for 13 more years, I know a lot of veterans. And, I must admit, most are men; however, more and more women are serving in military forces around the world. It's good to honor those who have served in the name of justice and freedom. November 11 is the anniversary of the armistice that was signed in the Forest of Compiègne by the Allies and the Germans in 1918, after four years of conflict. At 5:00 a.m. on Monday, November 11, an order was issued for all firing to cease at 11:00 a.m. (the eleventh hour of the eleventh day of the eleventh month), ending the hostilities of World War I. It was supposed to be the war to end all wars. (It wasn't until the 1950s that the day was changed to Veterans Day.)

Oh, how I wish it really had been the end of wars, but we know it was not. And there is another war being fought as well, a spiritual war. There are many veterans in that war as well, and I know many of them. I would say that there are more women than men who are veterans in that war. It's interesting, however, that as one reads the history of the Christian church all the way back to Bible times, and of our own churches, you will undoubtedly read of more men than women. But you can be assured that the women were there—sometimes struggling alongside their spouses, sometimes as single women, and many times as widows, completing work begun by their husbands. I think of my own mother, who served beside my father in numerous churches and the mission fields for so many years. These women, too, need to be honored. They, too, fought for justice and freedom. Unfortunately, there's not a day set aside to celebrate these women, but we can each honor their memory by telling their stories. We can give credit where credit is due. And we can reach out to women in our midst and say, "Thank you for a job well done!" Many women who write for these devotional books are veterans of this war, as are many of you reading this. "Thank you, and may you enjoy peace and honor."

ARDIS DICK STENBAKKEN

Our Lives Are Pictures

But whoever lives by the truth comes into the light, so that it may be seen plainly that what he has done has been done through God. John 3:21, NIV.

BOTH OF MY MATERNAL and paternal grandparents either immigrated to the United States or were first-generation Americans. German was the language that was spoken in their homes. They lived in communities comprised of German-speaking people where there was no emphasis placed on learning the English language.

My parents grew up speaking German. It wasn't until they went to school that they learned English. Both German and English were spoken in our home when I was growing up. However, my brother and I weren't allowed to speak German, because English was supposed to be our language. So while I learned to understand German, I didn't learn to speak or read it. When we visited my grandparents, they spoke to me in German, and I answered them in English.

English as a second language (ESL) is now included in the curriculum of many schools for both children and adults. Teachers are encouraged to illustrate the new words that are included in each lesson with pictures to help the students to associate the English word with a picture. In that way they start thinking in English.

I've been considering that concept and believe that we are called to be pictures on a page, individually drawn sketches of God's grace and love. The way we live out the gospel becomes a picture that should remind those around us of God's love.

Near the end of the Sermon on the Mount as recorded in Matthew, Jesus says, "Let your light shine before men, that they may see your good deeds and praise your Father in heaven" (Matt. 5:16, NIV). And in the Gospel of John His words are even more direct: "Whoever lives by the truth comes into the light, so that it may be seen plainly that what he has done has been done through God."

That means it is our responsibility to demonstrate God's grace through lives of service and devotion. We are pictures that remind people of our Father's love. If you compare that to teaching ESL, our lives—how we live every day—make up the pictures that will start people thinking about the gift of eternal life that was given to us through Jesus' sacrifice.

CLARICE BRENNEISE TURNER MURPHY

Airport Security

For he will rescue you from every trap and protect you from the fatal plague.
. . . He will shelter you with his feathers. . . . His faithful promises are your
armor and protection. Ps. 91:3, 4, NLT.

SINCE SEPTEMBER 11, AIRPORTS around the world have taken more steps in security. Passengers are supposed to be screened more carefully. But as with everything else, there is failure with all efforts that human beings put forth.

As I was catching a plane, I had on a lightweight winter coat. We had checked our bags and gone through the security line without being called for a secondary screening. We enjoyed a safe flight. After checking into the hotel and unpacking, we went out for a while. It was a bit cool, so I put on my coat. While waiting for the elevator, I reached in my pocket and felt an unusual object—a bullet! I pulled it out and showed it to my husband. To this day I don't know how that thing got into my pocket. This was the first time I'd worn the coat after getting it from the cleaners, so when I returned home I reported it to the management of the cleaners.

I immediately threw the bullet into the trash can. All sorts of thoughts ran through my mind. What would have happened to me had that bullet been detected while I was going through the security line? Would I have been able to board the plane? Would the authorities have thought I had concealed a weapon? Would I have been taken into custody for having it in my possession? Frankly, I think that bullet would have prevented me from continuing with my travel plans. I just thank God that my guardian angel kept that bullet hidden from all the cameras and other high-power X-ray screening equipment.

Just as the eyes of the security personnel and equipment were blinded to that bullet in my pocket, Satan blinds our eyes. We can't see the rose for the thorn. We can't be thankful because we are so busy complaining. And we wouldn't appreciate the sun if we didn't have some rain in our lives.

Lord, keep our eyes open to the many traps that Satan places in our path.
Keep our eyes fixed on You so that we will walk in the light of Your will. Help
us to always see clearly so that we may have eternal security in You.

MARIE H. SEARD

God Provides

But my God shall supply all your need according to his riches in glory by Christ Jesus. Phil. 4:19.

MORNING BROKE, AND THE mind-boggling problem I had retired with jolted my mind again. *Oh, I have no money!*

I got up, had devotions, and prayed—again—about the situation, then decided to stay home for the day in the hope that some delinquent debtor would appear on my doorstep. All I needed was 50 cents to pay my bus fare. Lunch was served at work, so food was no problem, and I usually walked from home to the bus stop (the shorter distance) and took the bus to work (the longer distance).

The day passed uneventfully. Night came, and still no money, so I resigned myself to the situation and simply prayed and went to bed.

The next morning when I awoke, I had worship and prepared for work. Since I hadn't received any money, I decided to borrow two quarters from a special mission offering I'd been saving. Then I prayed, locked the door, and began my 15-minute walk. Before I got to the main road a friend saw me and stopped, and gave me a ride straight to work. I was pleased that I had arrived earlier than usual.

I shared my problem with my coworker at the dental clinic of the José Martí School so that she could understand what was happening. When evening came, we packed away a few items, locked the door, and bade goodbye to workers in other departments. As we walked toward the gate to take the bus, another miracle unfolded. Another friend, on his way home, saw us walking and gave us both a ride home.

On reaching home, I quickly returned the two quarters to my mission offering and fell on my knees to praise God for the marvelous way He had provided for me that day. I thought I needed money, but my God knew I needed a ride.

Lord, please help us to trust You, even when the day seems dark and we cannot see clearly. BULA ROSE HAUGHTON THOMPSON

Even Birds

How good and pleasant it is when brothers live together in unity. Ps. 133:1, NIV.

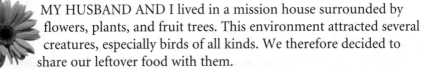

MY HUSBAND AND I lived in a mission house surrounded by flowers, plants, and fruit trees. This environment attracted several creatures, especially birds of all kinds. We therefore decided to share our leftover food with them.

Every morning we filled pots with fresh water and spread bread crumbs, rice, and overripe fruit for them. Soon I realized that more than 50 birds were coming to eat in our garden every day. This gave me the opportunity to study them from a hiding place, since they tended to fly away if they saw me try to come too close.

I noticed that the birds tolerated each other and never fought. While the ravens, crows, partridges, pigeons, and doves picked the bigger crumbs, the sparrows, robins, and nightingales concentrated on the tiny little crumbs. There wasn't a time that a bigger bird pecked at, stepped on, or maltreated a little one. From what I could see, they hopped about and ate what they could get at as they chirped on. It was a beautiful, peaceful scene worth watching.

Then I thought, *If birds that don't read or hear about God's love can mingle peacefully with understanding, why can't we humans do the same?* I don't think they have families as we do—sons, daughters, friends, in-laws, and tribes—yet they have no problem being together. We read the Bible; prophets and pastors preach to us and teach us to love each other as Christ loves us, yet we allow worldly tensions and sin to overcome us. We quarrel, bicker, argue, fight, and detest each other, even killing one another at times. In church we Christians try our best to find fault with each other. We move from church to church, full of malice and complaints.

But I have discovered that even birds of all sorts can mingle, share, and relate peacefully. That's how God wants us to live—in unity—as it will be in our eternal home. If we're not able to do that here on earth, how can we do it in the New Jerusalem?

Dear Father, thank You for using the behavior of birds to open my eyes. Please help me learn how to live pleasantly with others, just as it will be when You take us home.   MABEL KWEI

Just What You Said

And it shall come to pass, that before they call, I will answer; and while they are yet speaking, I will hear. Isa. 65:24.

IT WAS ALMOST 7:00 before I realized that I had overslept and that the school bus would arrive in 30 minutes. The rule in our home was that no one could be late for school without a vital reason. So I hurriedly put on my clothes and shouted to my dad in the bedroom to ask for lunch money. He responded, "You money is on the stereo." I continued getting dressed, gulped down breakfast, grabbed my books, flung open the door, and reached back with my right hand to grab the money from the stereo, never looking back.

The bus drove up to the stop, and we were seated. As we rode down the street, I checked my pockets to see how much money Daddy had left me for lunch. I remember thinking, *Yes, it's enough for lunch, with some change left over.*

A question then flashed through my mind: *What would happen if I trusted God like that?* We were always taught that our parents were examples of God's love and care toward us. I never questioned Daddy concerning when he put the money on the stereo, how much money he left, or how he knew I needed money. Nor did I go to check and make sure he left it on the stereo. I simply believed what he said and trusted him. I didn't even think about the money until it was time to leave and catch the bus. Never looking back, I simply reached for the money, and it was there. I believed Daddy because whatever he said, he did.

That morning my faith in God intensified. I was persuaded that whatever He said in His Word, I would trust and do, more so even than trusting Daddy—without question, reservation, and follow-up. I would take hold of God's Word through daily study, with an open heart, and count His blessings in my life.

SELITA FAY ATCHLEY HARPE

(?) Thought: Some Bible characters implicitly believed and followed God and His Word. Others asked for signs, or even doubted and refused His messengers. Think about some of these people and how you may, or may not, be like them. Here are some names to begin your thinking: Noah, Hannah, Gideon, Rahab, Sarah and Abraham, Peter, and the woman at the well. You may also want to think about what it means to really trust and believe.

Don't Forget to Do Good

But do not forget to do good and to share, for with such sacrifices God is well pleased. Heb. 13:16, NKJV,

IN MY RECENT TRAVEL to my country of birth, I saw so much poverty. It seemed that the rich had become richer, and that the poor had become poorer. I saw it everywhere, and I wished I were a millionaire so that I could help alleviate the condition and suffering of the poor. The saying that "God must love the poor because He made so many of them" must be true. Wherever I turned my eyes I saw the abject poverty of the people of my country. I couldn't believe my eyes—squatters were everywhere.

One afternoon when we were getting ready to go to our meeting place, five haggard children came to the gate of the home where we were housed. The young man who was helping us translate our presentations into the local vernacular asked the children what they wanted. They said they were begging for some money so they could have some food. I hurriedly invited them to come to the dining table. We had just finished our lunch, and I felt very fortunate that the cooks had made so much spaghetti. (Coincidence? I believe the Lord knew that those children would be coming.) I set the spaghetti and the sauce on the table, picked up a hand of bananas, and brought out the young coconuts from the refrigerator. The children were so famished that they ate all the food I set on the table. While they were eating, I asked them if they'd had some breakfast that morning. They answered that they had not. It was already past 2:00 in the afternoon—no wonder they were hungry.

I was so touched that I went to our room and got some money to give each of them. Oh, how they thanked me again and again. Their faces glowed with smiles, revealing that they were truly grateful for the little act of kindness I had shown them. The admonition "But do not forget to do good and to share, for with such sacrifices God is well pleased" meant so much more to me.

To me it wasn't a sacrifice. A little kindness shown to those hungry children was a privilege, for Jesus said that if we could do something good to the least of them, we were truly doing it for Him (Matt. 25:40). And wouldn't Jesus do the same if He were here on this earth today? Don't we want to be like Him? OFELIA A. PANGAN

My New Bibles

Thy word is a lamp unto my feet, and a light unto my path. Ps. 119:105.

ON A WARM, SUNNY DAY in November the temperature was several degrees above the norm in Battle Creek, Michigan. Lewin and I enjoyed the tour of Adventist Village and were extremely grateful to Bessie for inviting us to join the group for the trip.

After the tour the group decided to go to the mall. This gave us an opportunity to dine at the Old Country Buffet and shop as well. Among the numerous stores were two that struck our fancy—the Dollar Tree and the Family Christian Book Store.

As Lewin entered the bookstore, she was told that the store was closing; we would have to come back another time. We were disappointed and proceeded to the Dollar Tree.

The next morning as we left the city to return home, we stopped by the mall again. This time we were among the first customers in the Family Christian Book Store. While browsing through the merchandise, I mentioned to Lewin that I hadn't brought my Bible with me on the trip because it was too big and heavy. My small Bible had fallen apart, so I desperately needed a new one. I was holding a beautiful small leather-bound Bible in my hand as I spoke, indicating that I really liked the Bible but would try to find it at a more reasonable price when I returned home.

"Where is home?" asked a young man who had obviously overheard our conversation. When I told him New York, he asked why we were in town and about the Bibles we were looking at. "The print isn't bad," I said, and he agreed. We chatted, and I moved on.

As I was making a decision about items I'd planned to purchase, the store clerk came over to me with a bag in her hand and said, "That young man that just left the store asked me to give this Bible to you and to tell you 'God Bless You.'"

I was in total shock. "Pass the blessings on," she said. I assured her that I would. Then she asked me if I would like a free gift and said I could have anything on the table behind me, including several small Bibles. I now own one of those as well.

CORA A. WALKER

Hungry?

But the fruit of the Spirit is love, joy, peace, patience, kindness, goodness, faithfulness, gentleness and self-control. Against such things there is no law. Gal. 5:22, 23, NIV.

THE UNITED STATES IS one of the wealthiest nations of the world, and it shows. The majority of the diseases we suffer from are the result of fat. Because of this, weight loss, diet, and exercise are a huge industry, making millions of dollars a year. Yet we have obese children and adults suffering from malnutrition. It sounds as if this country is eating itself to death on all the wrong foods.

This starvation, however, is not limited to our physical existence. One of the other leading industries in America is entertainment. Whether it's movies, TV, books, or some form of video games, this industry walks away with billions of dollars.

So the question is Why? Why do we spend so much money on food and fun? Most people say it's because it makes us feel good. Food and fun are both necessities of life, but an excess of either usually indicates that something else is missing. In fact, all people are missing something in their life when God isn't in it. Filling this void has become a major moneymaker. But even with all that food and fun, people still feel the void when the meal or the show is over.

We Christians have heard that "people need the Lord," and it is completely true. However, in God's great scheme of things, we are a vital link in filling that need. The problem is that most of us don't realize how to do it.

A while back I was part of a discussion group in which we realized that all of the fruits of the Spirit are expressed through our attitudes, the way we act and respond to those around us 24/7. Family, friends, coworkers, and strangers alike are craving these fruits. It doesn't matter whether or not they are Christians—they still need to experience these fruits.

Have you ever craved an orange? Or a peach, or a watermelon? I have. Just as you and I may crave sweet fruit, so those around you crave the sweet, succulent taste of kindness and gentleness. Now the question is What kind of fruit are you going to serve today? Remember: everyone is craving it, and God gives it to you freely. I hope you share it in the same way.

JULI BLOOD

Claiming God's Promises

And this is what he has promised us, eternal life. 1 John 2:25, NRSV.

TWO SUMMERS AGO, after my secondary education gradua-tion, I began to worry and become discouraged. For me, higher education was not just a mere dream—it was a goal, despite hard-ships. There were nine children in our family, and my mother had been a single parent since I was 7 years old. So I started to pray hard that I would be able to pursue my studies in college. For us to survive, my broth-ers planted vegetables at the back of our house, and sometimes they would fish. My mother would go to the farm to harvest rice for our family. But I remembered God's promises that He would not leave or forsake us, and that He was true to His promises. So I said to myself, *Why should I worry? I have a God who listens and knows my needs.*

Then one day I heard about the women's scholarship program funded by the women's ministries devotional books and donations. The scholar-ships were for women who wanted to pursue their college education but didn't have the finances.

With the help of my aunt, I wrote to ask about the requirements, and we sent the forms in right away. After a year, however, it seemed that every-thing had been in vain. I hadn't heard a response, nor had I been given any hope. One day, though, I learned that my aunt and my mother were still praying hard for this scholarship.

One afternoon someone handed me a letter—it was from the scholar-ship committee. My eyes got bigger. I couldn't believe it! The only words I could utter were "Yes, my prayers have been heard! Praise the Lord; He re-ally listens to our prayers."

Too many of us are creeping through life with extreme caution regard-ing the promises of God! We are afraid and anxious that what God has promised might not be sufficient for our need. We step out in faith, but lightly. But the promises of God are not fragile and about to cave in when you stand on top of them.

We are to stand on the promises, just as the song "What a Friend We Have in Jesus" says. We are to appropriate them, use them, and stand firmly on them! They are foundational! They will not break with your need. It's God we're dealing with, and God is God! Believe what the Word of God says! He has promised! LOURDES VEHIGA

Changes

For I am the Lord, I change not. Mal. 3:6.

THERE ARE SO MANY changes here on earth. Just go away from home for a few weeks, and you can see changes that were made while you were gone. New buildings go up, roads are made on land to be developed, and so much more. And there are many changes in our lives, too. One day is full of laughter and sunshine; the next can bring pain and heartache.

As I was taking my grandchild to school one morning, as I do each day, I passed a house where some very dear friends used to live. I thought about this family with their two children. In this house were laughter and tears, joy and sorrow, good times and hard times. The mom and dad were some of the very first people I met when I moved to Michigan. Their oldest son was the same age as our oldest son, and they became best of friends. Their daughter was only two days younger than our daughter (I used to call them my twins, Kathy and Cathy), and they too were very good friends.

The children went to school together and had many fun times at our house on the farm. They loved to come to the farm! They were like my own kids, and I really enjoyed them.

Somehow, change took place, and all the children grew up. Oh, we would see them now and then, but they all went different directions. They all had children of their own, and life went on. Their mom and dad decided to move into a condo and sell their house that held so many memories. Then the mother died, and the father later remarried. A short time after the mother's death my husband died, and there were more changes.

Somehow, as I pass that house each day of the school year, I'm filled with sadness. Even though there are changes all the time in our lives, it makes me think of our God, who never changes. I am thankful that my heavenly Father is always the same yesterday, today, and tomorrow. He is constant and never changes. We can always depend on God to be there for us each step of our lives, a present help in times of trouble.

Thank You, Lord, for always being with us and for never changing. Thank You for Your love and support—a help we can always depend on.

ANNE ELAINE NELSON

Ask in My Name

And I will do whatever you ask in my name, so that the Son may bring glory to the Father. You may ask me for anything in my name, and I will do it. John 14:13, 14, NIV.

MY 13-YEAR-OLD FORD had carried me all over California, moved with me from California to Oklahoma, faithfully carried me from Oklahoma to Tennessee, to Michigan, and back to Tennessee over the past four years. It now had more than 100,000 miles on it, and the headaches that inevitably come with car ownership were increasing. This summer especially seemed to be filled with one problem after another.

One particularly early morning I was to meet a friend to walk. As I drove to her house, the car emitted some new noise. I'd had enough. I turned to my Best Friend with my complaint. "God, please make a way for me to get a different car." Just that morning I had read the above text in John 13, so I added, "I ask it in Jesus' name!"

This was no easy task, for at the time I was your typical "starving college student." Oh, I paid my bills and had plenty to eat, but my income left little or no extra to save from month to month. Nevertheless, I trusted my God because He had come through so many times before.

I'd almost forgotten my request until a day or two later when my mom called with a great idea she'd had. "Why don't we look for a car for you, and I can use the money I've been sending you every month toward a car payment instead?"

As usual, when I get a response to a direct answer to prayer like this one, I was moved to tears and couldn't speak for a moment. I explained to her about the prayer I'd sent up in exasperation a few mornings before, and she became as excited as I. We agreed that she and my dad would look for a car.

Two months later I was still driving my Ford and, frankly, was wondering if that grand answer to prayer was going to materialize after all. When yet another car problem cropped up, I called my dad to complain. "Guess what?" he responded. "I bought you a new car today!"

God had led them to the exact make and model of car I wanted. It was in excellent condition, and had all the features I wanted—and then some. It had low mileage for its six years, and they had paid at least $2,000 less than the going price.

Glory to the Father, indeed! I asked in His name; I'll praise in His name!

EMILY THOMSEN

Old Tree

And on the morrow . . . he was hungry. . . . And seeing a fig tree afar off
having leaves, he came, if haply he might find any thing thereon: and when
he came to it, he found nothing but leaves. Mark 11:12, 13.

SITTING BEFORE AN ENORMOUS glass window, I could observe in the distance an old dry tree attempting to maintain itself
upright under the cold wind. At one time this had been a beautiful tree with green leaves and luxuriant branches.

Like that old tree, I too was sad and attempting through my own efforts
to avoid being blown away by the whirlwind of life. I didn't see any prospect
for improvement, and weakness allied itself with discouragement and pro-
foundly dominated me. I didn't have even the strength to ask for help, and I
remained there lifeless, waiting to be consumed by the coldness of life.

Pray? For what reason? I had already prayed so much, and it seemed
that I hadn't obtained any answer. Friends? Yes, I had some, but they
wouldn't be able, even with their kindness, to fill the emptiness that dominated me.

The Lord, then, made a great light shine in my mind. I remembered the
fig tree that had been cursed by Jesus. I felt like that fig tree—dry, and without any fruit. However, contrary to what He did with the fig tree, I could
feel Christ by my side to give me life. I recovered my courage, and I
strengthened myself in His promises because He Himself said that He is the
way, the truth, and the life. And He gave me life!

Now when He draws near to me again He will find a "tree" full of fruit,
with bright-green leaves and beautiful buds and flowers. This miracle can
be accomplished only by Him.

Yes, this is really what I expect. When the Lord Jesus draws near to Me, I
don't want Him to find a sad and lifeless servant, because His light and power
reinvigorate me to the depths of my soul. In Him we have joy and peace. In
Him we can overcome sadness, discouragement, and feelings of defeat and depression. "He shall be like a tree planted by the rivers of water, that bringeth
forth his fruit in his season; and his leaf also shall not wither" (Ps. 1:3).

Lord, make us leafy, fruit-bearing trees to honor Your name on this earth.
Give us always the blessing of witnessing to, taking in, and serving others.

KELITA DE SOUZA SILVA

The Mysterious Escape

The angel of the Lord encamps around those who fear him, and he delivers them. Ps. 34:7, NIV.

I AM A COLLEGE TEACHER who gives lectures to all students in the school of education in my subject area of counseling, guidance, and psychology. At the end of a session examinations are set and the papers are marked. All such papers must be submitted at a scheduled time. Usually I try to mark all the papers and turn in grades before the deadline.

One year something very remarkable happened to me—something that has reinforced my belief and trust in the Lord. I had just finished marking the first paper when I heard a voice say, "Stop marking! Go there and lie down and rest!" Since I had just started marking, I thought, *Let me finish this one.* Then the same voice said emphatically, "Get out of here!" Immediately I found myself hurled from my seat, and I landed some distance from my desk.

I quickly called my sister to come to my side. Simultaneously there appeared before me something like a red-hot balloon, which engulfed the area where I had sat. There was a deafening clap of thunder that destroyed all the electrical appliances in the room and left charred marks in its path. The smoke that engulfed the house we live in took some time to clear.

The thunderclap, which had left me in a state of shock, was heard in the entire neighborhood—and I had been saved by an unseen hand!

Yes indeed, the words of the Lord now ring in my ear: "The angel of the Lord encamps around those who fear him, and he delivers them."

The Lord's angels have been stationed to look after us, and they are really at work in our lives. Our God is good—blessed is the woman who takes refuge in Him. Those who trust themselves in His omnipotent hands cannot be plucked out. Even when the dry winds of life sap our spiritual lives, when we feel oppressed or lost and far from God's presence, we can pray with the psalmist and we need not remain lost, nor must we try to find our way home on our own. He is the one who cares for us.

We can petition our loving Father to send forth the divine light and truth we need to guide us. The Lord is our light; He is the strength of our life. We need not be afraid (Ps. 27:1). SAL OKWUBUNKA

Life Is Uncertain

You don't even know what your life tomorrow will be! You are like a puff of smoke, which appears for a moment and then disappears. James 4:14, TEV.

LIFE IS SO UNCERTAIN. For years you may travel the same roads each day, see the same homes or landmarks, wave at the same person sitting on her front porch. Then tomorrow comes, and one of them may not be there. Remember September 11? Who can forget, right? We are never really prepared for change. Many times changes can be upsetting to us. We like to feel secure.

A couple months ago a number of acres of land across the road from us changed hands. I had heard rumors that there were going to be lots of changes made there. On this particular property was an old house that sat on a knoll. Some friends of ours had even lived there once. But it had been used only for storage for the past few years. So I didn't always look at it when I went down the road, but I knew it was there. It was a tiny piece of security in my rush of life.

One morning I drove to work, and everything was in place. All was right with my road. When the time came to drive back home again, something was definitely not right. I couldn't believe my eyes! Where the house had been, there was nothing. Not too far away, however, was a huge hole in the ground. It had obviously been dug by the earthmoving machines that were sitting nearby. A small spiral of smoke ascended upward. The old house had met its demise and had been pushed into the huge hole in the ground. Though the house had no sentimental value to me, it was something that I had counted on to be there. Now it was gone. Life is so uncertain.

Most days now, when I drive by, there is smoke making its way heavenward. The newer house that had been down in the valley has now been moved to the place that the old house used to occupy. I have imagined standing on its deck and looking out over the field. It must be a beautiful view, especially in the early mornings.

Someday there will be other houses where I can stand on a deck and look over fields of spectacular glory that far surpasses any ever seen on earth. And it will be in a place where life won't be so uncertain.

DONNA SHERRILL

Through My Camera's Eye

For the eyes of the Lord range throughout the earth to strengthen those whose hearts are fully committed to him. 2 Chron. 16:9, NIV.

AFTER YEARS OF USING a throwaway point-and-shoot camera, I yearned to graduate to a digital camera. Several of my friends already had one. When my husband asked me what I would like for my birthday, I didn't even have to think about it twice. I wanted one of those digital cameras with its own stand, the kind I had read about in the Sunday's colorful glossy advertisements. The vision of my photo shots going right into my computer made this great-grandmother feel as if I was really entering into that world of high technology. I was hooked!

But now I found out that I needed glossy photo paper, and lots of it. I also would need a new color printer that scans, prints, and several other things that I haven't learned about yet. I'm sure that with a little practice I'll be able to dazzle my family with my expertise.

As I reflect on this new era that I am about to enter, I realize my eyes are not the sharpest, my hands are not the steadiest. I really do have a burden to take pictures. When my mother died seven years ago at the age of 90, I inherited all her photo albums and boxes full of black-and-white photographs. It is our family history. Photos tell a story. I want to continue this family photographic history for my children.

Cousins living in other states also have family photos. We began to trade and send each other copies of old photos to expand our family history. Photos were being mailed to and from Florida, Ohio, Tennessee, and Illinois. I soon learned how expensive reproducing old photographs at the local photo store could be.

I'm learning now to scan old pictures into my computer and print them out. And better yet, I can e-mail photographs to my cousins and in the same way receive family photographs from them.

In contemplating this modern miracle of digital cameras, computers, printers, and scanners, I am drawn to the real miracle of a family history that my Bible tells me about. From Genesis to Revelation, I have learned that I'm part of God's family, and I have met the Savior.

My camera can't take in the whole picture, but I'm glad God's eye can.

MARIANNE TOTH BAYLESS

Seeking a Complete Life

But seek ye first the kingdom of God, and his righteousness; and all these things shall be added unto you. Matt. 6:33.

I WAS HAPPY. I had everything I wanted, and joy was in our home. I was 13 years old; my parents had a great amount of money that they spent on parties. But it didn't take long for our castle to crumble, and all that we had was transformed into emptiness because we trusted in money to make us happy. All of the money, my father's work, the private school, and, finally, our house disappeared. We sold the house to survive, and we went to live with my grandmother.

This entire situation left me without answers to my questions. Only tears were a relief to my heart. When I was hungry, I had to ask my grandmother for a plate of food, because my father was working in another city and my mother didn't know what to do.

My heart felt more and more anguished. I suffered because of the way we lived. It hurt to see my mother crying, and I suffered because of my father's absence. I wanted to find comfort, but I didn't know where to look.

It was during these days of sadness and despair that I accepted an invitation to visit a church. In this church I found peace and comfort. I became a new person. I realized that everything that had happened—the fact that we had lost everything, the lack of food, all of this—was the consequence of human error, because we had never stopped to think about God. We were far from Him, and we didn't realize that He had His eyes set on us. "I call on the Lord in my distress, and he answers me" (Ps. 120:1, NIV), states the beautiful psalm.

I was baptized at 14 years of age. That was a very happy day for me, although my parents weren't present at my baptism. I knew that God, through me, had planted a little seed that would later produce fruit within my home.

Now I'm 22 years old, and I'm happy to have my family with me. Everyone has accepted the Lord Jesus in their life, and I exalt this marvelous God who always cares for us. Our life has returned to normal. All that we had lost, today we have received double. However, the most important thing is the love of God that filled that empty place that had existed in our home. When we seek Him with all of our heart, we are certain to find Him.

MÔNICA MEDRADO VIEIRA

The Lord Is My Shepherd

I will fear no evil. Ps. 23:4, NKJV.

WHENEVER I THINK OF Psalm 23 I think of my favorite pastor, Pastor Papu. I like the way he explains the poem behind the psalm. "He makes me to lie down in green pastures; He leads me beside the still waters" (Ps. 23:2, NKJV). Pastor Papu describes that as something sweet and wonderful—in other words, in good times it's nice to know that the Lord is with us. Then we see a transition when the writer says, "Yea, though I walk through the valley of the shadow of death, I will fear no evil."

Pastor Papu's explanation of Psalm 23 became more significant to me when a good friend of mine, Calvin Masuku (Mr. C), and his two daughters, Pamela and Ayanda, left their house for an outing. They didn't pray as they set out, but Pamela, who was sitting in the front of the car, remembered that they had forgotten to pray, so she kept on asking her daddy to stop to pray. Mr. C decided to stop the car and asked her to pray.

Just when they finished praying, they saw four men with guns ready to fire. Shocked as he was, Mr. C managed to start the car. Keeping his head down and not even knowing where he was driving, he pressed on, with shooting all around them. He drove the car with one hand while holding on to his daughter with the other one, trying to push her head down while she struggled to see what was going on. He drove until he heard no more gunshots—and to his amazement, the hijackers had disappeared.

When Mr. C gave this testimony in the Mtata Central church, the first thing he said was "Really, the Lord is my shepherd, because He saved us from the valley of death." As I listened I also realized that when we Christians pray it doesn't mean that we won't face trials, tribulations, or the valley of death. But God has promised to be with us in those problems if we trust Him.

It was just like the story of Daniel's friends when King Nebuchadnezzar said to them, "I will throw you into a furnace of fire, and no one will be able to save you from my hand" (see Dan. 3:15). It's true that no one saved them from that hand, but the living God saved them in that hand.

Dear Lord, thank You for Your mercies that never cease to end, for without You where would we be?

DEBORAH MATSHAYA

Caught Up

For the Lord himself shall descend from heaven with a shout. . . . Then we which are alive and remain shall be caught up together with them in the clouds, to meet the Lord in the air: and so shall we ever be with the Lord. 1 Thess. 4:16, 17.

I SPENT MY HIGH SCHOOL years at a girls' boarding school, Westwood High in Stewart Town, Trelawny. The school was affiliated with three churches—Baptist, Anglican, and Methodist—where alternate visits would be made to them on Sundays.

When I got to fourth form, I became part of the Methodist group and would attend that church every Sunday rather than alternating with the other two. As part of the Methodist group, I'd get to church early to assist with the preparations for service, sing in the choir, and participate otherwise as it became necessary.

One Sunday morning the bell ringer didn't show up. Being one of the strongest in the group, I decided to take on the task. I mustered up all my strength and pulled on the rope. Down tipped the top of the bell, and on its way back up I was caught up in the air. I held on for dear life.

Whenever this story is recalled, it evokes some amount of amusement. However, serious reflection reminds me of the text for today. In this verse we're told that Jesus will descend to this earth, and the faithful will be caught up, and so shall we be with Him forever.

In my so-called caught-up experience, I was taken up without undergoing any changes such as those recorded in 1 Corinthians 15:51-54, such as "this mortal must put on immortality" (verse 53). Hence my experience was a little frightening, and I was extremely happy to return to earth.

In contrast, when Jesus comes to take us home, the Bible says that "in the twinkling of an eye" (verse 52) we will be changed. Then our "caught-up" experience will be so enjoyable that if our bodies were not changed, we wouldn't be able to contain the joy. What a day!

This is the hope that keeps me going each day, and my prayer is:

Loving heavenly Father, thank You for the joy of knowing that You have prepared a place for us to be. One day soon You will be coming for us to be with You in heavenly places. Amen.   CHRISTINE SHAND

341

The Best Place in the World

In the midst of the street of it, and on either side of the river, was there the tree of life, which bare twelve manner of fruits, and yielded her fruit every month: and the leaves of the tree were for the healing of the nations. Rev. 22:2.

IT SEEMED THAT WE were the only two who were awake. Dazzled by the rainy day, I moved my attention from the water that ran down the window—and there he was, on top of the tree, hopping, free, and happy, indifferent to the gray day that had just begun outside.

I can't say how long he stayed there. It was long enough for my memory to record the beautiful scene of a noisy bird on a frozen morning on the farm.

Insignificant? Perhaps. But the presence of that bird took me very far from my own reality. I felt alone and abandoned when he left. I missed him, wanted him to return, and desired the freedom that he enjoyed. Like this bird at the top of the tree, I also wanted to be on top of the world, recognized, loved, important, happy, and able to squander money. I was tired of poverty and felt that I had been rejected by God because I was still here and so alone.

In a short time our Father in heaven helped me to understand the price of true happiness. So that we could be free one day like that little bird in the tree, His Son became a slave to this world. Our liberty cost the life of His Son. The emptiness of my soul is filled only when the Savior becomes the most important part of my life.

In the midst of all the riches that many mortals dream of and run after, I came down from unrealistic ambitions and goals to become happy and to worship at the feet of the Savior.

Revelation 22:2 describes a tree that will serve to heal the nations. And it is under the tree of life, beside Christ and our loved ones, that we will finally be living in the best place in the universe. There we will not have the desire to be at the center of attention, because Christ will occupy His rightful position as the first and the only one worthy of honor, praise, and glory.

Thank You, Lord, because You continue to teach us lessons of courage and hope through Your Word. Thank You because, in addition to all the trees, there is the tree that is a shelter for all people, where You are waiting for us, and we will be together with You forever!   JUDETE SOARES DE ANDRADE

The Candy Cane Maker

I am the good shepherd; I know my sheep and my sheep know me. John 10:14, NIV.

"BUT I WANT SOMETHING original!" Melissa's voice wasn't exactly a whine, but it was close to it.

Taking a risk, I asked, "Do I hear anger squeezing out through a small opening?" That's my definition of whining.

"If I'm very honest, yes!" she said with a frustrated laugh. Her teacher had assigned a holiday show-and-tell using candy, and Melissa couldn't come up with an "original idea."

"There's always the story of an original idea," I suggested in what I hoped was an offhanded manner to avoid sounding as if I had the solution. Melissa's face showed interest.

"You know, the confectioner who invented a candy to remind his customers of the reason for the season." Melissa was hooked! Now her face reflected a so-what-are-you-waiting-for expression.

"According to legend, the candy cane maker started with a recipe for white hard candy, because Christ is pure and the Rock of Ages. He flavored it with peppermint (similar to hyssop, an herb that was used in the Old Testament for sacrifice), and fashioned the mixture into the shape of a shepherd's staff, because Christ is also the Good Shepherd. Next he twisted in a red stripe to represent Christ's shed blood, and three thinner red stripes for whippings from the Roman soldiers. Voilà! Candy canes."

Trust Melissa to want to know why some have a green stripe, too! "Sometimes the candy-cane maker added a green stripe as a reminder that Christ is a gift from God," I said in answer to her question. Well, that is what the legend said. Melissa jumped up and did her little victory jig. She stopped as suddenly as she had begun. "And the stripes go right through the candy cane. They're always there, right to the end."

She headed for the phone. Her little voice was clear and sweet as she said, "Mom, I need 27 candy canes with red *and* green stripes." Pause. "For show-and-tell." Pause. "And Mom, after Friday, candy canes will always remind them of Christ, the Rock of Ages, the Good Shepherd, a pure gift from God—who is with us to the end." Wonderful description!

ARLENE TAYLOR

Unseen Help

He reached down from on high and took hold of me; he drew me out of deep waters. 2 Sam. 22:17, NIV.

WHAT A GREAT RIVER for swimming! It was the month of December, and the heat was suffocating. At just 6 years of age, I was thinking of only one thing—jumping into the river that flowed near my neighbor's backyard. The river continued under the railroad overpass and formed a deeper pool of water—"the lake," as we called it. Certainly the lake was a great place to swim.

Since I was very mischievous, I was also very carefully watched. On that afternoon it was already after 5:00, and I hadn't been able to get away from the adults, who hadn't taken their eyes off me. As soon as there was a little distraction, I happily slipped down the stairs, then ran through the guava trees and through the weeds on the banks of the river until I reached the lake.

Although I didn't know how to swim, I loved to get in the water and play there joyfully. The river was almost seven feet (more than two meters) deep in some locations and full of rocks and some whirlpools where the water flowed beneath the rocks. I didn't realize that I'd been taken by the current to the deepest part of the river. In a short time I found myself in a huge whirlpool, pulling me to deeper water.

Suddenly there was no ground under my feet, and I had the terrible sensation of being sucked down farther and farther. I went to the bottom several times. I was swallowing a great quantity of water and desperately struggling, trying to get air that was now in short supply. This vigorous activity was all in vain—my small body continued to be pulled under. I was alone and afraid. I was tired. My arms hurt, my nose stung, and the whirlpool pulled my helpless feet with great force.

Suddenly something gave me a strong push under my feet, taking me from the bottom of the river and carrying me to the shallow water, where I fell, facefirst, onto the sand. Not understanding what had happened, I slowly returned to the neighbor's house.

That day God showed me directly, however in an unseen manner, the immense love that He has for me and how precious my life is to Him. May I give honor and glory to this wonderful God my whole life!

ROSENI M. CÂNDIDO

Reunited

Suppose a woman has ten silver coins and loses one. Does she not light a lamp, sweep the house and search carefully until she finds it? And when she finds it, she calls her friends and neighbors together and says, "Rejoice with me; I have found my lost coin." Luke 15:8, 9, NIV.

I WAS READING THROUGH our local newspaper when I came across an appeal from Linda, a woman who was looking for a long-lost school friend she had last seen 30 years before. I recognized the name of the "lost" friend and the address given where he had resided many years ago. I knew the family very well. We had lived in the same suburb, attended the same school and church, and went camping together annually. The parents were now deceased. When the children grew up and got married, each went their own way, and I lost track of this large family.

So I called the number given and told Linda that I'd be able to help her make contact. She said she'd been out of the country for several years and had therefore lost contact with her school friend and was now making this effort to find him.

This event reminded me of the Bible story in today's text. The coin didn't know it was lost, just as Terence didn't know he was "lost" to Linda. The Bible woman needed her coin—that's why she had to find it.

Like the coin, we can become lost, going our own way, rolling more and more into the dark where we can't be seen, maybe even by our friends and family. We may even think that we can get away from God at times. We need a Hand to pick us up. Linda needed help to find Terence. I was the hand that stretched out to help her. We can't get up on our own.

Jesus searches us out and rejoices with all heaven when He has found us. Linda said she was going to organize a great reunion party to celebrate with her family and friends because she had found her long-lost friend.

We may not always realize we are lost, but I thank my Savior, who came to search for me, found me, and rejoiced that He found me. I'm glad that He didn't give up searching for me and that I can be His precious treasure once more. After all, I'm more precious than gold!

PRISCILLA E. ADONIS

(?) **Thought:** Right now would be the perfect time to ask God to find you if you feel lost, or to thank Him for finding and treasuring you.

The Good Shepherd, Even in Emergencies

The Lord is my shepherd; I shall not want. Ps. 23:1.

ANOTHER SHIFT WAS BEGINNING, and I was at my office to see patients as usual. I greeted the cardiologist who had just arrived, and offered him cake and tea. Suddenly I had the sensation of intestinal discomfort and nausea. I went to the restroom, but I felt dizzy and was perspiring a great deal. I thought of taking a shower to feel better, but I gave that up. I returned to my office, lay down, and called the nurse.

After my blood pressure normalized, I thought, *I could take a little bit of IV solution and that would make me better quickly.* A male nurse came to see me and decided to follow my case closely. I felt as though I was on a roller coaster—my blood pressure went down, causing me to feel bad; but later my blood pressure improved, only to drop once more and make me feel bad again.

Vomiting didn't bring any relief, and even after several bottles of IV solution the low blood pressure and paleness continued, indicating something more serious. Examinations confirmed pregnancy and acute anemia. There was no blood bank at this location, so I had to be moved to another hospital 50 miles away.

My colleagues, in anguish, attempted to call a special ambulance to transport me because the situation was very serious. I didn't have any pain, but I felt a tremendous indisposition and was very sleepy. I knew it was necessary to keep myself awake.

I decided to envision the first verse of Psalm 23 without stopping. During the entire trip—which seemed like an eternity—I was not in want of calmness or protection. I was not wanting for a dedicated husband or a friendly and agile medical team—they were waiting for me in the operating room. Neither did I want for five pints of blood of the right type to compensate for the serious internal hemorrhage. The left fallopian tube had burst because of an ectopic pregnancy.

After three days of recovery without further problems, I was released from the hospital and could witness to all that the Lord is our shepherd and doesn't leave us in want of anything, even in the times of greatest affliction.

EDILENE YULE DE MACEDO TERRA PAES

Angels Watching Over Me

For he will command his angels concerning you to guard you in all your ways. Ps. 91:11, NIV.

FOR MANY YEARS I had driven the same old car, and it had served me well. It was special to me because my father had purchased it for my mother just before he died of cancer. She serviced it on time and never drove over the speed limit, so the car was still in good shape 18 years later when she died. I was happy to inherit it, but after another 17 years it really needed a rest.

Then our daughter came home to spend Thanksgiving with us and decided we should go car shopping. Since none of our family had experience in buying a car, we were relieved when a friend offered to accompany us. His help was especially welcome since he had been a used-car salesman and knew all the tricks of the trade. After test-driving several models, we finally settled on a car that was much nicer than we'd ever had before (and much nicer than I thought we really needed); however, our friend was able to help us get it at such a good price that we couldn't resist.

We live out in the country about a half hour from town over a narrow road that winds down to the river, crosses a one-way bridge, and continues with more sharp curves up the other side of the canyon. I always say a prayer for protection as I start down the hill from our home.

About two weeks after we got the new car, I was driving to town, and, as usual, had prayed for God's guidance. A mile later I came to a T intersection at which I needed to turn left to go to town. At this time of morning most of the traffic was coming from the right, so I looked only briefly to the left before starting out onto the main road. As I did so, I realized a red pickup truck was speeding up the hill on my left. Before I had time to react, it seemed that an unseen hand gave my car a push, just enough to get past the truck. I knew it was a very close call because the other driver was so frightened that he stopped in the road after he passed the intersection. I kept on going, thanking God for what I knew was a direct answer to my prayer of a few minutes before. I also thanked Him for saving my "new" car.

This was a good lesson for me—I not only thanked God for His protection but also vowed to always be more careful at that intersection.

BETTY J. ADAMS

Just a Breath

If my people, who are called by my name, will humble themselves and pray and seek my face and turn from their wicked ways, then will I hear from heaven and will forgive their sin. 2 Chron. 7:14, NIV.

SINCE THE TIME I was small I had watched my father working. He made cookies to sell as a means of income. Mother woke up early, prepared breakfast, took care of the housework, and then woke me. I got dressed, ate breakfast, then helped them roll out ring-shaped cookies. My parents were strong and worked hard.

At that time I didn't understand how they struggled to give us all that we needed. Sometimes I got up in a bad mood, but soon my humor improved.

Mother had married very early and didn't require anything of Dad; she knew what he could offer her. The difficulties were great, but they overcame them. Today their family is all grown; they've celebrated their diamond wedding anniversary and are always together.

I visit whenever I can, helping them and giving my affection. They have many years of experience in life and will soon be 90 years old. My father spends most of the day in bed and has to have sessions of hemodialysis. I never imagined taking care of my father, that strong man who worked hard, but today he is weak and totally dependent on the care of his family.

Life is just a breath; we are here in passing. The strength of youth doesn't last long. Regardless of age or strength, God doesn't want any of His children to be lost. He gives each of us the opportunity to know Him and to serve Him on this earth. He gives us everything, and we should return our praise and worship to Him. It's my desire to see my father and mother in heaven so that together we can praise and worship our God.

I can only thank God for everything He has done for me. I'm weak and totally dependent on Him. Each day I place myself in His hands. When we do His will, He hears us, because the promise is: "If my people, who are called by my name, will humble themselves and pray and seek my face and turn from their wicked ways, then will I hear from heaven and will forgive their sin." That's what is important—not the length of life, as life here on earth is but a breath.

LEONÍZIA GENEROSO

God Answers

If any of you lacks wisdom, he should ask God. James 1:5, NIV.

I'D BEEN ASKED TO serve my local church as an elder. I was told that the church needed me. I could imagine I could serve God with my gifts in this way, but I already had too many things to do. How could I take on another heavy responsibility? I asked other elders how much time they needed for their church responsibilities, and considered whether I'd be able to do that. I sought counsel of a friend, but above all I prayed about it. I asked God to show me what I could give up. I enjoyed all my tasks—I really didn't want to give up anything. And when my friend said I should say no, it seemed clear. I couldn't be an elder.

My pastor had made an appointment to hear my answer. That morning I reached for my devotional book and started to read. The text for the day was "But as for me and my house, we will serve the Lord" (Joshua 24:15). I swallowed hard. Why did I have to read that text just then? I wished I hadn't even picked up the book. I had wanted to decline the offer, and now it was clear that God wanted me to accept. The whole day I pondered the question, and that evening I told the pastor about the answer to my prayer and said I would take up the challenge.

But this was only half the answer. I still hadn't found anything I could give up. *God will give me enough strength to do what He wants me to do,* I thought. At a women's ministries retreat I spoke about this experience. One of the women asked me the next day what I had given up. "You have to re- duce your load," she said. Then I told her about all my projects and tasks. She picked one and said, "Other people could do that." Who was she to tell me that? That was something I loved to do. I passed on to other topics, but my mind was reeling. She was right. Others *could* do that. After a while I said, "You're right—others can do that. I have to give this responsibility up. Thank you for pointing that out to me." God had used her to speak to me. He wanted to answer my prayer through her.

Sometimes we think that God doesn't give us clear answers. But could it be that we pass on to other topics and don't listen to what He is saying? Sometimes we have to wait for a while until we recognize God's answer. But it's worth it. Knowing that we walk with God and hear His voice gives us strength. I wouldn't want to do without that for anything!

HANNELE OTTSCHOFSKI

God Has the Last Word

I will go before thee, and make the crooked places straight: I will break in pieces the gates of brass, and cut in sunder the bars of iron. Isa. 45:2.

MY NIGHT OF ANXIETY had passed. I greeted the new day with heartfelt thanks. I was alive and well enough to think that I could go to my job for a few hours. Then I remembered the Holy Spirit's words: "You will be OK, but you must go and see the doctor."

It was still too early to call the doctor's office to make an appointment, so I drove the 45 minutes to work and waited for the minute that the doctor's receptionist would answer the phone.

"The earliest the doctor can see you is Thursday," she told me. I knew that wouldn't do—Thursday was two long nights away. All I needed was for the doctor to order a bronchodilator for me. I was still having difficulty breathing, and I was too scared to go through another night without it.

"I will convey your message to the doctor," the woman said politely. As a nurse, I was bothered by an unsettling question: "Since the doctor has never treated me for this problem before, would she prescribe the medication?"

I was in my car with the key in the ignition when the Holy Spirit advised me to call the doctor's office again to see if the doctor had received my message. "Hold on," said the person who answered the phone after hearing why I called. She returned shortly with another question. "Did you leave a message on the answering machine, or did you speak to someone?" I told her I had spoken to someone. "Hold on," she said again, indicating that she was having a problem locating my message. Then she asked, "Can you come in today?" You know my answer was yes!

The doctor saw me that afternoon and treated my problem. And I got the bronchodilator and the other medications without having to pay for them!

We serve a God who is almighty and all-powerful. He creates. He destroys. He is always capable of fulfilling His promises in our lives. Oh, if only we could comprehend just a little of His power we would trust Him completely. Then our worries, cares, and anxieties would fade away, not at all impacted by our environment of fear.

When God speaks, He does have the last word.   MADGE S. MAY

God Answers Prayer

This sickness will not end in death. No, it is for God's glory so that God's Son may be glorified through it. John 11:4, NIV.

"YOUR HUSBAND HAS LYMPHOMA of the stomach and bone marrow. Without chemotherapy he could die." Shocked by what the doctor was saying, we sat in silence, trying to absorb the words. What did this mean for us? How would we deal with it?

The effects of the chemotherapy concerned us, but the doctor assured us that this chemotherapy didn't have the usual side effects. We asked the Lord to direct us, and my husband, Len, believed that the Lord spoke to him, telling him to have this chemotherapy.

Confident that the Lord was leading, we made the necessary arrangements. Len was to go to the hospital for five consecutive days to receive the treatment intravenously. All went well for three days. On the third night he began to experience heart palpitations that kept increasing in strength. I drove him to the hospital, where he was monitored for a few hours, then allowed to return home.

The next morning at his usual treatment he mentioned that he'd been to the hospital during the night. Several doctors conferred and decided not to give him his treatment that day but to admit him to the hospital. I returned home feeling exhausted. The tension and strain got the better of me, and I burst into tears. I began to pray, imploring God to help me deal with the situation. In my distress I opened my Bible, searching for some words of comfort and direction. The words of John 11:4 leaped out at me: "This sickness will not end in death."

A feeling of relief swept over me as I immediately thanked God for answering my prayer, giving me the very words I needed to hear at exactly the right moment. I packed some clothes for Len and returned to the hospital. On the way I stopped in to see a friend and relayed my experience. Together we knelt down and thanked God again for His answer to prayer.

The heart palpitations were a side effect from the anti-nausea drug Len had been given. He resumed his treatment and has made a full recovery. We praise God for not only answering our prayers but for His healing and interest in each one of us.   ANNE TINWORTH

? **Thought:** Do you think God always, never, or sometimes gives us an answer with a random text?

Ask, Seek, Knock

Ask, and it shall be given you; seek, and ye shall find; knock, and it shall be opened unto you. Matt. 7:7.

MANY YEARS AGO I was a vibrant 20-year-old living a life outside of what I knew to be the right way to live. During my years in the desert God had blessed me with a beautiful baby boy. When this child was still a newborn, the doctors said that he needed an operation on his skull. He was diagnosed with a condition known as craniostenosis. This meant his soft spots had closed too early, which would continue to restrict his brain growth. The local children's hospital recommended that he, my firstborn, undergo an operation—a bifrontal craniotomy. His little head was the size of a large orange, and they wanted to remove bone from the front of his skull to provide room for growth for his future. This couldn't be!

I had no family or friends to call on for support. I stood on the hospital veranda with a sense of hopelessness, loneliness, and desperation. Where could I go, who would support me, where was love? In absolute despair I searched within myself. I was reminded of those things I'd been taught as a child at church. God will never leave me; ask, seek, knock, and you will find; and that old favorite, John 3:16: "For God so loved the world, that he gave his only begotten Son, that whosoever believeth in him should not perish, but have everlasting life." Right then and there I said to God, *If You want me back, then bring my baby through this operation, and I will go back to church, turn my back on my current life, and raise my son in a way that he will personally know that You, God, saved Him.* My son did survive, and I have kept my covenant with God.

If your life seems to have dealt you some trials, or if you feel sad or alone, believe that God has a plan for a good life. All you need to do is to ask, seek, knock, and know (believe). I did, and now my son has a daily relationship with the God who saved Him.

Father God, You, and You alone, are the source of my future, the confidential keeper of my past, and the maker of my future. Thank You for reminding me of my spiritual responsibilities as a mom. Please bless my family as You have planned. Please bless the significant people in the life of the reader of this piece.

JULIE NAGLE

Divine Cure

They that trust in the Lord shall be as mount Zion, which cannot be removed, but abideth for ever. Ps. 125:1.

BROUGHT UP IN A POOR family, I always had to struggle to survive. Without money or any support, I many times fought against the mountain of difficulties that I had to overcome. I was not able to see the strong hand of God that guided me constantly and in all places.

At the most crucial time of my life I asked God to reveal Himself to me because pain and the fear of death surrounded me. I felt weak and overcome by suffering and deception. As if this wasn't enough, the doctors had confirmed my disease. This was the beginning of the end.

Many times I compared myself to that woman with the blood disease whom Jesus cured. In the same way I nurtured the hope of being touched by His hands and of also being cured. By passing through the valley of the shadow of death I learned to trust in the Master. I experienced extraordinary things because I felt His arm around me and His powerful hand in mine. I heard His sweet voice speaking softly to my heart: "Do not be afraid; I chose you."

One day, thinking that I'd already received the blessing of being cured, I went to the doctor to have new examinations performed. To the surprise of the medical team, after all possible examinations were done, the tumor could no longer be located. Certainly this illness would have taken my life within three years, because at an earlier examination cancer in its advanced stage had been detected. My chances of survival were minimal, and the physicians didn't want to risk surgery. It was really the final phase.

My children suffered and pleaded with God for my life. What gave us strength in the midst of so many tribulations was the love that united us, and we humbly asked the Lord for my cure. Death could not overcome this time. It was then that Jesus and His "team" came on the scene and freed me from the hands of the enemy because of the high price He had paid for me.

Today I don't have all material things that I've longed for, but I'm happy, and I always say to my God, "Father, I love You, and I want to make an effort to follow Your commandments because I know that You can do everything and that You chose me to serve You." CECÍLIA FRANCISCA NUNES

The Promise!

I am going to prepare a place for you. . . . When everything is ready, I will come and get you, so that you will always be with me where I am. John 14:2, 3, NLT.

FOLLOWING OUR SCHOOL tradition, faculty and students assemble together at the beginning of each new school year for the annual handshake. It was my smile that attracted his attention, or so says my dearly beloved. We simply introduced ourselves there at Gem State Academy. Ron came from British Columbia, Canada, and my home was in Oregon. We graduated class of '69, got married 19 months later, had two kids, Andrea and Sonny, and recently we celebrated our thirty-third wedding anniversary.

Ron promised that he would always take me home for Christmas, if we could afford it. He has faithfully kept his wedding promise, driving us 2,000 miles (3,200 kilometers) round-trip year after year. I can recall only three times that we stayed home.

Life hasn't been easy for Ron and me, especially after the birth of our son in 1986. Sonny is severely mentally challenged. The responsibilities we share are mind-boggling! With Ron's blessings, Sonny and I go on vacation every summer. We visit family and friends on both sides of the border. I sincerely believe that I wouldn't have endured being Sonny's mommy without the miraculous support of my blessed family.

Reluctantly Ron and I decided it wouldn't be wise to go to Oregon for Christmas one recent year. The widespread outbreak of flu in the United States caused us concern. However, we would chance going to British Columbia. Christmas Day came and went, and we were content with our decision.

I was sitting at Andrea's desk the day after Christmas, reading a book, when I was embraced from behind. In total surprise, I turned to see my mother's beautiful face. Grandma Lila's gesture of love was followed with more kisses, hugs, and smiles from Grandpa Bill, Aunt Jan, and Uncle Jess. They had driven to Canada because "Christmas just wasn't the same without you!" Andrea and Bill had kept their surprise a secret. Sonny was chattering and dancing for joy! Ron was snoozing, but soon joined our celebration!

Every day I think about Jesus and His promise, anticipating His glorious return!

DEBORAH SANDERS

Home Sweet Home

Speaking to yourselves in psalms and hymns and spiritual songs, singing and making melody in your heart to the Lord. Eph. 5:19.

HAVING GROWN UP IN a loving and caring Christian home, I'm more than convinced that our homes should be the place where we belong, where we feel understood, accepted, and loved unconditionally. As C. D. Brooks says in his sermon on love: "Essential to our spiritual development are peace in the home and love relationships." This statement holds real value and weight in our lives. I'm sure nobody wants to experience hell in the home. Hell so hot that we burn one another with accusation and false witnesses. Hell so hot that we burn one another with words of discouragement and cut through each other with sarcasm. Hell so hot that our communication lines go off as the electricity wire of peace is disconnected. I'm sure no one wants such a life here on earth.

Home should be a place of comfort and refuge, where you and I are accepted just as we are, and where we are loved unconditionally without any trace of rejection or gossip in our absence.

Loving God is the key to the door of a peaceful home. When we truly love God, then loving others comes easy for us, for we are simply obedient. Are we united in His mission in the home? God looks at the heart, and He understands each one of us. When the peace of Jesus is in the home, we won't hurt each other intentionally. When the peace of Jesus is in the home, we will have large hearts for one another. When the peace of Jesus is in the home, we will help one another in planning, and we won't tell tales on each other. We'll be ready to serve one another, and rejoice at the victory others achieve. With this peace in the home we will give of our time and gifts freely. And with peace in the home God naturally comes first in everything, my neighbors come second, and I come third. But I take care of myself, too. Love is the key.   BERYL ASENO-NYAMWANGE

? **Thought:** Do you feel as though you have this peace in your heart and home? The Scriptures, especially the New Testament, have a lot to say about how to have this peace. You may want to begin an in-depth study on it today.

Heights of Hierarchy

Go to the ant, you sluggard; consider its ways and be wise! Prov. 6:6, NIV.

WE WERE IN MEXICO for a Christmas holiday when I glanced down to see a string of ants busily scurrying across a crack in the sidewalk. They were noticeable only because of the big green pieces of leaves on their backs. *Pretty large cargo,* I thought.

A verse I learned as a child popped into my head: "Go to the ant, you sluggard; consider its ways and be wise! It has no commander, no overseer or ruler, yet it stores its provisions in summer and gathers its food at harvest" (Prov. 6:6-8, NIV). As we hurried to catch up with the others, I wondered how God could use this small creature to teach us such an important lesson. We're so much bigger than that!

The next day I joined the girls in a "canopy" tour that had us swinging through the tops of jungle trees that were 90 feet above the ground. As I looked down, many of the small creatures were no longer visible. Our group carefully followed the guide's instructions, trusting him to make sure that our cables were safely attached, and had an exhilarating ride, noticing things only visible from such an exalted level.

I love to be up high, and as we left for our return to Texas I watched the ground slowly disappear as the airplane nosed its way into the vast sky. The sights and sounds that had seemed so vivid over the past week now melted into oblivion as the plane pierced the puffy white clouds.

My thoughts turned again to the ants. How small they were now as I soared above the earth and the towering trees. How small was I to God, in His magnificent heaven? Even though I was higher than ever, I suddenly felt like one of those tiny ants. *God, do I look like a little ant, scurrying around with a big load on my back?*

God created wonderful things of nature to delight and inspire, yet we are so much more important to Him. And that's the best "high" of all!

The Bible says, "Are not two sparrows sold for a penny? Yet not one of them will fall to the ground apart from the will of your Father. And even the very hairs of your head are all numbered. So don't be afraid; you are worth more than many sparrows" (Matt. 10:29-31, NIV).   SANDRA COLE

You Want It or Not?

If you, then, though you are evil, know how to give good gifts to your children, how much more will your Father in heaven give good gifts to those who ask him! Matt. 7:11, NIV.

RUMMAGING THROUGH BOXES of Christmas decorations, I came upon a large package wrapped in bright Christmas paper. *Oh, no!* I thought. *Do I still have that?*

"That" was a gift I'd purchased years before for a nephew. I couldn't remember why I'd wrapped it but never given it to him. Perhaps I'd belatedly learned that he already had a Goodyear Blimp kit. So I'd stashed it in the basement and forgotten about it.

I considered donating it to a needy family through our church. But when the gift list was posted, a model blimp kit was not on it. I'd have handed it to a waif on the street, but I wasn't sure how to tell a real waif from an unkempt rich kid.

The blimp kit shares the shelf with some Christmas activity books—all dressed up in finery and going nowhere. I bought them on sale the year my youngest child outgrew them. Then there are the things I bought at bargain prices to be prepared for bridal or baby showers. Bargains outnumbered showers.

Thinking of all the gifts I've never given is downright embarrassing. But there is something worse: gifts that are given but not received. How terrible it must be to lovingly offer a gift, only to discover the receiver won't even open it! I've never refused another person's gift, but I'm afraid I can't say the same about God's gifts.

I've become freshly aware of God's overwhelming generosity. Of course, God's greatest gift is the Christ Child. All Christians accept that gift. But do we ignore other gifts God has in store for us?

Scripture clearly teaches that God wants to give us peace, joy, courage, faith, and much more. But how many of God's gifts will we bother to "unwrap" this Christmas? If we don't slow down and focus our attention on them, God may have to "put them back on the shelf," with the hope we'll want them another time.

God's gifts are beyond counting. And not only are there no "Do Not Open Till Christmas" tags affixed, but the gifts don't stop on December 25. God keeps on giving, giving, giving.

DOLORES KLINSKY WALKER

A Piece of Cake

Pleasant words are like a honeycomb, sweetness to the soul and health to the bones. Prov. 16:24, NKJV.

ON THE FIRST DAY of a scheduled 10-day trial, counsel for the defendants brought a charter application before me. They claimed their clients' right to a speedy trial had been infringed by unreasonable delay pursuant to section 11(b) of the Canadian Charter of Rights and Freedoms. They sought remedy by way of a stay of proceedings. This meant I had much evidence, statutory and case law, and legal argument to review before rendering my decision, which was required before the trial could proceed.

It was 4:30 p.m. I expected dinner guests at 7:00, and my judgment was due at 9:00 the following morning. As I breezed through the doors of the supermarket, a woman whom I recognized as a worker from the floral department called out to me. "Have a piece of cake!" There are always in-store promotions at this spot, so without breaking my stride I called back, "No thanks!" As I passed I noticed through my peripheral vision one huge, uncut cake, and another from which she was serving. I then heard someone say, "Good luck on your retirement!"

By then I had reached the produce section and was about to throw items into my cart when it dawned on me that this was Donna's retirement party. Words fail to describe how terrible I felt. Donna is a strikingly beautiful woman who always appears well-groomed. Her smile seems genuine even when I'm certain, given her age, it must hurt to be on her feet all day. She had assisted me many times in choosing floral arrangements for special occasions. She appeared to give more than her job specification required. Yet there I was, on her special day, thoughtlessly rushing by without a word of gratitude or congratulations. When I recognized my blunder, and with a deep sense of embarrassment, I hurried back to visit.

This incident makes me wonder how often, in my rush to accomplish my "must do" tasks, I have thoughtlessly and carelessly slighted and hurt someone. I finished writing my judgment at 1:30 a.m. Clearly, the five minutes spent speaking with Donna made no significant difference to my tight schedule. I hope it made a difference to her; it certainly made a difference to me.

AVIS MAE RODNEY

Familiar Faces

By this all men will know that you are my disciples, if you love one another.
John 13:35, NIV.

HE WAS OLD AND a little disheveled as he sat heavily on the ancient wooden bench. His chin rested on his chest, which rose and fell with the rhythm of his breathing. Occasionally the monotony was broken with a jerk as his rounded body struggled to remain upright. The old man drew warm glances from joggers and children playing on the jungle gym equipment from a bygone era. Tots giggled as their parents pushed them in strollers along the moist dirt path. He looked familiar, but almost no one spoke as he snoozed in the balmy afternoon sun.

Even in the shabby costume of the indigent, his weather-worn red cheeks, white beard, and full head of snowy hair sparked a memory of childhood fantasies with talking reindeer, toymaking elves, and trees laden with gifts. Without a single word or gesture, these strangers were transformed by who they thought he was. Few drew close enough to experience the combined scents of body and alcohol odors emanating through his pores. They hadn't seen his drunken rages the night before, or seen him rummaging through trash bins. Through a childhood tale they painted the picture of a man far different from the one who sat before them. He was not jolly, as they imagined. His voice was not calm and comforting, but no one knew.

Christians are called to be recognizable to the world around them. God wants others to notice us not by our designer clothes or fancy haircuts, but by the way we care for one another. Others won't know to whom we belong by the cars we drive or the colleges we attend. God is not even looking for our wealth or talents, but love. It is our love that will attract others. When we love the way Christ loved, others will smile or remember how life should be. Exhibiting God's love creates a lasting impression that goes beyond the fairy tale. Christian love is an adventure in reality with grace. It is acceptance without denial of our faults. It soothes the soul and draws others to hope—hope in salvation. SHIRLEY KIMBROUGH GREAR

(?) Thought: Scripture has a good deal to say about appearance but very few rules. Some people think Christians should all look a certain way, but is this what the Bible talks about? You may want to do a study on this, including a study of what the Bible says about pride and stewardship.

Hope Full

But the angel said, "Don't be afraid! I have good news for you, which will make everyone happy. This very day in King David's hometown a Savior was born for you." Luke 2:10, 11, CEV.

I SAW THEM—175 university students, weary but bright-eyed, wearing winter jackets and ball caps, struggling with luggage. Exams finished, they were heading home for Christmas. We awkwardly maneuvered baggage and bodies onto the buses. I was the last one on the last bus. Amazingly, I got a front seat.

At the next stop I watched her board the bus. Blond head lowered, eyes red from crying, she took the first available seat—right behind me. Soon I heard, "I'm on the bus. It should arrive at noon. Is he opening his eyes? Is he talking? How is Mom?" Later her phone rang. "Yes, I'm on my way. Will you pick me up? Barb is trying to arrange flights."

My heart went out to her. I knew what she was going through. Twice that year the doctor's diagnosis numbed me. "Your father might not make it. We have to treat his condition aggressively with medication, and his heart might not be strong enough." Five months later: "Your mother has had massive heart failure. She's on life support. You'd better call the family home." Both parents rallied, but it's hard to stare death in the face.

Yes, it was all too familiar. I wanted to talk with this woman, pray with her, but we weren't sitting together. I took a Christmas card from my bag, wrote a note of encouragement, and silently prayed for her and her family. Turning around, I handed her the card.

The bus pulled off for a quick stop. She stood by the double seat and, leaning over, said, "I was just asking God to send me an angel. Thank you." I was glad to be a blessing but amused at the thought of being an angel. When she reached her destination, she quietly commented as she passed by, "God used you today. Thank you." Later I pulled out another Christmas card—same style. I stared at the picture. There on the front was an angel.

Hope-filled students heading home for the holidays. A passenger hoping to get a good seat on the bus. A woman in crisis, hoping to have an angel sent by God to encourage her. It seemed that everyone had some hope. But the ultimate hope was summed up in the simple card with the powerful message: "Fear not. Jesus is born—the Hope of the World."

DIANE BURNS

Hope and Courage

The Lord shall preserve thee from all evil: he shall preserve thy soul. The Lord shall preserve thy going out and thy coming in from this time forth, and even for evermore. Ps. 121:7, 8.

I WAS RETURNING HOME to our apartment in a 24-story building that had two elevators. The lobby was crowded with people coming from school and work. Both elevators came down at the same time, and all of the adults, except for me, got into one elevator. My daughter, Evelyn, and I got in the other one, with the children. Just as the elevator door was closing, one of the girls pushed the open button to allow a man who had rushed into the building to enter.

My daughter introduced me to a friend of hers, and the girl and I talked while we made several stops. I was facing the back of the elevator while my daughter and the girl faced the front, where the man was. When we reached the seventh floor, I heard loud cursing. I was unaware that the man was demanding my purse and jewelry. He was yelling, "Give me all your money." I turned around to find myself looking into the barrel of a gun. I said, "Excuse me; I didn't hear you," and threw my shoulder purse on the floor near his feet.

As he was leaving he picked up the purse, then demanded my jewelry. I showed him my hand and ears, letting him see that I didn't have any. He warned us not to scream or make a sound or he would blow our heads off.

When we reached our apartment door, my daughter began to scream. I remained calm throughout the whole ordeal of the robbery, police investigation, and hours of looking at mug shots. But when I tried to sleep, sleep wouldn't come. Every time I closed my eyes I would see the barrel of the gun in my face.

Neither Evelyn nor I could eat or sleep. But after three days we decided to finish our Christmas shopping anyway and went our separate ways. As soon as I got off the bus panic seized me, and I took a cab home. Soon Evelyn came in, reporting the same panic experience.

I could no longer go on like this. I knew I needed help. My mind turned to Psalm 121. Throughout the next couple months I recited this psalm and prayed that God would take this fear away. God's Word gave me hope and courage.   MARY J. FELDER

? Thought: Read Psalm 121 to see what it says about sleep. What other assurances does it give?

O Come, Let Us Adore Him

When the Son of Man comes, will He find faith on the earth? Luke 18:8, NIV.

FOUR DAYS BEFORE CHRISTMAS I went to the mall to find an appropriate gift. Just inside the main mall entrance, in the open area of the food court, a five-piece brass band was playing "O Come, All Ye Faithful." And the crowds were coming to shop! I've never seen the mall so crowded; the aisles were full of busy, happy people. I pushed my way along, store to store, and finally found an appropriate gift. Then, tired and weary, I started toward the far exit.

As I walked through the aisles, listening to the carols being played, *I thought to myself, I wonder how many of these shoppers really are celebrating the true meaning of Christmas and are truly faithful to the Savior of whom we sing in the carols?* I found myself deciding that I would donate more of my time to the reason for the season, worshipping Jesus who came as a babe to live among us.

Suddenly I came upon the Giving Tree. On the branches were colorful felt cutouts, with stick-on labels pinned to them. I stepped closer and began to read the labels. Each tag had a first name and age and gender, plus first and second choices of a gift. There were many children's names, as well as those of some seniors. I found an 81-year-old woman who wanted a warm blanket. I could do that! I took an instruction sheet and read it as I walked along. Buy one choice of gift and wrap it. Attach the stick-on label, and return the gift to the tree. I would never meet the woman, nor she me. But God knew her needs, and that was good enough for me.

It was fun being an anonymous donor to a child of God whom I knew not. I like to imagine her snuggled into the fluffy blanket I bought and wrapped for her. Perhaps that's the real meaning of Christmas, sharing our means to help others who have less. I hoped many of those busy shoppers at the mall took time to share their Christmas with the names on the Giving Tree. It certainly gave a glow to mine! I knew God would bless them too.

Dear Lord, thank You for the chance to share Your love with a stranger I may never know. Bless that poor soul and keep her warm. And may You find many of Your faithful followers blessing others when You come to earth again.

BESSIE SIEMENS LOBSIEN

An Angel's Hand

Whatever things you ask in prayer, believing, you will receive. Matt. 21:22, NKJV.

IT WAS CHRISTMASTIME. My husband, Jerry, some friends, and I were invited to a Christmas party being held 20 miles away in the Dallas, Texas, area. To get there, we would be driving through heavy traffic, and it was raining. We had to decide who was going to drive; Jerry was reluctant because of the heavy traffic. About a month earlier I had taken a defensive driving class, so I was elected to drive.

We started out, and sure enough, there was a lot of traffic, and the roads were wet. But the roads don't usually ice over, and since traffic was moving at the recommended speed, we didn't anticipate any problem.

Suddenly, about three cars ahead of us, cars started to swerve and collide into one another. "Steer! Don't jam on the brakes!" my mind screamed. But steer where? Cars were all over the road. "God, help us," I breathed.

With no time to look, I steered to the right, into the slow lane. I felt— and heard—a thud. There was an off ramp, so I steered the van off the main highway and pulled to the side. I looked at our friends. One was speechless. One was crying. Jerry was just sitting there, staring straight ahead.

"What did I hit?" I asked.

They all said, "Nothing. You didn't hit anything. You did well. God must have been watching over us! We'll let you drive anytime we go with you!" But I knew what I had heard and felt on the right side of the van.

A few days later as I was getting into the van, on the passenger side I noticed a dent about four feet up on the rear door the size of a medium-sized hand. Right in the area that I felt the thud. I knew an angel had helped us that day.

We always make it a habit to pray when we go on a trip. We prayed that day before we left, and we prayed when we pulled over. God sent an angel to be there for us.

God is good! All the time!

JANET THORNTON

The Greatest Gift of All

If ye then, being evil, know how to give good gifts unto your children, how much more shall your Father which is in heaven give good things to them that ask him? Matt. 7:11.

PARENTS LOVE TO GIVE gifts to their children. Mine did too. When I was 3 I'd often ask, "When can I have a big teddy bear?" I looked longingly at them in the store windows. Christmas Eve came—a foggy, cool evening in California's San Fernando Valley. Mother and I were sitting in the living room by the fire, eating cookies and drinking hot chocolate.

A quiet knock sounded at the door. Mother smiled and said, "You may open the door." A large man stood in the doorway—I remember his hat and tan coat. It was my father, and in his arms was a huge brown-and-cream teddy bear. "Merry Christmas," he said, handing it to me. I was so delighted; I couldn't stop hugging that bear. I kept it through grade school, high school, and college. Today he sits in my bedroom in the little chair I sat in as a child.

Another time I opened the door on my birthday to find a wiggly, furry puppy. "Happy birthday," Mother said. I named him Kokoma and kept him 17 years.

College years arrived, and at my high school graduation my father's gift, added to my savings, was enough to buy a small car.

Dad, of course, wanted to help me select it. He wanted a four-door conservative car for me. I envisioned a two-door sportier something. We negotiated. My first car was a white four-door car with red seat covers and a stick shift on the floor. It was my transportation through college and into my first job. (My second car was a red two-door Camaro with bucket seats.)

As wonderful and special as these gifts were, the greatest gift my parents gave me was telling me that Jesus was my friend, praying with and for me, and showing by their lives that Jesus cared—that no matter what happened, He would always be there for me.

As an adult when I had a question or hurtful things happened, instead of dumping God and going out on my own I took Him with me on a journey to find answers and comfort—that was their greatest gift to me, the gift of God.

EDNA MAYE GALLINGTON

What's in a Name?

And knew her not till she had brought forth her firstborn son: and he called his name JESUS. Matt. 1:25.

FOR CENTURIES NAMES HAVE had many meanings, for various reasons. Babies have been named after famous people—presidents, movie stars, athletes, singers, or Bible characters, as well as family members.

Through the years I became curious as to why people choose various names, and took it upon myself to do a little research. I found some answers to my "why" questions. I was given the name Annie after my dad's mother. I didn't like it very much during my early childhood years, but as I grew up and got to know my grandmother, I didn't have to ask my dad why he gave me that name. It was obvious. My grandmother was a kind, loving person who loved Jesus very much. And my dad loved her too.

My husband longed for a son after our daughter was born. He envisioned having a son named after him. And we were blessed with a baby boy who was given his dad's name.

I recall two coworkers who gave me interesting reasons they were given their names. One said her mother had tried to conceive for several years but never gave up having faith that one day, in God's time, her prayers would be answered. After six years she had a 7½-pound baby girl. They named her Faith.

The other coworker said she was given her name because after having five boys, her mother longed for a baby girl. Upon giving birth at last to a girl, she couldn't think of a better name than Jewel, the long-awaited gift of life.

I realize that names have become important in our lives, but there's a name I didn't have to research. It's a name I love to hear, that sounds like music to my ear. As the songwriter says: "It's the sweetest name I know." That name is the name of a special baby Boy born long ago in a manger, and His name was called Jesus, and He would save His people from their sin.

Thank You, Jesus, for being You and giving me loving parents who gave me my name. Help me to forever realize, along with your other children, that there's nothing important about our names unless we're linked with God and living in harmony with You. ANNIE B. BEST

Kindness Comes Back

And she said unto her husband, Behold now, I perceive that this is an holy man of God. . . . Let us make a little chamber . . . and let us set for him there a bed, and a table, and a stool, and a candlestick. 2 Kings 4:9, 10.

I'M SURE THAT THE MAN and woman of Shunem, who re-modeled their home and added a room for the prophet Elisha, had no idea what their simple act of kindness would lead to. Not only was a child born to their childless home, but the resurrection of that same child several years later was added recompense for the kindness they had shown.

Just as the ripples extend out from a stone thrown into a pond, we never know how just a small act of honesty and kindness can reflect out to encompass many others. A wonderful story like this unfolded here in the Kansas City region.

On the first of December a young server named Heidi, working in an Applebee's Restaurant, found an envelope of money at a table she had waited on. She counted out 33 $100 bills. She knew who had forgotten the envelope, because the customer had paid with a $100 bill.

Now, Heidi could have pocketed that cash and used it to pay bills. She and her husband were deeply in debt. Surgery on their young son had left them with a huge medical bill, and it was a grim Christmas they were facing. It must have been a huge temptation to keep the money.

But Heidi was an honest young woman. The next day the customer called back, frantically trying to trace his money. What a relief to hear that the money had been found and was safe. When the customer came back to pick up his money from Heidi personally, he rewarded her with one of those $100 bills.

After the story appeared in the Kansas City *Star*, there was a flood of support for the young couple. Money and Christmas gifts and toys were sent for the honest young woman and her family. The story hit national wires, and newspapers across the country carried the tale. A follow-up story in the *Star* related that the family continued to receive the reward for Heidi's act.

The restaurant chain awarded her a check for several thousand dollars and also created an ongoing fund for employees who were facing financial difficulties. Ripples in a pond—a good deed. It flows out to those around you, and eventually comes back to bless the giver.   FAUNA RANKIN DEAN

The Real Story

Now this is eternal life: that they may know you, the only true God, and Jesus Christ, whom you have sent. John 17:3.

MY READING WAS INTERRUPTED when the train stopped at a station and four children came rushing in, followed by their mother. When the train began to move again, I decided to resume my Bible-year reading, but before long the restless children began switching from one seat to another until one of them landed in the empty seat by my side. Immediately I gave approval to his move with a smile.

"Is that book the Bible?" he asked.

"Yes! How did you know?" I asked

"I saw a book like that at Grandma's house, and she says it's called the Bible."

"Has she told you any stories from this book?"

"She didn't tell me yet; maybe next time I go to her house she will."

"The Bible is about Jesus, you know. Do you know who Jesus is?"

"Yep. I have a Jesus in my house, and He's about this big," he said, holding his little fingers about two inches apart. "We put him in a manger every year, by the Christmas tree."

He continued to describe with emotion all the pieces that composed his Nativity set. The restless child calmed down while staring out my window at the passing trees as I began to tell him the story of Baby Jesus.

"Is Jesus for real?" the boy interrupted.

"Yes, He is," I replied. This came as a surprise to him. With that he jumped up and gave me the OK sign and said, "'Bye!" He then went back to his mother.

There are many around us like this child, who still know Jesus only as a symbol. They have seen Jesus in a manger, Jesus on the cross, Jesus in the Passion movie. But many still ignore the reality that Jesus lives and forgives our sins, and that He died so that we may be saved. Jesus' last prayer on earth was for us to know Him as the real one and only true God, so that we may have eternal life. Time is crucial; let us tell the real story.

GEORGINA ALMEDA

Isabella—The Adored

Many, O Lord my God, are thy wonderful works which thou hast done. Ps. 40:5.

SHE WAS THE LATEST addition to our family of five. She arrived on a cold winter evening, a bundle of joy, so soft and warm. Her fair face, shining eyes, and rosy lips made her look lovely and adorable. She looked like royalty, so we name her Isabella. Isabella cried only when she was hungry or uncomfortable. She slept for long hours and woke up only at feeding time.

As she grew day by day we were there to assist her. We kept her from falling when she took her first steps. She went through different stages of growth from infancy to maturity, and they were new and thrilling experiences for us and taught us fresh lessons. We loved Isabella. The responsibility for her proper growth rested with us adults. We took turns caring for her, seeing to her nutritional needs, making her bed as cozy as possible, keeping her bath warm and comfortable, and giving her timely immunization shots to keep her healthy at all times.

Isabella's wants and needs changed as she grew. Sometimes she was more demanding than obedient. At other times her indifference to respond to our call irritated us. But she loved us to talk to her, pet her, and let her remain on our laps as long as she pleased. She loved to play with anything moving, even as tiny as a bug. We loved Isabella, in spite of all her tricks and pranks.

Isabella has grown into maturity. She looks more majestic, walking around with her head held high. Her cleanliness is commendable. She makes new acquaintances, and they engage most of her time. She doesn't respond to our calls often. Lying on the softest couch in the hall, she now takes only "cat naps." She's now more of a cat than a kitten. Oh—the secret is out!

Yes, our Isabella is a lovely pet cat that we adore so much. Now that the secret is revealed, let me share another surprise. The long whiskers and snow-white hair suited Isabella well, but it didn't take long for us to realize that our Isabella is not a *she* but a *tom—a he!* He grew strong, looked handsome and clean, and is accepted as the most eligible mate in the feline neighborhood. We still love Isabella, and he still gets our love and attention as a most adored pet.

MARGARET TITO

?Thought: Why do you suppose God gave us pets? What spiritual lessons can they teach?

Thoughts in the Shower

At that time many will turn away from the faith. . . . But he who stands firm to the end will be saved. Matt. 24:10-13, NIV.

"OH, WHAT A BLESSED RELIEF!" I exhaled aloud as the force of the shower's hot spray pounded into the muscles of my aching back. This simple treatment brought some relief and helped the muscles in my back relax.

The shower is especially helpful since lumbar number one was broken in a fall. Unfortunately, this accident has slowed my once very active life considerably. Standing with the bountiful hot water massaging my 87-year-old back, I turned my thoughts to my early childhood. Taking a bath in those days was a weekly event instead of a daily occurrence, as it is today. When I say "event," I mean it was a major production; hence, it was undertaken only once a week.

Our water was supplied by an outside well, pumped into a pail, and carried, one pail at a time, into the kitchen, where it was poured into a large boiler pot on top of our wood-burning stove. When the pot was full and the water was heated, it was then transferred to a small round tub placed in the middle of the kitchen floor.

Each of us five sisters would squeeze into the tub and scrub up, one at a time. After each girl finished, she poured her soapy water outside, and the process began again for the next one, and finally Dad and Mom. It was an all-afternoon event every Friday, as we wanted to be our cleanest for the coming Sabbath. Now you can see why it was a once-a-week event!

While I stood in my comfortable shower, reminiscing about those days past, a more serious thought entered my head. With all the conveniences that I now take for granted, will I be able to leave them when the time comes to "flee into the mountains" (Matt. 24:16)? Will I have the courage to leave my warm bed, comfortable home, and hot shower to endure the hardships that are inevitable? Will my faith, trust, and love for God be strong?

Knowing God and experiencing His presence daily in my life assures me that He will be my strength in every situation if I stay close to Him and in His care. The Bible gives us many such promises: "I will say of the Lord, He is my refuge and my fortress: my God; in him will I trust" (Ps. 91:2). "God is our refuge and strength, a very present help in trouble" (Ps. 46:1).

ANNETTA M. JOERS

Meditation

Let the words of my mouth, and the meditation of my heart, be acceptable in thy sight, O Lord, my strength, and my redeemer. Ps. 19:14.

IT WAS A TERRIBLE experience! My husband and I lived in Groveland, Florida, but I was begging to move back to our summer home in Tennessee.

One night after I had taken my shower, the hot water wouldn't shut off. Since our neighbor is a fix-it person, we called him for help. When Doug came, he brought his son-in-law, Denver, along, and together they repaired the water problem. While there, Denver explained that he and Wendy had just returned from Ohio and were looking for a place to rent.

I appealed to Bill to help this young couple and their 6-year-old son by renting them our place furnished. They had come from Ohio with only what was in their car. They were delighted, and as soon as we left to go north, they moved in. The house was complete with furniture, pots and pans, dishes, silverware, and linen. A contract was signed for the rent payment, and we felt good about helping someone in need.

The first month's rent was several days overdue, as was the second and third. The check in payment for the fourth month's rent was returned for insufficient funds, and our account was charged $6.50. A letter was sent expressing our disappointment and requesting that they move. After a few more months with no response, we made a trip to Florida.

Imagine our surprise to find the house empty of furniture. The washer and dryer were gone, the electric fan was off the ceiling, the screen was torn completely out of the porch door—in short, the whole mobile home was trashed.

This experience was very disturbing, and I found myself brooding over it and rehearsing it to others. Then one day the Lord reminded me of the text that I prayed every morning: "Let the words of my mouth, and the meditation of my heart, be acceptable in thy sight, O Lord, my strength, and my redeemer." The Lord said, "It is not good for you to meditate on this mistreatment that you have suffered. Remember what they did to Me when I was on earth?"

Although I have yet to understand fully the reason for this traumatic experience, I am determined to put it behind me and praise the Lord and meditate on His goodness to me.

RUBYE SUE

Some Miracles of God

[The Lord's] mercies are great. 2 Sam. 24:14.

MANY PEOPLE TALK ABOUT the sad things of the world. I've taken the position that the bad last days will come only too soon, so I'm going to try to concentrate on the miracles that God has done in my life. Here are some of them that I recall.

I can now see that it was a miracle that I was privileged to grow up in a hardworking Lutheran Christian family in which Bible study, prayer, and regular church attendance were practiced. It wasn't always easy for my farmer parents with a large family of eight children.

It was a miracle that as a teenager I was allowed to leave my family and farm life to attend high school in town, to live with and work for a lovely Seventh-day Adventist family. It was here that I learned more wonderful Bible truths and witnessed their practical Christian faith that led me to join the Adventist Church. Through the years I've been privileged to meet and work with many other sincere, God-loving people. It has been truly inspirational.

Another very big miracle in my life was meeting my future husband while we were attending a class in public speaking. We became acquainted, and soon he invited himself to join me in attending Sabbath church services. After two years of study we were married. We have now been happily together for 52 years and are both active in church and mission projects.

I love making nice religious education visual aids for children in countries around the world. It's a miracle to see how God has blessed this work. It's also been very rewarding to receive reports from missionaries, such as those who said they shed tears of joy when our material arrived.

Thank You, God, for helping us to be a part of telling the world about You and Your love for each of Your children. FRIEDA TANNER

(?) Thought: As we come to the end of another year, this would be a good time to recount God's special blessings to us personally. It is also a good time to make sure that we are each doing something for God and for those around our neighborhood and our world who do not yet know Jesus or His love.

Free at Last

I was in prison, and ye came unto me. Matt. 25:36.

I WORKED IN PRISON ministries for many years. God allowed me to touch the lives of thousands of individuals behind prison walls; however, many of them also touched my life. One week I had promised the women that I would arrive early on my next visit, in the event that they wanted to talk to me or that they needed counseling.

On that particular day a young woman came to hear me speak. I'd never seen her before, but as I spoke, her eyes were getting wider and wider. She listened attentively but said nothing.

After the service was over, I began gathering my material. She said that she had listened to the call every Saturday morning to join our service but thought that our representatives were "a group of nuts" who wanted them to hear us. She continued, "This morning a voice said to me, 'Why don't you go down and hear for yourself?' I decided to come, and I must tell you that I am so happy I came." She had discovered, after marrying her husband, that he was a drug addict. She was taking the rap for him. Though she had served several years, he had never come to see her. What devastated her even more was that he was currently in a relationship with someone else. Tears were streaming down her face as she spoke softly to me. I couldn't hold my tears back either.

She continued, "I was thinking of taking my life tonight, as well as my baby's. Your words were very encouraging. You have given me hope. You have saved our lives."

I silently gave God all the glory and all the praise. I knew that I didn't do anything of my own but that God used me to direct her to Him. God loves us all and doesn't want to see any of us lost.

We communicated frequently, and eventually she was released from prison. She was also released as a prisoner from depression, guilt, fear, and the sin that caused her to become incarcerated.

Satan has a way of making us prisoners for him. God has a way of making us free, if we surrender our lives to Him through His Son. This young woman made that choice, and she is now free at last. Freedom awaits you, too.

DAISY SIMPSON

Nothing but Junk

Don't store up treasures here on earth where they can erode. . . . Store them in heaven where they will never lose their value. . . . If your profits are in heaven your heart will be there too. Matt. 6:19-21, TLB.

I WAS IN MY STORAGE shed, sorting out some unused belongings and planning a garage sale. Among the forgotten treasures I came upon two boxes of trophies I'd won in bowling and competitions. I didn't want to put them in the trash, as they represented the hours of practice, sweat, and tears I'd put into gaining those awards. I thought that maybe I could sell them and regain a measure of reimbursement for all my time and effort. (I'm in the habit of not throwing anything away—it could be useful for something sometime.)

Among the piles of stuff I had collected were lots of artificial flowers of every color and size (in case I needed to put together a bouquet sometime). There were antique lamp parts, old cameras, chairs to be refinished, two extra fans (in case mine broke down). Some of the things may even be worth money—someday. Some folks may think this is being frugal. Basically, I had a shed half full of junk.

This all reminded me of a child's poem called "Hector the Collector." It describes all the things that Hector collected over the years. He "loved them more than shining diamonds, loved them more than glistenin' gold." Then Hector called to all his friends, "Come and share my treasure trunk!" And all the people "came and looked . . . and called it junk" (Shel Silverstein).

So it will be at the end of our lives. All our possessions, the things we've spent a lifetime working to acquire that is over and above what we need for daily living, will be nothing but junk. That's when we'll surely know that the best things in life are not things. Paul said, "What things were gain to me, those I counted loss for Christ" (Phil. 3:7). Because we possess the greatness of knowing Jesus our Lord, we can dedicate all that we have to Him and keep the clutter out of our lives. He will help us keep everything in balance. I'm reminded of the words to the song "I'd rather have Jesus than silver or gold, I'd rather be His than have riches untold; . . . I'd rather have Jesus than anything this world affords today" (Rhea F. Miller).

VIDELLA MCCLELLAN

AUTHOR BIOGRAPHIES

Betty J. Adams, a retired teacher with three grown children and five grandchildren, is active in community service, prayer ministry, and women's ministries, and contributes to her church newsletter. She's been published in *Guide* magazine. Her interests include traveling, gardening, writing, mission trips, and her grandchildren. **Aug. 11, Dec. 5.**

Priscilla E. Adonis has been married to the same man for more than 35 years. The women's ministries coordinator at her local church in South Africa, she enjoys sending notes of encouragement. She's written for the devotional book and sent recipes to various cooking publications. Her daughters live in California; she has one grandson. **Apr. 7, May 26, Dec. 3.**

Maxine Williams Allen lives in Orlando, Florida, with her husband and two small sons. She has her own computer and business consulting company and loves to travel, meet people, and experience different cultures. Her hobbies include writing, reading, and computers. She's especially interested in family, children's, and women's ministries. **Jan. 31, Oct. 29.**

Irina Jeanete Pires Almada, a resident of Corroios, Portugal, enjoys helping to care for a home for orphans and needy children. She's also involved in several missionary projects in her local church. She likes to travel, read, camp, and care for her home and children. **July 20.**

Georgina Almeda writes from Miami, Florida. She's a first-time contributor to the devotional book, and a former worker in the Inter-American Division of Seventh-day Adventists. **Dec. 25.**

Judete Soares de Andrade is married and the mother of two children, Jean and Jennifer. She works with the sale of religious and health-related books. She enjoys waking up early, reading, making friends, and receiving and writing letters. **Nov. 30.**

Mirlène André is currently a United States Peace Corps volunteer, serving in The Gambia, West Africa. When she returns to the United States, she plans to provide computer and career training for women who are trying to come off welfare. **Jan. 15, July 23.**

Mary J. Wagoner Angelin and her husband, Randy, live in Ooltewah, Tennessee. Her hobbies include therapeutic humor, exercising, hiking, writing, and vegan cooking. A stay-at-home mom to two children, she works one day a week as a social worker. She volunteers with the Make-a-Wish Foundation, deaf services, and Regeneration, a Christ-centered 12-step group. **Jan. 1, Sept. 21.**

Marilyn Joyce Applegate writes from Walla Walla, Washington. She happily abides with her husband and an assortment of grateful dogs from the animal shelter. **June 30, Nov. 4.**

Beryl Aseno-Nyamwange lives in Togo, is from Nairobi, Kenya, and has worked in Somalia with an international nongovernmental organization. Beryl has a master's degree in communication and enjoys writing, cross-cultural experiences, reading, mission projects, and keeping a daily journal. An accomplished swimmer, she made it to the nationals in her country in 1992. **Feb. 7, Dec. 13.**

Viorica Avramiea, an office secretary at her church's headquarters in Romania, holds a B.A. in theology from the Romanian Adventist Theological Institute. She is a church leader, Sabbath school superintendent's helper, and Sabbath school teacher. Hobbies include teaching, training people for Vacation Bible School, reading, fitness, gardening, cooking, climbing, and translating. **Apr. 4.**

Rosemary Baker, a freelance writer living in Iowa, is author of the children's book *What Am I?* and has contributions in *Shining Star, Kids' Stuff,* and other magazines. She's a member of the Iowa Poetry Association and the Quint City Poetry Guild. Active with her church and volunteer work, she enjoys working with children. Her hobbies are arts, crafts, music, and painting. **Sept. 22, Oct. 31.**

Audrey Balderstone and her husband operate a garden landscaping company in England. Both are involved in church and community activities. Audrey raises thousands of dollars for charity through Flower Festivals and is president of ASI Europe, a business and professionals' association with chapters throughout Europe. **Aug. 5.**

Jennifer M. Baldwin writes from Australia, where she works in clinical risk management at Sydney Adventist Hospital. She enjoys church involvement, travel, and writing, and has contributed to a number of church publications. **Feb. 3, Sept. 15.**

Mary Barrett and her husband are in pastoral ministry in England. She is a writer and speaker, and the mother of two daughters. For relaxation she loves to be with family and friends. **Apr. 6, May 10.**

Tânia Micol S. Bartalini is a religious education teacher in Niterói, Rio de Janeiro, Brazil. She is a pianist and director of the local church Community Services center. **Feb. 25, Sept. 30.**

Marianne Toth Bayless had some changes in her life this past year: she retired from 17 years working in a local high school as a secretary, she became a great-grandmother, and she recently married. Marianne has been women's ministries director at her church in south Florida and enjoys creative scrapbooking (a new hobby for her). A family heritage album is in progress. **May 31, Nov. 26.**

Dawna Beausoleil lives with her husband in an isolated area of northern Ontario. Besides rural life, she enjoys their cats, reading, scrapbooking, and flower gardening. She's been published in many magazines and books. **May 6.**

Susan Berridge is a registered nurse and teaches health occupations at a vocational school. She has four daughters and three grandchildren. Her hobbies include painting, gardening, and outdoor activities. **July 15.**

Annie B. Best is a retired teacher, widow, and mother of two grown children. She enjoys being with her three grandchildren, reading, and listening to music. She enjoys working as leader in the children's departments of her church. **Apr. 10, May 7, Dec. 23.**

Nelda Bigelow is a widow with two daughters, six grandchildren, and three spoiled cats. She became Sabbath school secretary at age 14 and has been a superintendent for more than 50 years. She retired for nine months 10 years ago but went back to work, part-time, because she enjoyed being with people. She enjoys reading, cross-stitch, and writing letters. **Jan. 29.**

Dinorah Blackman lives in Panama with her husband and daughter, Imani. They own an educational consulting agency. **Feb. 28.**

Juli Blood is a young mother who has been happily married to Gary since 1994. They were missionaries in Korea for a year. Juli fills her days with reading and writing. She has a cat, Sandy, who didn't enjoy Korea as much as she and her husband did. **July 31, Nov. 19.**

Evelyn Greenwade Boltwood is a busy wife, mother of two young adults, career woman, Pathfinder area coordinator, and a member of the National Kidney Foundation Board of Upstate New York and the Kidney Kids committee. A member of Akoma, an African-American community gospel choir, she loves reading and exploring God's world. **Jan. 30.**

Ani Köhler Bravo retired from the Brazil Publishing House after 24 years and returned to college to get a degree in translation and interpretation. She lives with her husband and son in Engenheiro Coelho, Brazil. Her pastimes include reading, cooking, playing the piano, entertaining friends, and writing. She enjoys her church, music, and women's ministries. **Apr. 27, Sept. 20.**

Lorian Lenise Bridgeforth graduated from Oakwood College in 2001 and is currently a secondary English teacher. She enjoys reading, playing tennis and basketball, and working with the Pathfinders at her church. She has one daughter, Breanne. **July 9.**

Diane Burns delights in spending time with close friends and encouraging others in their walk with Jesus. She cherishes the adoration of her husband, Lawrence; loves exhilarating hikes on the beautiful trails around Corner Brook, Newfoundland, Canada; enjoys other people's pets and children; and takes life seriously yet loves a good laugh. She is a first-time contributor. **Dec. 18.**

Betty R. Burnett, retired and "retreated," lives in Michigan's beautiful Upper Peninsula. She has shared her life's experiences in previous devotional books and eagerly looks forward to continuing her life with Papa in a heavenly country. **June 11, Oct. 6.**

Roseni M. Cândido enjoys writing texts and poetry from her home in Brazil. She has experienced great personal satisfaction in publishing a small book. **Dec. 2.**

Maria Costa Sales Cardosa worked as a missionary in Angola and is currently a secretary in her church headquarters in Portugal. She is a widow who has two children and four grandchildren. She enjoys writing poetry, reading, traveling, and walking in nature. **Jan. 7, May 19.**

Joyce Bohannon Carlile works part-time for her dentist husband, is mother to four adult children, and has two grandchildren. She volunteers at Tulsa Adventist

Academy, is director of women's ministries of her church, and is one of its youth leaders. **June 16, Aug. 18.**

Marísia Oliveira H. Carvalho is studying at Northeast Brazil College. She dreams of becoming an educator and finishing her degree in education. Her husband is in his third year of theology studies. **Mar. 21.**

Virginia Casey is a retired municipal clerk residing in Conception Bay South, Newfoundland, Canada. She takes great pleasure in church-related duties. Her hobbies include reading, writing, and outdoor activities. She especially enjoys interacting with people. **Apr. 25.**

Aucely Corrêa Fernandes Chagas, a nurse, holds a master's degree in collective health. She works in the hospital in Campo Grande, Brazil, and is coordinator and professor in the graduate nursing course at the Dom Bosco University. She enjoys listening to music, doing handicrafts, and caring for plants. **Mar. 25, Nov. 5.**

Beth Vollmer Chagas is a pastor's wife and mother of two teenagers, Andrew and Juliana. She lives in Brasilia, Brazil, and works for the South American Division of Seventh-day Adventists as a translator. Her favorite pastimes are reading, sewing, and cooking. **Jan. 13, June 17.**

Birol Charlotte Christo is a retired teacher. During her active service she also worked as an office secretary and statistician. She lives with her husband in Hosur, India. The mother of five grown children, Birol enjoys gardening, sewing, and creating craft items to finance her projects for homeless children. **Apr. 28, July 29.**

Hercilia M. Coelho worked in the Silvestre Adventist Hospital in Rio de Janeiro, Brazil, for many years. In 1970 she moved to the United States, and sends donations for the construction of a church and a sports complex for youth camps in Trimonte, Minas Gerais, Brazil. She admires nature and likes flowers. **July 5.**

Clareen Colclesser, a retired nurse, and a widow since 1994, has two children, seven grandchildren, and six great-grandchildren. She enjoys family, quiet times with a good book, and her summer retreat near Lake Huron, Michigan. Clareen stays active in her church, enjoys writing letters and short stories, and perusing her collection of interior decorating magazines. **Apr. 9, Aug. 8.**

Sandra Cole is married and has three daughters and a son-in-law. About four years ago she resigned as business manager in her husband's practice. She has been editor of Burton Academy's newsletter for more than 11 years and editor of her church's newsletter in Texas. She is also head deaconess in her church and cares for her 80-year-old mother. **Dec. 14.**

Adriana Azevedo da Costa is a phonoaudiologist at Parana Adventist Academy, Brazil. Adriana takes care of the kindergarten class at the church she attends. She likes to read, listen to music, and work with children. **July 25.**

Eva Alice Covey is in her eighth decade of life. She lives alone, has been a teacher, raised a family, and written books. God has given her a young mind and a love for words, and as long as she is able, she will try to fulfill the purpose for which she is here. **Mar. 4.**

Anne Cram is married with two married sons, one daughter, and four grandchildren. For the past 11 years she has been involved with fly 'n' build projects to the Solomon Islands, Vanuatu, and Kiribati in the South Pacific. Hobbies include knitting, crocheting, patchwork, reading, and gardening. Anne lives in Sydney, Australia. **May 21, Oct. 15.**

Celia Mejia Cruz is a pastor's wife, mother of five adult children, and grandmother of eight. A church elder and women's ministries leader, Celia works at the church that her husband, Mario, pastors. She is also a Shaklee distributor and enjoys entertaining, reading, playing with her dog, and collecting Siamese cats. **June 27, Aug. 22.**

Winsome Dacres is a podiatrist who lives in England with her husband, two guinea pigs, and a mouthy dog who thinks she owns the home. Winsome is the women's ministries leader and communication secretary for her local church. In her spare time she enjoys sports and reading. **June 2.**

Becky Dada is principal of a secondary school in Ibadan, Nigeria. She and her pastor husband have four children. She's been involved with women's ministries and development, publishing Bible games and youth magazines, and is now writing the history of Adventist women in west Nigeria. Her hobby is conducting Revelation seminars, giving talks, reading, and writing. **Feb. 5, May 5.**

Elizabeth Davis was a freshman at Southern Adventist University, going for her Bachelor of Science with a biology major, when she wrote this devotional, her first published item. She is still looking for an Adventist church in the area that fits her personality. She loves anything to do with animals, especially horses, and loves to read. **Feb. 12.**

Fauna Rankin Dean, a published freelance writer-photographer, lives near Kansas City with her husband. They have one adult son, two teenagers, and 10 golden retrievers who make every day interesting. She is currently working on a book, and serves as president of her local Toastmasters Club. **Feb. 21, Dec. 24.**

Winifred Devaraj is a retired teacher and women's ministries director from Bangalore, India. Her only son is a medical director at the Adventist hospital in Kerala, India, and has given her twin grandsons. Her hobbies include listening to music, telling stories, helping her pastor husband with visitation, and giving Bible studies. **Mar. 2.**

Kim DeWitt is a mother and pastor's wife who lived in Kenya, Lebanon, Cyprus, and Singapore while growing up. She and her husband recently returned after six years of mission work at Maxwell Adventist Academy in Kenya. They now pastor in Michigan. She loves baking, nature, camping, snake catching with her husband, and sports. This is her first contribution. **June 20.**

Laurie Dixon-McClanahan, a retired Bible instructor for the Michigan Conference of Seventh-day Adventists, likes to write, research for genealogy, read, and correspond via e-mail. **Jan. 18, Sept. 11.**

Leonie Donald moved back to New Zealand in 2003 with her husband to be near elderly parents. She enjoys reading, exercise, and gardening. Leonie takes an active part in church activities at the retirement village where her parents reside. **Jan. 8, June 12, Oct. 11.**

Goldie Down passed away in December 2003. She and her husband, David, spent 20 years in evangelistic work in Australia and New Zealand, and served as missionaries in India for another 20 years. Goldie was a prolific writer, with 23 books and numerous articles to her credit. She was the mother of six children, whom she home-schooled. **Apr. 29, Sept. 7.**

Louise Driver lives in Beltsville, Maryland, with her pastor husband, Don. They have three grown sons and four grandchildren. At church she is involved with praise music. She's head of the children's department at the Potomac Adventist Book Center. Her hobbies include singing and music, reading, gardening, and traveling to historical places. **Sept. 9.**

Donna M. Dunbar is a registered dietitian who works for the Department of Juvenile Justice in Arcadia, Florida. She and her husband, Clarence, run the Lighthouse Outreach Center, now a multidenominational soup kitchen. She has two sons, three stepchildren, and four wonderful grandchildren. **Oct. 17.**

Mary E. Dunkin holds degrees in home economics and business administration, and is working on a master's degree in business administration/human resources, as well as being president of her high school alumni association. Her passions are God's will, being Doc and Nellie's daughter, 40 years of Pathfindering, and her four precious "muttlets." **June 4, Oct. 16.**

Gloria Stella Felder works as administrative assistant in Queens, New York. She and her pastor husband are the parents of five adult children and five grandchildren. Gloria enjoys singing, listening to music, writing, speaking, and spending time with her family, especially her grandchildren. She is currently working on her second book. **Feb. 24, May 9, Sept. 29.**

Mary J. Felder, who resides in Georgia, is a first-time contributor. **Dec. 19.**

Maria de Lourdes Fernandes is a clinical and organizational psychologist who specializes in bioethics and has a master's degree in biological sciences. She has two children, a boy and a girl, and likes to collect pens and miniature elephants. **Oct. 12.**

Clara Hornus de Ferreyro is a Bible instructor in Argentina. She supports the work of her pastor husband in their work in various provinces of Argentina and Uruguay. She has two children and two grandchildren and enjoys reading and walking. **Mar. 17, Oct. 8.**

Valerie Fidelia, a wife, mother, and grandmother, works as a department director in the Middle East Union of Seventh-day Adventists, based in Cyprus. She loves her work with women's ministries, and in her local church is involved in small groups and music ministry. **June 24.**

Edith Fitch is a retired teacher living in Lacombe, Alberta, Canada. She volunteers in the archives at Canadian University College and is a member of the Lacombe Historical Society. She enjoys doing research for schools, churches, and individual histories. Her hobbies include writing, traveling, needlework, and cryptograms. **Apr. 23, Sept. 14.**

Lana Fletcher is a homemaker living in Chehalis, Washington, with her husband. She has one adult daughter. Her younger daughter was killed in a car accident in 1993. She is the church clerk, has attended Toastmasters for several years, and enjoys gardening, writing, and making Creative Memories albums. **Apr. 11, Nov. 3.**

Sharon Follett writes from Dunlap, Tennessee, a small town in the beautiful Sequatchie Valley, where she teaches music and supports her husband, Ron, who pastors three Seventh-day Adventist churches in the valley. They are devoted to their ministry and to their family, and desire all to be ready to meet Jesus when He comes. **Jan. 28, July 4.**

Edit Fonseca lives in Curitiba, Parana, Brazil. She is a minister's wife, piano teacher, and director of women's ministries for the South Parana Conference. She has two sons—a physician and a minister—and enjoys music, writing, and walking. **July 14.**

Heide Ford is a pastoral counselor with Centre Pointe Counseling. A registered nurse and former associate editor of *Women of Spirit* magazine, Heide lives in Maryland with her husband, Zell. She enjoys leading Bible study groups, reading, and whale watching. **May 8.**

Sônia Regina Friedrich has been a secretary at the Diadema Adventist School in São Paulo, Brazil, for 14 years. She likes to listen to music, write, and go for walks. She is a first-time contributor. **May 14.**

Vinita Gaikwad is from India but presently works in Uganda as head of the English Department at Bugema University. She has worked as a teacher at Spicer Memorial College and assistant editor at the Southern Asia Division of Seventh-day Adventists in the Communication Department in Hosur, India. **Feb. 17.**

Edna Maye Gallington is part of the communication team in the Southeastern California Conference of Seventh-day Adventists and is a graduate of La Sierra University. She's a member of Toastmasters International and the Loma Linda Writing Guild and enjoys freelance writing, music, gourmet cooking, entertaining, hiking, and racquetball. **Mar. 28, Dec. 22.**

Leonízia Generoso is married and the mother of two children, Lucas and Rafael. She enjoys singing and doing cross-stitch pictures. **Mar. 12, Dec. 6.**

Marybeth Gessele is a pastor's wife living in Gaston, Oregon. She has a degree in home economics and is currently working as a caregiver. Her joys in life include ministry with her husband, recipes, quilting, country living, and her two granddaughters. **Mar. 20.**

Evelyn Glass and her husband, Darrell, love having their grandchildren live next door to them in northern Minnesota, on the farm where Darrell was born. Evelyn is active in writing for her local church paper and is a member of a local writers' group. Since retiring, she's added quilting to her list of hobbies. She continues to speak for various events. **June 3.**

Mary Jane Graves and her husband, Ted, are busy retirees in North Carolina, where they spent their last working years on the staff of a Christian boarding high school. They are involved in delivering meals to shut-ins, church business, gardening, and other activities. **July 2, Aug. 27.**

Shirley Kimbrough Grear writes from New Jersey, where she lives with her husband, Carl. She is the mother of CJ and Michelle, and has four grandchildren. She's active in women's ministries, writes, lectures, and provides workshops. **Aug. 19, Dec. 17.**

Carol Joy Greene writes from Florida, where she has retired. She is the mother of three adult children and the grandmother of four. She's active in women's ministries in her church. **Feb. 26, Sept. 28.**

Glenda-mae Greene is a chronicler of the everyday moments in her life and the author of the recently published devotional *Green Pasture Moments for Frazzled Urban Dwellers.* She writes from Palm Bay, Florida, where she's actively involved in women's prayer circles and teaching Sabbath school classes at her church. **Feb. 1, Apr. 13.**

Janet M. Greene is a cardiac rehabilitation nurse, wife, and mother to two girls. Her major objective is that her daughters see Jesus in everything every day. She is active as an associate Pathfinder director, with the expanded goal of having 25 other young people also see Jesus in everything. And yes, she is still a shopaholic. **Oct. 2.**

Takara Greene writes from Palm Bay, Florida, where she lives with her family. An active Pathfinder, she loves volleyball and playing the cello. When she wrote this story, she was a 13-year-old eighth grader. **July 27.**

Gloria Gregory is a director of admissions at Northern Caribbean University in Jamaica. She enjoys encouraging others, writing, and handcrafts. Her two adult daughters and her husband, Milton, are her writing inspirations. She is a frequent contributor to the women's devotional. **Apr. 5, June 15.**

Maria Bellezi Guilhém lives in São Carlos, São Paulo, Brazil, with her husband, a retired pastor. She likes to visit those who are elderly and sick, walk in the morning, and listen to birds singing at daybreak. **Oct. 21.**

Dessa Weisz Hardin and her husband live in Maine. She enjoys traveling, writing, reading, working, and teaching children. An added dimension is grandparenting. **June 10, Aug. 29.**

Selita Fay Atchley Harpe is a graduate of Oakwood College with B.S. degrees in nutrition and human environmental sciences. Her hobbies include reading, creating new vegan dishes, drama, travel, interior design, househunting, and playing word games. She is the Adventist youth leader for her church in Birmingham, Alabama, where her husband, Michael, pastors. **Jan. 6, Nov. 16.**

Marian M. Hart, a retired elementary teacher and nursing home administrator, works with her husband doing property management. As a member of the Battle

Creek Seventh-day Adventist Tabernacle for 28 years, she has served as a volunteer in many different capacities. Six grandchildren make her a proud grandmother. **Apr. 26, Aug. 7.**

Ursula M. Hedges passed away in September 2005 in Australia. She was a secondary school teacher-administrator. Born of missionary parents in India, she and her Australian principal husband gave 10 years of mission service in the Pacific, Australia, and New Zealand. Ursula was active in women's ministries, and published books, stories, and articles. **Aug. 28.**

Karen Holford works beside her husband, Bernie, as an associate director of family and children's ministries in southern England. They have three teenage children. Karen has written several books and is training to be a family therapist. In spare moments she likes to make quilts. **June 13, July 28.**

Jacqueline Hope HoShing-Clarke has served in the field of education as principal and teacher. She is the director of the precollege department at Northern Caribbean University, Jamaica, and is currently studying for a Ph.D. Jackie is married and has two children, Deidre and Deneil. She enjoys writing, teaching children's Sabbath school, flower gardening, and housekeeping. **Jan. 9, Oct. 26.**

Lorraine Hudgins-Hirsch lives in Loma Linda, California. She has worked at Faith for Today, the Voice of Prophecy, and the world headquarters of the Seventh-day Adventist Church. Her articles and poems appear frequently in various publications. She is the mother of five grown children and 10 grandchildren. **May 28.**

Muriel Huguenin is a wife, mother, and grandmother who originally comes from Switzerland—hence, her love of languages. The young people she has taught in a Christian high school inspire her walk with the Lord. Her hobbies include music involvement with her church and hiking on the 40 acres she and her husband live on. **Mar. 29.**

Bonnie Hunt, retired from 20 years of teaching, coordinates a learning assistance program for nursing students. She coauthored a book with David Gerstle, *Inspiration PRN: Stories About Nurses—A Collection of Spiritual Lessons.* Hobbies include her children, grandchildren, reading, writing, traveling, and building houses. **Feb. 15.**

Ramona L. Hyman, assistant professor of English at Oakwood College, is a writer and speaker. Her articles have appeared in such magazines as *Adventist Review* and *Message.* She has served as a speaker for the Alabama Humanities Foundation. Presently she is a doctoral student at the University of Alabama. **June 5.**

Shirley C. Iheanacho, originally from Barbados, now resides in Huntsville, Alabama, with Morris, her husband of more than 34 years. She has had the unique privilege of working in the office of the president of Oakwood College for 20 years, assisting four college presidents. She enjoys her two grandsons, playing in the handbell choir, singing in the church choir, and encouraging people. **May 29, Sept. 2.**

Emralina Pangan Imperio is a retired unit clerk, married, with four children and nine grandchildren. She loves sewing for the less-fortunate children in the

Philippines. She plays the piano for self-entertainment and loves traveling to other countries. **Apr. 14, Oct. 13.**

Avis M. Jackson is a mother of five, and a balloon artist by trade. She owns a little shop in her town and sells balloons and party stuff. She is an Adventist by calling. **June 19.**

Consuelo Roda Jackson, Ph.D., devotes her retirement days to her family and hobbies. She is a conservationist and environmentalist who enjoys music, reading, and writing. Consuelo volunteers to play the piano and lead the singing at a skilled nursing facility. A perpetual student, she looks forward to sitting at the Master Teacher's feet. **Feb. 8, July 6.**

Madeia Jacobs is a nurse who loves the Lord and attends Mizpah Adventist Church in Philadelphia, Pennsylvania. She is always writing in the recesses of her mind. **Oct. 14.**

Phoebee Jocelyn-Muscadin was born in Haiti and now lies in Florida. She is a respiratory therapist who also works as volunteer chaplain-coordinator for the Florida Adventist Prison Ministries team. She spends her free time gardening and writing sacred songs in both English and French. This is her first submission. **Apr. 1.**

Annetta M. Joers, of Reedsport, Oregon, was 89 years old at the time she wrote her devotionals—by hand. She is a first-time contributor. **Apr. 30, Dec. 27.**

Lois E. Johannes is retired from overseas service in southern and eastern Asia. She lives near a daughter in Portland, Oregon, and enjoys knitting, community service work, patio gardening, and her four grandchildren and two great-grandchildren. **Apr. 16.**

Angela C. Hardin Jones recently married Donald, the love of her life. Together they have three children and two grandchildren. Her passions include writing, sharing God's love with others, and spending time with family. She has written six children's picture books and hopes to be a published author in that genre soon. This is her first attempt at publishing adult material. **Mar. 15.**

Emily Felts Jones began Bring Forth Ministries in 1996. Through music, writing, and speaking, she loves sharing God's desire to work in and through each one of us—no matter what our age or background may be. She loves being a wife, mother, and grandmother. **Mar. 30.**

Sonja Kalmbach is a first-time contributor. At the time of this writing she was a 25-year-old taking German, American, and Scandinavian studies at the University of Tübingen, Germany. She teaches languages at a Swedish school and is about to obtain her teacher's degree for English and German. **Oct. 3.**

Barbara Ann Kay is first a child of God and is happily married, is the mother of three grown children (four, including her son-in-law). She is retired from home schooling and works in her greenhouse business growing ivy. She loves spending time with her two grandchildren and, for fun, goes riding with her husband on his four-wheeler. **Aug. 9.**

Gladys S. (Guerrero) Kelley, from the Dominican Republic, came to the United States when she was 17 years old. She has a bachelor's degree in English education and is currently working on a master's in second-language acquisition. She teaches Spanish as a second language, loves to write, swim, read, play volleyball, and do extreme sports (bungee jumping and skydiving). **Feb. 10.**

Hepzibah G. Kore lives in Hosur, India, with her husband. She is the Shepherdess coordinator and women's ministries director for the Southern Asia Division of Seventh-day Adventists. She delights in serving the women and enjoys gardening, reading, and listening to music. **Mar. 31.**

Betty Kossick is a columnist and freelance correspondent for Zephyrhills *News.* During her more than 30 years as a writer she's had the opportunity to give honor to the Giver of Talents. "I'm a very ordinary woman who has been allowed some very unordinary opportunities to praise Him through writing." She remains a busy great-grandmother. **Mar. 24, Oct. 10.**

Patricia Mulraney Kovalski is a retired teacher, widow, mother, and grandmother. She likes to swim, give English teas, travel, and work for the Lord. **May 27, Nov. 2.**

Annie M. Kujur served her church organization for 43 years as an elementary teacher. Now retired, she and her husband, with the help of the Asian Aid Organization, run a family orphanage, teaching more than 53 orphans from kindergarten to class 3. She has authored four books for the elementary school, and teaches piano to students from all walks of life. **Apr. 12, Oct. 27.**

Mabel Kwei works with her pastor husband, who is the president of the Seventh-day Adventist Gambia Mission Station in West Africa. She is director of women's ministries, a lecturer at Gambia College and the University of Gambia, and enjoys reading. **June 25, Nov. 15.**

Nathalie Ladner-Bischoff, a retired nurse, lives with her husband in Walla Walla, Washington. Besides homemaking, gardening, and volunteering at the Walla Walla General Hospital gift shop, she reads, writes, knits, and crochets. She's published several magazine stories and a book, *An Angel's Touch.* **Jan. 16.**

Mandy LaFave-Vogler is a registered nurse working part-time at a local health department. Her young children bring her great joy—and challenges. She and her husband live in Manton, Michigan, and attend church in Lake City, where she helps with cradle roll and kindergarten classes. She enjoys gardening. **Aug. 10.**

Sally Lam-Phoon, from Singapore, is the director of women's ministries at the Northern Asia-Pacific Division of Seventh-day Adventists in Seoul, Korea. Her passion is to help women discover their potential in following God's will. She's married to Chek Yat Phoon, and they have two daughters, Michelle and Rachel. **Feb. 13, Sept. 16.**

Iani Lauer-Leite has a bachelor's degree in administration and a master's degree in psychology. She works as a professor at a Seventh-day Adventist college in Brazil. She likes to read and talk, and is active in the music ministry of her church, rehearsing with groups and playing the piano during worship services. **Apr. 24, Aug. 6.**

Arlete Francisco Leão worked for 22 years in education with her husband. Even though she's retired and has difficulty getting around, she likes to present seminars and special weeks of spiritual inspiration for children near her home in Brazil. **Feb. 4, July 30.**

Gina Lee has had more than 750 articles published, mostly in Christian magazines. She enjoys working at the library and caring for her family of cats. **June 22, Sept. 25.**

Ruth Lennox has retired three times. In 1995 she retired from active medical practice, in 2003 from leading women's ministries in British Columbia, and in 2004 from leading women's ministries for the Adventist Church in Canada. Ruth and her husband have three married children and four delightful granddaughters. **June 26, Oct. 28.**

Cecelia Lewis writes from Huntsville, Alabama, where she is a Bible instructor and teaches baptismal classes for adults, youth, and children at the Oakwood College Seventh-day Adventist Church. She enjoys tutoring at the elementary school, reading, writing, gardening, and being a member of the bell choir. **July 16.**

Cordell Liebrandt lives in Cape Town, South Africa. She is a paralegal with an interest in working with people, women's ministries, and evangelism. She is happily married and enjoys the outdoors, walks in nature, and being with family and friends. Her greatest desire is to serve God. **Aug. 12.**

Olga I. Corbin de Lindo, retired from the United States Air Force, was born in Panama. She and her husband, Richard, have one adult daughter and three grandchildren. She serves her church as a pianist and a women's ministries member, and during her 60-plus years of service has helped in almost every department. She enjoys giving Bible studies, reading, writing, gardening, and playing the piano. **July 8.**

Bessie Siemens Lobsien, a retired missionary librarian, has been writing short essays, poems, and stories since girlhood, some of which have been published in church papers. She likes to sew quilts and clothes for her grandchildren and great-grandchildren, as well as for her local Adventist community center. **Jan. 4, Dec. 20.**

Sharon Long (Brown) is from Trinidad, West Indies. She is a social worker executive manager with child and family services in Edmonton, Alberta, Canada. She and her husband, Miguel, have three adult children, one teenager, and two granddaughters. Sharon is active in her church and sings in two choirs. She enjoys writing, entertaining, cooking and baking, and sewing. **Mar. 5, May 24, Oct. 22.**

Isabel Cristina de Almeida Machado is a widow and mother of three children. She has worked with the sale of educational and religious literature for 23 years and enjoys reading and taking nature walks. **Mar. 14, Sept. 26.**

Amy Smith Mapp, a retired public educator, is a part-time adjunct instructor, aerobics instructor, and reader for McGraw-Hill Publishing Company. Married to C. Bernell Mapp, they have three children and six grandchildren. **July 21.**

Tamara Marquez de Smith writes from Bay Shore, New York, where she lives with her husband, Steven, and their two daughters, Lillian and Cassandra. At her church Tamara serves where the Lord can use her. **June 29, Sept. 4.**

Peggy Mason lives in Wales with her husband and one of her two adult sons. She is a teacher of English and a writer whose hobbies include dried flower growing and arranging, cooking, sewing, gardening, and reading. Peggy is also a pianist and composer who enjoys working for her church and community. **Nov. 1.**

Soosanna Mathew has been a teacher for many years and is now an office secretary. She and her pastor husband have two grown children, David and Hannah, and one grandchild, Dana. Soosanna enjoys writing and music. **Apr. 19.**

Deborah Matshaya is a teacher at Marian High in Elsies River in Cape Town, South Africa. Previously she taught at Bethel College. She has had several devotionals published and loves gospel music. **Aug. 2, Nov. 28.**

Madge S. May practiced nursing in Canada—from Quebec to the Northwest Territories—and Saudi Arabia before moving to Florida, where she now works. She is the director of the Emmanuel Gazelle Adventurers Club at her church in Plant City. **May 3, Dec. 8.**

Vidella McClellan is a homemaker and caregiver for the elderly in British Columbia, Canada. A mother of three and grandmother of seven, her hobbies are gardening, crossword puzzles, playing Scrabble, and writing. She belongs to the Toastmasters Club and is active in her church. Her interest in writing began by recording her experiences for casual family reading. **Feb. 27, Dec. 31.**

Hilda McClure is a retired secretary-bookkeeper who lives with her husband, Warner, in the state of Washington. Together they care for a 94-year-old friend in their home. Hilda is a deaconess and works with some committees in her church. She enjoys reading, knitting, embroidery, and traveling. **Nov. 8.**

Patsy Murdoch Meeker has enjoyed the company of Tibby, her long-haired calico cat, for a number of years. She likes to read and e-mail friends. Most of all, she likes to talk to her heavenly Father and Big Brother. **Oct. 20.**

Gay Mentes writes and does her artwork, Heavenly Reflections, from Kelowna, British Columbia, Canada. She and her husband, Alex, who is also an artist, have two children, Sharlet and A.J. Her artwork has been in the local art gallery, and she makes greeting cards, does artist trading cards, is a member of the Red Hat Society, and belongs to Toastmasters. **Apr. 2.**

Christel Mey is an author of several volumes of poems and has written articles for various periodicals. She is a vocal soloist and painter, is married, and has two adult children. She lives in Germany and Turkey. **Jan. 3, June 23.**

Quilvie G. Mills is a retired community college professor who is actively engaged with her pastor husband, H. A. Mills, in the operation of their church in Port St. Lucie, Florida. She has a deep interest in young people and finds joy in helping them achieve their goals. Her hobbies include music, reading, traveling, word games, and gardening. **May 22, Sept. 3.**

Susen Mattison Molé was born in India to missionary parents and spent most of her early life in eastern Asia. She is a full-time mother and teacher to two home-schooled daughters. Occasionally she finds time for her hobbies, which include reading, trekking, and needlepoint. She's married to a naval officer and continues to travel the world. **Nov. 6.**

Marcia Mollenkopf, a retired schoolteacher, lives in Klamath Falls, Oregon. She is active in local church programs and has served in both adult and children's divisions. She enjoys reading, crafts, hiking, and bird-watching. **May 18.**

Mildred Ellen Moore, born in Sanford, Florida, is the seventh of nine children and a third-generation Seventh-day Adventist. She attended church schools in Florida, Pennsylvania, and New York. She is retired and a member of the Beltsville Adventist Church. She enjoys singing and reciting poetry. **Aug. 21.**

Esperanza Aquino Mopera is the mother of four adult children and a grandmother of six. She is on the staff at Lake Taylor Transitional Care Hospital as a charge nurse. She enjoys gardening. **Mar. 26, Aug. 31.**

Walkíria Vespa S. S. Moreira, a pastor's wife, is an educator and enjoys traveling. She has three children and lives in Colatina, Espirito Santo, Brazil. **July 10, Sept. 8.**

Barbara Smith Morris is executive director of a nonprofit retirement center and presents devotional talks over the speaker system daily. She served for seven years as a Tennessee delegate, representing housing and service needs of low-income elderly. Barbara presents seminars on elder life issues. She has four grown children and six grandchildren. **Feb. 16, Aug. 25.**

Bonnie Moyers lives with her husband and three cats in Staunton, Virginia. She's a musician for a Methodist church, works as a laundry assistant for a nearby bed-and-breakfast, and freelance-writes whenever she can fit it in. She has two adult children and one granddaughter. Her writing has been published in many magazines and books. **Jan. 25, June 7.**

Ethel D. Msuseni is a single parent, professional nurse and teacher, and pensioner member of her church in Umtata, South Africa. Her hobbies include baking, sewing, gardening, and listening to gospel music. **Feb. 11, June 8.**

Clarice Brenneise Turner Murphy lives in the mountains of western North Carolina. She is the mother of a grown son, a social worker by profession, and the CEO of a hospice. **Jan. 22, Nov. 12.**

Lillian Musgrave and her family have made northern California their home for more than 40 years. She enjoys family and grandchildren, and now has a great-grandchild, too. Other interests include music, writing (including poetry and songs), and church responsibilities. **Mar. 6.**

Julie Nagle is a wife and a mother of three who works for the Australian Public Service. She's dedicated to service for God and with God, and is an ordained elder for Christ. Julie is an indigenous Australian who is involved in many ministries, including those to women and the general public. She enjoys public speaking and continual learning. **Mar. 11, Dec. 10.**

Sibusisiwe Ncube, a native of Zimbabwe, Africa, is currently in the United States for further studies. She enjoys listening to gospel music, reading, cooking, and visiting. Previously she worked as a missionary with her husband in Kenya for several years. **Mar. 22, Nov. 10.**

Anne Elaine Nelson, a retired teacher, is doing tutoring and testing for schools, and has written the book *Puzzled Parents.* Her four children have blessed her with 11 grandchildren. Widowed in 2001, she lives in Michigan, where she stays active as women's ministries leader in her church. Her favorite activities are sewing, music, and photography. **May 17, Nov. 21.**

Maria Sinharinha de Oliveira Nogueira was born in Brazil. She's a retired teacher who is married and has two daughters and four grandchildren. She serves as a deaconess in her church and enjoys reading good books, writing poems, crocheting, crossword puzzles, walks, and physical exercise. **Apr. 22.**

Cecília Francisca Nunes is a farmer who lives in the state of Paraiba, Brazil. She has seven children and two grandchildren and serves as a deaconess in the Vila Queimadas church. She supports women's ministries and enjoys crochet and knitting. **Dec. 11.**

Beth Versteegh Odiyar lives in Kelowna, British Columbia, Canada, where she manages the family chimney sweep business. She has twin sons and a daughter in college. Beth enjoys mission trips and road trips to visit family in the United States. She loves creativity—sewing, cooking vegan, home decorating, organizing—and hopes to be a writer. **Mar. 19.**

Sal Okwubunka, a counseling psychologist, contributes for the first time. She writes from Nigeria, where she is women's ministries and education director for the East Nigeria Conference. **May 2, Nov. 24.**

Regiane Ramos Oliveira is the mother of Wilson and Gabriela. She works for Epidemiological Vigilance in Sorocaba, São Paulo, Brazil. She is women's ministries and youth department director in the Parque Laranjeiras church. **Apr. 15.**

Jemima D. Orillosa works in the Secretariat Department of the world headquarters of the Seventh-day Adventist Church. She is active in her local church in Maryland, where she lives with her husband and two daughters. She enjoys gardening and making friends. **Jan. 23, Oct. 24.**

Rócio Ortiz is a dentist in Brazil. Married, she includes reading, meditating, and writing as her hobbies. **Aug. 15.**

Brenda D. Ottley is a real Caribbean person: born in Guyana and married to a Trinidadian. She is a secondary school teacher on the island of St. Lucia in the West Indies. She's involved in a Friday evening radio ministry with her husband, *Our Time Together.* She is a first-time contributor. **Jan. 12.**

Hannele Ottschofski lives in Germany, where she is an elder of her local church. She loves to prepare PowerPoint presentations, and speaks at women's retreats and evangelistic campaigns in the Ukraine. **July 19, Dec. 7.**

Edilene Yule de Macedo Terra Paes, 42, a surgeon, and her husband, a biologist, live in Rio Bonito, Rio de Janeiro, Brazil. They are the parents of Anna Carolina, who just turned 3 two days after the incident she writes about in her devotional. She helps in the beginners' class in the Rio Bonito church and enjoys physical activity, music, books, travel, and photography. **Dec. 4.**

Ofelia A. Pangan and her husband are stationed at Mission College in Thailand, where she teaches in the English Second Language school and her husband is the senior pastor of the college church. She loves her family of three professional adult children, their spouses, and nine grandchildren, and enjoys reading, walking, gardening, traveling, and playing Scrabble. **July 26, Nov. 17.**

Revel Papaioannou and her pastor husband work in Greece. They have four sons and 10 grandchildren. She loves teaching and for years has given Bible studies and taught all ages in Sabbath school, Bible seminars, Pathfinders, Vacation Bible School, and English as a foreign language. **Aug. 4.**

Abigail Blake Parchment is wife of Sean, sister of Rachel and Asenath, daughter of Frieda and Albert and the King of kings. She is active in women's ministries in her church in the Cayman Islands. Her ultimate career goal (as yet unrealized) is to be a full-time wife and mother. Until that time, she is a family nurse practitioner, working in women's health. **Oct. 4.**

Eve Parker is a secretary in the Education Department at the Georgia-Cumberland Conference of Seventh-day Adventists. She enjoys reading, writing, and working with animals—especially horses. **Jan. 21.**

Betty G. Perry lives in Fayetteville, North Carolina, with her retired pastor husband. They have two adult children and four grandchildren. An anesthetist for 27 years, she is now semiretired. Hobbies include sewing, new recipes, piano, and interior decorating. **Jan. 27, Apr. 8.**

Kelly Piceno is a homemaker who lives in Montevallo, Alabama, with her husband, John, and their three children. She enjoys singing, reading, writing, exercising, planning, and organizing. Kelly relies on the promises of God's Word to help her in her daily struggles. One of her favorites is Isaiah 40:11: "He gently leads those that have young" (NIV). **Oct. 18.**

Birdie Poddar lives in northeastern India. She and her husband enjoy retirement but keep busy. She gardens, cooks, bakes, sews, reads, writes, and does handcrafts. They have a daughter, a son, and four grandsons. **Jan. 20, Aug. 24.**

Lanny Lydia Pongilatan, from Jakarta, Indonesia, works as a professional secretary. She was an English instructor for Indonesian Professions in the Indonesian-American Foundation. She enjoys playing the piano, listening to Christian gospel songs, reading religious books, playing tennis, and swimming. **Aug. 14.**

Daisy B. Princesa, a senior at Adventist University of the Philippines, is pursuing a Bachelor of Elementary Education degree. She's been a church choir member and active in other campus groups. Every Christmas vacation and summer vacation she joins the Voice of Youth. Her interests are singing, playing guitar—and a little piano. **May 30.**

Judith Purkiss is a secondary school teacher, originally from Birmingham, England, who currently lives and works in London. She is the Sabbath school leader in her local congregation and enjoys reading, singing, cooking, and running. **Jan. 19, Sept. 23.**

Edileuza Nascimento Ramos is a housewife, mother of three, and an avid reader. She is missionary director at her church, as well as an assistant in women's ministries in her district; she also serves as a member of the executive committee of the South Bahia Conference, Brazil. Her greatest pleasure is making friends for Jesus. **Aug. 13.**

Vicki Macomber Redden was the desktop and Web content coordinator for *Insight* magazine at the Review and Herald Publishing Association in Hagerstown, Maryland, until she got a promotion—full-time mommy to Elaina Noel. When she has a free minute she enjoys cooking, scrapbooking, and photography. **Apr. 17, Sept. 17.**

Lílian Borreli dos Reis lives in Brazil with her pastor husband and her teenage children, Laurie and Liander. A nursing auditor, she enjoys listening to music, reading, traveling with her family, and getting to know new cultures, typical foods, and customs. **May 25.**

Odnar Lima dos Reis is a retired teacher who has two children. She enjoys decorating with flowers, walks, reading, and music. **Aug. 20.**

Darlenejoan McKibbin Rhine was born in Nebraska, raised in California, and schooled in Tennessee. She holds a B.A. in journalism, and worked in the plant at the Los Angeles *Times* for 21 years before retiring in 1995. A retired writer, she now lives on an island in Puget Sound, Washington, and attends the North Cascade Seventh-day Adventist Church. **May 11, July 18.**

Charlotte Robinson is a wife and mother of three. She's had stories published in *Our Little Friend, Primary Treasure, Guide,* and *Insight,* as well as children's stories in the *Adventist Review.* Between taking her junior and early teenage children to school and cleaning two post offices, she likes to mow lawns, write letters, and do almost anything but clean house. **July 13.**

Avis Mae Rodney, a justice of the peace for the province of Ontario, is possibly the first, and only, Black female justice of the peace in Canada. She is the first ombudsperson appointed by the Adventist Church in Canada. Wife and mother of two adult children, Avis enjoys long walks, gardening, reading, crocheting, and spending time with her five grandchildren. **Aug. 30, Dec. 16.**

Aurísia Silva Brito Rodrigues is the women's ministries director of the Vila Nova Nanuque church in Minas Gerais, Brazil. She is 23, married, and has a 5-year-old daughter. She likes to read, listen to music, go places, talk, and raise animals. **Feb. 18.**

Terrie Ruff is a team social worker/supervisor with Alexian Brothers Community Services PACE Program in Chattanooga, Tennessee, and an adjunct professor at Southern Adventist University. Terrie enjoys public speaking, writing, singing, and traveling. Her goal is to be a "beneficial" presence in the lives of all she meets. **Apr. 21, Oct. 1.**

Samyline P. Samaillano is 19 years old and the first child of Samyu and Gemma Samaillano. She is a nursing student in Northern Luzon Adventist College, Philippines. She is an avid reader of books, and also enjoys drawing, playing guitar, and indoor games. **Oct. 30.**

Deborah Sanders shares from her personal journal, *Dimensions of Love,* which has become a writing-prayer ministry. She lives in Canada with Ron, her husband of 36 years. They've been blessed with two children, Andrea and Sonny. Sonny is mentally challenged with psychomotor retardation and autism. "Thank you for caring," says Debbie. **July 7, Dec. 12.**

Lilith R. Scarlett serves as dean of women at Northern Caribbean University in Mandeville, Jamaica. She enjoys early-morning walks, loves helping people, and finds joy in entertaining, listening to good music, and reading. She's still learning to wait on the Lord. **Mar. 1.**

Marie H. Seard is a repeat contributor to the devotional book project—she and her husband enjoy their ministry of giving these books as Christmas gifts to other women. She writes a personal message to each woman who receives a book. Additionally, she and her husband travel, and visit their children—a son and daughter-in law—in California. **July 12, Nov. 13.**

Christine Shand is a first-time contributor to the devotional book series. She enjoys reading *Women of Spirit* in her spare time. **Nov. 29.**

Donna Lee Sharp is a retired minister's wife who enjoys playing the piano and organ at various churches and community organizations. Bird-watching, walking, and traveling across North America to see six children, seven grandchildren, and many friends makes life exciting. **Feb. 6, Nov. 9.**

Donna Sherrill lives in Jefferson, Texas, and manages a small country store close to Jefferson Adventist Academy. She's working on an album of songs she's written, and is publicist for a Christian country recording artist. She enjoys making cards, doing newsletters, and spending time with her grandchildren, who live close by. **Nov. 25.**

Carrol Johnson Shewmake and her pastor husband are now retired but still active in prayer ministry. Carrol is the author of seven books and often speaks at camp meetings, prayer conferences, women's retreats, and churches. She is the mother of four adult children, eight grandchildren, and one great-grandson. **Mar. 7, Sept 10.**

Judy Musgrave Shewmake and her husband, Tom, live in northern California. They have a married daughter, a married son, and a son and daughter she teaches at home. Judy is editor of *The Adventist Home Educator,* a newsletter for Adventist home-schoolers. Her favorite hobby is writing, and she also enjoys reading, genealogy, and making memory scrapbooks. **June 6, Sept. 18.**

Janet McKinon Sigh, from Fairbanks, Alaska, is a first-time contributor to the devotional book series. **Jan. 2.**

Rose Neff Sikora and her husband, Norman, live in the mountains of western

North Carolina. A registered nurse at Park Ridge Hospital for the past 20 years, her interests includes camping in a travel trailer, writing, spending time with her three grandchildren, and helping others. Rose has been published in magazines and books. **May 15, Sept. 5.**

Maria Cleuza Rodrigues da Silva is a Brazilian and has been married for 32 years. She works in a laboratory of clinical analysis. During her free time she enjoys reading, crochet, cooking, and singing. She has two daughters and two grandchildren. **Sept. 12.**

Kelita de Souza Silva resides in São Paulo, Brazil, with her husband and daughter. She likes to work with children and enjoys painting canvases and porcelain as a hobby. **Nov. 23.**

Carolina Kuntze Silveira studies nutrition at Brazil Adventist University, Campus 1, in São Paulo, Brazil. She plays clarinet in the youth symphonic band and participates in the university's bell choir. She likes piano, volleyball, and spending time with her family. **Aug. 23.**

Judy Good Silver lives with her husband, Phil, in Stanley, Virginia, on her great-great-grandfather's home place in the Shenandoah mountains. She has two children, Jill and Joel, and two grandchildren, Jonah and Mary. She was a home-care nurse for more than 20 years and has written a book of about her home-care patients, *Forget-me-nots.* **Jan. 10, Aug. 16.**

Sandra Simanton is a full-time mom in Sioux Falls, South Dakota, where she lives with her husband and three children. **Mar. 3, Sept. 27.**

Darlene Simmonds writes from Hempstead, New York. She is the Sabbath school superintendent for her church, as well as the Bronx/Manhattan district leader for women's ministries. Darleen enjoys singing and playing the piano for relaxation. In her spare time she ministers to needs of seniors. **Sept. 19.**

Daisy Simpson has, for more than 40 years, been a member in a local Seventh-day Adventist church in Queens, New York. She has been active as a choir member, deaconess, Sabbath school secretary, treasurer, and teacher. She has worked as a counselor and instructor in prison ministries for more than 30 years. She enjoys gardening and giving Bible studies. **Feb. 20, Dec. 30.**

Rebecca Singh is an English professor at Roorkee Adventist College in India, and is also a women's ministries director in Varanasi, Uttar Pradesh, India. She is a first-time contributor. **Apr. 3.**

Taramani Noreen Singh serves in Roorkee Adventist College, India, as the librarian. She has two young sons. **Oct. 7.**

Heather-Dawn Small is the director for women's ministries at her church's world headquarters. A native of Trinidad and Tobago, she has a young adult daughter and a high school-age son. She says she loves travel, reading, embroidery, and stamp collecting. *Joy* is her favorite word. **Feb. 2, May 4, July 1.**

Yvonne Curry Smallwood is a scientist who works as a director for diversity programs in science for underserved populations. As a single mom of two teenagers, she enjoys running, crocheting, reading, and writing. **May 12, Oct. 23.**

Thaís Rainha de Souza is 12 years old and lives in Rio de Janeiro, Brazil. She likes to read, play basketball, and spend time with her friends, observing the heavens. **Aug. 3.**

Ardis Dick Stenbakken and her husband, Dick, a retired Army chaplain, live in Colorado, near their son and daughter-in-law and their granddaughter, Aubrey. She misses her daughter and son-in-law, who still live in Maryland. Ardis especially enjoys helping women discover their full potential in the Lord. **Feb. 14, Aug. 1, Nov. 11.**

Risa Storlie enjoys reading, writing, cooking, hiking, and observing and learning lessons from nature. **Feb. 19, Sept. 1.**

Iris L. Stovall, a certified personality trainer through CLASS (Christian Leaders Authors and Speakers Services), especially enjoys speaking to women. An ordained elder, Iris has worked in women's ministries at her church's world headquarters for 11 years. She has three grown children, Greg, J.T., and Jhovonnah; and three granddaughters. **Mar. 8, June 9.**

Rubye Sue, a retired secretary and a great-grandmother, works at a small self-supporting school, where she enjoys interaction with the students. Rubye, 83, and her husband, 90, still travel, and look forward to visits with their children, grandchildren, and great-grandchildren. **June 14, Dec. 28.**

Carolyn Rathbun Sutton, freelance writer and speaker, lives in Tennessee with her husband, Jim. They enjoy camping, gardening, and sharing Jesus in practical ways, such as through their Building for Christ Ministries. **Mar. 16, Sept. 24.**

Loraine F. Sweetland is retired in Tennessee with her husband, 98-year-old mother-in-law, and three dogs. She chairs the school board and the Family Life Center building committee, as well as volunteering as treasurer for her local food co-op. In her spare time she works on genealogy. **May 23, Aug. 26.**

Frieda Tanner, a retired nurse, keeps busy by sending Bible school materials all over the world. She lives in Eugene, Oregon, near her two grandchildren. **Dec. 29.**

Arlene Taylor is director of infection control and risk management at St. Helena Hospital in California. As founder-president of her own corporation, she promotes brain function research. She is a professional member of the National Speaker's Association and has received the American Biographical Institute's American Medal of Honor for brain function education, 2002. **July 22, Dec. 1.**

Rose Thomas grew up in Haiti. She is a first-grade teacher who enjoys reading, cooking, signing, and writing. She lives in St. Petersburg, Florida, with her husband, her two children, her younger sister, and cousin. She teaches the youth class, coordinates the children's story time, and writes for the church's newsletter at Elim Adventist Church. This is her first published work. **Mar. 13, Oct. 19.**

Sharon M. Thomas is a retired elementary school teacher. She and her husband,

Don, a retired social worker, have two sons, who are graduates of Oakwood College. She enjoys reading, walking, biking, and shopping. Sharon and Don are enjoying the time and freedom to pursue a variety of interests that retirement allows. **Sept. 6.**

Stella Thomas works as an administrative assistant in the Global Mission office of her church's world headquarters. She enjoys meeting people and sharing the good news of God's love. **Feb. 23, Sept. 13.**

Emily Thomsen is a massage therapist and wellness professional. She loves being self-employed and working from home. She enjoys cooking, home decorating, music, reading, writing, and photography—but backpacking is her passion. In the summer of 2003 she hiked more than half the Appalachian Trail. **Nov. 22.**

Bula Rose Haughton Thompson is a dental assistant who works at the Mandeville Comprehensive Health-Care Centre in central Manchester, Jamaica. She is a couturière par excellence whose other hobbies are singing, reading, and meeting people. **June 28, Nov. 14.**

Janet Thornton moved to the small community of Berea in Jefferson, Texas, from Farmingdale, Maine, in 1978. Now retired, she worked as a food service director. She has five children, nine grandchildren, and two great-grandchildren, and enjoys reading, quilting, walking, and doing anything to help where help is needed. **Mar. 9, Dec. 21.**

Anne Tinworth is a mother and grandmother living on the Sunshine Coast of Australia. She enjoys taking part in the spiritual and social welfare of the retirement village where she works. She is interested in knitting, sewing, and serving in various capacities in her local church. **Dec. 9.**

Margaret Tito works in the Southern Asia Division of Seventh-day Adventists in India. She's enjoyed being an educator of children of various ages for almost 28 years. She and A.J., her pastor husband and communication director of the Southern Asia Division, have three grown children. She is a first-time contributor. **Jan. 26, June 21, Dec. 26.**

Nicéia Triandade lives in Niteroi, Brazil. She's married, the mother of three adult children and grandmother of five. She enjoys friends, sewing, cooking, and writing poems. Her greatest joy is to travel with her family and to meditate by looking at the sea. At church she is the women's and family ministries director and associate Sabbath school leader. **May 16, Aug. 17.**

Gloria Lindsey Trotman is the women's ministries director of the Inter-American Division of Seventh-day Adventists. The Trotmans have four children and four grandchildren. Gloria enjoys reading, writing, music, people-watching, and having fun with her grandchildren. Her motto is "Making a Difference." **Jan. 5.**

Eunice Urbany was raised on a Seventh-day Adventist academy campus in east Indonesia. She has worked as a nursing instructor and supervisor, taught pediatric nursing and nursing history in west Indonesia, and worked in nursing in Singapore, Hong Kong, and Germany. She has also lived in Toronto, Canada;

Chile, South America; and the United States. **Mar. 27, Oct. 9.**

Rebecca L. Usoroh lives with her husband, Isaac, in southern Florida. They are the proud parents of two young sons. They are recent graduates of Andrews University in Berrien Springs, Michigan. **Nov. 7.**

Nancy Van Pelt, a certified family life educator, best-selling author of more than 20 books, and internationally known speaker, has traversed the globe for 20 years, teaching families how to love each other. Her hobbies are getting organized, entertaining, having fun, and quilting. Nancy and her husband live in California and are the parents of three adult children. **Jan. 11, June 1.**

Cereatha J. Vaughn has lived in Detroit, Michigan, all of her life, where she is employed by the board of education as a teacher's aide. A second-generation Adventist, she has strong conviction for the spiritual welfare of God's children. She has a passion and talent for writing sermons, short stories, and poems. She is single, and devotes her time to serving God wherever she is. **Feb. 22.**

Lourdes M. Vehiga writes from San Pablo, Philippines. She is a first-time contributor and a recipient of a scholarship from the profits of the sale of books in this series. **Nov. 20.**

Ellen Andrade Viana is an administration student at Faculdade Adventista da Bahia, Brazil. She likes to read, listen to music, and participate in activities involving adventure. She is a member of the group Jovens Amigos (Youth Friends) in her religious community. **Mar. 18.**

Ivonete Viana is the wife of a retired pastor, Mozaniel Viana. They live in Pernambuco, Brazil. **Mar. 10.**

Mônica Medrado Vieira, 22, is a student in Brazil. She enjoys music, singing, and writing, and has already had some articles published. **Nov. 27.**

Donna Meyer Voth is a substitute teacher and volunteer for the American Cancer Society. She enjoys giving Bible studies, watercolor painting, traveling, and camping. She and her husband live in Vicksburg, Michigan. They have a daughter in college. **Apr. 20, Oct. 5.**

Cora A. Walker is a retired nurse, editor, and freelance writer who lives in Fort Washington, Maryland. She is an active member in the little country church she attends in Charles County, Maryland. She enjoys classical music, reading, writing, swimming, singing, and traveling. She has one son, Andre V. Walker. **Mar. 23, Nov. 18.**

Dolores Klinsky Walker is known by family, friends—and even strangers—as a "pusher." She pushes words, writing everything from book reviews to plays, and lending books left and right. An active United Methodist in Walla Walla, Washington, she has retired from raising three praiseworthy children and now nurtures her husband of 42 years and their fat cat. **Jan. 24, Dec. 15.**

Anna May Radke Waters is a retired high school administrator. She's an ordained elder in the Meadow Glade church, where she serves as a greeter. Among her many hobbies are her seven grandchildren (at the top of her list) and her husband, with whom she likes to travel. She enjoys Internet Bible studies and responding to prayer requests for Bibleinfo.com. **Jan. 17, July 17.**

Dorothy Eaton Watts is an administrator for her church headquarters in India. Dorothy is also a freelance writer, editor, and speaker. She has been a missionary in India for 26 years, founded an orphanage, taught elementary school, and written more than 20 books. Her hobbies include gardening, hiking, and birding (with more than 1,400 in her world total). **Jan. 14, June 18.**

Daniela Weichhold is from Germany, but works at the European Commission headquarters in Brussels, Belgium. She likes being with friends, enjoys God's wonderful nature, and traveling. At church she's involved in health ministries. She likes learning foreign languages and discovering different cultures. Singing and playing the piano are important parts of her life. **July 24.**

Lyn Welk-Sandy works with bereaved children and aids young offenders attending court. She has a full-time pipe organist position at a church in Adelaide, South Australia, and enjoys choir work and Christian fellowship. She loves caravanning and photography in the outdoors. She is the mother of four adult children and has eight grandchildren. **May 1, July 3.**

Mildred C. Williams is a retired physical therapist who lives in southern California. She enjoys studying and teaching the Bible, writing, gardening, public speaking, sewing, and spending time with her family. **May 13.**

Tricia Williams, a first-time contributor, is a freelance writer, proofreader, and photographer. Although she misses her home state of Oklahoma, Tricia is learning to enjoy the Cumberland Mountains of southeast Kentucky, where she, her husband, and young Hannah Rose live. Her hobbies include reading, drafting, and playing the piano for church. **Apr. 18, Oct. 25.**

Nilse Toledo Woerle is a teacher who helps in assistance work to needy families, and works as a volunteer in adult literacy classes. **Feb. 9.**

Aileen Young is a retired teacher, community volunteer, and church member in Aiea, Hawaii. She and her husband, Thomas H.T. Young, have two sons, Gregg and Gary, and three grandchildren, Spencer, Ashley, and Liliane. Besides writing and walking, she is actively engaged in music, traveling, and dabbling in watercolors. **May 20.**

Leni Uría de Zamorano directs a cafeteria for seniors that's operated by her church and helps in the music department, directs a Sabbath school class, and is involved in women's ministries. She has two married children and a 3-year-old granddaughter she enjoys caring for and playing with. She likes walking with her husband in the mornings, reading, and traveling. **July 11.**

prayer requests

_____

_____

_____

_____

_____

_____

_____

_____

_____

_____

**Whatever spiritual blessing we need,
it is our privilege to claim through Jesus.**

—Ellen G. White, _Thoughts From the Mount of Blessing,_ p. 133.

prayer requests

_____

_____

_____

_____

_____

_____

_____

_____

_____

_____

Whatever spiritual blessing we need,
it is our privilege to claim through Jesus.

—Ellen G. White, *Thoughts From the Mount of Blessing*, p. 133.

prayer requests

_____

_____

_____

_____

_____

_____

_____

_____

_____

_____

Whatever spiritual blessing we need,
it is our privilege to claim through Jesus.

—Ellen G. White, _Thoughts From the Mount of Blessing,_ p. 133.

prayer requests

_____

_____

_____

_____

_____

_____

_____

_____

_____

_____

Whatever spiritual blessing we need,
it is our privilege to claim through Jesus.
—Ellen G. White, *Thoughts From the Mount of Blessing*, p. 133.